THE INTERNATIONAL ORDER OF ASIA
IN THE 1930s AND 1950s

Modern Economic and Social History Series

General Editor: Derek H. Aldcroft

Titles in this series include:

Alfred Herbert Ltd and the British Machine Tool Industry, 1887–1983
Roger Lloyd-Jones and M.J. Lewis

Rethinking Nineteenth-Century Liberalism
Richard Cobden Bicentenary Essays
Edited by Anthony Howe and Simon Morgan

Governance, Growth and Global Leadership
The Role of the State in Technological Progress, 1750–2000
Espen Moe

Triumph of the South
A Regional Economic History of Early Twentieth Century Britain
Peter Scott

Aspects of Independent Romania's Economic History with Particular Reference
to Transition for EU Accession
David Turnock

Estates, Enterprise and Investment at the Dawn of the Industrial Revolution
Estate Management and Accounting in the North-East of England, c.1700–1780
David Oldroyd

Across the Borders
Financing the World's Railways in the Nineteenth and Twentieth Centuries
Edited by Ralf Roth and Günter Dinhobl

Economics in Russia
Studies in Intellectual History
Edited by Vincent Barnett and Joachim Zweynert

Mining Tycoons in the Age of Empire, 1870–1945
Entrepreneurship, High Finance, Politics and Territorial Expansion
Edited by Raymond E. Dumett

British Conservatism and Trade Unionism, 1945–1964
Peter Dorey

The International Order of Asia in the 1930s and 1950s

Edited by
SHIGERU AKITA
Osaka University, Japan
and
NICHOLAS J. WHITE
Liverpool John Moores University, UK

Routledge
Taylor & Francis Group

LONDON AND NEW YORK

First published 2010 by Ashgate Publishing

Published 2016 by Routledge
2 Park Square, Milton Park, Abingdon, Oxfordshire OX14 4RN
711 Third Avenue, New York, NY 10017, USA

First issued in paperback 2016

Routledge is an imprint of the Taylor & Francis Group, an informa business

British Library Cataloguing in Publication Data
The International Order of Asia in the 1930s and 1950s. —
  (Modern economic and social history)
  1. Asia—Economic conditions—1918– 2. Asia—Foreign economic relations.
  I. Series II. Akita, Shigeru. III. White, Nicholas J., 1967–
  330.9'5042-dc22

Library of Congress Cataloging-in-Publication Data
Akita, Shigeru.
  The international order of Asia in the 1930s and 1950s / Shigeru Akita and Nicholas J. White.
    p. cm. — (Modern economic and social history)
  ISBN 978-0-7546-5341-7 (hardcover : alk. paper) 1. Asia—Economic conditions—20th century. 2. International cooperation. I. White, Nicholas J. II. Title.

  HC412.A375 2009
  337.5009'041—dc22

                                                              2009010367

ISBN 13: 978-1-138-27589-8 (pbk)
ISBN 13: 978-0-7546-5341-7 (hbk)

Contents

PART 2   THE INTERNATIONAL ORDER OF ASIA AND ASIAN REGIONAL ECONOMIES

List of Tables

List of Figures

Notes on Contributors

Shigeru Akita is Professor in the Department of World History, Graduate School of Letters at Osaka University, Japan, where he specializes in the history of the British Empire and Commonwealth. He has published in Japanese: *International Order of Asia in the 1930s* (Hiroshima: Keisui-sha, 2001) (coed. with Naoto Kagotani), and *The British Empire and International Order of Asia* (Nagoya University Press, 2003). His publications in English include *Gentlemanly Capitalism, Imperialism and Global History* (ed., Palgrave-Macmillan, 2002). He is also involved in research on Global History.

Bruce Cumings is Gustavus F. and Ann M. Swift Distinguished Service Professor at the Department of History, University of Chicago. His research covers 20th-century international history, U.S.-East Asian relations, East Asian political economy, modern Korean history and American foreign relations. He is the author of *The Origins of the Korean War* (Grupo Ilhsa S.A., two volumes, 1981, 1990); *War and Television* (Verso Books, 1993); *Korea's Place in the Sun: A Modern History* (W. W. Norton, 1997); and *Parallax Visions: American-East Asian Relations at the End of the Century* (Duke University Press, 1999).

Naoto Kagotani is Professor of Economic History at The Institute for Research in Humanities, Kyoto University. He works on the history of Japan's foreign trade. He has published in Japanese: *The Asian Trading Orders and Modern Japan, 1880–1945* (Nagoya University Press, 2000) and edited two volumes. He has also published four papers in English, including 'The Chinese Merchant Community in Kobe and the Development of the Japanese Cotton Industry, 1890–1941,' in *Japan, China and the Growth of the Asian International Economy, 1850–1949* (Kaoru Sugihara ed., Oxford University Press, 2005).

Yoichi Kibata is Professor of International Relations at the Faculty of Law, Seijo University. He specialises in the history of the British Empire in the age of decolonisation. He has published in Japanese: *Price of Imperial Rule: Imperial Mentality and the Break-up of the British Empire* (Tokyo University Press, 1987); *The Twilight of the Empire: British Policy towards Japan and Malaya, 1947–1955* (Tokyo University Press, 1996) and *The British Empire and Imperialism* (Yushisha, 2008). His publications in English include: (ed. with Ian Nish) *The History of Anglo-Japanese Relations, 1600–2000*, Vol. 2, *The Political-Diplomatic Dimensions, 1930–2000* (Macmillan, 2000) and (ed. with Philip Towle and Margaret Kosuge) *Japanese Prisoners of War* (Hambledon, 2000).

Toru Kubo is Professor of Asian History at the Faculty of Liberal Arts, Shinshu University. He works on the economic history of modern China and East Asia. He has published in Japanese: *China's Quest for Sovereignty in the Interwar Period: Tariff Policy and Economic Development* (Tokyo University Press, 1999) and *Chinese Cotton Industry and Management in the Interwar Period* (Kyuko Publishing, 2005). His articles in English include 'The Tariff Policy of the Nationalist Government, 1929–36: A Historical Assessment', in *Japan, China, and the Growth of the Asian International Economy, 1850–1949* (Kaoru Sugihara ed., Oxford University Press, 2005).

Toshiro Matsumoto is Professor of Asian Economic History at The Graduate School of Humanities and Social Sciences, Okayama University. His research focuses on the aftermath of Japanese colonial administration, particularly in China. He has published in Japanese: *Japanese Colonial Occupation and Economic Development in China* (Ochanomizu Shobou, 1988) and *From Manchukuo to Communist China: the Industrial Reconstruction of Northeast China observed through the Iron and Steel Industry in Anshan, 1940–1954* (Nagoya University Press, 2000). He has also published many articles in Japanese, including 'Industrial Development in Northeast China from 1949–1988', *Studies on North-East Asian Economics*, no.4 (2007).

Man-houng Lin is Senior Research Fellow at the Institute of Modern History, Academia Sinica, Taipei and Professor at the Department of History, National Taiwan Normal University. Lin's main area of research focuses on treaty ports and modern China, empires and Taiwanese merchants, and East Asian overseas economic networks, 1860–1961. She has published 5 books and about 70 articles in Chinese, English, Japanese and Korean, including *China Upside Down: Currency, Society and Ideologies, 1808–1856* (Cambridge MA: Harvard Asian Center, 2006). Since 2008, she has served as the President of the Republic of China (Taiwan)'s Academia Historica (State History Academy).

Catherine R. Schenk is Professor of International Economic History at the University of Glasgow. Her research has focused on international monetary and financial relations since 1945 with particular emphasis on the UK and East Asia. Her recent books include *Hong Kong as an International Financial Centre* (Routledge, 2001), *Hong Kong SAR's Monetary and Exchange Rate Challenges* (Palgrave, 2008) and *The Decline of Sterling as an International Currency* (Cambridge University Press, 2009).

Tomoko Shiroyama is professor at the Graduate School of Economics, Hitotsubashi University. Her research interests include business history, the history of finance and banking in modern China, and the world economy in the nineteenth and twentieth centuries, with a special interest in China and other East Asian countries. Her major publications include in Japanese, 'China in the 1930s and the International Monetary System', *International Relations*, no.146 (2006). She recently authored *China during the Great Depression: Market, State, and the World Economy, 1929–1937* (Cambridge, MA: Harvard Asia Center, 2008).

Kaoru Sugihara is Professor of Economic History at the Center for Southeast Asian Studies, Kyoto University. He works on the history of intra-Asian trade as a historian of the modern international economy. He has published in Japanese: *Patterns and Development of Intra-Asian Trade* (Mineruva Shobou, 1996), *The Rise of the Asia-Pacific Economy* (Osaka University Press, 2003), and edited three volumes. He has also published four books in English, including (ed.) *Japan, China, and the Growth of the Asian International Economy, 1850–1949* (Oxford University Press, 2005), and is preparing (ed. with Gareth Austin) *Labour-intensive Industrialization in Global History* (Routledge, forthcoming).

Nicholas J. White is Reader in Imperial and Commonwealth History at Liverpool John Moores University. His research specialism is in the modern economic and business history of 'Commonwealth' Southeast Asia, i.e. Malaysia, Singapore and Brunei. His publications include *Business, Government and the End of Empire: Malaya, 1942–57* (Oxford University Press, 1996), *Decolonisation: the British experience since 1945* (Longman, 1999), *British Business in Post-Colonial Malaysia, 1957–70: 'neo- colonialism' or 'disengagement'?* (RoutledgeCurzon, 2004), and *The Empire in One City? Liverpool's Inconvenient Imperial Past* (ed. with Sheryllynne Haggerty and Anthony Webster, Manchester University Press, 2009). He is currently working on a book on the relationship between Liverpool's twentieth-century decline and the process of decolonisation.

Acknowledgements

This volume is the result of four international conferences: the workshop on 'The International Order of Asia in the 1930s and 1950s', held in London in September 2001, a session of the 13th International Economic History Congress in Buenos Aires in August 2002, and sessions of the Association of Asian Studies (AAS) in Tokyo in June 2003 and in San Diego in March 2004. The London workshop was financially supported by a fellowship from the Japan Foundation for 2001.

Eleven papers were submitted to the London workshop and the session of the International Economic History Congress in Buenos Aires. Each paper has been revised in the light of further exchanges that have occurred since then, especially at the two sessions of the AAS, which attracted the interest of American scholars in our joint research project. We would like to express our appreciation to our discussants, Profs Brian R. Tomlinson (SOAS, University of London) and Peter Cain (Sheffield Hallam University), and Drs Antony Best (LSE) and Gareth Austin (LSE).

A Visiting Professorship at Liverpool John Moores University (LJMU) in March 2007 enabled Akita to be attached to the History Department, School of Social Science, LJMU to edit this volume and to further exchange ideas with colleagues in Liverpool.

We are also grateful to the generosity of the Photo Archive of *The Asahi Shimbun* [Newspaper] (Tokyo, Japan) to allow us to use some of their collections for this book. We especially appreciate the kind arrangements made by Mr Yasuji Nagai, who is a staff writer and in charge of collections at the Osaka Head Office of *The Asahi Shimbun*.

Finally, we would like to thank Mr Tom Gray and Ms Ann Allen of the Ashgate Publishing Group for their long patience and gracious support of our editorial work.

Shigeru Akita and Nicholas J. White
October 2009

Modern Economic and Social History Series
General Editor's Preface

Economic and social history has been a flourishing subject of scholarly study during recent decades. Not only has the volume of literature increased enormously but the range of interest in time, space and subject matter has broadened considerably so that today there are many sub-branches of the subject which have developed considerable status in their own right.

One of the aims of this series is to encourage the publication of scholarly monographs on any aspect of modern economic and social history. The geographical coverage is world-wide and contributions on the non-British themes will be especially welcome. While emphasis will be placed on works embodying original research, it is also intended that the series should provide the opportunity to publish studies of a more general thematic nature which offer a reappraisal or critical analysis of major issues of debate.

Derek H. Aldcroft
University of Leicester

Introduction
The International Order of Asia in the 1930s and 1950s: Contexts, Hypotheses and Scope

Shigeru Akita and Nicholas J. White

Analytical Viewpoints

The principal aim of this edited volume is to reconsider the nature and formation of the international order of Asia in the 1930s and 1950s in the light of new historiographical developments in the UK as well as in Japan. The chapters which follow are based upon the discussions and debates which took place at a panel of the XIII International Economic History Congress in Buenos Aires in July 2002 and on further speculations and exchanges of ideas thereafter. Before outlining the contents of the book, this chapter introduces the historiographical contexts and theoretical frameworks for these deliberations.

Recently, several Japanese economic historians have offered a new perspective for analyzing Asia's economic history.[1] They have argued that the economic growth of Asian countries was led by the phenomenon of intra-Asian trade which began to grow rapidly around the turn of the nineteenth and twentieth centuries. Alternatively, the British imperial historians, P.J. Cain and A.G. Hopkins, have presented their own controversial interpretation of 'gentlemanly capitalism' in which they have emphasized the leading role of the service sector rather than that of British industry in explaining the nature of British expansion overseas.[2]

---

[1] Kaoru Sugihara, *Ajiakan Boeki no Keisei to Kozo* [*The formation and structure of Intra-Asian trade*], (Kyoto,1996); Naoto Kagotani, *Ajia Kokusai-Tsusho Chitsujo to Kindai Nihon* [*The Asian International Trading Order and Modern Japan*], (Nagoya, 2000); Shigeru Akita, *Igirisu Teikoku to Ajia Kokusai-Chitsujo* [*The British Empire and International Order of Asia*], (Nagoya, 2003).

[2] P.J. Cain and A.G. Hopkins, *British Imperialism, 1688–2000* (Second Edition, Harlow and New York, 2001). For critical assessments of 'gentlemanly capitalism' in East, Southeast and South Asian contexts see ibid., pp. 16–17; Shigeru Akita, 'British informal empire in East Asia, 1880–1939: a Japanese perspective' in Raymond E. Dumett (ed.), *Gentlemanly Capitalism and British Imperialism: The New Debate on Empire* (London and New York, 1999), Ch. 6; Maria Misra, 'Gentlemanly capitalism and the Raj: British policy in India between the wars' in ibid., Ch. 7; Nicholas J. White, 'Gentlemanly capitalism and empire in the twentieth century: the forgotten case of Malaya, 1914–1965' in ibid., Ch. 8;

These approaches are not necessarily incompatible, and an overarching objective of this volume is to investigate whether it is possible to integrate intra-Asian and 'gentlemanly capitalist' perspectives and so present a fresh interpretation of the international history of Asia in the 1930s and 1950s.

Within this general framework, there were three specific areas of enquiry at the Buenos Aires conference,[3] which continue to inform this volume and which were closely related to each other. The first was to reconsider the metropolitan-peripheral relationship in Asia in the 1930s and 1950s, focusing on the role of the sterling area and its implications for Asian economic development. Cain and Hopkins have identified the financial and service interests of the City of London as Britain's core economic interest. As such, they have emphasized the importance of the sterling area or bloc for the reassertion and extension of British influence on a global scale in the 1930s.[4] To make their case in the Asian context, Cain and Hopkins focused on British India and China in the inter-war years.[5] Moreover, Cain and Hopkins asserted that imperial history could be viewed as a bridge to global history – the final chapter of their second edition of *British Imperialism* argued that the empire and the imperial system should be regarded as modernizing and globalizing forces.[6] In Buenos Aires and in their subsequent chapter submissions, the authors were encouraged to explore the economic linkages between the British Empire, the sterling area and South, Southeast and East Asia, and considered the economic implications of these interconnections for the development of Asia, and especially for the process of Asian industrialization.

The second focus was on revealing the formation of inter-regional trade relations within Asia in the 1930s and their revival and/or transformation in the 1950s. This theme emphasized the importance of Asian indigenous forces in creating and sustaining the international order of Asia both before and after the Pacific War. The concept of 'intra-Asian trade' has been discussed several times at international conferences since the IX Congress of the International Economic History Association in Bern in 1986.[7] Moreover, the Japanese economic historian, Kaoru Sugihara, has written numerous articles and a well-received book on this

---

Shigeru Akita (ed.), *Gentlemanly Capitalism, Imperialism and Global History* (London and New York, 2002).

[3]   Some of these themes had already been developed in Shigeru Akita and Naoto Kagotani (eds), *1930-nendai Ajia Kokusai Chitujo* [*International Order of Asia in the 1930s*] (Hiroshima, 2000).

[4]   P.J. Cain and A.G. Hopkins, *British Imperialism, 1688–2000*, parts 5–7.

[5]   Ibid., Chs 23 and 25.

[6]   Ibid., 'Afterword: Empires and Globalization'. Cain and Hopkins's interpretation is distinct from that recently presented by Niall Ferguson. Ferguson is more positive and legitimizing in his presentation of the British Empire as a hegemonic and globalizing force. Cf. Niall Ferguson, *Empire* (London, 2003) and Niall Ferguson, *Colossus: the rise of America's Empire* (New York, 2004).

[7]   Wolfram Fischer et al. (eds), *The Emergence of a World Economy, 1500–1914, Beitrage zur Wirtschafts und Sozialgeschichte, Band 33–2* (Wiesbaden: Franz Steiner, 1986).

subject, based on multi-archival research on trade statistics.[8] The Buenos Aires panelists attempted to consider further the economic impact of intra-Asian trade on the international order of Asia, and to reveal intra-Asian linkages with the capitalist world-economy.

The third area of enquiry concentrated on continuities and discontinuities within the international order of Asia between the 1930s and the 1950s. On the surface, there appears to be little continuity between the pre- and post-war eras in Asia's international history. After the Second World War, 'political decolonization' or independence was the dominant issue in most Asian countries. A host of new Asian nation-states arose in the course of the 1940s and 1950s, while, concurrently, the Cold War established new international divisions in post-colonial East and Southeast Asia. However, from the perspective of international economic relations, it might be possible to identify some key elements of continuity before and after the Asia-Pacific cataclysm of 1937–45. The authors attempted, therefore, to reveal those aspects of continuity and their significance from both global and regional perspectives.

At the same time, to provide a framework for discussion in Buenos Aires and for the contents of this volume, Shigeru Akita and his colleague, Naoto Kagotani, put forward the following three hypotheses:

(1) Economic nationalism, the 'imperial division of labour' and 'complementarity'

First, Akita and Kagotani attempted to reconsider the historical significance of Asian industrialization in the 1930s via a global perspective. It has often been assumed that trade frictions in the 1930s represented a contested and bitter scramble for Asian markets on the part of British and Japanese cotton textile industries – an all-too-obvious clash of manufacturing interests. However, the recent arguments of Cain and Hopkins suggest that the financial and service sectors had always dominated British economic interests and that manufacturing was secondary. The UK's external economic policies reflected this peculiar structure of the British economy, and the 'gentlemanly' inclinations and biases of UK policy-makers. Cain and Hopkins placed much emphasis on the payment of interest and dividends from the colonies, and the defrayal of administrative costs by these dependencies. They stressed that the maintenance of sterling's credibility was imperative for the British 'official mind'.[9] The same logic could be applied in the case of The Netherlands and Dutch colonial rule in the Indonesian archipelago.[10] Drawing upon these

---

[8] Sugihara, *Intra-Asian trade*; Kaoru Sugihara, 'International Circumstances Surrounding the Postwar Japanese Cotton Textile Industry', in D.A. Farnie and D.V. Jeremy (eds), *The Fibre that Changed the World: The Cotton Industry in International Perspective, 1600–1990s* (Oxford, 2004), Ch. 17.

[9] Cain and Hopkins, *British Imperialism*, Chs 17, 23 and 25.

[10] Naoto Kagotani, 'Japanese Cotton-textile diplomacy in the first half of the 1930s: the case of the Dutch-Japanese trade negotiation in 1934', *Bulletin of Asia-Pacific Studies*, vol. VII (1997).

interpretations, Akita and Kagotani noted a 'coexistence' of economic interests, which tended to arise between British and Dutch financial concerns and Asian manufacturing interests, bolstered and not obstructed by the rise of nationalism. The industrialized nations of Britain and Holland began to transfer labour-intensive textile industries to Asian countries, especially in East Asia, and the European metropoles concentrated instead on the economic activities of the financial and service sectors. Although there was strong opposition from Lancashire's textile industry, this shift of British economic interests permitted the industrialization of Asia, and according to Akita and Kagotani, was one of the prominent features of the international order of Asia in the years leading up to the Pacific War.

Hence, especially for Akita, economic 'complementarity' between the Western imperial powers and South, Southeast and East Asia was a central element in Asian industrialization. The development of manufacturing industry in Asia during the 1930s is not solely explicable, therefore, by a confrontation or rivalry between 'Core' and 'Periphery' of the global economy. In the case of British India, the Lancashire textile industry's loss of competitiveness in the colonial market has been interpreted as an 'economic triumph' for Indian nationalism.[11] However, in Akita and Kagotani's hypothesis, the industrialization of India was achieved by utilizing Britain's 'imperial order' even under the colonial administration.[12] In the 1920s, the Government of India gradually raised the level of import duties in order to attain more revenues and to balance Indian finances. That increase in Indian tariffs had the effect of smoothing the payment of administrative levies to the UK (the remittance of the so-called 'Home Charges'). In that sense, the British government implicitly permitted the raising of Indian import duties and confirmed the protective effect of duties for Indian industries, even when London enforced 'Imperial Preference' after the Ottawa Agreement of 1932. Import-substituting industrialization commenced in British India during the 1930s through a complementary economic relationship between British financial interests and India itself. From the British financial point of view, Indian industrialization was useful for the collection of Indian debts since the subcontinent could produce a trade surplus with the UK by reducing imports (import-substitution) and the export of gold, and by establishing a favourable balance of payments position. The Indian nationalists apparently recognized this logic in their political negotiations for tariff autonomy.[13]

---

[11]   Basudev Chatterji, *Trade, Tariffs and Empire: Lancashire and British Policy in India 1919–1939* (Delhi, 1992).

[12]   Nobuko Nagasaki, 'Hi-bouryoku to Jiritsu no Indo [India under Non-violence and Independence]', in Naoki Hazama and Nobuko Nagasaki (eds), *Sekai no Rekishi [Series of World History]* 27: *Jiritsu ni mukau Ajia [Asian movements towards Independence]* (Tokyo, 1999).

[13]   The disputes between the Government of India and Indian nationalists continued, however, in the field of Indian financial policy, especially in regard to the fixed exchange rate of the Indian rupee to sterling. Indian nationalists insisted that the official exchange rate

Akita also pinpointed a similar complementary relationship between China and the UK during the 1930s, especially surrounding the Chinese currency reform of 1935. The Nationalist (Guomindang) government of China suffered financially from a heavy outflow of silver between 1933 and 1935, caused by fluctuations in silver prices in the American market. Chiang Kai-shek's regime received some advice from American financial counsellors such as the Kemmeller Commission and A.N. Young concerning possible remedial action. However, in the end, Chinese ministers of finance, T.V. Soong (1928–33) and H.H. Kung (1933–47), largely completed the planning of monetary reform by themselves and carried it out resolutely in November 1935, and notwithstanding Japanese obstructionism. The British Leith-Ross Mission visited Japan and China on the eve of the currency reform to persuade the Japanese government to agree to a joint loan to China. The Nanjing government tacitly took advantage of this opportunity, and successfully obtained cordial support from the leading British financial interest in China, the Hongkong and Shanghai Banking Corporation (HSBC). On the other hand, just after the announcement of reform, the Guomindang regime smoothly sold huge amounts of nationalized silver bullion to the United States in accordance with the Chinese-American Silver Agreement which was signed with the American Department of the Treasury on 2 November 1935.[14] Through these actions, the market value of the new Chinese dollar stabilized without officially pegging either to sterling or the US dollar.[15] The success of monetary reform led to the acceleration of import-substitution industrialization and the increase of Chinese exports. This masterly implementation of Chinese currency reform depended on a shrewd political calculation of the balance of power and the utilization of Anglo-American rivalry in order to enlarge the economic influence and financial autonomy of the Chinese regime – the Nationalists took the initiative in currency reform and achieved considerable economic success in the late-1930s.[16]

---

of 1 rupee equaling 1s 6d be reduced to 1s 4d. Tight money control and this high exchange rate imposed by the Government of India was a major obstacle to the further expansion of Indian exports of cotton goods, especially yarn, to Asian countries. On Indian financial policies, which were crucial for preserving the international role of sterling, the British authorities would not make concessions to the demands of Indian nationalists.

[14]   On the Chinese currency reform see Arther N. Young, *China's Nation-Building Effort, 1927–1937: The Financial and Political Record* (Stanford, 1971), Chs 7 and 8; Yutaka Nozawa (ed.), *Chugoku no Heisei-Kaikaku to Kokusai-Kankei [Currency Reform in China (1935) and China's Relations with Japan, Britain and America]*, (Tokyo, 1981); P.J. Cain, 'British Economic Imperialism in China in the 1930s: The Leith-Ross Mission', *Bulletin of Asia-Pacific Studies*, vol. VII (1997).

[15]   Kaoru Sugihara has revealed the *de facto* linkage of the new Chinese currency with sterling through the careful financial management of the Chinese authorities, and its stabilizing effect on the new currency. See Ch. 3 in this book.

[16]   Toru Kubo, *Senkan-ki Chugoku Jiritsu eno Mosaku: Kanzei-Tsuka Seisaku to Keizai-hatten [China's Quest for Sovereignty in the Inter-war Period: Tariff Policy and Economic Development]* (Tokyo, 1999), Ch. 8.

These two examples from British India and Guomindang China reflect the unique features of the economic development of Asia in the 1930s, and a similar relationship has been discerned by Akita between Japan and the UK at the turn of the nineteenth and twentieth centuries.[17] Hence, especially for Akita, 1930s India and China demonstrate the need to reconsider Asian economic development from a new angle of complementary relationships with, rather than antagonisms against, the Western powers. Asian industrialization made steady progress by taking full advantage of the imperial world order of the inter-war era.

(2) The 'Openness' of the Imperial International Order and Asia

It has been conventional to argue that the European powers and Japan divided Asia into spheres of influence through exclusive 'bloc' economies during the 1930s and that this economic rivalry became a background cause of the Second World War in Asia and the Pacific. However, for the Akita and Kagotani thesis, European policies towards Asia in the 1930s were not as exclusionary as is often argued and the Ottawa Trade Agreement and the UK-led sterling area possessed a degree of 'openness'. In this sense, Akita and Kagotani accepted the Cain and Hopkins paradigm on a crucial issue: the Ottawa Agreement was intended primarily to promote the financial and service interests of the City of London rather than British manufacturing interests, through smoothing the payment of interest and dividends from the colonies and the Dominions to the metropole.[18]

In order to achieve that smooth payment of interest, it was imperative to increase and maintain the trade surpluses of the colonies and the Dominions. Therefore, the metropolitan country needed to be the largest purchaser of primary products from the colonies. As a consequence, the Ottawa agreement gave priority to the expansion of colonial exports of primary products rather than to the export of manufactures from the UK.[19] A contemporary publication by the Royal Institute of International Affairs clearly pointed out this central logic which lay behind the sterling area in the late-1930s.[20] Yet, it proved difficult to maintain a large trade surplus for the colonies by relying only on the sterling area. The imperial economic bloc had to be complemented by the growth of exports to other advanced industrial nations, such as the United States and Japan, from the empire-Commonwealth. As Akita argued, India had industrialized in the 1930s by taking full advantage of the protection provided by Imperial Preference. The main concern of the United Kingdom was not to implement tariff policies for the protection of British domestic

---

[17]   Akita, *British Empire and International Order of Asia*, Chs 5 and 6.

[18]   Cain and Hopkins, *British Imperialism*, Ch. 20.

[19]   See Ian M. Drummond, *British Economic Policy and the Empire 1919–1939* (London: Allen and Unwin, 1972) and Ian M. Drummond, *Imperial Economic Policy 1917–1939: Studies in Expansion and Protection* (London: Allen and Unwin, 1974).

[20]   The Royal Institute of International Affairs, *The Problem of International Investment* (London, 1937).

industries, but to maintain the international role of sterling along with the financial and service interests of the City. The empire-Commonwealth of the 1930s was not a 'closed' bloc protected by preferential tariffs. It was alive and responsive to the global economy in order to promote British finance and services. Britain heavily depended on a relatively free 'free trade' regime, balanced budgets and low military expenditure in the 1930s. A 'closed' empire usually increased the cost of maintaining an imperial system,[21] and the British Empire provides a classic example of how costs could be reduced through imperial 'openness'.

(3) Continuities between the 1930s and the 1950s

Notwithstanding the vast turmoil of World War Two in Asia and the Pacific, as well as 'political decolonization' and the spread of the Cold War in post-war Southern and Eastern Asia, elements of Akita and Kagotani's international order may well have survived into the 1950s, helping to explain the pattern of rapid economic growth in East and Southeast Asia particularly. Hence, for example, Christopher Bayly and Tim Harper have pointed to central facets of pre-war economic life in British Southeast Asia, which were largely recreated and expanded from the early-1950s onwards, and notwithstanding the on-going operation of the sterling area in the region:

> Japanese trade and investment in this period [the 1920s and 1930s] is a crucial link in the history of the modern economic dynamism of Southeast Asia. Japanese goods were at the heart of the consumer boom in Malaya in the later 1930s ... In 1941, Japanese investments in British Malaya totaled 85 million yen. Japanese firms attempted to corner the market in goods from matchboxes to condensed milk; they imported over half of Malaya's everyday goods. The people of Singapore marvelled at the new technology in a 'Japanese Commercial Museum'. Children in Malaya grew up with toys from the 'ten-cent' stalls on Middle Road in Singapore and elsewhere; the small army of Asian clerks depended on Japanese stores ... for the cheap white shirts and ties they were required to wear in European offices. The Japanese were responsible for what was perhaps the most revolutionary innovation within the rural economy of Southeast Asia at this time: the bicycles with which country people could get their own goods to market ....[22]

---

[21] Patrick K. O'Brien with Leandro Prados de la Escosura, 'The Costs and Benefits of European Imperialism from the Conquest of Ceuta, 1415 to the Treaty of Lusaka, 1974', *Revista de Historia Economica*, Ano XVI, Invierno 1998, No.1; Avner Offer, 'The British empire, 1870–1914: a waste of money?', *Economic History Review*, 2nd ser., 46 (1993).

[22] Christopher Bayly and Tim Harper, *Forgotten Armies: Britain's Asian Empire and the War with Japan* (London: Penguin, 2005), pp. 5–6.

Recognition of such continuities from pre- to post-war Asia might allow recent works on the international economic history of the 1950s to be developed, modified or challenged. Noriko Yokoi, for example, has explored Britain's sterling and trade policies towards Japan from 1948 to 1962, challenging the conventional view of British opposition to Japan's economic recovery in the 1950s.[23] Even so, however extensive her research was, Yokoi's study was still dominated by the reactions of British home industries to Japanese competition. In particular, she emphasized the negative attitudes of the Manchester Chamber of Commerce and the Board of Trade towards Japan's economic recovery, and the fears of these private and public bodies concerning a revival of severe Japanese competition along the lines of the 1930s. At the same time, Yokoi's study remained within a framework of bilateral relations between the UK and Japan. Kaoru Sugihara, on the other hand, has revealed the revival of 'intra-Asian competition' in the 1930s for cotton goods markets on a wider Asian scale, and the rapid recovery of the Japanese cotton textiles industry in the 1950s.[24] Here, Akita tried to relocate these two pioneering works within a wider global context, since as Catherine Schenk clearly pointed out, the sterling area – as the financial expression of the British imperial system – obviously covered much more than Eastern Asia in the post-war era and reflected the economic interests of both London and the empire-Commonwealth.[25]

As for reconsideration of British sterling policies during the 1950s, the recent historiographical developments in imperial and Commonwealth history also need to be borne in mind. The work of Cain and Hopkins additionally deals with the UK's post-war international economic policy, as well as the survival of the so-called 'gentlemanly order' in the City, focusing primarily on the role of the sterling area.[26] Strongly influenced by Cain and Hopkins, Gerold Krozewski has, meanwhile, presented us with a new analysis of the end of empire in the 1950s, located at the intersection of British imperial policy and international relations. In the late-1940s and early-1950s, when political control was feasible, discriminatory management of the colonies and the sterling area sustained Britain's post-war recovery. However, subsequently, the emergence of liberal multilateralism, in the new international economic order dominated by the United States, exerted a strong influence on Britain's overseas position and policies, and led to the rapid

[23]   Noriko Yokoi, 'Searching for a Balance: Britain's Trade Policy towards Japan, 1950–1954' (Unpublished Ph.D. thesis, University of London, 1998); Noriko Yokoi, *Japan's Postwar Economic Recovery and Anglo-Japanese Relations 1948–1962* (London and New York: Routledge Curzon, 2003).

[24]   Kaoru Sugihara, 'International circumstances surrounding the Post-war Japanese Cotton Textile Industry', in Farnie and Jeremy (eds), The *Fibre that Changed the World*, Ch 17.

[25]   C.R. Schenk, *Britain and the Sterling Area: From Devaluation to Convertibility in the 1950s* (London: Routledge, 1994); see also Economic Cooperation Administration Special Mission to the United Kingdom, *The Sterling Area: An American Analysis* (London, 1951).

[26]   Cain and Hopkins, *British Imperialism*, Ch. 26.

dissolution of the empire from the late-1950s.[27] Akita suggested that greater incorporation of an eastern Asian perspective, and from Japan particularly, was required in these new evaluations of the later transformation of the sterling area.

The Book in Outline

This volume is divided into two parts. The chapters in Part I discuss the linkages between the international order of Asia, the British empire-Commonwealth, and the sterling area, beginning with Shigeru Akita's study of Britain and the international order of Asia during the 1930s. As the *de facto* structural power, Akita argues that the UK played a central role in inter-war industrialization in India, China and Japan, and that there was a greater degree of complementarity between the British presence in Asia and Japanese economic development in the 1930s than might be supposed. Admittedly, previous complementarities between Britain and Japan – in the export of British machinery and the provision of the City of London's financial services – were on the wane, not just in Japan but in the Japanese colonial empire as well. Nevertheless, drawing upon a wealth of British official reports from the various trade commissioners and commercial counsellors in the field, Akita reveals the complementary relationship between the export of British capital goods and Chinese and Indian industrialization, the complementarity between the City and the financial requirements of India and China, and the mutual economic interdependence of Japan and the British colonies and dominions 'East of Suez' – notably India as a market for Japanese textiles and Malaya, Australia, as well as the subcontinent, as suppliers of raw materials for Japan's 'second industrial revolution'. Hence, coexistence rather than contention pervaded the complex multiple economic relationships between Britain, Japan, China and India in the 1930s, and the intra-Asian trade and 'gentlemanly capitalism' theses are both combined and reconciled in Akita's analysis. This revisionism is mirrored, to a certain extent, by Yoichi Kibata's study of political relations between Britain and Japan from the 1930s to the 1950s. He stresses that from the Japanese occupation of Manchuria in 1931 to the outbreak of the Sino-Japanese war in 1937, British policy-makers were content to co-exist and cooperate with Japan in China as a means of checking the excesses of Guomindang nationalism, and so long as British financial and commercial interests in Shanghai were not overly threatened. '[T]here is room for [us] both' as Neville Chamberlain wrote to his sister as late as 1935, and British trade and financial missions looked forward to 'imperialist economic cooperation' with Japan in China. Kibata moves on to emphasize the very changed circumstances of the post-1945 international order in Asia, most

---

[27] Gerold Krozewski, *Money and the End of Empire: British International Economic Policy and the Colonies, 1947–58* (London and New York: Palgrave, 2001); Gerold Krozewski, 'Gentlemanly Imperialism and the British Empire after 1945', in Akita (ed.), *Gentlemanly Capitalism*, Ch. 4.

obviously exhibited in Britain's retreat from China and India. Nevertheless, an element of Anglo-Japanese cooperation survived the Pacific War in Southeast Asia, at least, where the British were anxious to utilize first post-imperial Japan's manpower and subsequently its revived economic capacity to prop up UK interests in the region.

That Japan was not isolated from the British-led international economy in Asia during the 1930s, is re-emphasized in Kaoru Sugihara's analysis of the interconnection between the sterling area and East Asia's industrialization. In particular, he explores the 'linking' of Japan in 1932 and China in 1935 to the sterling area, and assesses the extension of sterling's influence outside the British Empire during the 1930s in the broader context of global history. At the same time, however, there is no denying the tremendous transformative power of Japanese colonialism, irrespective of the attachment to sterling. Focussing on Korea, but with reference to and implications for the 'Northeast corner' of the world economy as a whole, Bruce Cumings's chapter emphasizes that Japan's stress on heavy industrialization and the development of sophisticated transportation networks in its East Asian colonies changed the face of the region, inducing remarkably high industrial growth rates and a division of labour which have had a profound influence on East Asia's economic development to this day. In this sense, Cumings brings to the fore important continuities between the pre- and post-war economic interconnectedness of Japan, Korea and Taiwan. Despite the tectonic hegemonic shift of regional power towards the United States, evinced by the on-going American military presence in Japan and South Korea, the Cold War anxiety to re-build these two countries as bulwarks against communism tended to encourage the revival of certain aspects of the pre-war economic order. Cumings's fascinating chapter thus ends with the visit of veteran Korean industrialist, Pak Hung-sik, to Japan in 1950 and his advocacy of a resurrection of the pre-war 'economically combined .... organic whole' that was Japan, Korea, Taiwan and Northeast China.

Yet, notwithstanding the arrival of US hegemony and far-reaching political changes in the context of decolonization and the Cold War, the British post-war presence in Asia also played its part in the revival of intra-Asian trade and investment flows in the post-Pacific War era. As Catherine Schenk reveals, the close financial and commercial relationship between Hong Kong and China during the 1930s, and Hong Kong's special position in the international monetary system, was replicated in the post-war period. The 'Hong Kong gap' within the sterling area (whereby the British colony operated a free foreign exchange market while, at the same time, its currency remained convertible with sterling), combined with US-led embargoes on trade with communist China after 1949, permitted Hong Kong to both survive and revive as mainland China's 'window on the West'. Anxious to preserve its business interests in communist China and to prevent Beijing falling completely into the arms of Moscow, Britain not only recognized the People's Republic but also resisted placing controls on China's use of sterling. As such, sterling transactions through Hong Kong became a key device whereby the People's Republic maintained its international economic connections. At the same time, Hong Kong's relative political stability and loose financial regimen, as well as the liberalism of its international currency exchange, made the British-maintained territory a central hub of intra-Asian trade, payments and capital flows. Indeed, Nicholas White's chapter picks up on the significance of Hong Kong for the economic development of 1950s Malaya. Moreover, that the *Pax Americana* was not absolute, and that British activities in Asia could continue to exercise a considerable influence over the nature and pattern of the post-war economic order, is also stressed by White. His chapter begins by outlining the enduring value of Malaya's US dollar earnings for metropolitan Britain throughout the 1950s. However, the sterling area regime in Malaya became more 'open' as the decade progressed, and a continuity of greater significance for Malaysia's and Singapore's international economic history, linking the 1930s to the 1950s, lay in the existence of the sterling area alongside burgeoning intra-Asian trade and investment flows. Wide-scale evidence of smuggling points to a considerable volume of intra-Asian trade which was hidden from the official statisticians. At the same time, White points to Malaya's re-engagement with, and growing incorporation into the regulated Asia-Pacific economy. Here, the chapter places particular emphasis upon the resurrection and expansion of Japanese economic interests in Malaya and Singapore during the 1950s. Like Kibata, White points to the importance of British officials in encouraging this phenomenon, as they fell into line with US Cold War strategies (as also described in Cumings's chapter). Additionally, the revival of Japan in Commonwealth Southeast Asia owed much to the decisions of Malayan politicians and business leaders against the backdrop of decolonization.

The chapters in Part II of the book are principally concerned with the international order of Asia and the Asian regional economy. Naoto Kagotani opens the second act by returning to the relationship between Japan and the European occupancy of South and Southeast Asia in the 1930s, through a focus on the cotton trade negotiations with British India and the Netherlands East Indies. Hence, Kagotani provides a link between the two parts of the book by confirming that Japanese trade with colonial India and Indonesia was maintained at very high levels throughout the 1930s, and, in line with the earlier arguments of Akita and Sugihara, demonstrates that before 1937, at least, Japan was not divorced from the global economy. Moreover, in further defence of the complementarity thesis, Kagotani argues that a certain degree of interdependence was maintained between Japan, British India and the Dutch East Indies based upon the linking of sterling and the yen after 1932, the revenues which colonial governments gained from import duties on Japanese goods, and the profits derived by European and Asian merchants from commercial exchanges with Japan. Japan remained a significant engine of Asian regional development then, even for areas under European colonial control in the supposedly protectionist, bloc-economy-ridden 1930s; and, if anything, Japanese trade sustained European imperialism in both South and Southeast Asia. In this, Kagotani challenges much recent Japanese historiography on the relationship between Japanese commercial expansion and the road to Pearl Harbor by counter-arguing that the trade diplomacy of the Japanese government was more inclined to meet British and Dutch financial interests than those of its own industrialists.

The final four chapters are concerned with China (including Manchuria and Taiwan) in the 1930s and the 1950s. Tomoko Shiroyama utilizes the Chinese currency reform of 1935 to investigate China's relationship with the international financial and political systems. Shiroyama's analysis would seem to support the arguments of Akita and Sugihara about the continued significance of British 'gentlemanly capitalism' in the East Asian economy – the linkage with the pound sterling in the 1930s permitted intra-Asian trade and investment flows to flourish, and encouraged import-substitution industrialization. However, as Shiroyama's chapter also establishes, there is a danger of exaggerating the degree of 'hegemony' or 'informal imperialism' which Britain exercised in the region, since she effectively demonstrates the 'agency' of the Guomindang government. Chinese politicians and officials were able to skillfully play off the competing interests of Britain, the United States and Japan in China to achieve the currency reform that they wanted, and so avoided a constraining peg either to the US dollar or the pound sterling. Concurrently, however, Shiroyama's chapter does reveal the Nanjing regime's acute awareness of the close integration of the pre-war Chinese economy with the world economy in terms of trade and capital flows, and the stabilized exchange rate was a principal factor in the expansion of international trade after 1935. Had the Sino-Japanese war not intervened in the summer of 1937 one is tempted to speculate that the fate of the Guomindang regime may have been quite different. Notwithstanding war and revolution, however, Toru Kubo demonstrates that China was never completely estranged or cut off from the international economy, and particularly the Asian regional economy. It is clear that China followed very different development strategies under Nationalist, Japanese and Communist rule (and that under these very different regimes the sources of imports varied immensely as well). However, supported by a wealth of statistical evidence, Kubo emphasizes a consistent trend in the geographical destination of China's exports from the 1930s through to the 1950s. With the exception of the Pacific War period, large volumes of light industrial goods and primary products were exported annually from China to Southeast Asia. To confirm Schenk's earlier assertions, Hong Kong provided a vital gateway for mainland China's ongoing exchanges with Southeast Asia under CCP rule. Moreover, export surpluses with Hong Kong and Southeast Asia were significant as an instrument for earning foreign exchange which could be re-deployed to buy in foreign-produced capital goods, thus underpinning the drive to heavy industrialization. Kubo's irresistible conclusion, therefore, is that, even in the 1950s under CCP socialization of the domestic economy, Chinese economic development must be viewed within a pan-Asian context.

Moreover, communist China's heavy industrialization also owed something to Japanese colonial rule, as disclosed in Toshiro Matsumoto's detailed case-study of the Anshan iron and steel complex in Manchuria. This is not to minimize the dramatic changes in the international order of Pacific Asia between the 1930s and the 1950s: as Matsumoto elucidates, the influence of the UK in Northeast China had been minimal since the 1930s, while Japanese authority was eliminated in August 1945. The Soviet Union and the United States emerged as the new superpowers in the region and, clearly by the end of the 1940s, military hegemony within China itself had shifted from the Guomindang to the communists. But that does not mean that there was a complete absence of political and, particularly, economic continuity between 1930s and 1950s Manchuria. As hinted at by Cumings too, the legacy of Japanese colonialism could still be profound for post-war Northeast China's economic modernization under both Nationalist and Communist control through the retention and transfer of Japanese technology, know-how and equipment and, at Anshan particularly, the presence of a quantitatively small but qualitatively highly significant group of Japanese engineers and their families until March 1953. Post-war economic linkages between Japan and an ex-colony in East Asia, this time Taiwan, are also persuasively presented in the final chapter by Lin Man-houng. Through the biographies of a number of leading Taiwanese merchants engaged in trade between Japan and Taiwan during the 1950s, Lin demonstrates that the pre-war economic elite survived the purges of the Guomindang period on the island. Indeed, not only did this economic elite maintain its strong Japanese identity, but the pre-war entrepreneurs co-existed quite comfortably with the new Republic of China government in Taipei. As such, it is not surprising to discover that from as early as 1950 Japan was reinstated as Taiwan's most import export market. Like Cumings, Lin also points to the significance of the Cold War, and US policy, in galvanizing and re-soldering these intra-Asian links as Taiwan joined Japan and the Republic of Korea in the front line of defence against communist expansion in Asia. Significant here was the locus of interaction which Taiwanese business leaders provided Japanese exporters to reach overseas Chinese entrepreneurs in Southeast Asia. Moreover, Lin concludes that the revived Taiwan-Japan relationship in the post-war époque helped boost the island's industrialization, and its wider integration with the international economy in the 1950s and 1960s.

Indeed, Lin's chapter provides a fitting finale for the whole book since it points to two fundamental intertwined issues which emerge (albeit in different degrees) from all the chapters in this volume: firstly, the Second World War in Asia and the Pacific, for all its ghastliness and destructiveness, was not necessarily a grand watershed in Asian international history, and that over the longer-term the continuities which link the 1930s to the 1950s may be more significant than the discontinuities; secondly, throughout the twentieth century, and notwithstanding often gaping and apparently insurmountable international political divisions – colonialism in the 1930s, the Cold War in the 1950s – there was a high-level of economic interaction and interdependence between almost all the countries of South, Southeast and East Asia.

PART 1
The International Order of Asia, the British Empire and the Sterling Area

Chapter 1

British Economic Interests and the International Order of Asia in the 1930s

Shigeru Akita

Structural Power and the History of Economic Relations

The purpose of this chapter is to reconsider the nature and formation of the 'International Order of Asia' in the 1930s in the light of new historiographical developments in Great Britain as well as in Japan,[1] and to present a framework for the reconsideration of the 'International Order of Asia' in the 1950s from the perspective of the continuities from previous decades. The main focus of the argument is to evaluate the role played by the United Kingdom in the formation of the 'International Order of Asia' in the 1930s.

Recently, in an attempt to take the debate on British imperialism beyond the confines of the formal/informal empire discourse, Tony Hopkins has distinguished between two forms of power in the international system and made use of the concepts of 'structural power' and 'relational power', as a means of interpreting the British presence in Latin America, especially in Argentina, in the nineteenth century. 'Structural power' allows its possessors to determine, or at least exert, a predominant influence, and to lay down the general rules of the game governing international relations and can be seen in this context as fundamentally a manifestation of the core values and policy priorities of the British liberal state, with its preference for free trade, low taxation and sound money. On the other hand, 'relational power' deals with the negotiations, pressures and conflicts that determine the outcome of particular contests within this broad framework.[2] These

---

[1] See Shigeru Akita and Naoto Kagotani, 'International Order of Asia in the 1930s', *Discussion Paper of Osaka University of Foreign Studies*, 2000. The first section in this chapter on Japan overlaps with this 'Introduction'. For a critical comment on our views, see Antony Best, 'Keizaiteki Yuwa-seisaku ka, Keizaiteki Nashonarizumu ka [Economic Appeasement or Economic Nationalism?]', *Jinbun Gakuho* [*The Journal of the Institute of Research in Humanities, Kyoto University*], No. 85 (2001).

[2] A.G. Hopkins, 'Informal Empire in Argentina: an Alternative View', *Journal of Latin American Studies*, 26 (1994), pp. 469–84; P.J. Cain and A.G. Hopkins, 'Afterword: The theory and practice of British imperialism', in Raymond E. Dumett (ed.), *Gentlemanly Capitalism and British Imperialism: The New Debate on Empire* (London and New York, 1999), pp. 204–6.

concepts of 'structural power' and 'relational power' originate with Susan Strange, an eminent specialist in international political economy. She identified four aspects of structural power: control over credit, control over production, control over security, and control of knowledge, beliefs and ideas.[3] Let us try and apply these concepts to the broader context of global history.

British imperial history increasingly is being seen as a bridge to global history. In the last chapter of the second edition of *British Imperialism, 1688–2000*,[4] Cain and Hopkins suggest that imperialism and empire can be viewed as globalizing forces. Furthermore, in the introduction to his recent edited volume on globalization, Tony Hopkins emphasizes the importance of 'imperial' or 'modern' globalization as a driving force in the world order.[5] This chapter will analyze the British economic relationship with three Asian countries in the 1930s, that is, with Japan, China and British India, and try to economically connect these countries with each other as well as with Great Britain. In the context of British imperial history, British India has usually been recognized as a core colony or dependency in Britain's 'formal empire', while China has been regarded as a typical example of 'informal empire' in the nineteenth and the early twentieth centuries. The term 'informal empire' was mainly applied to areas and regions of the non-European developing world, as the original definition of the term assumed the unequal political and economic status of these countries. However, the overseas influence of Great Britain ranged far beyond the confines of formal and informal empires, due to the global network of the City of London and the influence of its financial and service sectors in the capitalist world-economy. For example, after the conclusion of the Anglo-Japanese Alliance in 1902, Japan was treated as an ally of Great Britain rather than as part of the British informal empire.[6] Nevertheless, even in the 1930s, the United Kingdom continued to exert financial influence upon Japan and the colonies of other Great Powers through the establishment of the sterling area, by setting 'the rules of the game' for international finance in East Asia. At that time, as we will consider later in the third section, the Chinese Nationalist Government strengthened its political authority, and partly manipulated the balance of power in East Asia as a newly emerging nation-state. Thus debates continue about the validity of applying the concept of informal empire to China. Juergen Osterhammel favours analyzing the dynamic interactions between the British government, the Nationalist Government of China and her 'bureaucratic capitalism', as well as the evolution of a Japanese informal empire in East Asia,

---

[3]   Susan Strange, *States and Markets* (London, 1988), Ch. 2.

[4]   P.J. Cain and A.G. Hopkins, *British Imperialism, 1688–2000* (2nd Edition, Harlow and New York, 2001).

[5]   A.G. Hopkins (ed.), *Globalization in World History* (London, 2002), Introduction.

[6]   Ian H. Nish, *The Anglo-Japanese Alliance: The Diplomacy of Two Island Empires 1894–1907* (London, 1966).

by using a more sophisticated version of informality.[7] But perhaps the best way to consider these interactions is to use the newer concepts of 'structural power' and 'relational power', which incorporate these types of autonomous activities by the non-European countries, and which allow us to understand the extent to which the United Kingdom exerted its influence upon international relations.

In this analysis of economic relationships in the 1930s, three series of data sets, published by the Department of Overseas Trade will principally be drawn upon. They are the *Reports on Economic and Commercial Conditions in Japan, China and British India*. To foster British overseas trade, the Department of Overseas Trade maintained the following commercial representation abroad. In the British Empire, it had the Trade Commissioner and Imperial Trade Correspondent Services. In the 1930s, there were 16 Trade Commissioners' offices, including British India (Calcutta and Bombay, which also covered Ceylon). Sir Thomas M. Ainscough (the Senior Trade Commissioner) represented the department in India. In foreign countries, there were 38 commercial diplomatic posts, situated in all of the more important foreign markets of the world. They consisted of 'Commercial Counsellors' and 'Commercial Secretaries', and both were members of the staff of the British Embassy or Legation in which they served. In certain countries where no commercial diplomatic officer was stationed, the senior consular officer undertook duties of a similar character. H.J. Brett and L.B.G.S. Beale (Commercial Counsellors) represented the department in China, and Sir George Sansom (Commercial Counsellor) did the same in Japan. Related materials at the Foreign Office and the Bank of England archives, which are concerned with financial matters and the interests of Great Britain, will also be referred to.

British Perceptions of Japanese Economic Development in the 1930s

(1) The Changing Perspective of 'Complementarity'

In a previous article, the present author has emphasized the existence of a complementary relationship between the United Kingdom and Japanese industrialization at the turn of the last century.[8] *The British Consular Reports* expressed high expectations of growth in the Japanese capital goods market, and encouraged the formation of a highly developed 'commercial nation', which would lead the rapid growth of intra-Asian trade in the early 1910s. This more favourable

---

[7]   See C.M. Turnbull, 'Formal and Informal Empire in East Asia', in Robin W. Winks (ed.), *The Oxford History of the British Empire*, vol. V, *Historiography* (Oxford, 1999) and Jurgen Osterhammel, 'China', in Judith M. Brown and Wm. Roger Louis (eds), *The Oxford History of the British Empire*, vol. IV, *The Twentieth Century* (Oxford, 1999).

[8]   Shigeru Akita, '"Gentlemanly capitalism", intra-Asian trade and Japanese industrialization at the turn of the last century', *Japan Forum*, 8(1) (1996), pp. 51–65.

attitude of British officials towards the expansion of the Japanese export trade coincided with the financial interests of the City of London.

However, during the inter-war years, this complementarity tended to diminish, especially in the case of British exports of machinery. Just after World War I, it was noted that 'American competition is being keenly felt and threatens to become a permanent danger.' 'The pre-war positions of Great Britain and America have been reversed and a recapture of the market will be a matter of the greatest difficulty,' while 'a great advance was made in local [Japanese] manufacture.'[9] The rapid growth of the Japanese manufacturing industry was accelerated in the 1920s[10] and the early 1930s 'under the stimulus of a vigorous campaign for the encouragement of home products'.[11] This reflected 'the increasing ability of Japan to supply her own machinery requirements',[12] and indeed Japan started to export its machinery and machine tools to Manchuria in the 1930s (and especially after 1934). Therefore, the competitiveness of British machinery was lost in the Japanese import-market and led to the weakening of a recognized sense of complementarity, given the difficulties of keeping pace with the higher development of Japanese industrialization.

At the same time, British financial interests witnessed a diminishing share of Japanese business. Japan reopened its foreign-bond issues in 1923, especially for the reconstruction projects following the Great Earthquake. Japan raised $536,000,000 (£57,000,000) from foreign capital markets up to 1931, when the country was forced to re-adopt an embargo on sales of gold following the abandonment of the gold standard by the British government. This period in the 1920s was referred to as the second introductory period of foreign capital.[13] However, the proportion of British capital was reduced owing to the heavy inflow of American money in the 1920s. In these processes, the financial presence and influence of the City of London declined significantly. Moreover, the Japanese government adopted new monetary and financial policies from 1932.

---

[9]   Department of Overseas Trade, *Report on Economic and Commercial Conditions in Japan, 1919*, p. 39.

[10]   On British perceptions of Japanese economic development in the 1920s from a different angle, see John Sharkey, 'British Perceptions of Japanese Economic Development in the 1920s: with special Reference to the Cotton Industry', in *The History of Anglo-Japanese Relations, 1600–2000*, vol. IV, Janet Hunter and S. Sugiyama (eds), *Economic and Business Relations* (Basingstoke, 2002), Ch. 7.

[11]   Department of Overseas Trade, *Report on Economic and Commercial Conditions in Japan, 1932*, p. 68.

[12]   Ibid., *1932*.

[13]   On the loan issues on the London capital market by Japanese governments in the 1920s, see Toshio Suzuki, 'Japanese Government Loan Issues on the London Capital Market during the Interwar Period', in Hunter and Sugiyama (eds), *Economic and Business Relations*, Ch. 5.

(2) Changes in the Character of Japanese Import-Trade

On the eve of the Great Depression of 1929, Japanese economic development was described as 'remarkable and well-sustained',[14] notwithstanding the Financial Crisis of 1927. Over half of Japan's imports were raw materials, and it was noted that 'Japan's position is not unlike that of Great Britain.... She must purchase abroad the raw materials of industry, and with her profits buy such finished goods as she requires'.[15] This changing character in Japan's import-trade gradually increased the value of imports from British India (raw cotton and pig-iron), Malaya (iron ore and rubber), Australia (wool) and the Dutch East Indies (sugar). 'As her manufacturing capacity advances, she buys more raw materials and less finished products, to the advantage of those countries which supply such commodities as raw cotton, wool, wheat, iron, oil and timber.'[16] Accordingly, the importance of the British Empire, especially that of British India, increased greatly, whereas the imports of manufactured goods from the United Kingdom to Japan dropped drastically.

In the late 1920s, Sansom observed that 'this appears to be an inevitable tendency in world trade ... the sale of vast quantities of raw materials by these regions increases, in the long run, their purchasing power and their consumption of manufactured goods'.[17] He also pointed out that 'disturbed conditions, or any other causes which reduce purchasing power in China or British India, affect seriously the total volume of her [Japanese] exports and, indirectly, her purchasing power in foreign markets in general .. The defeat of a customer in one market may mean the loss of a customer in another'.[18] His remarks reveal the so-called 'final demand linkage effect', which promoted industrialization in Japan. Kaoru Sugihara explained its logic as follows: Southeast Asian countries, such as Burma, the Straits Settlements, and the Dutch East Indies, specialized in the production and export of primary products to European countries; in return, they earned hard currency, sterling, and imported cheap consumer goods from Japan or British India.[19] Through the process of its rapid recovery from the Great Depression, Japan became an important buyer in the world's markets for raw materials and 'one of

---

[14] Department of Overseas Trade, *Report on Economic and Commercial Conditions in Japan, 1929*, p. 1.

[15] Ibid., *1929*, Foreign Trade.

[16] Department of Overseas Trade, *Report on Economic and Commercial Conditions in Japan, 1930*, p. 18.

[17] Department of Overseas Trade, *Report on Economic and Commercial Conditions in Japan, 1927*, p. 64.

[18] Department of Overseas Trade, *Report on Economic and Commercial Conditions in Japan, 1929*, p. 18.

[19] Kaoru Sugihara, 'Japan as an Engine of the Asian international economy, c.1880– 1936', *Japan Forum*, 2(1), (1990).

the most important consumers of raw materials'.[20] Therefore, Japanese demands and imports of raw materials contributed, to a great extent, to the economies of the primary-producing countries. In this sense, Japanese economic development had a vital link with and influence upon the recovery of the world economy in the early 1930s.

(3) The Strong Competitiveness of Japanese Exports

As mentioned before, achieving rapid economic development in 1928, 'Japan has already ... developed from an importer, through an intermediate stage of production for domestic needs, into an exporter.' She was 'not only ... an importer of manufactured products but also ... a potential competitor in other markets.'[21] This trend continued in spite of the Great Depression, and in 1932 Sansom observed that 'Japan offers less and less prospect as a market for the manufactured goods of other countries. ... She is now established as one of the most serious competitors of those countries, and is at the same time one of the most important consumers of raw materials.'[22]

The Japanese export market changed drastically in the early 1930s. On 11 January 1930, the Japanese government lifted the gold-embargo under deflationary policies and its economy fell into unusual difficulties. Sansom pointed out at the time that 'her main economic interests are in two regions, the USA and Asia ... which must have an important bearing upon her foreign policy.'[23] However, owing to the financial depression in the USA and political unrest in China, combined with the development of the Chinese manufacturing industry, by 1934 Sansom was forced to observe that 'the two leading markets have lost their relative importance' and that 'it is somewhat surprising to find 1934 exports to British India valued at 238 million yen, whereas exports to what is described as China in the Japanese trade returns were only 117 million yen.'[24] British India became the largest trade-partner of Japan in 1933 and this development led to the trade dispute with India. Sansom was already insisting in 1930 that 'Japan must turn more and more to the production of finished goods to supply not only her present markets, but also to attempt to push far afield into Africa, Near Eastern, and South American areas

---

[20]   Department of Overseas Trade, *Report on Economic and Commercial Conditions in Japan, 1932*, p. 39.

[21]   Department of Overseas Trade, *Report on Economic and Commercial Conditions in Japan, 1928*, p. 34.

[22]   Department of Overseas Trade, *Report on Economic and Commercial Conditions in Japan, 1932*, p. 39.

[23]   Department of Overseas Trade, *Report on Economic and Commercial Conditions in Japan, 1930*, p. 16.

[24]   Department of Overseas Trade, *Report on Economic and Commercial Conditions in Japan, 1933–34*, p. 103.

hitherto supplied mainly by Lancashire.'[25] *The Economist* also pointed out that 'under pressure of boycott in China and restrictions in India, Japan has been forced to seek new markets for her goods, and has been successful in opening new connections in Central and South America, Africa and Eastern Europe.'[26]

In the early 1930s, several Japanese commercial missions were dispatched to these latter regions in order to open new export-markets, which took about one-quarter of total Japanese exports in 1934. Through the rapid recovery from the Great Depression, the export trade of Japan diversified. New exports such as rayon (artificial silk), woolen tissues and steel ingots increased, and 'tinned and bottled foodstuffs, chemicals, instruments and machinery, lamps, iron manufactures and glass ware'[27] were added. Sansom observed that this trend 'has reduced Japan's dependence upon the sale of a single preponderant commodity [silk]', and he noted 'important progress in heavy industry, hitherto perhaps the weakest point in Japan's industrial economy'.[28] The quality of Japanese exports greatly improved and competition with high quality foreign goods commenced, especially in the case of cotton textiles. Sansom was highly impressed by these transformations.

(4) The Positive View of Japanese Economic Nationalism

Sansom put much emphasis and high estimation upon the Japanese economic and financial policies, which were introduced from 1932 by the Finance Minister, Korekiyo Takahashi. His economic policy was characterized as 'a policy of State expenditure financed by State borrowing', reflation and liberal spending. 'The loan-financed expenditure of the Government has set in motion economic factors which were awaiting release and has thus produced those favourable conditions.' 'It is at least true that a country which is rapidly increasing its production can more safely depart from financial orthodoxy than one where production is stationary.' 'It may be regarded as an experiment in recovery from depression by an un-orthodox programme of public works financed by public loans.'[29] The Japanese government issued domestic bonds of £200,000,000 [about 3 billion Yen]. According to Sansom's judgement, these bonds were 'not an excessive price to pay.' Takahashi's

---

[25]   Department of Overseas Trade, *Report on Economic and Commercial Conditions in Japan, 1930*, p. 27. Cf. *The Economist* (2 March 1935), 'Japan – Workshop of the Orient'.

[26]   *The Economist* (3 June 1933), 'Japanese Export Competition'; *The Economist* (16 February 1935), 'Prosperity – Japanese Style'.

[27]   Department of Overseas Trade, *Report on Economic and Commercial Conditions in Japan, 1933–34*, p. 93. Cf. Osamu Ishii, *Sekai-Kyoukou to Nihon no Keizai-Gaikou 1930–1936* [*The Great Depression and Japanese Economic Diplomacy*], (Tokyo: Keisou-shobo, 1995).

[28]   Department of Overseas Trade, *Report on Economic and Commercial Conditions in Japan, 1933–34*, Major Industries, p. 68.

[29]   Ibid., *1933–34*, pp. 14–15. Cf. *The Economist* (28 September 1935), 'Loan Expenditure in Japan'.

financial policies might be called Keynesian, even in the first-half of the 1930s. Of course, Sansom also pointed out that the loan-financed expenditures mainly poured into military spending, leading to the poverty of Japanese farmers, and that 'the capital resources of Japan do not suffice for the economic development of Manchuria at the pace which it has hitherto maintained.' 'A Japan-Manchuria economic bloc has not yet been constituted.'[30]

However, the depreciation of the yen and a fall in the exchange rate gave a great advantage to Japanese exports. 'Most exporting industries benefited' and a 'spectacular revival in foreign trade'[31] was achieved within a short period. Sansom also tried to analyze other secrets of Japanese competitiveness. He referred to the 'rationalization' of industries, the bid for increased efficiency and the beneficial role of government assistance, especially subsidies for shipping. Such economic policies of the Japanese government, and the positive role played by the state, were most impressive because they contrasted sharply with the poor performance of British governments.[32]

British Perceptions of Chinese Industrialization in the 1930s

(1) The Growth of Chinese Cotton Industries and the Export of British Capital Goods

This chapter will now move on to reveal British perceptions of Chinese industrialization, which started in the middle of the 1920s around Shanghai. In September 1929, Commercial Counsellor, H.H. Fox reported in the aftermath of China's political upheavals as follows: 'during the recent troubled times in China the foreign-controlled settlements of Shanghai have been the one area within which life and property have been, comparatively speaking, safe and where confidence could be felt in the investment of capital, an immunity of which the Chinese themselves have taken full advantage. There has been in consequence a great concentration of wealth in the port, a rapid increase of population, and every incentive for establishing industries ... Shanghai has now become, what at one time it was predicted Hankow would be, the industrial centre *par excellence* of China'.[33]

Chinese cotton industries developed rapidly in the inter-war years. First, Chinese cotton-yarn production acquired a dominant position in the early 1920s in the domestic market, and from the middle of the 1920s, an intensive triangular struggle between European, Japanese and local Chinese textiles emerged for the Chinese cotton-piece goods market. The share of British cotton piece goods

---

[30]   Ibid., *1933–34*, p. 16.

[31]   Department of Overseas Trade, *Report on Economic and Commercial Conditions in Japan, 1932*, pp. 12 and 17.

[32]   Cf. G.C. Peden, *Keynes, the Treasury and British Economic Policy* (London, 1988).

[33]   Department of Overseas Trade, *Economic Conditions in China to September 1st, 1929*. Report by H.H. Fox, assisted by H.J. Brett (London, 1930), p. 33.

declined heavily, and Japanese cloths increased their sales (although the latter's turnover was exceeded by local products after 1927). Therefore, there was a keen price competition within the Chinese cotton goods market. *The Report of 1928* mentioned rivalry between British and Japanese mid-range quality textiles and the rapid rise in Chinese production of coarser quality goods. It also pointed out that 'the lot of the British piece-goods importer has been and still is further embarrassed by the greatly increased competition from local and Japanese mills ... and it is quite impossible for Lancashire to successfully compete with the eastern mills in some lines.'[34]

On the other hand, the development of cotton and woolen industries led to the growth of imports of machinery and industrial plants in China. *The Report of 1929* pointed to the vast potential of the Chinese market for the export of capital goods: 'This country may within the next decade go far towards making herself independent of foreign supplies in the matter of clothing and foodstuffs, but it will be many years before she can attempt to make herself the various forms of delicate and complicated machinery which her industries will require. I can see no reason why Great Britain, if she can quote competitive prices and reasonably prompt deliveries, should not hold her own in the Chinese machinery market.'[35] The same expectations continued to grow in the 1930s. *The Report of 1931–33* emphasized that 'the greatest market in China from now forward will undoubtedly consist mainly of capital goods, and the loss to our trade in consumable goods will, or can be, much more than offset by the volume of machinery and equipment we supply.' 'On the principle that the best markets of the United Kingdom are the most developed countries, progress in China should lead to increased imports of higher class goods, materials, machinery and equipment from the United Kingdom. It must therefore be in the ultimate interest of Great Britain to co-operate with the Chinese in the establishment of industries calculated to meet the needs of the masses'.[36] In this sense, there existed a complementary relationship between British exports of capital goods, especially machinery, and Chinese rapid industrialization. This type of economic relationship had first appeared at the turn of the century between Japan and the UK, as mentioned in the former section. Now in the early 1930s, China started to follow the path of industrialization paved by Japan, and there appeared two dynamic economic centres in East Asia.[37] In the 1930s, new exporters from Italy, Belgium and Czechoslovakia participated in the Chinese capital goods market. The competition for capital goods exports

---

[34] Department of Overseas Trade, *Economic Conditions in China to September 1st, 1928*. Report by H.H. Fox (London, 1929), p. 47.

[35] Department of Overseas Trade, *Economic Conditions in China to September 1st, 1929*, p. 50.

[36] Department of Overseas Trade, *Trade and Economic Conditions in China 1931–33*. Report by Louis Beale and G. Clinton Pelham (London, 1933), pp. 10–11, 81.

[37] Kaoru Sugihara, *Ajia kan Boeki no Keisei to Kozo* [*The Formation and Structure of Intra-Asian Trade*], (Kyoto: Mineruva Shobo, 1996), Ch. 4.

to China became intensive, and China emerged as one of the most price-oriented export markets in the world. *The Report of 1930* pointed out that 'the days of large profits in old-established lines of trade are gone, and only the closest co-operation between the manufacturer and the agent or merchant here can help British trade to regain its former preeminence.'[38]

(2) The Development of Chinese Consumer Goods Exports

At this initial stage of industrialization, China began to export her home-produced consumer goods (for example, cotton piece goods and matches) to the Straits Settlements, the Dutch East Indies, Egypt, Arabia and Morocco.[39] In 1927, Chinese exports drastically increased and the Chinese trade deficit with the United Kingdom markedly decreased. In the early 1930s, this trend was hindered by the Great Depression and by newly erected tariff barriers. However, even under such unfavourable conditions, Chinese exports to British India increased in the items of cotton yarns, piece goods and raw silk, from 1.8 to 5.19 per cent of the country's share of Chinese exports. These home-produced consumer goods were also exported to Southeast Asian countries such as French Indo-China, Siam, the Straits Settlements, the Dutch East Indies and the Philippines. In this period, to a limited extent, China became an exporter of light consumer goods, including hosiery, matches, soap, lamps and glasses, and these exports amounted to £6 million in 1930.[40] In 1931, the import value of raw cotton exceeded that of manufactured cotton goods for the first time in China. The British Reports identified this trend as a consequence of the rapid development of the Chinese cotton industry. This increase in the Chinese export trade contributed to the development of intra-Asian trade in the 1930s.

In the inter-war years, the United Kingdom occupied the third position in the share of Chinese external trade, compared with its dominant position before World War I. Japan and the United States engaged in a fierce competition for the biggest share. However, the share of the British Empire as a whole, including Hong Kong, British India, Australia and Canada, averaged about 35 per cent, and occupied the top place in Chinese external trade in the 1930s (although admittedly the empire's share did tend to decrease). *The Report of 1931–33* analyzed the reasons for the competitiveness of Japan and the US and pointed out a linkage effect between the export trade and imports: 'They [Japan and the US] are by far the greatest importers of Chinese produce. Thus the trade between China and Japan, and China and the United States is a two-way trade. Together Japan and the United

---

[38]   Department of Overseas Trade, *Economic Conditions in China to August 30th, 1930*, Report by E.G. Jamieson (London, 1930), p. 70.

[39]   Department of Overseas Trade, *Economic Conditions in China to September 1st, 1928*, Industry and Production, p. 36.

[40]   Department of Overseas Trade, *Trade and Economic Conditions in China 1931–33*, p. 8.

States of America normally take 40 per cent of Chinese exports.'[41] The increase of imports from China led to more exports to China, and there was a correlation between import and export. In this sense, the expansion of Chinese exports and increased absorption of Chinese goods provided foreign exchange for China, thus contributing to the servicing of Chinese debts. Moreover, *The Report of 1931–33* suggested the possibility of acceleration in Chinese economic development – indeed, China might even catch up with Japan.

(3) Tariff Autonomy and the Policies of the Chinese Nationalist Government

From 1 February 1929, the Nationalist Government in Nanjing recovered China's tariff autonomy and raised the level of import tariffs for revenue purposes.[42] The tone of the *British Commercial Reports* was sympathetic towards Chinese tariff policy. The import duties of 1931 were regarded as revenue tariffs, because the increase on capital goods was gradual and the rates for railway materials and machinery were reduced in order to encourage industrial development. In 1932–33, it became clear that the Chinese government had further raised the level of tariffs in order to protect domestic industries, although the rates for machinery and vehicles remained unchanged. This introduction of the so-called 'protection tariff' gave strong impetus to the domestic production of consumer goods and, to some extent, accelerated the development of import substitution. *The Report of 1931–33* commented that 'there is nothing to retard this development except China's internal political situation, and it is reasonable to expect that with the growing national consciousness, the efforts already being made towards a settled economic policy will now be greatly accelerated.'[43] As far as the exports of British capital goods were guaranteed, the British commercial secretaries and counsellors gave positive support to the policies of the Nationalist Government. China was an emerging market where a high rate of economic growth was widely expected. However, the British officials in China were worried about the intensive competition between the United States, Germany and the UK for capital goods exports, and became more sensitive towards the declining share of British exports of capital goods.

Indeed, once the high expectations in the Chinese market turned to disappointment, thanks to the poor record of British exports, criticisms of the economic policies of the Chinese Nationalist Government soon followed. For example, China's hasty import-substitution policies and its discriminative treatment of foreign capital were regarded as inopportune at a time when it was essential for China's development to be assisted by foreign countries, particularly the UK. Moreover, the Nationalist

---

[41]   Ibid., p. 10.

[42]   Toru Kubo, *Senkanki Chugoku Jiritsu eno Mosaku: Kanzei-Tsuka Seisaku to Keizai-hatten* [*China's Quest for Sovereignty in the Inter-war Period: Tariff Policy and Economic Development*], (Tokyo: Tokyo University Press, 1999).

[43]   Department of Overseas Trade, *Trade and Economic Conditions in China 1931–33*, p. 58.

Government's state-oriented industrialization programme[44] was criticized, since it was detrimental to the free access of Chinese entrepreneurs to the market. *The Report of 1931–33* expressed wariness at the excessive economic nationalism of the Guomindang government. The barter trade of machinery between Germany and China was also criticized as a deviation from multi-lateral trade.[45]

However, British economic interests in China covered the broader service sector as well as trade interests. The British Commercial Secretary in Shanghai, H.J. Brett, sent an insightful letter to the Commercial Counsellor in Beijing on 10 May 1927:

> I take it that from the home point of view, China is chiefly important (a) as a market for British goods, and (b) as a field for the profitable investment of British capital. My own opinion is that the real importance of China to us is potential rather than actual, for she is undoubtedly the largest undeveloped market in the world, and the main reason (apart from any political considerations) for trying to keep our end up out here is that we may be in a position to get our fair share of the enormous trade that is bound to come sooner or later. From this point of view, the British firms, shipping companies, & etc., which have developed trade in China appear to me to constitute valuable assets which it is worth our while to protect not only for their own sakes but also with an eye to the future.[46]

This opinion was fully supported by Sir M. Lampson, the British Minister to China. As he insisted:

> British companies in China engaged in the business of local shipping, banking, insurance, shipbuilding, mining, and the big distributing companies who have built up-country wide organizations for the manufacture and sale of oil, tobacco, sugar and other commodities ... These important but largely intangible financial interests which we have in China are apt to be overlooked ... The real importance of maintaining and protecting British interests, as Mr. Brett points out, lies rather in the fact that China is, beyond question, the largest undeveloped market for British goods in the world, and that the existence of old-established and well-organized British trading communities in various parts of the country is an asset which, when normal conditions are restored, cannot fail to be of the greatest value to British merchants and manufacturers both in the United Kingdom and other parts of the British Empire.[47]

---

[44]   See Toru Kubo, 'China's Economic Development and the International Order of Asia, 1930s–50s' in this volume.

[45]   Department of Overseas Trade, *Trade and Economic Conditions in China 1933–1935*. Report by A.H. George (London, 1935), pp. 2, 32, 34–5.

[46]   Commercial Secretary, Shanghai, to Commercial Counsellor, Peking, 10 May 1927. Enclosure in No. 1, F6353/1566/10, F4047, I.O.L.C., L/P&S/10/1201, File1, pt 16 (1927).

[47]   Despatch. Sir M. Lampson to Sir Austen Chamberlain, No. 569, 27 May 1927, F6353/1566/10, in Ibid.

The remarks of Brett and Lampson appear partly to reflect the beginning of market penetration by British firms through direct investment in the interior of China.[48] Moreover, these quotations indicate the intimate connections between British economic interests in China, the network of British expatriate businesses, and the British Empire.

(4) Chinese Currency Reform in 1935 and British Financial Interests

China escaped from the severe impact of the Great Depression in 1929 given its silver currency standard. However, since September 1931, the pound sterling, Indian rupee and Japanese yen seceded from the international gold standard one after another, and the value of Chinese currency appreciated relatively in terms of these currencies. This process was accentuated when the US dollar followed the same course in April 1933. 'From October 1931 to May 1934, prices fell, trade was further handicapped by drought, famine, war and the loss of the Manchurian provinces, exports were reduced ... the adverse balance of trade increased, and in 1932 for the first time for many years there was a net export of silver, reflecting the adverse balance of payments'. The US's Silver Purchase Act promoted the drain of silver from China after June 1934, and the Chinese economy fell into a period of severe deflation. This monetary crisis had a very serious effect on imports. *The Report of 1933–35* fretted about this situation, because the UK had the paramount interest in China in every field of foreign economic activity. This was especially the case in investments,[49] reflecting the UK's position as East Asia's structural power.

The Nationalist Government's currency reform of 3 November 1935 overcame these difficulties and paved the way for further development of the Chinese economy.[50] As for the role played by the UK in Chinese currency reform, there exists an academic debate about the following subjects: (1) the initiative of the Guomindang government and its relationship with the Leith-Ross Mission of 1935, and (2) the implications of the international great-power rivalry for currency

---

[48]   Jurgen Osterhammel, 'Imperialism in Transition: British Business and the Chinese Authorities, 1931–37', *China Quarterly*, LXLVIII (1984); Jurgen Osterhammel, 'China', in Judith M. Brown and Wm. Roger Louis (eds), *The Oxford History of the British Empire*, vol. IV, *The Twentieth Century* (Oxford, 1999).

[49]   Department of Overseas Trade, *Trade and Economic Conditions in China 1933–1935*, pp. 72–80.

[50]   Arthur N. Young, *China's Nation-Building Effort, 1927–1937: The Financial and Political Record* (Stanford, 1971), Chs 7 and 8; Yutaka Nozawa (ed.), *Chugoku no Heisei-Kaikaku to Kokusai-kankei [Currency Reform in China (1935) and China's Relations with Japan, Britain and America]*, (Tokyo, 1981). On American influence and Chinese responses, see Tomoko Shiroyama, 'China's Relations with the International Financial System in the 20th Century: Historical Analysis and Contemporary Implication' in this volume.

reform.[51] Here, we will try to reveal briefly the original British intentions for Chinese currency reform. In April 1935, the British trading and financial interests in China requested that their home government take the lead in the Chinese financial crisis: 'The present crisis in Chinese currency and finance offers HMG an opportunity of offering constructive assistance in a manner which will both alleviate the financial difficulties of China and bring Great Britain more actively in to the field. A British initiative taken today will appear, not as a protest against encroachment on British interests and, therefore, not as a hostile move against either party in the Far East, but as a realistic measure designed for practical ends.'[52]

The British government decided to despatch Sir F. Leith-Ross, the chief economic adviser to the British government, to China in June 1935. Before his departure to China, Leith-Ross exchanged several notes with Montagu Norman, the Governor of the Bank of England. Through their exchange of opinions, we can ascertain the original aims of British policy. In response to the points raised in Leith-Ross's 'Questions on China', the Governor carefully replied as follows:

> [Question] (1) If the Chinese Government decided to abandon silver, should her currency be linked with gold, sterling or yen?;

> [Answer] Linking to sterling would be best, and the Sterling Exchange Standard would be the best solution with a rate not above 1s/2d ... It seems most probable that they [Japan and the United States] would refuse financial assistance to inaugurate a sterling scheme, whereas China would probably regard a loan as a necessary condition;

> [Question] (2) Is it indispensable for China to raise a foreign loan or credit before attempting to place the dollar on a foreign currency basis?;

> [Answer] It may be necessary to provide China by means of a loan with (a) the substantial external cushion, and (b) the means of effectively regulating their exchange.[53]

The Governor seemed to suggest three related but 'opposing' targets to Leith-Ross: (1) the search for the possibility of a sterling exchange standard, (2) the

[51]   Cain and Hopkins, *British Imperialism*, Ch. 25; Shigeru Akita, 'British informal empire in East Asia, 1880–1939: a Japanese perspective', in Dumett (ed.), *Gentlemanly Capitalism*, Ch. 6; Peter Cain, 'British Economic Imperialism in China in the 1930s: The Leith-Ross Mission', *Bulletin of Asia-Pacific Studies*, vol. VII (1997).

[52]   Bank of England Archive, G1/298, 2524/5, *The Note Presented to the Chancellor of the Exchequer, 3rd April 1935*, 'Note on Policy in China'.

[53]   Bank of England Archive, OV104/1 3138–2, 38A, 38B and G1/300 2525/2, Confidential. From Leith-Ross to the Governor, 'Question on China', 3 July 1935; OV104/1 3138–2, 43A, Confidential. 'Provisional Answers to Questionnaire on China', 17 July 1935.

effective cooperation of the four powers of the international consortium to China, and (3) the exercise of strong influence over the Chinese Nationalist Government. In trying to create 'the rules of the game' in China's international financial affairs, Britain had to pay much attention to the reactions from Japan and, especially, from the US, whose silver purchasing policy had greatly influenced the need for currency reform in the first place. The Governor also agreed that 'trading interests were very important and he thought it quite likely that the trading interests of this country desired HMG to follow a much stronger policy than hitherto'.[54] These original intentions of the British government for Chinese currency reform reflected the mixed character of British economic interests in China.

The currency reform led not only to the stability of the Chinese currency and its exchange rate, but also to the enlargement of the central government's authority. It enabled the government in Nanjing to consolidate external debts and to solve the problems of defaults on Chinese railway loans. Therefore, the rating of the Chinese government in international money markets was greatly improved. *The Report of 1935–37* appreciated the success of the currency reform and commented in an optimistic manner that:

> The outstanding feature is the increasing and justified confidence which the Chinese themselves, as well as the world at large, have in the future of this country ... the magnitude of China's needs in her economic development – communications, industries, and technical skill – provide an opportunity for the United Kingdom to contribute to the building up of a modern China on sound foundations, a task of the greatest importance and value to China and to the rest of the world. It is for us to grasp the opportunity by assisting China in the fields of planning and creating her public utilities, communications and basic industries.[55]

These remarks reflected the economic positions of the UK and the British Empire, which dominated Chinese external trade and foreign investments in China.

British Perceptions of the Indian Economy in the 1930s

This chapter has analyzed British perceptions of Japan and China in the 1930s, mainly by referring to commercial reports and related materials. We will now examine British perceptions of Indian economic development in the same period, and compare the case of British India with East Asia. In the course of the 1930s,

---

[54]   Bank of England Archive, G1/300 2525/2, 14A. CHINA, 24 July 1935.

[55]   Department of Overseas Trade, *Report on Economic and Commercial Conditions in China,* by Sir Louis Beale, *April 1935–March 1937* (London, 1937), pp. 5–6.

British India was incorporated into the so-called 'Ottawa System', that is, imperial preference and the sterling area.[56]

(1) The Impact of East Asian Industrialization: the Development of 'Intra-Asian Competition'

The economic developments in Japan and China in the 1930s were mirrored in the *Reports on economic and Commercial Conditions in India*. In particular, the Japanese export drive of the early 1930s became a major threat to British manufactured exports. *The Report of 1930–31* clearly analyzed 'Japanese competition' in cotton piece-goods as follows: 'Japan has been able to turn the boycott of UK goods to her own advantage and has increased her share of the total trade to 36 per cent ... Japanese competition is based simply and solely on the price factor ... the leaders in control of the highly-centralised and closely-knit cotton industry of Japan have realized the need throughout the East for standardised cloth at rates which are within the limit of the restricted purchasing power of the impoverished masses of India, China and Africa ... Even the Indian mills are suffering most severely from Japanese competition in plain goods.' 'For the first time in the history of the trade, imports of Japanese piece goods [Grey Goods] have exceeded, both in quantity and value, the imports from the UK.'[57] The British *Reports* pointed out that the depreciation of the exchange value of the yen and the drastic decrease of the purchasing power of India were the main causes of Japanese penetration into the Indian market. This development led to the cotton trade negotiations between Japan and the Government of India in 1933, and to the subsequent signing of the Indo-Japanese cotton trade agreement in April 1934.

The cheap consumer goods from Japan penetrated into the Indian market through the tariff barrier erected by the Government of India. *The Report of 1933–34* pointed out as follows:

> The results last year would have been much more striking had it not been for the onset of Japanese competition, which had a dual effect. In the first place, Japanese exporters secured a certain amount of trade formerly enjoyed by the UK and, secondly, they succeeded in capturing a much greater volume of trade from Continental exporters, much of which would otherwise have been diverted to suppliers in the UK. The disparity between the respective price levels of the UK and Japan is too great to be bridged by a 10% preference ... The additional alternative minimum specific duties imposed on a limited range of foreign imports under the provisions of the Indian Tariff (Amendment) Act, 1934, have

---

[56]   See B.R. Tomlinson, *The Political Economy of the Raj 1914–1947: The Economics of Decolonization in India* (London, 1979); idem., *The New Cambridge History of India, III–3, The Economy of Modern India 1860–1970* (Cambridge, 1993), Chs 3 and 4.

[57]   Department of Overseas Trade, *Conditions and Prospects of United Kingdom Trade in India 1930–31*, Report by Thomas M. Ainscough (London, 1932), pp. 67–73, 148–9.

checked, to some extent, the flood of Japanese imports in those items, but it is to be expected that Japanese competition will increase in intensity and will cover a constantly widening range of goods.[58]

These remarks reflected the limited capacity of tariff policies to restrict the inflow of cheap consumer goods, which formed a major part of the development of intra-Asian trade.

At the same time, Chinese cotton goods, especially yarns, were exported to India in the early 1930s: 'It will be noted that the weight of yarn imported from China actually increased, but there was a drop in values due to lower prices.'[59] 'The incursion of mills in China into trade in counts of 40's [yarns] and upwards is a recent significant development.'[60] The Japanese and Chinese cotton goods competed in the Indian market: 'in 11's to 20's [cotton yarns], the increase was almost entirely secured by Japanese yarns at the expense of China ... In two-fold spinning, the Chinese mills were out of the market in the earlier part of the year, but re-entered it after October, when Japanese arrivals tended to fall off.' 'Japan has almost completely ousted the product of the Chinese mills from the market [of Grey Goods] as a result of the depreciated yen'.[61] Here was merely one aspect of 'intra-Asian competition' for cotton goods in the 1930s. However, as we will see later, the import of cotton yarns in India was negligible, when compared with the large and rapidly growing production of the Indian mills. By involving Indian manufacturers, intra-Asian competition evolved on an even larger scale.

The growth of Japanese exports to India was not confined to cotton goods. The British *Reports* referred to the increase of other consumer goods, such as porcelain, glass and glassware, and boots and shoes: 'So widespread is the sale of Japanese rubber footwear that even the Indian shoemakers of Cawnpore, Agra and Delhi are finding it difficult to compete'.[62] In addition to these miscellaneous light industrial goods, the export of capital goods from Japan commenced steadily from the middle of the 1930s: 'Imports from Japan have shown steady expansion during the past few years and include such items as cotton textile machinery, sewing and knitting machines, and cheap industrial equipment for the lesser industries ... Intensified competition must be expected in the future and greater efforts will be required to secure business.' 'Japanese competition is now severe in galvanised

---

[58]   Department of Overseas Trade, *Conditions and Prospects of United Kingdom Trade in India 1933–34*, pp. 111–13.

[59]   Department of Overseas Trade, *Conditions and Prospects of United Kingdom Trade in India 1930–31*, pp. 140–42.

[60]   Department of Overseas Trade, *Report on Economic and Commercial Conditions in India 1935–36*, by Sir Thomas M. Ainscough (London, 1936), pp. 116–17.

[61]   Department of Overseas Trade, *Conditions and Prospects of United Kingdom Trade in India 1932–33*, Report by Sir Thomas M. Ainscough (London, 1933), pp. 120–21, 129.

[62]   Department of Overseas Trade, *Conditions and Prospects of United Kingdom Trade in India 1930–31*, pp. 208–9.

sheets and wire nails and is also increasing in tubes.'[63] These miscellaneous cheap goods were also important items of intra-Asian trade and they were necessities for the everyday life of the poor inhabitants of British India.

Table 1.1   The Sources of Supply of Yarns to India and Indian Mills Production (lbs)

Countries	1930–31	1931–32	1932–33	1933–34	1934–35
UK	10,314,913	11,912,546	13,357,065	9,952.435	9,792,311
Netherlands	15,015	–	–	–	–
Switzerland	73,600	51,201	65,900	13,500	–
Italy	64,435	142,489	5,444	18,090	–
China (incl. Hong Kong)	11,743,238	13,215,238	13,325,400	10,229,275	12,767,925
Japan	6,894,903	6,206,197	18,148,809	11,683,936	11,339,411
Others	33,811	47,429	200,764	157,927	122,203
Total	29,139,915	31,575,100	45,103,382	32,055.163	34,021,850
Indian Mills	867,279,000	966,407,000	1,016,418,000	921,061,000	1,000,756,000

Sources: Department of Overseas Trade, *Commercial Reports on India, 1930–35* (N.B. these are all current figures and are not adjusted by constant figures.)

(2) The Ottawa Trade Agreement, Imperial Preference and Indian Benefits

British India was an essential part of the 'formal' British Empire. *The Reports of 1932–33* and *1933–34* appreciated the positive effects of the Ottawa Trade Agreement upon British trade relations, and allocated special sections to an analysis of the Ottawa Agreement: 'This momentous agreement gives effect, for the first time in the history of the trading relations of the two peoples, to the principle of Imperial Preference and thereby inaugurates a new era in Indo-British economic relations which, it is hoped, will strengthen the bonds of mutual interest and will contribute to the material welfare of the two nations'. 'The outstanding advantage of the Ottawa Trade Agreement is the acceptance by India of the principle of Imperial Preference and her realisation that it is to her material interest to take her part in the economic *bloc* of the British Commonwealth of Nations'.[64] From the British point of view, the Ottawa Trade Agreement was recognized as an initial step in the formation of an economic bloc with India and the other Dominions. It was further expected, in 1933, that the British

---

[63]   Department of Overseas Trade, *Report on Economic and Commercial Conditions in India 1935–36*, pp. 142, 156.

[64]   Department of Overseas Trade, *Conditions and Prospects of United Kingdom Trade in India 1932–33* (London, 1933), pp. 74, 87–8.

Commonwealth might act as a group of nations in preserving a favourable regime for mutual trading.[65] It was a peculiar expectation from the Indian point of view, because British India was not a formal member of the British Commonwealth, and the Indian government was reluctant to accept the principle of imperial preference. Indian preferences on British cotton goods were only conceded in 1931 (at a 5 per cent margin), and were not intentionally discussed at the Ottawa Trade Agreement for political reasons.[66]

The Report of 1932–33 included a detailed analysis of the working of the Ottawa Trade Agreement. According to its data, the total advantage to the UK was Rs.551 lakhs or £4,132,500. Of this total, no less than Rs.337 lakhs (£2,527,500) was derived from differential duties, which were imposed prior to the Ottawa Agreement in order to protect the Indian consumer from the effects of the policy of discriminating protection. Therefore, the total advantage to the UK which might be directly attributed to the preferences conceded by the Ottawa Trade Agreement amounted to Rs.214.5 lakhs or £1,608,750. This total sum was compared with the figure of Rs.802 lakhs or £6,015,000, which was the total advantage accruing to India from the preferences granted by the UK.[67] As these statistics indicate, the introduction of preferences was followed by a relative improvement in the competitive position of the UK. However, British India received far greater benefits from the Ottawa Trade Agreement through the increase of Indian exports to the British home market: 'When the effects of the valuable preferences accorded to Indian products such as tea, linseed, rice, jute manufactures, pig iron and semi-manufactured steel are felt in a normal year, it may be presumed that the UK market will be a still more valuable outlet for India's exportable surplus and that the percentage will probably advance still further. This will be a development of the greatest importance in binding the economic interests of the two countries still closer.'[68] In this sense, the 'Ottawa System' (cotton goods preferences plus the Ottawa Trade Agreement) produced quite one-sided benefits for British India. This tendency was confirmed by a contemporary publication of the Royal Institute of International Affairs,[69] and Cain and Hopkins also insist that the Ottawa Agreement was more beneficial to primary-producing colonies than to British industries. The British home market became the largest open market in the world, which enabled British colonies to earn sterling for servicing their debts to the City

[65] Department of Overseas Trade, *Conditions and Prospects of United Kingdom Trade in India 1933–34*, p. 55.

[66] Basudev Chatterji, *Trade, Tariffs and Empire: Lancashire and British Policy in India 1919–1939* (Delhi, 1992), chs 7–8.

[67] Department of Overseas Trade, *Conditions and Prospects of United Kingdom Trade in India 1932–33*, pp. 90–124.

[68] Ibid., p. 31.

[69] The Royal Institute of International Affairs, *The Problem of International Investment* (Oxford, 1937), p. 326.

of London.[70] In 1936–37, 'on account of very heavy shipments of Indian produce … the favourable balance [to India] attained the record figure of Rs.16 crores … It is abundantly clear that India now enjoys a substantial and increasingly favourable balance of trade in merchandise with the United Kingdom'.[71]

However, this was only one aspect of the 'Ottawa System'. The 'openness' of the trade regime was more conspicuous for the international order of Asia in the 1930s, especially in the case of British India. A typical example of such 'openness' was the huge export of Indian raw cotton to Japan in the 1930s. The fiscal year of 1932 was a 'nadir of India's economic history' and the disastrous fall in prices continued unchecked. However, 'shipments to Japan, remained constant at just under Rs.14 crores' in 1932–33.[72] Indian raw cotton was vital to the rapid development of Japanese cotton industries, and a huge amount of imports offered the Japanese government a critical bargaining chip in its economic diplomacy in the 1930s. In April 1933, the Government of India raised the import duties on Japanese cotton goods to 75 per cent, and denounced the Indo-Japan Commercial Convention of 1904. In retaliation against these measures, the Japanese Cotton Spinners' Association boycotted the import of Indian raw cotton. In order to seek a solution to this trade friction, the Indo-Japan cotton trade negotiations were held in Simla and Delhi from September 1933 to January 1934.[73] Two experienced specialists in trade, who had been the authors of the *Commercial Reports* on Japan and British India, participated in these negotiations. Sir Thomas Ainscough, Senior Trade Commissioner in India, Burma and Ceylon, played a key role in matters affecting the British Empire and Great Britain, while Sir George Sansom, Commercial Counsellor in Japan, joined in the negotiations as an adviser to the Government of India and as an observer of the British Government, 'particularly as regards [the] effect of negotiations on relations between Japan and the British Empire'.[74] Ainscough and Sansom cooperated intimately for the benefit of British

---

[70]   P.J. Cain and A.G. Hopkins, *op. cit.*, Chs 18 and 20; P.J. Cain, 'Was it Worth Having? The British Empire 1850–1950', in P.K. O'Brien and L.P. de la Escosura (eds), *The Costs and Benefits of European Imperialism from the Conquest of Ceuta to the Treaty of Lusaka, Revista de Historia Economica*, 16–1 (1998).

[71]   Department of Overseas Trade, *Conditions and Prospects of United Kingdom Trade in India 1937–38*, Report by Sir Thomas M. Ainscough (London, 1939), pp. 32–5.

[72]   Department of Overseas Trade, *Conditions and Prospects of United Kingdom Trade in India 1932–33*, pp. 16–19.

[73]   For Japanese economic diplomacy in the 1930s, see Naoto Kagotani, *Ajia Kokusai Tsusho Chitujyo to Kindai Nihon* [*The Asian International Trading Order and Modern Japan*] (Nagoya: Nagoya University Press, 2000), Chs 6–7; Naoto Kagotani, 'Japan's Commercial Penetration and the Cotton Trade Negotiations in the 1930s' in this volume.

[74]   Telegram from Mr. E. Crowe (Department of Overseas Trade) to Mr. Snow (British Ambassador to Japan), 21 August 1933, No. 174, F5407/1203/23, FO 371/17161 (The National Archives of the UK, hereafter TNA). I am indebted to Prof. Kagotani for bringing the material in notes 74–6 to my attention.

India by taking advantage of their well-informed positions. In particular, Sansom recognized that 'the cotton boycott was Japan's strongest, if not her only card; and she would wish to play it with the greatest effect', and judged that the export of raw cotton to Japan was indispensable to Indian agriculturalists and the Government of India. Therefore, he saw the importance of a linkage between the quotas on Japanese cotton goods and Japan's purchase of Indian raw cotton at the critical stage of negotiations in October 1933.[75] Sir George Schuster, the Finance Member of the Government of India, also shared the same opinion and thought that 'it was important to encourage the Japanese to buy large quantities of Indian cotton, by giving them a high "ceiling" for the textile quota, linked to a high figure for raw cotton'.[76] The negotiations reached an agreement in January 1934.

Table 1.2   Exports of Indian Raw Cotton and Home Mills Consumption in the Early 1930s. Unit: Thousand bales (400 lbs)

	1929	1930	1931	1932	1933
To the UK	233	286	274	125	242
Continent (Europe)	1,429	1,505	1,003	424	862
China	456	555	626	243	169
Japan	1,722	1,409	1,753	757	1,426
Others	93	113	73	33	42
Total	3,933	3,868	3,729	1,582	2,741
Home Mills	1,992	2,373	2,271	2,346	2,360

Sources: Department of Overseas Trade, *Commercial Reports on India, 1930–34.*

By virtue of the 'Ottawa System', India's export trade recovered steadily, and in 1935–36, the revival of exports was distributed over practically the whole range of India's export staples. India's export trade to the UK increased by 35.2 per cent, while her trade with other countries advanced by not more than 14.75 per cent. 'Her exports to countries other than the UK were assisted by abnormal purchases of cotton by Japan to make up for the short purchases during the 1933 boycott.'[77]

---

[75]   Official Diary of Mission to Simla Conference, 1933, by Sir George Sansom, 7, 11 and 14 October, F6645 (20 October 1933), FO371/17163, TNA; Report from Sir George Sansom to Mr. E. Crewe, 20 November 1933, F7394 (27 November 1933), FO371/17164, TNA.

[76]   Official Diary of Mission to Simla Conference, 1933, by Sir George Sansom, 28 October, F7030/1203/23, FO371/17164, TNA.

[77]   Department of Overseas Trade, *Report on Economic and Commercial Conditions in India 1935–36*, pp. 4–7.

Japan remained the principal buyer of Indian raw cotton, and the UK occupied the second position, in spite of the Lees-Mody Pact of 1933 and the efforts, made by the Lancashire Indian Cotton Committee, to encourage the use of Indian cotton.[78] In this context, the 'Ottawa System' was an open trade regime, even for non-member countries.

(3) Indian Industrialization, Economic Nationalism and Capital Goods Exports

An impressive phenomenon in British India during the 1930s was the progress of industrialization, especially the rapid development of cotton industries, and its severe contest with foreign goods. There appeared in this period a three-cornered competition between British, East Asian and Indian cotton goods. In 1931, one year before the Ottawa Trade Agreement, the Government of India gave preferences to British cotton products vis-à-vis foreign competition, and Indian preferences were renegotiated in 1934 and 1936. But the growing competition from Indian industries became even more severe than Japanese competition. Every *Commercial Report* on India in the 1930s emphasized the encroachment of the Indian mills. Moreover, in 1936–38, when quotas were imposed on Japanese goods in foreign markets, 'the Indian mills are now not only securing almost the whole of the domestic market but are competing keenly with U.K. and Japanese goods in the overseas markets of Burma, Ceylon, Nigeria, Egypt, Iraq, Iran, the Straits Settlements, Tanganyika Territory and elsewhere'.[79] With the rapid development of the Indian cotton industry, the new intra-Asian competition commenced for exports of cotton piece goods to the countries of the Indian Ocean Rim.

There were several reasons for the rapid development of the Indian cotton industry. Earlier in 1930, *the Report* recognized the inevitability of Indian economic development as follows: 'There is little doubt that a self-governing India will take full advantage of her fiscal autonomy in order to promote her industries ... [Lancashire's] efforts to regain a footing in the Indian market may be frustrated by the fiscal policy of an autonomous India.'[80] Above all, the heavy surcharge (25 per cent) in 1931 had a severely restrictive effect on imports. Moreover, the surcharge had a protective effect, which was not intended, and it stimulated a large number of nascent local industries. *The Report of 1933–34* briefly summarized the outlook of the Indian import trade as follows: 'The competition of Indian industries, stimulated by the protective and revenue duties, the 'swadeshi' movement, which is one of the most potent manifestations of economic nationalism, and the preferences accorded by Indian Government Departments when making purchases of stores, cannot fail to restrict the Indian market for imported goods ... In the

---

[78]   Chatterji, *Trade, Tariffs and Empire*, Ch. 8.

[79]   Department of Overseas Trade, *Conditions and Prospects of United Kingdom Trade in India 1937–38*, pp. 9, 180–81.

[80]   Department of Overseas Trade, *Conditions and Prospects of United Kingdom Trade in India 1930–31*, p. 72.

near future, UK industries will have to rely on the combined effects of preferential duties and industrial co-operation to enable them to secure, at the expense of other overseas competitors, a greater share of a limited market.'[81]

Although facing severe competition from Indian industry, the British Reports on India were not completely pessimistic about the future of British exports. They expressed a realistic and positive view that the industrialization of India was an inevitable process, promoted by economic nationalism, and that the British might take advantage of this opportunity to cooperate with India. Even in the early 1930s, the more advanced development of Indian industries was expected: 'It is inevitable that the Indian mills will encroach to a rapidly increasing extent upon the finer types of plain fabrics as they use more and more American and Egyptian cotton for the spinning of finer yarns.'[82]

> Although Indian mill competition is cutting into the market in an ever-widening range of fabrics, the Indian mills cannot as yet provide the variety of qualities, designs, colours and styles which consumers like to have if only they can afford to pay for them. In times of intense agricultural and industrial depression such as the past four years, the Indian consumer has been obliged to substitute the cheaper, coarser, less attractive fabric made in India for the finer imported article which has been in the habit of purchasing. It is not too much to expect that, as the prices of primary commodities rise thereby releasing purchasing power, we shall see a broadening of the demand for Lancashire staples of the finer qualities and for fancy styles.[83]

In this context, the events of 1933 fostered the prospect of future cooperation between British and Indian cotton industries: 'The visits of the delegations from the UK Textile and Iron and Steel Industries, and the Clare Lees-Mody Pact have permanently established the policy of industrial co-operation between the two countries; such a policy is calculated to have such far-reaching effects not only in the economic sphere but also in the political arena by removing the sources of economic rivalry and ill-feeling and by promoting a spirit of community of interest between the two peoples.'[84] At this very moment, Indian nationalists and the British Government were carrying on political negotiations for the revision of the Government of India Act of 1919, which led to the enactment of a new Act in 1935. It is worth mentioning that the pursuit of economic cooperation was

---

[81]   Department of Overseas Trade, *Conditions and Prospects of United Kingdom Trade in India 1933–34*, p. 11.

[82]   Department of Overseas Trade, *Conditions and Prospects of United Kingdom Trade in India 1930–31*, pp. 71–2.

[83]   Department of Overseas Trade, *Conditions and Prospects of United Kingdom Trade in India 1933–34*, General Forecast (June,1934), pp. 158–9.

[84]   Ibid., p. xiii, Covering Despatch from Thomas M. Ainscough to President of the Board of Trade, W. Runciman, 11 September 1934 and p. 75.

closely connected with the relaxing of political tensions in constitutional reform and that both Indian and British sides recognized this linkage to take advantage of each other.[85]

Furthermore, *the Report of 1935* contained a more far-sighted and long-term view of economic relations. It supported the rapid economic development of India, and expected an increase in British capital goods exports, such as machinery, chemicals, and transport vehicles as follows:

> A partial solution of the problem will be found in the rapid development of the country which is already resulting in a remarkable diversification of her economic requirements ... It is most encouraging to note that in the newer highly technical industries, UK manufactures are successfully meeting foreign competition and are reinforcing their efforts by adequate sales, technical and service organization on the spot. Fortunately, too, these classes of imports, which are capable of such great expansion, can be developed without competing with India's own natural industrial developments. The friendly co-operation of British manufacturing organizations, with their technical experience and knowledge of world-wide conditions, and Indian industries, with their knowledge of local conditions, should be most valuable in research work with the object of stimulating the consumption of their products ... I am convinced that we must rely more and more in future on the supply of capital products and technical equipment to India, thus aiding her own development with our experience and technique.[86]

From this long quotation, we may identify an expectation of the same kind of complementary relationship that existed vis-à-vis East Asian industrialization. In reality, in 1937, the imports of machinery outstripped the long-established supremacy of cotton textiles and accounted for 10 per cent of imports, the most important item in the list of imports into India of manufactured goods.[87] With progressive Indian industrialization, 'the demand for the most developed types of plant is likely to become even more insistent'.[88]

---

[85]   On the linkage between political and economic problems, see Nobuko Nagasaki, 'Gandhi jidai' [The era of Gandhi], in Naoki Hazama and Nobuko Nagasaki, *Sekaino-Rekishi 27: Jiritsu e mukau Ajia* [*A History of the World 27: Asian Countries towards Self-determination*], (Tokyo: Chuokouron-shinsha, 1999), Part 2, Ch. 8.

[86]   Department of Overseas Trade, *Report on Economic and Commercial Conditions in India 1935–36*, pp. 17–19. See also, Department of Overseas Trade, *Conditions and Prospects of United Kingdom Trade in India 1937–38*, pp. 25–7.

[87]   For the import of machinery into India and its economic implications, see A.K. Bagchi, *Private Investment in India 1900–1939* (Cambridge, 1972), Ch. 3.

[88]   Department of Overseas Trade, *Conditions and Prospects of United Kingdom Trade in India 1937–38*, pp. 190–93.

(4) British Financial Interests and Indian Industrialization

As mentioned earlier, the Great Depression and its severe impact upon India greatly reduced the purchasing power in India, mainly due to the decline in the prices of primary products. The deterioration of the balance of trade of India became a serious question, and could only be adjusted by the shipment of gold bullion. This was an abnormal phenomenon. The Indian Finance Member, Sir George Schuster, pointed out at the Ottawa Conference that 'India in order to maintain an even position requires a favourable trade of balance of at least Rs.50 crores (£37.5 million) annually.'[89] *The Report of 1932–33* also mentioned that, 'there can be no lasting improvement in the import trade until India's favourable balance of trade in merchandise is restored to a figure of at least Rs.50 crores, which she requires to meet her essential obligations in London ... [U]ntil India can obtain a favourable balance of Rs.50 crores *in merchandise* she cannot be considered to be on a sound foundation ... The seriousness of the fall in the trade balance is accentuated in the case of India, which, as a debtor country, needs to maintain a large favourable balance of trade in merchandise'.[90] The decrease of the trade margin had a negative effect on debt servicing, which was closely connected with the interests of the City of London.

In addition, a vicious circle arose between the decrease of imports and diminishing customs revenue: 'The decline in India's imports in five years from Rs.253 crores to Rs.115 crores ... had most serious repercussions on the revenue position ... As imports declined with corresponding shrinkage of revenue, fresh duties and surcharges were added to the revenue tariff to make good the deficiency. These, in turn, caused a further fall in imports until, in many cases, the law of diminishing returns began to operate. Moreover, the high tariff level resulted in the creation of new industries, which displaced imported goods and brought about a further restriction of imports and of Customs revenue.'[91] The emergency measures taken in 1931–33, in consequence, led to revenue difficulties resulting from the contraction of imports, and these seemed to aggravate the weak fiscal situation of the Government of India.

In the latter half of the 1930s, Indian exports to the British home market increased due to the Ottawa Trade Agreement, whereas the level of Indian imports did not recover to the same extent as its exports. *The Report of 1937* recognized the contraction of the Indian market as an outlet for overseas manufactured goods on account of rapid Indian industrialization. As a market for UK goods,

---

[89]   Statement made by Sir George Schuster at a meeting of the committee on monetary and financial questions on 28 July, 1932. Quoted in: Department of Overseas Trade, *Conditions and Prospects of United Kingdom Trade in India 1932–33*, Appendix 1, pp. 225–8.

[90]   Ibid., pp. 26, 37.

[91]   Department of Overseas Trade, *Conditions and Prospects of United Kingdom Trade in India 1933–34*, pp. 8–9.

British India now ranked third and had been surpassed by the Union of South Africa and Australia. *The Report* warned against excessive import-substitution industrialization in India in the following terms:

> Indian public men, both politicians and industrialists, seem to be imbued with the conviction that the more domestic production is substituted for imports until the latter are gradually extinguished, the more prosperous the country will become … The policy of maximum industrialization … must inevitably lead, firstly, to a serious clash of interest with the agricultural element, which constitutes nearly 70 per cent of the population, secondly, to a crisis in India's finances as the Government of India rely upon Customs receipts for some 60 per cent of their revenue, and, lastly, to the collapse of the financial and economic fabric of the Government of India which is dependent upon an excess balance of exports in order to meet India's financial commitments in London (amounting to some Rs.50 to 60 crores per annum) and to maintain the exchange.[92]

This serious warning from Thomas Ainscough was primarily directed towards the trade imbalance and deficit, caused by the decrease in Indian imports of manufactured goods. But the logic of his first point was not clear, that is, the clash between Indian agricultural and industrial interests. However, his second and third points revealed the clear relationship between British financial interests and Indian industrialization. Contrary to his warnings, the rapid progress of Indian industrialization was favourable to the City of London and British financial interests because industrialization guaranteed the smooth servicing of Indian debts by creating a surplus balance of exports.

Conclusion

We shall now sum up the arguments of this chapter. First, during the inter-war years, and especially in the first half of the 1930s, the British *Commercial Reports on Japan* tended to shift the focus of their attention from the British home economy to the markets of the British Empire. From the British point of view, Japanese economic development in the 1930s was a form of import-substitution industrialization. Although Japan emerged as the most formidable competitor in cotton goods markets, especially in China, the importance of British India greatly increased for the Japanese export economy in the early 1930s, as an expanding market for the Japanese cotton industry and as a vital source of raw cotton. On the other hand, for British India, Malaya and Australia, Japanese imports of primary materials also played an important role in the process of the recovery from the Great Depression and for the further expansion of export markets. Therefore, a

---

[92]   Department of Overseas Trade, *Conditions and Prospects of United Kingdom Trade in India 1937–38*, pp. 24–9.

complementarity of economic interests emerged in the 1930s between the British Empire and Japan rather than between Great Britain and Japan.

China was a hopeful export market for British capital goods, especially British-made cotton textile machinery. From the British point of view, the beginning of industrialization in China was a type of export-induced industrialization for British exports, which had been the case for Japan at the turn of the twentieth century. The British *Commercial Reports on China* emphasized the potential of the vast Chinese market and the keen competition for capital goods exports among the great powers, as well as for consumer goods from Chinese domestic industries. This sensitive observation seemed to reflect the importance of the Chinese market for British capital goods industries. In the 1930s, the economic development of China was centred on Shanghai, especially the foreign-controlled International Settlement, where the UK held the paramount position in regard to financial and service interests. The Chinese currency reform of 1935 was important not only for the Nationalist Government of China but also for Britain in order to exert and maintain its financial influence as the structural power.

In addition to industrialization in East Asia, even in the case of British India, the rapid development of cotton industries occurred in the 1920s and was accelerated under the Great Depression from the early 1930s. The Government of India introduced emergency measures, such as surcharges and increased tariff rates in 1931–33, to tackle the fiscal problems. These policies, in turn, unintentionally promoted the growth of Indian cotton industries, and the same tendency could be found in the case of Indian iron and steel, with the development of the Tata Iron and Steel Works. In this sense, Indian economic nationalism and British economic interests could also coexist with each other.

Therefore, we can identify in the 1930s a very unique complementary relationship between British economic interests and industrialization in Asia; that is: (1) complementarity between exports of British capital goods and Chinese and Indian industrialization; (2) complementarity between British financial interests, 'gentlemanly capitalism', and the financial needs of China and British India, and (3) mutual economic interdependence, or the Empire-scale 'final demand linkage effect', between Japan and the British Empire.

Of course, the progress of industrialization in Asia in the 1930s created economic frictions or 'intra-Asian competition', and led to the deployment of economic diplomacy, such as the Indo-Japanese Trade Negotiation in 1933. However, these economic tensions reflected only one aspect of the development of intra-Asian trade. Much more significant was the tendency towards the emergence of mutual economic interdependence during the 1930s. Moreover, all three aspects indicated above, were closely connected with Britain's economic interests, centred on the financial and service sectors, demonstrating that Britain played the role of the structural power in international relations. In this sense, the presence of Great Britain in Asia was an important determining factor in the formation of the industrialization-based 'International Order of Asia' in the 1930s.

Table 1.3-1 The Direction of China's Foreign Trade in the early 1930s (in thousands of Haikwan taels)

Country	Net Imports						Net Exports					
	1929		1930		1931		1929		1930		1931	
	Hk.Tls.	%	Hk.Tls.	%	Hk.Tls.	%	Hk.Tls.	%	Hk.Tls.	%	Hk.Tls.	%
British India	54,180	4.28	132,093	10.09	84,989	5.93	17,815	1.75	16,953	1.89	18,118	1.9
Canada	38,413	3.03	13,488	1.03	22,572	1.57	2,160	0.21	3,491	0.39	3,736	0.41
France	18,044	1.43	16,758	1.28	21,420	1.49	56,319	5.54	42,700	4.77	34,111	3.75
French Indo-China	14,263	1.13	27,831	2.12	11,364	0.79	5,754	0.57	3,882	0.43	2,394	0.26
Germany	66,753	5.27	68,799	5.25	83,168	5.80	22,458	2.21	23,361	2.61	23,138	2.54
Great Britain	118,657	9.37	107,118	8.18	119,344	8.33	74,334	7.32	62,669	7.00	64,526	7.09
Hong Kong	210,412	16.62	211,423	16.14	218,170	15.22	173,581	17.09	158,018	17.66	148,312	16.31
Japan (incl.Taiwan)	319,075	25.21	322,303	24.61	290,386	20.26	256,428	25.25	216,555	24.20	264,956	29.13
Korea	14,868	1.17	13,022	0.99	10,069	0.70	39,784	3.92	44,175	4.94	29,631	3.26
Netherlands	11,826	0.93	10,627	0.81	13,493	0.94	39,543	3.89	44,944	5.02	49,528	5.45
Netherlands India	54,262	4.29	47,450	3.62	54,201	3.78	12,459	1.23	11,707	1.31	12,987	1.43
Straits Settlements	11,096	0.88	8,831	0.67	8,390	0.59	23,560	2.32	19,177	2.14	15,916	1.75
USA	230,109	18.18	231,653	17.69	320,266	22.34	137,836	13.57	131,880	14.74	120,205	13.22
USSR (Russia)	18,148	1.43	18,461	1.41	24,565	1.71	55,986	5.51	55,413	6.19	54,657	6.01
Other Countries	85,673	6.77	79,899	6.10	151,092	10.54	97,670	9.62	59,919	6.70	67,261	7.40
Total	1,265,779	100.00	1,309,756	100.00	1,433,489	100.00	1,015,687	100.00	894,844	100.00	909,476	100.00

Source: China. Maritime Customs, Trade Reports for the Year 1931, vol. I, p. 41.
These are all current figures, and not adjusted by constant figures.

Table 1.3-2 The Distribution of China's Foreign Trade in the Middle of the 1930s (in thousands of standard dollars)

Country	Net Imports								Net Exports							
	1935		1936		1937		1938		1935		1936		1937		1938	
	St.$	%	St.$	%	St.$	%	St.$	%	St.$	%	St.$	%	St.$	%	St.$	%
British India	35,470	3.86	24,712	2.63	12,467	1.30	16,214	1.81	20,328	3.53	18,685	2.65	11,791	1.41	19,720	2.58
Burma	–	–	–	–	8,220	0.86	12,801	1.43	–	–	–	–	4,503	0.54	4,661	0.61
Canada	20,413	2.22	19,782	2.10	17,093	1.79	7,872	0.88	4,198	0.73	5,270	0.75	7,091	0.85	3,675	0.48
France	13,336	1.45	18,311	1.94	15,106	1.58	18,304	2.05	29,243	5.08	30,388	4.31	32,643	3.89	20,402	2.67
French Indo-China	59,648	6.49	17,922	1.90	29,991	3.14	27,351	3.06	5,643	0.98	9,891	1.40	12,827	1.53	15,816	2.07
Germany	103,184	11.22	150,051	15.94	146,374	15.31	112,939	12.64	28,926	5.02	39,173	5.55	72,477	8.64	56,440	7.39
Great Britain	98,070	10.67	110,332	11.72	111,695	11.68	70,606	7.90	49,458	8.59	64,882	9.19	80,380	9.58	56,769	7.43
Hong Kong	16,816	1.83	16,554	1.76	19,078	2.00	24,589	2.75	94,502	16.41	105,979	15.02	162,904	19.42	243,395	31.87
Japan	139,320	15.16	153,369	16.29	150,432	15.73	209,864	23.49	82,047	14.25	101,947	14.45	84,306	10.05	116,547	15.26
Korea	2,738	0.30	2,931	0.31	2,346	0.25	5,577	0.62	11,564	2.01	9,740	1.38	7,712	0.92	6,873	0.90
Netherlands	4,509	0.49	4,763	0.51	6,053	0.63	4,640	0.52	15,251	2.65	16,546	2.34	14,261	1.70	8,170	1.07
Netherlands India	58,345	6.35	74,359	7.90	80,718	8.44	45,744	5.12	4,987	0.87	4,733	0.67	6,228	0.74	6,664	0.87
Straits Settlements	10,245	1.11	10,761	1.14	10,362	1.08	7,313	0.82	12,896	2.23	15,644	2.22	19,213	2.29	17,546	2.30
USA	174,678	19.00	185,134	19.66	188,859	19.75	151,254	16.93	136,394	23.69	186,320	26.4	231,449	27.59	86,853	11.37
USSR (Russia)	7,687	0.84	1,221	0.13	704	0.07	5,491	0.61	4,239	0.74	4,210	0.60	4,915	0.58	613	0.08
Other Countries	174,752	19.01	151,342	16.07	175,795	16.39	172,941	19.37	76,133	13.22	92,333	13.07	86,070	10.27	99,587	13.05
Total	919,211	100.00	941,544	100.00	956,234	100.00	893,500	100.00	575,809	100.00	705,741	100.00	838,770	100.00	763,731	100.00

Source: China. Maritime Customs, Trade Reports for the Years 1936, vol. I, p. 55 and 1938, p. 35.
These are all current figures, and not adjusted by constant figures.

Table 1.4   Imports and Domestic Production of Cotton Piece-Goods in British India (million yards)

Year	UK	Netherlands	Italy	USA	Swiss	Japan	China	Others	Whole Imports	India	Amount
1913–14	3,068	25	23	9	6	9	-	19	3,159	1,164	4,323
1914–15	2,354	21	10	10	3	16	-	6	2,420	1,139	3,556
1915–16	2,022	21	13	14	4	39	-	5	2,118	1,442	3,560
1916–17	1,748	14	14	8	3	100	1	4	1,892	1,578	3,470
1917–18	1,404	6	7	7	1	95	1	3	1,524	1,614	3,138
1918–19	851	1	1	2	1	238	-	3	1,097	1,451	2,548
1919–20	963	8	1	6	2	76	-	8	1,064	1,640	2,704
1920–21	1,278	13	10	9	4	170	1	7	1,492	1,581	3,073
1921–22	947	12	2	21	1	90	1	6	1,080	1,732	2,812
1922–23	1,440	13	2	5	3	108	3	3	1,577	1,725	3,302
1923–24	1,306	11	6	1	7	123	6	7	1,467	1,702	3,169
1924–25	1,599	12	10	3	7	155	5	10	1,801	1,970	3,771
1925–26	1,275	16	11	3	7	217	2	9	1,540	1,954	3,494
1926–27	1,457	20	17	5	12	244	2	10	1,767	2,259	4,026
1927–28	1,530	20	26	5	15	323	7	10	1,936	2,357	4,293
1928–29	1,442	20	38	7	11	357	13	12	1,900	1,893	3,793
1929–30	1,236	22	25	9	10	562	10	8	1,882	2,419	4,301
1930–31	520	13	10	4	6	321	2	6	882	2,561	3,443
1931–32	376	7	11	3	8	340	4	4	753	2,990	3,743

1932–33	586	5	8	1	10	579	1	3	1,193	3,170	4,363
1933–34	415	2	-	-	1	341	-	2	761	2,945	3,706
1934–35	552	2	2	1	8	374	1	4	944	3,397	4,341
1935–36	440	2	1	1	6	496	-	1	947	3,571	4,518
1936–37	334	2	1	-	8	417	-	2	764	3,572	4,336
1937–38	267	1	1	-	9	308	-	5	591	4,084	4,675

Note: The data for 1937–38 does not include Burma.
Source: Department of Overseas Trade, *Conditions and Prospects of United Kingdom Trade in India 1937–38* (London, 1939), p. 170.

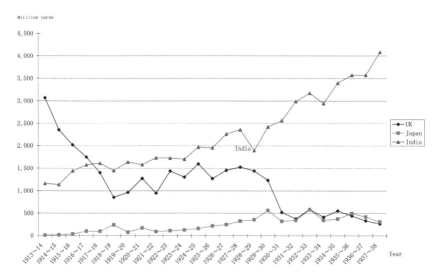

Figure 1.1   Imports and Domestic Production of Cotton Piece-Goods in British India

Figure 1.2   The Indo-Japan non-governmental Cotton Conference of 1933: The first meeting at The Cecil Hotel, Simla, 4 October 1933. © Asahi Photo Archive, 'Nichi-In Mengi Kyogikai [Indo-Japan Cotton Trade Conference'(No. 065178), *The Asahi Shimbun*, Tokyo.

Chapter 2

British Imperialism in Asia and Anglo-Japanese Relations, 1930s–1950s

Yoichi Kibata

Looking back from the year 1943, Stanley K. Hornbeck, an Asian specialist in the American Department of State who wielded a strong influence on American policy in East Asia, stressed the continuity in British attitudes towards Japan from 1902 to the time of the Manchurian Incident:

> [T]hroughout the period from 1902 to 1931 the British Government maintained and exploited [a] 'best friend' attitude toward Japan; and ... in 1931 there was a substantial body of opinion among leading figures in the British Government and in British financial and commercial circles to the effect that Japan was the one country in the Far East that could be relied upon for [the] maintenance of law and order ... and that it might be to British advantage were the Japanese to occupy and to become preoccupied with Manchuria and thereby to be caused to refrain from efforts to enlarge their activities, interests, and still further in the Yangtze Valley and regions southward therefrom.[1]

Needless to say, 1902 was the year when the Anglo-Japanese Alliance was formed. That alliance, which became the lynchpin of the imperialist world order in Asia at the beginning of the twentieth century, was terminated after World War I largely as the result of trenchant pressure from the United States, which expressed strong opposition to its renewal in the course of 1921.[2] The fact that Britain could not carry through its desire to continue the Alliance, which the Japanese side also wanted to be kept alive, signalled the relative decline of British power in Asia. Moreover, the international system created at the Washington Conference in the wake of the Anglo-Japanese Alliance, that is, the system under the nine-power treaty concerning China and the four-power treaty concerning the Pacific, made it clear that a naked alliance between imperialist powers was no longer viewed as a legitimate instrument in the international order.

---

[1]   Memo. by Hornbeck, 30 August 1943, Stanley K. Hornbeck Papers, Hoover Archives, Stanford University, Box 181.

[2]   The best account of the last phase of the Anglo-Japanese Alliance can still be found in Ian Nish, *Alliance in Decline: A Study in Anglo-Japanese Relations 1908–23* (London, 1972).

Various factors in international relations began to transform as the result of World War I, and the abolition of the Anglo-Japanese Alliance was a clear expression of this change. There are also grounds for arguing that the process of decolonisation started during or at the end of World War I. But, as has been pointed out by many historians, the basic stance of British imperial policy did not change dramatically. More than twenty years ago, John Darwin argued: 'the more closely we inspect the response of the policy makers towards the novel difficulties that had afflicted the imperial system after 1917 the less satisfactory it becomes to portray their dispositions as a conscious preparation for the final act of dissolution.'[3] More recently, P.J. Cain and A.G. Hopkins forcefully demonstrated that Britain continued to harbour imperialist ambitions which were underpinned by financial power.[4]

With such a view in mind, in this chapter, the author tries to throw light on an aspect of continuity in British imperial policy in examining British attitudes towards Japan in the 1930s, especially in the period between the Manchurian Incident and the outbreak of the Sino-Japanese War in 1937. Then the author briefly deals with British policy towards Japan after the end of World War II.[5] The picture drawn in this chapter will point to a clear discontinuity between the 1930s and the post-World War II period.

Britain, Japan and Asian Nationalism

Among the profound changes brought about by World War I, the most important factor that affected the imperialist world order was the rise of anti-colonial nationalism. In Asia, the force of nationalist movements in colonies or semi-colonies, especially those of China, Korea and India, gained momentum as the result of the war. It should be remembered that these countries were the objects of colonial domination under the Anglo-Japanese Alliance: the first Alliance in 1902 provided for the *status quo* in China and Korea, and the second Alliance in 1905 extended its scope to India.

It was the strengthening of nationalism in China that mattered most in Anglo-Japanese relations. The British stance vis-à-vis rising nationalism in China was revealed in the 'December Memorandum' of 1926 which was issued after the upsurge of anti-British nationalism during 1925 and 1926. This memorandum stressed the importance of dealing with Chinese nationalist movements with sympathy and displayed Britain's readiness to recognize China's right to enjoy tariff autonomy. But, as Harumi Goto-Shibata aptly explained in her study of Anglo-Japanese

---

[3]   John Darwin, 'Imperialism in Decline? Tendencies in British Imperial Policy between the Wars', *Historical Journal*, 23, 3 (1980).

[4]   P. Cain and A.G. Hopkins, *British Imperialism 1688–2000* (Harlow, 2001), Pts 5–8.

[5]   The section of this chapter covering the 1930s largely overlaps with the present author's 'Reasserting Imperial Power? Britain and East Asia in the 1930s' in Shigeru Akita, ed., *Gentlemanly Capitalism, Imperialism and Global History* (Basingstoke/London, 2002).

relations in Shanghai in the 1920s, the objective of this new policy was not to retreat from China, but to retain Britain's vital interests in China by surrendering only what was considered to be of secondary or peripheral importance, and by pacifying nationalists.[6] In a letter to Lloyd-George, Austen Chamberlain, the then British Foreign Secretary, explained the reason why it was imperative for Britain to preserve its position in China even by making such concessions: 'You will understand all that would be involved for our position throughout the Far East, in India, Afghanistan, Persia and even Turkey by a disaster at Shanghai.'[7] What was at stake in China was not only British interests in China itself but also the imperial influence of Britain in Asia more widely.

Even after the turmoil in the mid-1920s was calmed, British fears about the possible damaging outcome of active Chinese nationalism died hard, and British policy towards Japan during and after the Manchurian Incident should be viewed first and foremost in the light of this concern about Chinese nationalism. In the course of the Manchurian Incident, Britain continued to show magnanimity towards Japan. Britain adopted a relatively firm stance to rein in Japanese activities during the Shanghai Incident in early 1932, but it was only a temporary reaction, and, once Japan's threat to Shanghai, where British economic interests were heavily concentrated, receded, Britain went back to its accommodating attitude towards Japan.

It was thought that, as long as Japanese activities did not directly do harm to British interests in China, Japanese power could be utilized for restraining Chinese nationalism. For example, even during the period of the Shanghai Incident, Sir John Simon, the Foreign Secretary, stated in a Cabinet meeting: 'From the point of view of the security of the Settlement it appeared better that the Japanese should succeed than the Chinese.'[8] To provide another example, Admiral Sir Frederic Dreyer, the Commander-in-Chief of the China Station of the Royal Navy, wrote in 1933:

> We should admit that they [the Japanese], as a great Eastern people, have every right to a line of commercial expansion in the direction of China ... We should realise that they are Orientals and know how to deal with the Chinese far better than we do. We are not so competent to instruct the Chinese Government how to restore order out of chaos amongst 400 million Chinese.[9]

---

[6]   Harumi Goto-Shibata, *Japan and Britain in Shanghai, 1925–31* (Basingstoke/London, 1995), p. 38.

[7]   Sir Austen Chamberlain to Lloyd George, 19 January 1927, Lloyd George Papers, G/4/3/3, House of Lords Record Office.

[8]   Christopher Thorne, *The Limits of Foreign Policy. The West, the League and the Far Eastern Crisis of 1931–1933* (London, 1972), p. 262.

[9]   China General Letter No. 8, 3 November 1933, ADM 116/2973, The National Archives of the UK (TNA).

Such reasoning harks back to the function of the Anglo-Japanese Alliance in the heyday of imperialism. Under the Alliance, Japan's cooperation as a non-European 'Oriental' imperialist power helped Britain to maintain its far-flung empire in Asia. Japan came out of World War I in a much stronger shape than the other powers (including Britain) had expected, and began to demonstrate a desire to build an Asian empire by infringing upon the Euro-centred imperialist world order. But, the ruling circles in Britain continued to nurture the idea that Japanese activities could be utilized to buttress the imperialist order, in which Britain occupied the central position. This was not so much the defensive attitude of a retreating power as an undertaking to create a revised imperialist order in East Asia, using Japanese aggression in China as a means of curbing the further rise of Chinese nationalism.

In order to understand the historical meaning of British policy towards Japan at this juncture, it may be useful to consider the position of Indian nationalism in Anglo-Japanese relations. Nationalism in India was also gaining momentum during the 1930s and the British government was displaying some concession-giving gestures, leading to the new India Act of 1935. Unlike Chinese nationalists, Indian nationalists had as yet little to fear from Japanese aggression in their own country, and there was a marked tendency among some Indian nationalists to look to Japan as their friend or protector. This was a headache for British colonial administrators and the activities of Indian nationalists residing in Japan such as Rash Behari Bose were constantly kept under surveillance.[10] It was feared that a breach between Britain and Japan would lead to the strengthening of Japan's role in pan-Asiatic movements, and this would further stimulate Indian nationalism. In 1933, Hornbeck, whose observation was quoted at the beginning of this chapter and who was watching Britain's attitude towards Japan closely from the US, detected such a fear: 'It is very commonly argued in England that a strong Japan bound to England by contractual obligations is necessary for the maintenance of Britain's position in India.'[11]

This again brings us to the Anglo-Japanese Alliance. As was mentioned earlier, the area of application of the Alliance was extended to India at the time of its revision in 1905, and Japan came to commit itself to the defence of British interests in India. Though Britain and Japan maintained friendly relations after the end of the Anglo-Japanese Alliance, there was no guarantee for Britain to expect that Japan would take Britain's side against Indian nationalism. It is noteworthy that Hornbeck also pointed out that: 'The Tory element, with the Admiralty leading, in Great Britain keep bringing up the idea of renewing the Anglo-Japanese alliance.

---

[10]   For example see Clive to Simon, 8 November 1934, FO 371/18185, TNA. This is a detailed report about Indian activities in Yokohama, Tokyo, Osaka and Kobe. See also T.R. Sareen, *Indian Revolutionaries, Japan and British Imperialism* (New Delhi, 1993), Ch. 1. Rash Behari Bose should not be confused with Subhas Chandra Bose, who played the key role in the Indian National Army during the Asia-Pacific War.

[11]   Memo. by Hornbeck, 31 October 1933, Hornbeck Papers, Box. 12.

They ring the charges on the proposition, erroneous in fact, that Japan is the natural and the effective guardian of *peace* in the Far East' (emphasis in the original).[12]

Abortive British Attempts to Appease Japan in the 1930s

In fact, after the end of the Manchurian Incident in 1933, several attempts were made by Britain to bring about much closer Anglo-Japanese cooperation, if not a new alliance.[13] In 1934, Neville Chamberlain, the powerful Chancellor of the Exchequer in the British National Government, tried to conclude a non-aggression pact with Japan. This move was ardently supported by Sir Warren Fisher, Permanent Under-Secretary at the Treasury, and was pursued in spite of the reservation expressed by the Foreign Office, which feared that such a move would provoke adverse reactions in the United States, China and the Soviet Union. Though this attempt came to nothing in face of the negative attitude of Japanese policy-makers, who were not ready to enter into an agreement which might impinge on Japan's freedom of movement in international relations in Asia, especially in China, Chamberlain and Fisher did not give up their plan for building closer relations with Japan.

In 1935, with their strong backing, Sir Frederick Leith-Ross, a currency expert at the Treasury, was sent to China to help currency reform there. The significance of this Leith-Ross Mission has been stressed by Cain and Hopkins in their *British Imperialism* as a clear case supporting the theory of gentlemanly capitalism.[14] Shigeru Akita rightly criticized their argument, pointing out that the part played by the Leith-Ross Mission was relatively less important in the process of Chinese currency reform than was suggested by Cain and Hopkins, and the roles of China itself, as well as that of the United States, should be taken into account more fully.[15] The fact that Leith-Ross's actual role in the currency reform of November 1935 was not as significant as Cain and Hopkins suggest is borne out by a contemporary observation by Arthur N. Young, who was in a position to watch closely the process

---

[12]   Ibid.

[13]   For more detailed treatment of these attempts, see Yoichi Kibata, 'Anglo-Japanese Relations from the Manchurian Incident to Pearl Harbour: Missed Opportunities?' in Ian Nish and Yoichi Kibata (eds), *The History of Anglo-Japanese Relations, 1600–2000, Vol. 2, The Political-Diplomatic Dimension, 1930–2000* (Basingstoke and London, 2000), pp. 6–11.

[14]   Cain and Hopkins, *British Imperialism*, p. 608.

[15]   Shigeru Akita, 'British Informal Empire in East Asia, 1880–1939: a Japanese Perspective' in Raymond E. Dummett (ed.), *Gentlemanly Capitalism and British Imperialism: The New Debate on Empire* (London/New York, 1999), pp. 147–52; Shigeru Akita, *Igirisu teikoku to Ajia kokusai chitsujo* [*The British Empire and the International Order of Asia*] (Nagoya, 2003), Ch. 9. See also Yutaka Nozawa (ed.), *Chugoku no heisei kaikaku to kokusai kankei* [*Currency Reform in China (1935) and China's Relations with Japan, Britain and America*] (Tokyo, 1981).

of currency reform as a financial adviser to the Chinese government. In February 1936 he wrote to Hornbeck: 'You can take it quite definitely that the program of reform was not devised by Sir Frederick Leith-Ross. The plan was completed before he reached China, to be put into effect when the situation was ripe for it. Of course his presence here was quite helpful in inducing the influential British community to fall in line with the plan.'[16]

What should be stressed about the Leith-Ross Mission in the context of this chapter was that it also embodied a further attempt to bring about a new form of Anglo-Japanese cooperation in China. Leith-Ross carried a proposal to Japan concerning an Anglo-Japanese joint credit to 'Manchukuo', which could then be handed to China as compensation for the loss of Manchuria. This proposal elicited no positive response from the Japanese side, but in such a way Britain tried to maintain its influence in China in tandem with Japan through the *de facto*, if not *de jure*, recognition of Manchukuo, a puppet state created by Japan in the wake of the Manchurian Incident.

Neville Chamberlain's line of thinking in promoting this type of plan could be detected in a letter to his sister Hilda written in the spring of 1935 after a meeting with leading British industrialists in China:

> I have been astonished to find what confidence they all have in the future of the China market. They are also unanimous in thinking that while Japan will certainly take her place as China's mentor if she thinks we don't care, we have only to assert ourselves a little and she will be quite ready to work alongside of us *since there is room for both.* China too would be delighted if we would show that we meant to retain our interests in her country and a good deal of discussion has already taken place between Chinese and British as to the advantages of joint action in the development of railways which has only failed to materialise because of the doubts about British policy ... I told the men of business that I could not say what would be done for them but they might rely on it that some decision would be taken.[17] (emphasis added)

The view that the further participation in the development of railways would be beneficial to British interests in China was not unique to Chamberlain, but it is noteworthy that he put much emphasis on this point and that he believed in the possibility of British coexistence with Japan in China.

The same sort of reasoning was detected behind the despatch of a trade mission by the Federation of British Industries in the autumn of 1934. This mission was led by Lord Barnby, and it visited Japan and Manchukuo with the intention of promoting British trade with Manchukuo. The mission's overt aim was to probe into the chance of expanding British exports to Japanese-controlled

Manchuria, especially capital goods. But, just like the Leith-Ross Mission, the Barnby Mission had a strong political character. When Sir Charles Seligman, a member of the Mission, met Sir Montagu Norman, the Governor of the Bank of England before the departure of the Mission, Norman told him frankly that the Barnby Mission was political in nature despite it being dressed in industrial garb.[18] The Japanese government was well aware of this, and during the Mission's stay in Japan it tried to create the impression that the Mission was charged with the political task of promoting Anglo-Japanese rapprochement, and symbolized Britain's friendly stance towards the outcome of the Manchurian Incident. It should be added that recently published Japanese diplomatic records reveal that the Commercial Department of the Japanese Foreign Ministry was receptive to the overture of the Barnby Mission and was more than ready to cooperate with Britain in Manchukuo.[19] However, such an attitude did not prevail, and the Mission could not produce any positive results.

Both the Barnby Mission and the Leith-Ross Mission reveal the close links between economic and political motives in British policy in East Asia. In the case of the former, industrial interests occupied the central position, and in the latter, as was stressed by Cain and Hopkins, financial motivation to draw China into the sterling area was uppermost. Though propelled by different aspects of British capitalism, both missions embraced the same political purpose of achieving imperialist cooperation between Britain and Japan in China on the basis of the changed power relationships after the Manchurian Incident.

Another interplay of economic and political motives on the British side surfaced immediately before the outbreak of the Sino-Japanese War in an attempt to pursue what can be called 'economic appeasement' towards Japan. This centred on the proposal to abolish the import quota system in the British Empire, which had been laid down in 1934 to counter competition from Japanese goods, especially cotton products. For example, Sir Frank Ashton-Gwatkin, an economic specialist at the British Foreign Office, expected that the abolishment of the quota system would lead to an improvement in the political relationship between Britain and Japan.[20] Such a policy was actually recommended in the report of the Interdepartmental Committee on Trade Policy at the beginning of June 1937, in which it was agreed that: 'the government should inform the Lancashire industry that they desire to see an arrangement made by which the Colonial textile quotas are replaced by a voluntary restriction of Japanese exports.'[21]

---

[18] Robert A. Dayer, *Finance and Empire: Sir Charles Addis 1861–1945* (Basingstoke/ London, 1988), pp. 289–90.

[19] Nihon gaiko bunsho [*Documents on Japanese Foreign Policy*], *Showa Period, II-2–3* (Tokyo, 1999), No. 201.

[20] Memo. by Ashton-Gwatkin, March 1937, FO 371/21215, TNA.

[21] Report of the Interdepartmental Committee on Trade Policy, 7 June 1937, FO 371/21247, TNA.

It should be noted that this 'economic appeasement' was closely connected to the consideration of maintaining stability in the imperial order. When this quota system was introduced under strong pressure from the textile industries of Lancashire, severe criticism was voiced in some colonies, where the poorest classes would be badly hit by the exclusion of cheap Japanese goods, and the colonial authorities feared that discontent in those areas would nourish anti-British feeling.[22] Being not so popular from the outset and resulting in the increase in Japanese textile exports in markets outside the British colonies, this quota system could easily be singled out as a cumbersome factor, the removal of which would soothe the Japanese and bring 'moderate' pro-British elements in Japan towards a more friendly position.[23]

Opinions will differ as to the potential effect that such a policy might have had, for the outbreak of the Sino-Japanese war at the beginning of July 1937 prevented further discussion on this. But, given the fact that there were signs of increasing moderation on the Japanese side around this period, which was epitomized by the diplomacy of Naotake Sato, Foreign Minister in the Cabinet headed by Senjuro Hayashi, and by the ascertainable inclination towards a more conciliatory attitude towards China in the Japanese military,[24] it might be rash to belittle the meaning of this proposal. It seems that a change in Japanese attitude, if realized in actual policies, would have opened a way towards Anglo-Japanese cooperation in the manner which British policy-makers like Chamberlain desired: a situation in which Britain would maintain and even expand its interests in China, while securing friendly relations with Japan. 'Economic appeasement' might have assisted this process.

The Asia-Pacific War and Post-war Change

The outbreak of the Sino-Japanese War marked the beginning of the Asian phase of World War II, and in face of extensive military campaigns in China, Britain was deprived of manoeuvrability to plan out imperialist cooperation with Japan. Though there were attempts to appease Japan even after this period, they were not so much endeavours to create a new imperialist order hand-in-hand with Japan, but short-term reactions to Japanese military advances. It became increasingly clear during the course of the Sino-Japanese War that Britain had to follow the lead of the United States, which was emerging as Britain's successor as the hegemonic power in Asia.

Britain's position in Asia was damaged severely in the Asia-Pacific War, which occurred as a consequence of the Sino-Japanese War. Britain was given

---

[22]   For example, see 'Japanese Competition – Imposition of Textile Quotas in Ceylon', CAB 24/249, TNA.

[23]   Memo. by Beale, 6 April 1937, FO 371/20965, TNA.

[24]   See Katsumi Usui, 'Sato gaiko to Nitchu kankei (Sato Diplomacy and Sino-Japanese Relations)' in Akira Iriye and Tadashi Aruga (eds), *Senkanki no nihon gaiko* [*Japanese Diplomacy in the Interwar Years*] (Tokyo, 1984).

an enormous shock by the rapid defeat of its forces in Malaya and Singapore in the initial phase of the war between December 1941 and February 1942. The critical situation forced the British government to concede to the demands of Indian nationalists and the Cripps Mission in March 1942 promised to grant independence to India after the war, only to invite rejection from the leaders of the Indian National Congress who wanted an immediate solution to the political impasse. In China, Britain became virtually powerless and had both to relinquish its imperialist rights, and to give up its status as the predominant foreign power to the United States. As an example, Sir Frederick Maze was succeeded as Inspector-General of the Chinese Customs not by a British individual but by an American in 1943. This post had always been held by a Briton and had been the symbol of British influence in China.

The Asia-Pacific War for Britain was a war which was consistently fought with the aim of regaining its imperial interests and prestige. Although it was recognized that the complete recovery of the imperialist world order that had collapsed in the course of two world wars was impossible, strenuous efforts were made to rebuild Britain's imperial position. The question to be asked is: what sort of role did Britain expect Japan to play in Britain's attempts to recover its imperial position in the post-war world?

The first thing that Britain undertook after the end of the war was to get back to its colonial territories as fast as possible. It must be stressed here that, at the same time, Britain helped France and the Netherlands to return to their respective territories, Indochina and Indonesia, and in this way Britain attempted to rebuild the pre-war colonial order in Eastern Asia. In contrast to the British territories where there was no armed resistance against the return of Britain, France and the Netherlands faced powerful nationalist movements which had gained momentum during the war and these colonial powers had recourse to armed force in the re-establishment of their colonial rule. In providing assistance to the French and the Dutch, the British, in turn, had to depend on help from other peoples. During the heyday of the imperialist world order, and as late as the 1920s, Indian soldiers were widely used for such a purpose, but the change in the Indian situation now precluded this option. What is important in the context of this chapter is that many 'Japanese surrendered personnel' (JSP) were used by Britain not only in Malaya but also in Indochina and Indonesia. The scale of this reliance on ex-Japanese soldiers was depicted by Lord Mountbatten, who directed the South-East Asia Command, at the time of his visit to Sumatra in April 1946:

> I of course knew that we had been forced to keep Japanese troops under arms
> to protect our lines of communication and vital areas ... but it was nevertheless
> a great shock to me to find over a thousand Japanese troops guarding the nine
> miles of road from the airport to the town.[25]

---

[25]   Peter Dennis, *Troubled Days of Peace: Mountbatten and South-East Asian Command, 1945–46* (Manchester, 1978), pp. 225–6.

In Malaya, the JSPs were forced to work for various purposes, such as maintaining roads, preparing ground for farming and mending roads and railway systems for plantations.[26] In a situation, which transformed radically from that under the Anglo-Japanese Alliance, Japanese individuals were utilised by Britain to restore its imperial rule.

Britain found that it could restore its rule in Southeast Asia, and indeed it started to further consolidate its position there. We should bear in mind that the importance of Malaya and Singapore in the British imperial order after World War II increased significantly – both in economic and strategic terms – in the wake of the independence of South Asian countries. However, the situation in this region was far from stable. In Malaya, Britain had to fight a costly war, known as the 'Emergency', against the guerrillas led by the Malayan Communist Party. British policy-makers also watched anxiously the situation in Indochina, where France was facing acute difficulties. In a meeting held in Singapore in November 1949 British representatives in Southeast Asia and the Far East discussed the possibility of a kind of 'domino' phenomenon, in which a communist victory in Indochina would spread through Thailand and Burma to India, Pakistan and Malaya.[27] In order to prevent such a 'domino effect' from taking place increased economic assistance to this area was thought to be necessary (hence the Colombo Plan), and Anglo-Japanese relations came to be viewed against such a backdrop. It is noteworthy that, though apprehensions about Japanese trade competition were still strongly held in Britain, the concept of 'Japan as a development agent in British Malaya' began to emerge.[28]

To take an example of this discussion of Japan's role in Southeast Asia, in the autumn of 1951 shortly after the San Francisco Peace Conference, Malcolm MacDonald, who occupied the influential position of Commissioner-General in Southeast Asia, wrote to Kenneth Younger, Minister for Foreign Affairs, that it would be desirable to allow Japan to expand its economic relations with Southeast Asia, where, notwithstanding a strong antipathy towards Japan, the people of Southeast Asia had a desire to buy cheap Japanese goods, and where Japan's role as a provider of capital goods was also becoming important.[29] This view was accepted by Anthony Eden, Foreign Secretary in the Conservative government, which came to power in October. Eden admitted that Britain's negative attitude towards Japanese economic expansion in Southeast Asia would lead to the

---

[26]   See Yoichi Kibata, 'Japanese Treatment of British Prisoners of War' in Philip Towle, Margaret Kosuge and Yoichi Kibata (eds), *Japanese Prisoners of War* (London, 2000), pp. 146–7.

[27]   Conference of H.M. Representatives Held at Bukit Serene, 2–4 Nov. 1949, CAB 134/ 288, TNA.

[28]   See Junko Tomaru, *The Post-war Rapprochement of Malaya and Japan, 1945–61* (Basingstoke/London: Macmillan, 2000), p. 70.

[29]   MacDonald to Younger, 24 Sept. 1951, FO 371/92642, TNA.

'irritation of Asiatic opinion'.[30] Sir Esler Dening, who was to take up the position as the first British Ambassador to Japan after the war, also concurred, arguing that it was necessary to adopt a positive attitude towards Japanese economic activities in Southeast Asia 'both in our own interests and in those of Anglo-American relations in the Far East generally.'[31] It should be noted here that the American government was beginning to pay more attention to Southeast Asia around this period as an area for providing raw materials for Japan and as a market for Japanese manufactured goods.[32] British eyes, then, travelled from Southeast Asia, the epicentre of Britain's new post-war imperial order, to Japan, whereas American eyes travelled from Japan, the country occupying the pivotal position in US Cold War strategy, to Southeast Asia.

Thus, during the period immediately after World War II, it was in Southeast Asia that Britain sought Japanese cooperation. China, whose position was crucial in Anglo-Japanese relations in the days of the Anglo-Japanese Alliance and in the 1930s, receded from the scene. This is not to say that the problem of China lost its importance, and, as was shown in the difference in attitude between Britain and America towards Chinese participation in Japanese peace making, China still loomed large in British policy in Asia. However, China had changed radically. With a view not to losing a foothold in the area where Britain had long enjoyed a paramount position, the British government recognized the new regime in China at the beginning of 1950. Even so, it was no longer conceivable that China could be treated as an area for imperialist coexistence with Japan, as was the case in the past.

It should also be noted that in Japan during the period of peace-making (1951–52) much attention was paid to South Asia, especially to India, as the most attractive area for Japanese external economic activities, given the difficulty of expanding its trade with China.[33] Though Britain still had strong economic ties with India, such a Japanese interest in India seems to have elicited no reaction on the part of British policy makers. Since India had already become independent, Britain no longer had to pay attention to Indian reactions towards Japan.

In such a way, British policy and attitudes towards Japan after World War II clearly reflected the changed circumstances of the international order in Pacific Asia. When Japan began its economic penetration of Southeast Asia in the late 1950s and the 1960s, Britain was largely in retreat. The decision in 1967 to militarily withdraw from 'East of Suez' revealed that the basic framework of the old Anglo-Japanese Alliance, that is, the maintenance of British imperial influence

---

[30]   Eden to MacDonald, 16 Nov. 1951, FO 371/92642, TNA.

[31]   Dening to Eden, 17 Dec. 1951, FO 371/92642, TNA.

[32]   William S. Borden, *The Pacific Alliance: United States Foreign Economic Policy and Japanese Trade Recovery, 1947–1955* (Madison: Wisconsin University Press, 1984); Andrew J. Rotter, *The Path to Vietnam: Origins of the American Commitment to Southeast Asia* (Ithaca/London: Cornell University Press, 1987).

[33]   Hideo Kobayashi, *Nihon kigyo no ajia tenkai* [*The Activities of Japanese Enterprises in Asia*] (Tokyo, 2000), pp. 2, 43.

on the basis of military power, had finally evaporated. In 1966, the British Foreign Office produced draft 'guidelines for British policy towards Japan up to 1975', in which three key British interests vis-à-vis Japan were listed: that Japan should never again become a totalitarian power; that it should contribute to peace, stability and economic development in Asia; and that it should buy as many British goods as possible.[34] Though Japan's role in Asia was mentioned, Britain's interests were now concentrated on the last item, that is increasing UK exports to Japan. The days were gone when Britain tried to cooperate with Japan in Asia, whether in the form of imperialist cooperation in China during the period of the Anglo-Japanese Alliance, or in the 1930s, or in the form of utilizing the manpower and economic capacity of post-imperial Japan in Southeast Asia after World War II.

---

[34]   Chris Braddick, 'Distant Friends: Britain and Japan since 1958 – the Age of Globalization' in Nish and Kibata, *The History of Anglo-Japanese Relations, Vol. 2*, p. 279.

Chapter 3

The Formation of an Industrialization-Oriented Monetary Order in East Asia

Kaoru Sugihara

Introduction

In the period from 1929 to 1934, the volume of world trade fell sharply from 6.8 to 3.7 billion pounds.[1] This extreme shrinkage, described as the 'collapse of world trade,' was the first such experience in peacetime since the Industrial Revolution. Looking at the longer period from 1928 to 1938, world trade shrunk from 6.7 to 4.5 billion pounds.[2]

Table 3.1 shows that the impact of the drying up of world trade eventually spread to cover the entire world. More specifically, while the table shows that some intra-regional trade, like that in Latin America, was not heavily affected, overall, it is striking that the key links in the settlement patterns of multilateral trade were scaled down across the board.

However, the table, which was prepared by the League of Nations, fails to fully capture the magnitude of trade within East Asia, and within the yen bloc in particular. Most subsequent studies of world trade took little notice of this point. It was only relatively recently that recognition was made that among the major trade regions, only East Asia had experienced growth, which ended up facilitating the development of an international division of labour in Asia through intra-regional trade. More specifically, China proceeded with industrialization in the 1930s, generating an intra-regional competition that led to an upgrading of Japan's industrial structure. This relationship between Japan and China heralded the beginning of what is known as the 'flying-geese pattern of economic development' in both light and heavy industries. In addition, with the industrialization of India and China, the Japanese cotton industry lost the vast Asian market for low-grade cotton cloth, and began to advance into the Southeast and South Asian markets based on a specialization in processed cotton cloth and knitted products. In Korea, meanwhile, industrialization was pursued not only for immediate military goals but also as a means to boost the economic might of the Japanese Empire as a whole. Japan even attempted to facilitate the industrialization of Manchuria, though this

---

[1]   League of Nations, *International Trade Statistics, 1938*, Geneva, 1939, p. 9.
[2]   League of Nations, *The Network of World Trade*, Geneva, 1942, pp. 39, 172.

Table 3.1   Direction of World Trade, 1918 and 1938 ($ million)

	Africa		North America		Latin America		Asia		Soviet		Continental Europe		Non-Continental Europe		Oceana		Total	
	1928	1938	1928	1938	1928	1938	1928	1938	1928	1938	1928	1938	1928	1938	1928	1938	1928	1938
Export																		
Africa	23	16	23	10	–	–	8	10	4	–	146	125	66	49	–	–	270	210
North America	27	26	310	160	191	123	146	109	16	16	366	176	257	184	45	29	1,358	823
Latin America	4	6	228	110	60	74	2	6	2	–	228	135	129	82	–	–	653	413
Asia	23	33	240	113	16	10	425	288	23	6	193	125	92	88	21	20	1,033	683
Soviet	–	–	4	4	–	–	16	8	–	–	47	25	16	16	–	–	83	53
Continental Europe	131	123	173	100	140	106	130	109	35	16	1,362	941	356	243	14	10	2,341	1,648
Non-continental Europe	80	74	84	45	80	45	162	78	2	6	205	145	80	43	76	57	769	493
Oceana	4	–	16	6	–	–	23	14	2	–	64	26	74	100	8	12	191	158
Total	292	278	1078	548	487	358	912	622	84	44	2,611	1,698	1,070	805	164	128	6,698	4,481
Import																		
Africa	23	20	27	14	–	–	10	12	4	–	154	153	72	57	2	–	292	256
North America	33	35	310	162	212	135	160	129	21	19	401	208	247	194	51	35	1,435	917
Latin America	4	6	249	125	70	72	2	6	8	–	259	170	142	98	–	–	734	477
Asia	31	37	286	135	21	14	456	311	23	12	218	155	101	108	25	27	1,161	799
Soviet	2	–	4	6	–	–	14	4	–	–	49	29	18	16	–	–	87	55
Continental Europe	144	141	201	115	166	123	154	121	39	16	1,422	992	390	264	21	16	2,537	1,788
Non-continental Europe	92	82	95	51	90	49	175	88	2	6	218	164	82	45	80	67	834	552
Oceana	4	–	18	8	–	–	23	16	4	2	70	33	82	111	10	12	211	182
Total	333	321	1,190	616	559	393	994	687	101	55	2,791	1,904	1,134	893	189	157	7,291	5,026

Source and Note: League of Nations, *The Network of World Trade*, Geneva, 1942, p. 39.
Non-continental Europe refers mainly to United Kingdom and Ireland. Converted from US dollar to sterling, using the exchange rate cited in p. 172 of the same source.

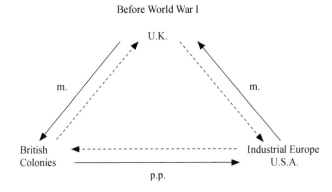

Before World War I

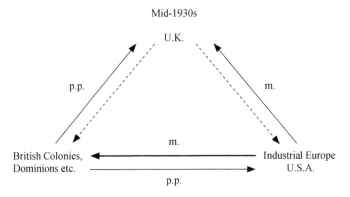

Mid-1930s

Note: m. refers to manufactured goods
        p.p. refers to primary products
        Broken lines refer to the flow of settlements

Figure 3.1   Changes in the Patterns of Multilateral Trade Settlements

was ultimately unfinished. Consequently, by the end of the 1930s, trade within the yen bloc, including Manchuria, had become the core of intra-Asia trade.[3]

Why, then, did East Asia alone succeed in rapid industrialization amidst the 'collapse of world trade'? It appears that previous studies of Japanese history have generally interpreted this success by tracing it to the closed yen bloc or to the expansion of Japan's colonies or its sphere of influence. The commonly accepted formulation, represented by Toichi Nawa's theory of 'three key trade

---

[3]   Kaoru Sugihara, *Ajiakan Boeki no Keisei to Kozo* [*Patterns and Development of Intra-Asian Trade*], (Kyoto: Minerva Shobo, 1996), Ch. 4.

links', described Japan's industrialization not as self-reliant but as one that faced a dilemma, namely that the deeper Japan advanced into the Continent, the greater its dependence on trade with the United States and the British Empire grew. While the emphasis on the importance of raw materials and resources for Japan's industrialization is an important insight in understanding the economic background of the Sino-Japanese war, it is problematic that the accepted theory regards the three key trade links, and in particular the relationship between the first two trade links (with the United States and with the British Empire) and the third (the yen bloc), in purely antagonistic terms.[4] The economic intentions behind Japan's imperialism, it seems to me, were to expand its sphere of influence in order to win a more stable status in, among other things, securing raw materials and resources while maintaining, whenever possible, free trade within the bounds of the imperialistic international order dominated by the European powers and the United States. The strategy behind the yen's devaluation was not only designed to make Japan's exports more competitive but also reflected the grave circumstances faced by Japan, which needed to expand the yen bloc and simultaneously seek to acquire foreign currencies.[5]

Meanwhile, previous studies of Chinese history have not fully appreciated the self-reliant and systematic nature of the policies followed by the Guomindang government. Studies by Toru Kubo, however, have found that China too pursued external economic policies for its industrialization while seeking cooperation with Britain and the United States. The Chinese currency was substantially devalued in 1929–31 in the wake of the fall of silver prices, and remained devalued after failing to fully recover in 1931–34 when silver prices shot up again due to U.S. policy. Following the Currency Reform of 1935, the Chinese government is understood to have sought to stabilise the currency at its devalued level.[6] Thus, in the mid-1930s, East Asia had the world's only 'devaluation zone', consisting of the yen bloc and China. Despite their political and military conflict, Japan and China continued to follow effectively mutually complementary industrialization policies, and a currency devaluation policy in particular, based on cooperation with Britain and the United States.

What is the origin of this trend, which may be characterised as the formation of an industrialization-oriented monetary order in East Asia? In what sense did

---

[4]   Kaoru Sugihara, 'The Economic Motivations behind Japanese Aggression in the late 1930s: Perspectives of Freda Utley and Nawa Toichi', *Journal of Contemporary History*, 32, 2 (1997), pp. 259–80.

[5]   Sugihara, *op. cit.*, Ch. 4.

[6]   Toru Kubo, *Senkanki Chugoku no 'Jiritsu eno Mosaku': Kanzei Tsuka Seisaku to Keizai Hatten* [*China's Quest for Sovereignty in the Interwar Period – Tariff Policy and Economic Development*], (Tokyo: Tokyo Daigaku Shuppankai, 1999). For an English summary of part of this work, see Toru Kubo, 'The Tariff Policy of the Nationalist Government, 1929–36: A Historical Assessment', in Kaoru Sugihara (ed.), *Japan, China, and the Growth of the Asian International Economy, 1850–1949* (Oxford: Oxford University Press, 2005), pp. 145–76.

it reflect the position of East Asia within the international order prevailing in the 1930s? This chapter addresses these problems by discussing several issues of contention that have been variously raised in Western economic history, international economic history, Asian economic history and Japanese economic history without being fully cross-referenced. In the next section, we will argue that the monetary order in East Asia was formed on the basis of, and in tandem with, the new international monetary system based on the British pound's departure from the gold standard in 1931. This chapter adopts a somewhat modified view of the world economy in the 1930s by taking stock of studies in more recent years. In the third section, we show that the currency devaluation by Japan and China in the period from 1929 to 1938 ended up facilitating the industrialization of East Asia. In the fourth and final section, we suggest that the monetary order in East Asia was quite different in nature from that in Continental Europe, because it assumed industrialization in cooperation with the Anglo-American bloc, and in this sense anticipated what was to come after World War II.

The International Currency Regime and the 'Devaluation zone' of East Asia

(1) The Collapse of World Trade and the 'Beggar-Thy-Neighbour' Policy

First, let us summarise the conventional theories regarding the 1930s. Technical factors and policy failures of the three principal players, the United States, Britain and Continental Europe were thought to have driven the economy towards the 'collapse of world trade'. More specifically, as a result of the second industrial revolution, Europe and the United States began to produce substitutes for the primary products that they had imported from tropical regions up to that time, including man-made fibre, artificial rubber and chemical fertilisers. In addition, government measures to stimulate domestic demand (particularly fiscal investment in infrastructure) replaced exports as the engine of economic growth. Consequently, the ratio of trade to GDP declined in the United States and Continental Europe, with the basic direction of development becoming increasingly oriented toward domestic markets (as well as markets of neighbouring regions over which each country's political power extended).[7]

The Great Depression beginning in 1929 put the brakes on the economic surge of the United States, which had appeared to be leading the world economy with its enormous economic power. With President Roosevelt giving clear priority to the domestic market, the post-Great Depression world lost its engine for the expansion of world trade. The United States accumulated massive gold reserves and attracted foreign capital seeking stability, making it difficult to secure international liquidity for the settlement of world trade. This era saw the implementation of the New Deal

---

[7]   James Foreman-Peck, *A History of the World Economy*, 2nd Edn (Hemel Hemstead (Hertfordshire): Harvester Wheatsheaf, 1995), Ch. 10.

and an attempt to reflate the domestic economy with a high-wage policy. Another notable development was the stagnation and shrinking of intra-regional trade in Continental Europe, which largely broke into three blocs: the exchange rate control bloc led by Germany; the 'gold bloc' comprising France and other countries holding firm to the gold standard, and the sterling area formed by Scandinavian and other countries who linked their currencies to sterling, whose exchange rate was devalued in 1931 with its departure from the gold standard. This is important because intra-regional trade in Continental Europe then still accounted for 21 per cent of world trade even in 1938, the largest share in regional trade. Excessively high exchange rates in France and some other countries narrowed the scope of policy measures to prevent deflation. The failure of international economic cooperation led to turmoil in the international financial markets through erratic flows of short-term capital, and also contributed to a rise in tariff rates. Capital by and large tended to flow back to home countries, and trade ties between Continental Europe and the United States weakened.[8]

Looking at a broader context, the transatlantic economies had served as the engines of the world economy since the end of the nineteenth century, thanks to the free movement of factors of production, which in turn made possible the development of the new world, endowed with abundant land resources. Also, prior to World War I, a multilateral trade settlement mechanism was in place, under which Britain had surpluses in merchandise and services trade with the developing countries and Continental Europe and the United States purchased primary products from the developing countries and exported manufactures to Britain. By the 1930s, however, the new world had lost its frontier and was no longer serving as a locomotive for expanded world trade. Already in the 1920s, major restrictions were placed on emigration and the free flow of factors of production (capital and labour), a prerequisite for the maintenance of the international gold standard, began to be done away with even among the developed countries. Continental Europe and the United States failed to move toward restoring a division of labour among themselves, instead tilting toward protectionism as they tried to protect agriculture and traditional industries by forming regional blocs. Needless to say, the multilateral trade settlement mechanism quickly became dysfunctional with the loss of just one of its vectors. The downturn in demand and fall of prices of primary products in Europe and the United States proved to be a critical impediment to the rebuilding of world trade.[9]

Thus, according to Kindleberger, the crucial strategic factor that transformed the depression in the United States into the Great Depression was the lack of leadership in maintaining the international financial system. The United States, though reeling from the Great Depression, did not follow Britain in moving off

---

[8]   Charles H. Feinstein, Peter Temin and Gianni Toniolo, *The European Economy between the Wars* (Oxford: Oxford University Press, 1997), Ch. 8.

[9]   A. Lewis, *Economic Survey 1919–1939* (London: George Allen and Unwin, 1949), p. 155.

the gold standard in April 1931, and continued to absorb international liquidity. It drew criticism for its devaluation of the dollar in September 1933, signaling a shift to a managed currency system, while keeping international liquidity in its hands. As a result, neither Britain nor the United States was able to seize the initiative as a hegemon. The 'competitive devaluation' only functioned as a 'beggar-thy-neighbour' policy that merely passed its own problems on to other countries. This recognition served as a background for the pursuit of a fixed exchange rate regime and U.S. leadership under the Bretton Woods system following the end of World War II.[10]

(2) The Sterling Bloc and East Asia

However, recent studies have led to some modifications to several aspects of the interpretations outlined above. Here, we present three specific points of contention. First, let us consider the significance of the establishment of the sterling bloc. Britain, which had the highest dependence on trade and international finance among the developed countries, tried to maintain economic relations with its colonies and self-governing dominions around the world, including in Asia, Africa, Australasia and Canada. The formation of the sterling bloc represented one of such major attempts. The sterling bloc (sometimes referred to as the sterling area) is a widely used term, and has no precise definition. When used to describe the situation before World War II, it usually covers the period from Britain's departure from the gold standard to the years just before the outbreak of World War II in 1939. Discussions in this chapter follow this practice.[11] The regions considered to belong to the sterling bloc include (1) Britain; (2) India, Malaya, Hong Kong and nearly all the other colonial territories; (3) the four dominions of Australia, New Zealand, South Africa and Ireland (excluding two other dominions of Canada and Newfoundland); and (4) Scandinavia, the Baltic countries, Portugal, Siam, Iraq, Egypt, Argentina and other peripheral countries (see Table 3.4 below).[12] The

---

[10]   Charles P. Kindleberger, *The World in Depression, 1919–1939*, 2nd Edn (London: Allen Lane, 1986). For the relationship between discussions on the Great Depression and Kindleberger's realist views of the U.S. role in the 1970s and onwards, see Kindleberger, 'International Public Goods without International Government', *American Economic Review*, 76 (1986), pp. 1–13.

[11]   Ian M. Drummond, *The Floating Pound and the Sterling Area, 1931–1939* (Cambridge: Cambridge University Press, 1981). Takao Kamikawa, 'Fukusu Kijiku Tsukaken no Kaiko' [Review of Multiple Key Currency Blocs], in Takao Kamikawa and Eietsu Imamatsu eds, *En no Seiji Keizaigaku: Ajia to Sekai Shisutemu* [*The Political Economy of the Yen: Asia and the World System*], (Tokyo: Dobunkan, 1997). Joji Kobayashi, *20-seiki Shisutemu 1: Koso to Keisei* [*The Twentieth Century System 1: Ideas and Formation*], (Institute of Social Science, Tokyo: Tokyo Daigaku Shuppankai, 1998).

[12]   Ragnar Nurske, *International Currency Experience: Lessons of the Inter-War Period, Geneva: League of Nations, 1944*, Ch. 3.

countries listed in (1) to (3) almost exactly correspond to the members of the tariff bloc at the time of the Ottawa Agreements, with some exceptions such as Canada. This tariff bloc formed the core of the sterling bloc, and had a degree of exclusiveness, but another major feature of the sterling bloc was the fact that many peripheral countries, as seen in (4), linked the value of their currencies to sterling. The sterling bloc was cohesive at the core, but at the same time remained open to the outside. Next, let us consider the significance of this two-tier structure.

Examining the core first, since the departure from the gold standard in 1931, Britain, in an effort to build an international financial system centered around the pound as a key currency, established a system under which colonies and dominions were required to hold reserves in sterling instead of gold, in London. British colonies, almost without choice, were forced to link their currencies to sterling. In India, for example, farmers reeling from the depression began already in 1929–31 to relinquish to the market gold that they had accumulated. Since India was prohibited from selling gold to countries other than Britain, in 1931–34 when the price of gold rose against the pound, massive amounts of gold flowed from India into London. Huge volumes were also hoarded in India, and this movement of gold could have crucial importance for London, as clearly pointed out by John Maynard Keynes during the gold standard years. According to Balachandran, contrary to the deflationary effect of gold stored away in India assumed by Keynes, Britain during that period did not want the Indian government to take antirecession measures domestically, rather hoping that the inflow of gold into London would bring with it a stronger position of the pound and some inflationary effects.[13]

Meanwhile, Australia and other dominions avoided deflationary pressure from gold shortages by shifting their reserves for trade settlements from gold to the pound, ensuring the expansion of the sterling bloc and also contributing to the stabilization of Britain's international balance of payments by keeping most of their sterling reserves in London. In addition, these dominions played an important role in reinstating London as the centre of international finance as they linked their currencies to the British pound and left the determination of the relative value of their currencies in the hands of British monetary authorities, thus following the initiative of the Bank of England through central bank intervention in the international financial markets. The inflow of gold produced in South Africa into London also enhanced the strategic importance of the dominions. All of these induced the flow of short-term capital into Britain, propping up the pound. Britain could not take similar measures toward Canada, a dominion that was becoming increasingly economically dependent on the United States. Nevertheless, the Bank of England tried to exercise its influence to a certain extent in the process of establishing the central bank in Canada.[14]

---

[13]   G. Balachandran, 'Gold and Empire: Britain and India in the International Liquidity Crisis in the Great Depression', *Journal of European Economic History*, 20 (1991), pp. 239–70.

[14]   Peter Cain, 'Gentlemanly Capitalism at Work: The Bank of England, Canada, and the Sterling Area, 1932–1936', *Economic History Review*, 49, 2 (1996), pp. 336–57.

Thus, the sterling bloc acquired a special international status as the core of the overall international trade and financial system, anchored in London but with its influence extending beyond the bloc. While Britain's current account surplus began to shrink, its external position strengthened remarkably as the recovery of capital proceeded smoothly partly due to the slowing of new bond issues overseas and increases in the balances of pounds held by other countries in the sterling bloc, along with foreign exchange equalization efforts. Specifically, at the end of 1931, Britain had net short-term external debts of 400 million pounds against gold and foreign exchange reserves of 120 million pounds. By the end of 1937, both had increased to approximately 800 million pounds. As a result, the ratio of its gold and foreign exchange reserves to net short-term external debts rose from 29 per cent to 102 per cent in the six-year period.[15] Thus, the value of the pound came to be determined basically by its strength as the key international currency, and it no longer necessarily reflected the actual conditions of Britain's external trade. With this, the pound transcended the strength of Britain as a nation-state and became a force aspiring for international cooperation in the world market.

In addition to British colonies and dominions, many independent countries linked their currencies to the British pound precisely because of its status as a key currency. During this period, with the weakening of the relative position of the dollar and European currencies, the number of countries with currencies linked to the pound increased.[16] This was the result of the functioning of a self-sustaining mechanism of expansion, under which the rise in confidence in the pound led to an expansion of the sterling bloc and the expanded bloc in turn led exchange rates to increasingly revolve around the pound, further enhancing the confidence in the pound as the key currency. In this way, the pound (and the pound and dollar from 1934 onward) rose above the 'competitive devaluation' for a given set of two countries and became the target against which other countries sought to set exchange rates. This allowed Britain to avoid making an immediate counter-devaluation of the pound when another currency was devalued against it. In other words, though the core part of the sterling bloc overlapped the tariff block formed under the Ottawa Agreements of 1932, the foundation for its existence, in effect, far surpassed the tariff bloc. For this reason, it was natural for the sterling bloc to promote cooperation rather than developing as an exclusive bloc. It appears that the commonly accepted theory fails to fully appreciate the international-cooperation-inducing nature of the sterling bloc.

Therefore, it is best to avoid calling it the 'sterling bloc,' making it appear to have clearly defined geographical boundaries, and to paint it with the same brush as the exclusionary 'mark bloc' and 'yen bloc' that spread in the late 1930s. In fact, Japan's decision to link the value of the yen to the pound beginning in 1932 was based on a strategy that was consistent and complementary with the idea of the formation of the *sterling area*. In addition, once the yen was linked to the pound, the yen bloc's expansion into the Continent simultaneously signaled an expansion of the sterling

---

[15] Kamikawa, *op. cit.*, p. 267.
[16] Nurske, *op. cit.*, pp. 50–54.

area there. Furthermore, as the value of the Chinese currency was also linked to the pound in 1935, East Asia was effectively incorporated into the sterling area. When the 'currency war' intensified amid the Sino-Japanese War and the confidence in the region's currencies became shaky, neither Japan nor China was powerful enough to restore full currency convertibility into gold and silver, and the East Asian currencies were increasingly left with no other choice than to maintain exchange rate links with the pound sterling to demonstrate their stability in terms of their international value. Only when the intensified inflation made this impossible did East Asian countries take steps to move toward full control of the exchange rates and trade.

(3) Preferential Tariff Blocs and East Asia

The formation and development of the sterling area seem to have played a role in facilitating trade between blocs rather than making them more exclusionary. Thus the second modification of the commonly accepted theory is to raise a degree of doubt about the understanding of the 'collapse of world trade.'

First, let us look at changes in Britain's balance of trade in the 1930s, as shown in Table 3.2.

Table 3.2   Regional Composition of UK Trade Balances, 1928 and 1938
            ($ million)

	1928	1938
Ireland	-9.04	-1.84
Dominions	-8.42	-75.06
India, Burma, Ceylon	28.56	-19.63
British Colonies and Protectorates	26.71	-2.25
Total of British Colonies, Dominions and others	36.99	-98.79
USA	-131.1	-91.42
Europe	-184.52	-115.56
Others	-72.54	-79.56
Total of Foreign Countries	-388.16	-286.54
Grand Total	-350.35	-385.32

Source and Note: The Network of World Trade, p. 91.

Converted to Sterling, as per Table 3.1

First of all, Britain's trade surpluses with its 'Empire' (hereafter denotes colonies, dominions and other regions which made up the categories (2) and (3) of the sterling bloc mentioned above) disappeared and turned into trade deficits. Particularly important was a sharp rise in the dependence of dominions on the British market for exports of primary products. Second, Britain's trade deficits with Continental Europe and the United States, in spite of declines, still underpinned the world's largest flow of trade settlement currencies. Britain, which registered trade deficits with almost every other country, emerged as the world's largest importer. In line with this, a comparison between the situation in the mid-1930s and the multilateral trade settlement structure prior to World War I shows that in addition to the two points described above, there also were changes in the relationship between industrial Europe and the United States and the British Empire. Specifically, as a third point to note, while imports of primary products by industrial Europe and the United States from the British Empire declined, exports of manufactures from the latter to the former increased, reducing the latter's trade deficit with the former. Thus a phenomenon emerged that can be called a trend toward bilateralism of world trade.[17]

However, these changes only involved settlement patterns, and did not necessarily represent a change in the structure of world trade itself. Seen from a different point of view, Table 3.1 can be interpreted as showing that there was no fundamental change in the trade structure between the developed industrial countries comprising Britain, industrial Europe and the United States on the one hand, and the British Empire that exported primary products on the other. Stated simply, the preferential tariff bloc built around Britain not only was unable to satisfy the Empire's demand for manufactures within the bloc but also forced it to rely on the purchasing power of countries outside the bloc as markets for primary products produced within the bloc.

Table 3.3   Geographical Composition of the Trade of Areas belonging to the Imperial Tariff Preference, 1928, 1935, 1938

	UK		Industrial Europe, USA		Japan		China		Total	
(Exports)	1928									
Egypt	106	37%	122	42%	8	3%	0	0%	288	100%
South Africa	114	47%	92	38%	1	0%	1	0%	245	100%
Canada	448	33%	673	49%	39	3%	19	1%	1364	100%
India	276	22%	479	38%	126	10%	38	3%	1250	100%
British Malaya	59	12%	254	53%	20	4%	17	4%	482	100%
Australia	244	38%	226	35%	56	9%	6	1%	646	100%
Total	1247	29%	1846	43%	250	6%	81	2%	4275	100%
(Imports)	1928									
Egypt	52	20%	112	44%	8	3%	2	1%	256	100%
South Africa	167	44%	131	35%	6	2%	1	0%	376	100%
Canada	192	16%	413	34%	13	1%	5	0%	1223	100%
India	447	47%	241	25%	60	6%	18	2%	953	100%
British Malaya	81	16%	47	10%	11	2%	35	7%	493	100%
Australia	280	41%	241	36%	21	3%	3	0%	678	100%
Total	1219	31%	1185	30%	119	3%	64	2%	3979	100%

[17]   League of Nations, *The Review of World Trade, 1935*, Geneva, 1936, pp. 63–9.

Table 3.3   Continued

	UK		Industrial Europe, USA		Japan		China		Total	
(Exports)				1935						
Egypt	57	31%	67	37%	9	5%	1	1%	183	100%
South Africa	59	41%	55	38%	2	1%	0	0%	145	100%
Canada	304	41%	310	42%	15	2%	7	1%	738	100%
India	186	31%	171	28%	84	14%	11	2%	607	100%
British Malaya	51	16%	161	49%	31	9%	5	2%	329	100%
Australia	226	50%	88	19%	60	13%	16	4%	453	100%
Total	883	36%	852	35%	201	8%	40	2%	2455	100%
(Imports)				1935						
Egypt	37	22%	59	36%	19	11%	1	1%	166	100%
South Africa	179	48%	116	31%	13	4%	0	0%	370	100%
Canada	119	22%	349	63%	4	1%	4	1%	552	100%
India	206	39%	121	23%	82	16%	9	2%	527	100%
British Malaya	44	16%	16	6%	17	6%	14	5%	270	100%
Australia	167	44%	96	25%	25	7%	2	1%	382	100%
Total	752	33%	757	33%	160	7%	30	1%	2267	100%
(Exports)				1938						
Egypt	47	31%	56	37%	9	6%	1	1%	152	100%
South Africa	64	36%	59	39%	2	1%	0	0%	151	100%
Canada	339	40%	336	40%	21	2%	5	1%	845	100%
India	240	36%	175	40%	59	9%	12	2%	662	100%
British Malaya	48	15%	149	40%	31	10%	4	1%	326	100%
Australia	282	54%	106	40%	10	2%	8	2%	525	100%
Total	1010	38%	881	40%	132	5%	30	1%	2661	100%
(Imports)				1938						
Egypt	43	23%	78	41%	5	3%	1	1%	188	100%
South Africa	203	43%	169	36%	13	3%	2	0%	468	100%
Canada	119	18%	461	68%	4	1%	3	0%	676	100%
India	206	38%	150	28%	63	12%	8	1%	538	100%
British Malaya	59	19%	29	9%	7	2%	19	6%	314	100%
Australia	224	43%	135	26%	23	4%	2	0%	515	100%
Total	854	32%	1022	26%	115	4%	35	1%	2699	100%

Source *and Note*: Calculated from *League of Nations: The Network of World Trade*, Annexe III.
Converted to sterling as Table 3.1. Industrial Europe refers to Austria, Belgium-Luxemburg, Czechoslovakia, France, Germany, Italy, The Netherlands, Sweden, and Switzerland. Japan includes Korea and Taiwan. China includes Manchuria and Hong Kong. India includes Burma.

Table 3.3 presents no more than a set of selected statistics collected by the League of Nations, which however makes it amply clear that it cannot be argued that the regions of the British Empire tilted rapidly toward an exclusive bloc. The table lists the ratios of major trading partners (countries and regions) in trade by six countries (regions) with 1928 total trade volumes in excess of 100 million pounds, out of colonies, dominions and others comprising the imperial regions of the British Empire, for 1928, 1935 and 1938.[18] As can be seen, a full 38 per cent of imports of these six countries/regions in 1938 was from industrial Europe and the United States, a much higher ratio than in 1928. Nor is that the whole story. Even in exports, while the ratio of their exports to Britain rose and the ratio of their exports to countries and regions outside the bloc declined, exports to industrial Europe and the United States still accounted for 33 per cent of their total exports in 1938.

Therefore, it seems only natural to assume that the preferential tariff bloc made up of Britain and its Empire was never intended to be a self-contained entity or a bloc, from start to finish, and that it tried to position itself as part of a new trade structure. Even within the new structure, while the weight of multilateral settlements declined, there was no change in the assumption of the maintenance of a multilateral trade structure in the sense that trade between two countries (or regions) are linked multilaterally.

How should the relationship between the preferential tariff bloc and Japan and China be understood in this context? Returning to Table 3.3, it is evident that for the preferential tariff bloc, the weight of East Asia was never large. In particular, that of China, including Manchuria, was extremely small. However, something similar to the bloc's relationship with industrial Europe and the United States can be discerned in its relationship with Japan, albeit on a much reduced scale. Specifically, the ratio of imports from Japan rose from just 2.8 per cent in 1928 to 7.1 per cent in 1935, and even in 1938 stood at 4.3 per cent, much higher than the 1928 level. For exports, the ratio of Japan declined slightly from 5.8 per cent to 5.0 per cent in the same 10-year period but registered a high 8.2 per cent in 1935, defying the characterization of a steady downward trend. As is widely known, this trading relationship between Japan and the British Empire was based on the exchange of manufactures for primary products, with Japan importing cotton and pig iron from India; rubber, tin and iron ores from British Malaya; wool, iron ore and zinc from Australia; aluminum from Canada; and wool from South Africa, and exporting cotton goods, rayon, sundry goods and others to these regions. This is what Toichi Nawa called the second trade link.[19]

For confirmation, this relationship weakened from 1937 onward, because of the tariff effects and also reflecting the limits of Japan's ability to earn foreign currencies. However, as argued by Nawa, it is true that this relationship was still important in that the dwindling trade ties included imports of raw materials and resources, which were crucial for the industrialization needs of the yen bloc. It should be pointed out

---

[18]   However, Hong Kong, which had a large quantity of re-exports and re-imports, was excluded.

[19]   Toichi Nawa, *Nihon Bosekigyo to Genmen Mondai Kenkyu* [*Studies on the Japanese Spinning Industry and the Raw Cotton Problem*], (Tokyo: Daido Shoin, 1937), pp. 467–70, Figures cited here are supplemented by *Statistical Abstract for the British Empire*.

here that seen from the preferential tariff bloc, the relationship with Japan was not at all an unnatural one from the perspective of the positional relationship of world trade. The members of the bloc hoped that purchases of manufactures from Japan for settlement in sterling would make it easier to export primary products (cotton in the case of India) to Japan. Needless to say, to industrial capitalists within the bloc, such as cotton spinners in Bombay, this appeared as an expression of the imperialistic international order that encouraged exports of primary products and tried to limit the marketing outlets for their manufactures to within the domestic markets. Therefore, this system had the potential to trigger nationalistic movements in India and could shake the very foundation of the Empire in some situations. In this respect, the fact that Japanese exports of manufactures remained at a high level until 1935 and stayed at a certain level even in 1938 was a matter of grave concern not only for Lancashire but also for the British Government of India.[20] Nevertheless, trade relations (as well as trade liberalism as an ideology justifying them) with regions outside the preferential tariff bloc provided the basic premise for supporting the entire economic strength of the British Empire and remained something that Britain could not categorically reject.

(4) Formation of the 'Devaluation zone' in East Asia

The third point of revision is that currency devaluations did not necessarily lead to the impoverishment of neighbouring countries but rather contributed to monetary stability and increased international liquidity. Today, a quarter century after the world economy shifted to the floating exchange rate regime, its merits are widely recognised, and accordingly, some modifications have been made to previous studies and theories concerning the 1930s. This development was triggered by a chapter written by Eichengreen and Sachs in 1985.[21] They argue that the departure from the gold standard freed central banks from the 'golden fetters' and enabled them to increase international liquidity without being held as strictly as they once had been to the constraints of gold reserves. This release from the 'golden fetters' was not designed for the implementation of Keynesian policies domestically (Keynesian policies in that sense might have been easier to carry out in countries with exchange controls such as Germany). Initially, for the country that was the

---

[20]   Naoto Kagotani, *Ajia Kokusai Tsusho Chitsujo to Kindai Nihon* [The Asian International Commercial Order and Modern Japan], (Nagoya: Nagoya Daigaku Shuppankai, 2000), Chs 5–7.

[21]   Barry Eichengreen and Jeffrey Sachs, 'Exchange Rates and Economic Recovery in the 1930's', *Journal of Economic History*, 45, 1985, pp. 925–46, included in Barry Eichengreen, *Elusive Stability: Essays in the History of International Finance, 1919–1939* (Cambridge: Cambridge University Press, 1990). For subsequent developments, see Barry Eichengreen, *Golden Fetters: The Gold Standard and the Great Depression, 1919–1939* (Oxford: Oxford University Press, 1992), and other books by Eichengreen that underscore the advantages of the floating exchange rate system.

first to devalue its currency (Britain in this case), the devaluation brought, in the short term, clear positive results in the form of increased exports and reduced imports. In addition, the devaluation of the dollar after the United States's effective departure from the gold standard in April 1933 restored the link between the sterling area and the dollar. The fact that the dollar eventually followed the pound helped accelerate the economic recovery and shored up confidence in the pound.

Table 3.4   Exchange Rates against Sterling, 1929–1938

	1929	1930	1931	1932	1933	1934	1935	1936	1937	1938
Germany	100	100	107.75	138.99	147.12	159.72	167.24	165.55	166.6	168.56
France	100	100	107.75	138.99	147.12	161.93	167.24	149.93	100.51	72.89
Netherlands	100	100	107.75	138.99	147.12	161.93	167.24	155.36	134.77	136.19
USA	100	100	107.75	138.99	114.58	96.58	98.77	97.78	98.39	99.55
UK	100	100	100	100	100	100	100	100	100	100
South Africa	100	100	107.75	135.99	99.09	98.96	99.37	98.94	99.04	99.04
India	100	100	99.99	100.28	100.32	100.24	100.48	100.67	100.67	99.8
Siam	100	100	104.63	114.28	101.14	100.71	100.86	100.89	100.51	100.93
Japan	92.34	99.04	105.67	77.04	59.29	57.5	57.13	56.99	56.81	56.72
China	98.35	70.7	54.97	69.91	72.13	78.15	85.84	69.66	69.06	49.09

Source and Notes: Calculated from League of Nations, *Review of World Trade, 1934–1938*, Annex, Geneva, 1935–1939.

Calculated by taking the 'parity-rate' of 1929, as defined by the League of Nations (arithmetic average of export and import rates), as 100.

Converted to Sterling as per Table 3.1.

Table 3.4 extracts major currencies from the exchange rate data of the League of Nations and recalculates them, changing the basis from the dollar to the pound. Figure 3.2, a plot based on the exchange rates calculated in the way described above, shows that among the developed countries, the so-called 'Anglo-American Group' with the pound and the dollar at its centre, formed the core of exchange rates at relatively low levels from 1934 onward. The pound and the dollar became the target currencies and succeeded in making other currencies converge to their levels. With this establishment of a multiple key currency system, the devaluation of the pound and the dollar put upward pressure on gold prices and led to an overvaluation of the currencies of countries that maintained links to gold. The Anglo-American Group succeeded in increasing international liquidity by changing the accounting unit of liquidity from gold to the pound and the dollar.

Needless to say, the managed currency system in the 1930s as a whole only achieved success on an extremely limited scale. The specific circumstances prevailing in those years prevented monetary authorities from promptly adopting policies in favour of international cooperation. In Europe and the United States

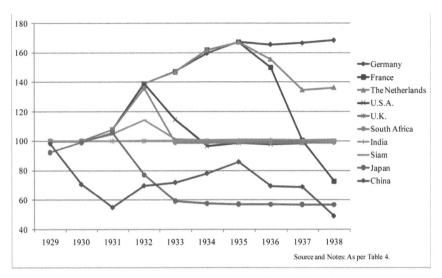

Source and Notes: As per Table 4.

Figure 3.2   Exchange Rates against Sterling, 1929–1938

following World War I, the significant emergence onto the political stage of groups with their own special interests, including industrial capitalists and trade unions, made the process of decision-making on economic policies more complex. In Britain, for example, balancing interests became difficult against the backdrop of massive unemployment, with the result that the central bank found it increasingly difficult to pursue an internationally coordinated macroeconomic policy by maintaining its independence. This is one of the reasons why Britain was unable to depart from the gold standard sooner. In the United States as well, as described earlier, President Roosevelt was preoccupied with promoting a domestic economic recovery. Another blow came from the split of developed countries into three large groups. The gold bloc, led by France, adhered to the gold standard, with its inflationary experiences in the 1920s still fresh in memory. Consequently, the currencies of the countries in this bloc became significantly revalued against the pound, contributing to a deepening of the economic stagnation in these countries. Meanwhile, another bloc of countries with exchange controls moved toward the imposition of trade controls, with their currencies remaining revalued against the British pound.

However, these developments do not suggest a simple cause-and-effect relationship under which currency devaluations by some countries helped to impoverish others through a beggar-thy-neighbour effect. If European countries had succeeded in the concerted devaluation of their currencies sooner, the temporary competitive advantages of the countries that devalued their currencies earlier may have been offset more quickly. Even so, the cooperative moves would not have ended simply in a zero-sum game. There would have been basically no change in the fact that the purchasing power of Britain was serving as an anchor maintaining the multilateral trade structure and contributing to a recovery of the global economy by increasing international liquidity.[22] The fact that currencies of the entire world were devalued against gold and freed from the 'golden fetters' at the initiative of the Anglo-American Group seem to have had the effect of promoting, to an extent, a recovery from the depression.

When seen in this way, it is evident that the incorporation of East Asia into the sterling area was a development consistent with the demands of the international currency regime for the stabilization of currency values and guarantee of international liquidity. However, just as they were incorporated into the sterling area, the currencies of East Asia were sharply devalued against the pound during those years. As shown by Figure 3.2, only East Asia, comprised of Japan, its colonies, Manchuria and China, moved in a totally different direction from what was happening in the rest of the world. This is precisely what is described in this chapter as the formation of the 'devaluation zone' in East Asia.[23]

How did this 'devaluation zone' come into being? Leaving the discussion on the process of the currency devaluation and its policy significance to the next section, we will present here a more general sketch.[24] First, as is commonly known, Japan returned to the gold standard in January 1930 right after the outbreak of the Great Depression. But since the repeal of the gold embargo at the old currency rate meant a revaluation of the exchange rate, the domestic economic situation deteriorated, causing the flight of capital overseas and a massive outflow of gold. When Britain departed from the gold standard in September 1931, foreign exchange banks, both domestic and foreign, and traders rushed into the exchange market to buy dollars. The Japanese government countered this by selling dollars but could not fight back the market pressures, and in December it decided to re-impose a ban on gold exports and departed from the gold standard once again. In this process, Japan lost massive amounts of gold. As much as 504 million yen worth of gold flowed out between May 1930 and January 1932, and the inadequacy of gold reserves constrained Japan's foreign exchange policy thereafter. Finance Minister Korekiyo Takahashi allowed the yen to fall rapidly, reasoning that the depreciation would adjust its exchange rate to the actual conditions of the Japanese economy and also help promote exports. Comparisons of the lowest market value of the yen between December 1931, just before exports of gold were banned again, and the end of November 1932, show that the Japanese currency dropped as much as 60 per cent against the dollar.

---

[22]   Eichengreen, *Golden Fetters*, Ch. 1.

[23]   This idea was first used in Sugihara (*op. cit.*, Ch. 4), and was elaborated by Kagotani, *op. cit.* However, they discussed the 'devaluation zone' mainly in the Asian context. This chapter attempts to extend it to an argument for the specificity of East Asia in the overall international currency regime.

[24]   Discussions on Japan are based on Nihon Ginko Chosakyoku Tokubetsu Shiryoshitsu, *Manshu Jihen Iko no Zaisei Kinyushi* [*Fiscal and Monetary History after the Manchurian Incident*], 1948, vol. 1, Ch. 4.

The lack of exchange rate stability constitutes an impediment to trade. But the lack of sufficient gold reserves leaves government intervention as the only means of stabilizing exchange rates at low levels. Thus, in July 1932, the Japanese government enacted the Capital Flight Prevention Law, restricting inflows and outflows of capital, and began in November 1932 to impose measures to prevent the yen's further depreciation, placing exchange transactions under nearly total control of the government. Then, in March 1933, the government shifted the basic exchange rate from the dollar-based to pound-based rate and linked the yen to the British pound at a low rate of one shilling and two pence. At that time, the pound was the only stable currency in existence, as the United States had slipped back into depression in 1933 and the value of the dollar had significantly fallen. From that time until the outbreak of World War II in 1939, the Japanese government all but succeeded in maintaining the yen's link to the pound. The maintenance of this link was an essential choice for Japan in order to maintain trade with countries outside the yen bloc and ensure the supply of raw materials and natural resources. Thus, it can be said that Japan, in effect, belonged to the sterling area during this period in that it depended on the confidence in the pound for the stability of the value of its settlement currency.

Meanwhile, the value of the Chinese currency, which was linked to silver, plummeted beginning in 1929 in tandem with the fall of the price of silver. Because of this, compared to other countries, China was not directly affected by the Great Depression. However, silver prices rose in the wake of departures from the gold standard by many countries from 1931 onward, leading to a massive outflow of silver from China. The depletion of silver reserves led to a credit crunch, and subsequently to deflation.[25] Furthermore, in addition to the problems associated with these short-term developments, amidst the shift to the international managed currency system, it became unrealistic for China to stabilise the value of its currency without exchange controls or monetary policy by a central bank. Even at this point of time, China had an assortment of different currencies, including silver bullions, various silver coins, copper coins and banknotes, and on top of that, exchange rates between them often fluctuated heavily. This situation not only hampered the inflow of foreign capital but also made it infeasible for the country to implement a rapid industrialization policy.

One of the main objectives of the currency reform in 1935 was to escape from the deflationary situation caused by the currency's link to silver and establish a new monetary system based on a linkage to the pound. Specifically, China restricted the right of currency issues to three governmental banks – the Central Bank of China, Bank of China and Bank of Communications – and designated only the standard dollar notes issued by these banks as legal tender. It also banned the use of silver as currency and tried to call in silver as early as possible to ensure the circulation of the national currency (yuan). Partly based on support from British banks, the replacement of silver with the new banknotes proceeded smoothly, and

---

[25]   Arthur N. Young, *China's Nation Building Effort, 1927–1937: The Financial and Economic Record*, Stanford: Hoover Institution Press, 1971, Ch. 8.

the concentration of silver in banks also made progress. As a result, from 1935 to early 1938, the value of the Chinese currency remained stable, with the exception of a short period of time.[26] It can be said that China in this period belonged to the sterling area, in the same sense as Japan did.

Even after the Sino-Japanese war broke out in 1937 and the central part of North China came under Japanese control, the yuan was not immediately driven out of circulation. As the yen-linked currency of continental China was not equivalent to the yen in value, precisely speaking, and its convertibility with the yen was also strictly regulated, its purchasing power was declining. On the other hand, the purchasing power of the yuan, contrary to Japan's expectations, was maintained for a considerable period of time.[27] It was only after April 1938 that the yuan's value depreciated rapidly due to the exhaustion from inflation and the war (for details, see the next section).

In summary, East Asia's shift to the managed currency system started in 1932, was completed in 1935, and was maintained until 1938. The shift was largely a response to the crisis that resulted from the currencies' links to gold and silver. What followed was an outflow of gold and silver from the region, instead of the absorption of gold for hegemony and stability as seen in the United States. Both Japan and China tried to stabilise the value of their currencies and secure liquidity in the region by joining the sterling area. Even after the Sino-Japanese war intensified, and the 'currency war' within the region and the political friction between Japan and the Anglo-American Group continued to deepen, the stability of the East Asian currencies in their relationships with countries outside the region seems to have become increasingly dependent on the confidence in the British pound as time progressed.

However, at the same time, the shift in both Japan and China to a managed currency system may be said to have also harboured their industrialization strategies by taking advantage of the new international currency regime. If a country devalues its currency substantially against the key currency of a country that will not implement a counter-devaluation, then it can potentially enjoy easier industrialization by making exports easier and imports more difficult for a reasonably long period of time. In this way the establishment of the new international currency regime provided East Asia with an opportunity that would have been inconceivable under the gold standard. The next section addresses these aspects of the shift to the managed currency system.

The 'Devaluation Zone' and Import Substitution Industrialization

(1) The Position of East Asia in the World Economy

How much weight did East Asia carry in the world economy in the 1930s?

---

26   Kubo, *op. cit.*, Ch. 8.

27   Takafusa Nakamura, *Senji Nihon no Kahoku Keizai Shihai* [*Wartime Japan's Control of the North China Economy*], (Tokyo: Yamakawa Shuppansha, 1983), pp. 209–13.

According to Table 3.5, which tallies the estimates made by Maddison using purchasing power parity, East Asia in 1933 accounted for 34 per cent of the world's population and 15 per cent of its total GDP (these shares would be slightly higher if the northern part of the Korean Peninsula were included). This means that East Asia, as a regional economy, ranked third in the world following Europe and the United States. However, in terms of standards of living, there was a major gap between East Asia and the advanced European countries and United States. Even Japan's per capita income was far below the lowest level in Europe and the United States, and that in the Japanese colonies was even lower. China's per capita income, meanwhile, was just 28 per cent of Japan's. In other words, there were major income gaps among East Asian countries as well.

Table 3.5   East Asia's Share in the World Economy, 1933

	GDP (in million 1990 dollars)		Population (in thousand)		GDP per capita (in 1990 dollars)
China	289,200	10%	500,000	29%	578
Japan	137,176	5%	67,182	40%	2,042
Korea	18,706	1%	14,266	10%	1,311
Taiwan	5,537	0%	4,995	0%	1,109
East Asia Total	450,619	15%	586,443	34%	768
USA	603,458	21%	126,180	7%	4,783
UK	234,409	8%	46,520	3%	5,039
Industrial Europe	630,742	22%	172,683	10%	3,653
Advanced Western Countries Total	1,468,609	50%	345,383	20%	4,252
World Total (40 countries)	2,912,869	100%	1,703,770	100%	1710

Source and Note: Angus Maddison, *Monitoring the World Economy, 1820–1992* (Paris: OECD, 1995), Table A, C. Do., *Chinese Economic Performance in the Long Run* (Paris: OECD, 1998), p. 158.
China includes Manchuria. Korea refers to present South Korea only. For the definition of Industrial Europe, see Table 3.3.

However, if the East Asian economy is looked at as a single entity, over 80 per cent of the total population was concentrated in China, placing Japan only in the periphery and making China its centre in terms of scale. Seeing Japan as peripheral was natural in a sense, considering that by around 1930 at least, China had accounted for two-thirds of the regional GDP. This relationship underwent a gradual change after the Manchurian Incident. A calculation of the yen bloc's GDP in 1933, adding Korea, Taiwan and Manchuria to Japan, shows that the bloc accounted for a little over 40 per cent of East Asia's combined GDP, with the ratio for China, excluding Manchuria, coming to just below 60 per cent.[28] Thereafter, as the economies in the yen bloc grew rapidly, the yen bloc's share in the East Asian economy grew by the mid-1930s, without much geographical expansion, as it took time for the yen-linked currency to take hold in North China and other areas. In other words, the yen bloc and the Chinese currency bloc came to stand almost on an equal footing in terms of the magnitude of the economies under their effective control. The 'currency war' between Japan and China was thus waged against the background of this change in relative economic might. Yet, the fact that the Chinese currency bloc until around 1937 still had an economic scale comparable to the entire Japanese Empire should be noted in understanding how Western countries treated Japan and China.

Now, let us move on to an overview of trade in East Asia. Table 3.6 shows that the share of European countries and the United States as a whole in East Asia's trade was lower than the shares held by India and Southeast Asia, and that the ratio was also declining. This can be said to reflect the growing ratio of intra-regional trade and East Asia's growing tendency toward a stronger degree of self-reliance. However, a closer look reveals that the share of trade with Western nations was the lowest in Japanese colonies and that for China (including Hong Kong and Manchuria), it remained as high as that of Southeast Asia until 1936. Moreover, the share of European countries and the United States fell sharply for both Japan and China only in 1938 and after. Thus, as far as the period until 1937 is concerned, it seems unlikely that East Asia was moving rapidly toward greater autonomy.

In qualitative terms too, East Asia's trade with Europe and the United States in this period had a non-negligible influence on the course of the East Asian regional economy. As the pattern of Japan's trade is relatively well-known, through Nawa's discussions and other sources, and was also addressed to a certain extent in the preceding section, here we will only look at China's trade as shown in Table 3.7, captured by the Chinese Maritime Customs (which generally covers areas falling under the Chinese currency bloc).[29]

---

[28] According to a comparative table of net domestic product in 1937, prepared by Yuzo Yamamoto, the net domestic product of Manchuria was equivalent to some 20 per cent of that of Japan proper. Yuzo Yamamoto, *Nihon Shokuminchi Keizaishi Kenkyu* [*Studies on the Economic History of Japanese Colonialism*], (Nagoya: Nagoya Daigaku Shuppankai, 1992), pp. 120–21. If the above ratio for Manchuria is applied to Maddison's data in Table 3.5 to obtain the ratios for the yen bloc and the Chinese currency bloc for 1933, they amount to 42 per cent and 58 per cent, respectively. These figures can be considered to represent the actual state of affairs relatively accurately, as Table 3.5 excludes the northern part of Korea while Manchuria's GDP must have grown substantially in 1933–37.

[29] According to Remer, the value of China's exports in this period was considerably underestimated and China had a surplus of exports over imports in 1930. C.F. Remer, *Foreign Investments in China* (New York: Macmillan, 1933), pp. 195–200, 204.

Table 3.6   The Share of the West in Asia's Trade, 1928–1938

	Japan		China		Korea		Taiwan		East Asia		Southeast Asia		India	
	Exports	Imports	Exports	Imports	Exports	Imports	Exports	Imports	Exports	Imports	Exports	Imports	Exports	Imports
1928	41	36	39	41	1	13	16	19	40	37	44	40	58	59
1929	40	37	38	41	1	15	23	30	39	38	45	41	57	58
1930	33	34	38	43	1	15	19	32	34	37	41	38	55	55
1931	35	30	36	49	1	14	23	29	35	37	40	34	57	52
1932	31	37	31	44	1	12	26	13	31	39	37	34	56	50
1933	28	35	36	40	7	6	36	16	30	37	40	31	63	49
1934	22	34	38	43	1	8	29	21	25	36	45	31	55	47
1935	23	33	45	35	1	12	20	18	28	33	44	32	58	47
1936	24	30	42	36	2	14	28	14	28	31	48	32	59	45
1937	23	34	45	29	4	23	32	13	28	33	53	36	55	47
1938	17	32	29	25	2	16	17	11	19	29	45	41	52	47

Source and Note: Kaoru Sugihara, *Asjiakan Boeki no Keisei to Kozo*, pp. 155–6. And *Teikoku Tokei Nenkan*. China includes Manchuria. The share of the West includes Asia's trade with the West via Hong Kong.

Table 3.7   Geographical Composition of Chinese Trade, 1928–1939
(in customs tael and standard dollar)

Exports	1928		1929		1930		1931	
UK	61,064	6%	74,334	7%	62,669	7%	64,526	7%
USA	127,205	13%	137,836	14%	131,880	15%	120,205	13%
Germany	22,825	2%	22,458	2%	23,361	3%	23,138	3%
Europe via Hong Kong	61,922	6%	36,452	4%	22,123	2%	20,764	2%
Total (Europe)	273,016	28%	271,080	27%	240,033	27%	228,633	25%
Asia via Hong Kong	103,811	10%	121,507	12%	121,674	14%	114,200	13%
Japan	228,602	23%	256,428	25%	216,555	24%	249,279	27%
Total (Asia)	332,413	34%	377,935	37%	338,229	38%	363,479	40%
Total	991,355	100%	1,015,687	100%	894,844	100%	909,476	100%

Imports	1928		1929		1930		1931	
UK	113,757	9%	119,149	9%	108,258	8%	119,986	8%
USA	205,541	17%	230,844	18%	232,406	17%	321,342	22%
Germany	55,697	5%	67,076	5%	69,105	5%	83,514	6%
Europe via Hong Kong	54,258	4%	21,448	2%	87,348	7%	86,610	6%
Total (Europe)	429,253	35%	438,517	34%	497,117	37%	611,452	42%
Asia via Hong Kong	162,775	13%	184,454	14%	122,287	9%	124,363	9%
Japan	319,293	26%	323,142	25%	327,165	25%	290,187	20%
Total (Asia)	482,068	40%	507,596	40%	449,452	34%	414,550	29%
Total	1,210,002	100%	1,281,321	100%	1,328,22	100%	1,448,187	100%

Table 3.7   Continued

Exports	1932		1933		1934		1935	
UK	37,584	8%	48,765	8%	49,806	9%	49,463	9%
USA	59,993	12%	113,146	18%	94,435	18%	136,410	24%
Germany	29,833	6%	20,795	3%	19,159	4%	28,926	5%
Europe via Hong Kong	12,106	2%	27,819	5%	25,250	5%	28,468	5%
Total (Europe)	139,516	28%	210,525	34%	188,650	35%	243,267	42%
Asia via Hong Kong	58,262	12%	84,668	14%	67,671	13%	57,885	10%
Japan	107,485	22%	95,806	16%	81,232	15%	82,059	14%
Total (Asia)	165,747	34%	180,474	29%	148,903	28%	139,944	24%
Total	492,989	100%	612,293	100%	535,733	100%	576,298	100%

Imports	1932		1933		1934		1935	
UK	119,192	11%	154,041	11%	124,647	12%	98,232	11%
USA	269,176	25%	297,486	22%	271,732	26%	174,930	19%
Germany	71,914	7%	108,016	8%	93,389	9%	103,385	11%
Europe via Hong Kong	24,190	2%	17,866	1%	10,374	1%	6,922	1%
Total (Europe)	484,472	46%	577,409	42%	500,142	48%	383,469	41%
Asia via Hong Kong	32,051	3%	27,524	2%	17,191	2%	11,808	1%
Japan	148,432	14%	132,349	10%	126,886	12%	139,593	15%
Total (Asia)	180,483	17%	159,873	12%	144,077	14%	151,401	16%
Total	1,062,617	100%	1,358,978	100%	1,038,979	100%	924,695	100%

Table 3.7   Continued

Exports	1936		1937		1938		1939	
UK	64,884	9%	80,380	10%	56,769	7%	90,863	9%
USA	186,321	26%	231,449	28%	86,853	11%	225,873	22%
Germany	39,174	6%	72,477	9%	56,440	7%	45,097	4%
Europe via Hong Kong	30,899	4%	55,387	7%	102,226	13%	79,956	8%
Total (Europe)	321,278	45%	439,693	52%	302,288	40%	441,789	43%
Asia via Hong Kong	63,928	9%	89,597	11%	111,962	15%	104,387	10%
Japan	102,367	14%	84,306	10%	116,547	15%	66,621	6%
Total (Asia)	166,295	24%	173,903	21%	228,509	30%	171,008	17%
Total	706,791	100%	838,770	100%	763,731	100%	1,030,359	100%

Imports	1936		1937		1938		1939	
UK	110,497	12%	111,695	12%	70,606	8%	77,860	6%
USA	185,512	20%	188,859	20%	151,254	17%	214,100	16%
Germany	150,238	16%	146,374	15%	112,939	13%	87,167	6%
Europe via Hong Kong	6,050	1%	7,440	1%	11,311	1%	13,458	1%
Total (Europe)	452,297	48%	454,368	48%	346,110	39%	392,585	29%
Asia via Hong Kong	10,499	1%	9,921	1%	10,819	1%	19,125	1%
Japan	153,577	16%	150,432	16%	209,864	23%	313,398	23%
Total (Asia)	164,076	17%	160,353	17%	220,683	25%	332,523	25%
Total	944,523	100%	956,234	100%	893,500	100%	1,343,018	100%

Source and Note: China Maritime Customs, *Report on the Trade of China. Trade of China.* The units are customs tael mp to 1932 and standard dollar after 1933. The figures after 1932 excluded the value of trade at the ports incorporated into Manchukuo. The estimates of final destination and countries of origin in Hong Kong trade derive from Sugihara, *Ajiakan Boeki no Keisei to Kozo*, p. 107.

First, it is noteworthy that the total value of China's trade, quoted in Chinese currency, did not show any remarkable decline, contrary to the impression given by the statistics expressed in sterling and displayed in Table 3.3. Secondly, China's trade with the West remained robust for both exports and imports and, if anything, was actually on the increase. It can be confirmed that in terms of exports, trade with the United States and trade via Hong Kong gained weight, while in terms of imports, the share of Germany increased. The discrepancy between Table 3.6 and Table 3.7 can be traced chiefly to the decreased share of Europe and the United States in Manchuria's trade. Examining the structure of the East Asian economy in terms of trade ties with Europe and the United States, it can be divided into two regions: (1) Japan and China (excluding Manchuria), which maintained comparatively strong trade ties with Western countries; and (2) Korea, Taiwan and Manchuria, which were deeply integrated into the yen bloc. In addition, in the same way as Nawa pointed out for Japan, in China, too, the harder the Guomindang government pushed for industrialization of the coastal region (in a bid to resist Japan), the more it had to import from Europe and the United States. Thus, in the pursuit of rapid industrialization through the currency devaluation, both Japan and China imported machinery and raw materials at high prices from Western countries while seeking to expand or defend their sphere of influence in order to secure market opportunities in Manchuria and North China.

Finally, we examine the impact of China's industrialization across the Asian economies. Viewed from the perspective of the cotton trade-centered system of intra-Asian trade, China's industrial development revolving around the cotton spinning industry in Shanghai signaled the emergence of a second core following Japan's cotton-spinning industry. China's import substitution industrialization led to a recapture of China's vast plain cloth market from Japan, and forced the Japanese spinning industry to make a switchover to processed fabrics and artificial silk as well as to move rapidly into the Southeast Asian and South Asian markets. The drop in China's trade amount in this process, when expressed in sterling, was not caused by the decline in importance of its industrialization in Asia's international division of labour but rather simply reflected a statistical bias defined by the sheer size of the Chinese economy. To begin with, the decline in imports that occurred naturally in the process of import substitution, particularly the decline in imports of cotton yarn and low-grade cotton yarn from Japan, translated into the drop in external trade and increase in domestic trade, just as was the case with the United States for the nineteenth century, since China could produce the bulk of the cotton it needed domestically, while the Industrial Revolution in Britain, and in Japan for that matter, was accompanied by imports of large quantities of raw cotton. From this perspective, the consequence of the competition between the Japanese and Chinese cotton-spinning industries, and the outcome of competition in the Chinese market, was the focal point of the overall process of East Asia's industrialization in the 1930s.

(2) Sino-Japanese Trade and Real Exchange Rates

What role, then, did the changes in exchange rates between the Japanese and Chinese currencies play? As shown in Figure 3.3, the exchange rate changes between Japan and China can be categorised into four periods: (1) the period from January 1929, when the Chinese currency was devalued sharply against the yen, to around September 1931, when Britain departed from the gold standard; (2) the period from the end of 1931 to October 1935, when the relationship between the Japanese and Chinese currencies was reversed with the yen's sharp devaluation and the Chinese currency's revaluation; (3) a period of stability from after the currency reform in China to after the start of the Sino-Japanese war (November 1935–March 1938); and (4) the period after the Chinese currency's re-devaluation. Here, we examine the first two periods until 1935.

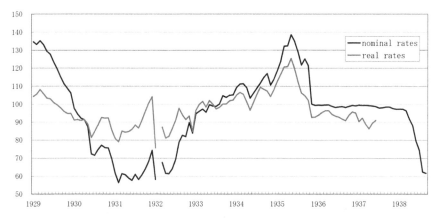

Figure 3.3   Movements of Japanese Exchange Rates against the Chinese Currency, 1929–1938

Source and Notes: Nominal rates derive from Nihon Ginko Chosakyoku (ed.), *Honpo Keizai Tokei [Economic Statistics of Japan]*, various years. Where necessary, I have referred to *Shokin Shuho [Weekly Reports of the Yokohama Specie Bank]* for the more detailed data. The index number of nominal rates to January 1932 was calculated from the inverse of exchange rates of tael per yen, and that from March to December 1932 from the inverse of the exchange rates of yuan per yen. The index number from 1933 was calculated from the exchange rates of yen per yuan, using the conversion rate of 1 tael to 1.588 yuan.

There are some technical problems that must be resolved in order to directly calculate the exchange rates between the Japanese and Chinese currencies. In China before the currency reform, there were a variety of silver coins in circulation aside from silver bullion, with monetary value higher than the value of silver they contained. Among them, the Shanghai tael, the most important silver coin in the market, was widely used as an accounting unit for large-lot commercial transactions and also served as the basis for foreign exchange calculations, while the silver yuan was used as the currency for domestic commercial transactions and in the consumption economy. Accordingly, the amount of tael in circulation tended to increase or decrease in response to fluctuations in foreign exchange rates and silver bullion prices, and yuan to depend on the quality of harvests of rural agricultural products and when these harvests came onto the market.[30] In the wake of the abolition of the tael and the adoption of the silver dollar after March 1933, exchange rates came to be generally quoted in the silver dollar (standard dollar) after about January 1933. The Chinese currency's exchange rates shown in Table 3.4, which is based on statistics compiled by the League of Nations, come directly from the rates provided by the China Maritime Customs Service, and are the rates for the customs tael (haiguan liang) until 1932 and the rates for the silver yuan (standard dollar) for 1933 onward. In the wake of the abolition of the tael and adoption of the silver dollar, Maritime Customs statistics were reconverted at the rate of one customs tael to 1.558 silver yuan (standard dollars) and the China Maritime Customs Service report on the trade of China in 1933 contain statistics converted at this exchange rate going back to the 1920s.[31] These calculations are significant for grasping trends in trade, but the adoption of these figures as exchange rates would give the impression that the Chinese currency was abruptly and dramatically devalued at the end of 1932 and early in 1933. Further, if the exchange rate between the Japanese and Chinese currencies is calculated on the basis of Table 3.4, it would produce a cross rate via the pound/dollar exchange rate. The exchange rate obtained in that way would be of some significance in its own right, but whether it reflected the direct exchange rate between the Japanese and Chinese currencies is another matter.

Given these circumstances, let us take a closer look at exchange rate movements around 1932. The data that served as the basis for Table 3.3 were taken from the direct exchange rates between the Japanese and Chinese currencies (yen per 100 units of Chinese currency) announced by the Yokohama Specie Bank, but they actually represent four different sets of aggregated data. More specifically, the Yokohama Specie Bank posted the quotations (the yen's exchange rate against the Shanghai tael) until November 1931, but abandoned the quotations after Japan departed from the gold standard in mid-December 1931. Thus, the market-quoted exchange rate between the yen and the Shanghai tael was adopted in the period from December 1931 to December 1932. However, data for February 1932 are missing, and the exchange rates from March to December 1932 were translated into the silver yuan at the rate of one tael to 1.558 yuan, as the yuan can be regarded as having assumed the principal role in exchange rates following the sharp rise of the yuan apparently in anticipation of the abolition of the tael and the adoption of the silver dollar. In Table 3.3, we use the inverses of the quotations provided by the Yokohama Specie Bank until 1932 to produce the Chinese currency's exchange rates vis-à-vis the yen and link them to the data for 1933 onward. Quoting of the yuan's exchange rates against the yen began in January 1933. Needless to say, the figures in Table 3.3 ignore the spread between bids and offers. However, given that they are the monthly direct exchange rates, this form

[30]   Tadao Miyashita, *Shina Kahei Seidoron* [*Treatise on the Chinese Currency System*], (Tokyo: Hobunkan, 1938), p. 79.
[31]   Detailed explanations can be found in China Maritime Customs Service, *Report on the Trade of China*, 1933, pp. 59–60. See also relevant pages of customs reports for other years.

of linkage may be of some significance. Considering that the exchange rates in Table 3.3 trace the tael's devaluation against the yen in the period from December 1931 to December 1932 and that the data links to 1933 appear to be natural, they can probably be regarded as reflecting the actual market rates rather than exchange rates quoted for Table 3.4. Since there is a gap larger than 10 per cent between the value of the Shanghai tael, which provided the basis for the calculations above, and the value of the customs tael, which is used as the accounting unit for official trade figures and customs duties, the rates quoted in Table 3.3 and those in Table 3.4 differ as well.

Needless to mention, the shift from the tael to the yuan was making gradual progress as part of the efforts toward currency system unification. Therefore, the significance of the tael's rates against the yen must have changed by the minute over time in accordance with changes in the relationship between the tael and yuan in China. But it cannot be argued definitively that the yuan had completely replaced the tael as the leading currency by 1932. While the amount of silver yuan in circulation was showing an upward trend, various types of silver coins, including Mexican silver coins, with a value in the vicinity of the yuan's value, could still be found on the market. Furthermore, in addition to silver coins, it goes without saying that there was a market for silver bullion in China. Therefore, the change in the currency base to the yuan in Figure 3.3 from March 1932 is simply a measure of expediency. Until 1931, this complicated situation was not considered as much of a problem in relation to exchange rates because the rates between the tael and the silver yuan were relatively stable at around 100 yuan to 72.3 taels. In 1932, however, the rates began to wildly fluctuate to the extent of going beyond normal predictive power, bringing home to market actors the risks inherent in the system. Further, an accelerated flow of silver yuan into Shanghai due to the rural depression led the relative value of the silver yuan, which was just beginning to gain an upper hand in the currency circulation, to decline, triggering people to melt the silver yuan coins, a development not welcomed by the government. These events helped boost the momentum for monetary unification in various quarters.[32]

What can be learned, then, from changes in the nominal exchange rates shown in Figure 3.3? In the first period (from January 1929 to September 1931), the value of the Chinese currency fell steeply as the fall in international silver prices which had continued since the 1920s accelerated further. Furthermore, as the fall in domestic prices of silver lagged behind the decline in international prices, silver flowed into China in massive quantities. As a consequence, credit conditions were eased, domestic prices rose and the economy turned up. On the other hand, the yen's value was moving almost in tandem with the pound and the dollar in this period as Japan had decided to return to the gold standard at the old value (the prewar rate) shortly before the collapse of stock prices on Wall Street in October 1929, and made good

---

[32]   Miyashita, *op. cit.*, Ch. 2 (Discussion on the Abolition of the Tael and the Adoption of the Silver Dollar), particularly pp. 97–8. The division by inverse numbers of the yuan's monthly exchange rates against the tael in 1932, shown on p. 97 of the above book, might produce figures that are slightly more accurate than the data in Table 3.3 obtained by the division by 1.558.

on the return in January 1930. This led to a steep rise of the yen and a sharp fall of the tael. In the period from December 1929 to February 1931, the tael plunged by 54 per cent against the yen. This doubtlessly boosted China's import substitution and the development of the Chinese cotton-spinning industry. Japan made an attempt to ride over this crisis through the development of *zaikabo* (Japanese owned cotton-spinning mills in China) and a shift to processed cotton cloth.[33]

With the beginning of the second period (from the end of 1931 to October 1935), however, the direction of exchange rates between the Japanese and Chinese currencies was reversed. First, Japan left the gold standard and devalued the yen against Western currencies. This also meant a weakening of the yen against the Chinese currency, which remained stable. In the following year, China experienced the sharp revaluation of its currency in the wake of a surge in international silver prices. As the United States purchased massive amounts of silver, partly at the request of silver producers, international prices of silver rose, lifting the value of the Chinese currency, which was linked to silver. In the latter half of 1934, as the United States continued to purchase silver under the Silver Purchase Act, nearly 200 million ounces of silver, equivalent to one-fifth of China's silver holdings, flowed out of the country in just six months or so, building momentum for currency reform.[34] As a result of these developments on both sides, by May 1935 the nominal exchange rate between the Japanese and Chinese currencies reverted to the level registered in early 1929. This must have acted as a disincentive for China's import substitution and export-oriented industrialization.

However, Figure 3.3 shows that the dramatic shift in exchange rates between the two periods actually was only an ostensible one, and that real exchange rates between the Japanese and Chinese currencies remained relatively stable as prices in the two countries moved in opposite directions.[35] More specifically, while prices in Japan fell significantly during the first period, those in Shanghai rose amidst the investment-led economic boom, keeping the changes in real exchange rates far smaller than those in nominal rates. While it is true that changes in real exchange rates were one of the

---

[33]   Naosuke Takamura, *Kindai Nihon Mengyo to Chugoku* [*The Modern Japanese Cotton Industry and China*], (Tokyo: Tokyo Daigaku Shuppankai, 1982), pp. 160–61.

[34]   Takeru Saito, 'America Gin Seisaku no Tenkai to Chugoku [U.S. Silver Policy and China]', in Yutaka Nozawa (ed.), *Chugoku no Heisei Kaikaku to Kokusai Kankei* [*The Currency Reform in China and its International Relations*], (Tokyo: Tokyo Daigaku Shuppankai, 1981), pp. 146–7. For details, see Tomoko Shiroyama, 'Shanghai Kinyu Kyoko (1934–1935) ni Kansuru Ichikosatsu: Kokusai/Kokunai Shijyo Renkan to Shijo/Seifu Kankei no Shikaku kara [Shanghai Financial Crisis in 1934–35: From the Perspectives of Market-State Relations and China's International Relations]', *Toyoshi Kenkyu*, 58, 2 (1999), pp. 377–418.

[35]   There are several previous studies on Japan's real exchange rates in the interwar period, but many of them take only prices in the United States and Britain into consideration. See, for example, Shinji Takagi, 'Senkanki Nihon Keizai to Hendo Kawase Soba' [The Japanese Economy in the Interwar Period and Floating Exchange Rates], *Kinyu Kenkyu*, 8, 4 (1989), pp. 109–40; Tetsuji Okazaki, *Kogyoka no Kiseki: Keizai Taikoku Zenshi* [*The Foundations of Industrialization: The Prehistory of an Economic Power*], (Tokyo: Yomiuri Shimbunsha, 1997), pp. 86–90.

factors that prevented Japan from increasing its exports, these fluctuations seem to be a relatively minor element at this point of time along with other factors including the boycott movement. In fact, Japan's exports of cotton goods, the biggest item in Sino-Japanese trade at the time, were robust in 1930. Though the Chinese cotton-spinning industry had already achieved considerable development in the 1920s, exports from Japan maintained an upward trend.[36] In the second period, on the other hand, Japan's exports slowed despite support from exchange rates and China's import substitution progressed rapidly.[37] A major factor behind this was the movement to boycott Japanese products, which had resumed in July 1931 and picked up steam after the Manchurian Incident in September of the same year. Tariff revisions in 1933 and 1934 also were effective in reducing China's imports.[38] In other words, China was unable to control exchange rates during this period, but was in a position to impose tariffs.

Thus, it is important to note that there was an element of openness to the yen bloc, similar to that observed for the sterling area. This is because Japan mainly responded to the growing trend toward economic blocs and China's import substitution strategy by devaluating the yen rather than imposing countervailing tariff hikes. As pointed out by Young, erratic fluctuations of the nominal value of currencies proved to be a major disturbing factor in trade.[39] At the same time, however, the currency devaluation in East Asia had the potential to promote trade through economic stimulus measures. The stagnation of exports due to China's tariff policy prompted Japan, it turns out, to cultivate export markets in Southeast and South Asia. But this was possible largely because structural adjustments of the Asian market as a whole were achieved, to a considerable extent, through changes in exchange rates. By joining the sterling area, Japan provided great sums of money for the growth of its colonies, contributing to a sharp rise in monetary aggregates in East Asia. Also, Japan's exports to the Dutch East Indies and India on the strength of the devalued yen were crucially important for the maintenance of the international division of labour within Asia.[40] It appears that Japan at this stage moved one step ahead of China in successfully stabilising the value of its currency and went on the offensive in establishing a monetary order.

(3) Structural Power and the Limits of Japan's Currency Strategy

Next, let us look at the third period (from November 1935 to April 1938). It was only after the currency reform of November 1935 that China escaped from the impact of large fluctuations in silver prices and the Chinese government became able, to a certain extent, to adjust exchange rates in accordance with its needs. In the meantime, the concentration of silver bullion at government-affiliated banks increased, and large

---

[36] China Maritime Customs Service, *Report on the Trade of China*, 1930, p. 42.

[37] Shou-Eng Koo, *Tariff and the Development of the Cotton Industry in China, 1842–1937* (New York: Garland Publishing, 1982), Ch. 6.

[38] Kubo, *op. cit.*, p. 160.

[39] Young, *op. cit.*, pp. 469–71.

[40] Sugihara, *op. cit.*, Ch. 4.

amounts of standard dollar notes were issued. The supply of banknotes is estimated to have reached slightly over 200 million yuan, a net increase of some 10 per cent in the estimated monetary aggregates. Also, after the currency reform, the Chinese currency (yuan) was linked to the British pound for a brief period. The stability of the currency's exchange rates enhanced the confidence in the legal tender and also contributed to the growth of its circulation. The yuan's exchange rate against the yen also stabilised, in sharp contrast to earlier periods. In the entire period from November 1935 to February 1938, during which the Sino-Japanese war had broken out, the yuan moved in an extremely narrow band of 102–106 yen.[41]

Thus, during this period, both the yen and yuan were linked to the pound and East Asia as a whole belonged to the sterling area, albeit only for a brief period. Seeing an opportunity in China's economic plight, Britain sought to maintain its influence in the Chinese market, supporting the spread of the standard dollar and actively resuming investment. As a consequence, the relationship between Japan and China became a relatively equal one in the sense that China's currency system came to adopt a shape befitting a nation state. At the same time, Britain repeatedly proposed the establishment of partnership with Japan.[42] It is important to note that this proposal was linked with its motivation to maintain and expand the sterling area. The stability of China's exchange rates at low levels, coupled with rising wholesale prices in Britain and the United States, made Western exports to China difficult.[43] Nevertheless, Britain, on the strength of its 'structural power'[44] (the ability of a country with hegemony to lay out rules in international relations using its key currency status, investment, military might, and so on, or the clout that stands above relational powers among nation states) and from the standpoint of protecting an imperialistic international order as a regime, was able to obtain certain support from other powers for China's currency reform.

However, behind East Asia's apparent exchange rate stability was a very destabilising factor: the relative rise in Japan's economic power and the expansion of the yen bloc in the Continent, which were taking place simultaneously. In the face of Britain's repeated calls for partnership, Japan had to weigh the merit of remaining within the regime (keeping itself in the group of powers and keeping China out of it) against the potential demerits of the yen bloc's expansion into the Continent possibly being blocked or at least facing interference by Britain and other Western powers. For this reason, Japan could not immediately follow the initiative of Britain, unlike other powers. However, if it refused to cooperate with Western powers, it risked having China use the opportunity to take advantage of the conflict

---

[41]   Based on *Honpo Keizai Tokei* (Economics Statistics of Japan).

[42]   Yoichi Kibata, 'Risu-Rosu Shisetsudan to Eichu Kankei (The Leith-Ross Mission and Sino-British Relations)', in Nozawa ed., *op. cit.*, pp. 199–230.

[43]   Chang Kia-Ngau, *The Inflationary Spiral: The Experience in China, 1939–1950* (New York: Technology Press of Massachusetts Institute of Technology and John Wiley & Sons, Inc., 1958), pp. 11–12.

[44]   For a detailed definition, see Susan Strange, *States and Markets* (London: Pinter, 1988), Ch. 2.

of interest among those powers. Such a situation would raise the risk of Japan being pitted against the 'structural power'. These were the circumstances that made Japan still hesitant at this stage about choosing a path of all-out confrontation.

Therefore, the recovery of trade through stable exchange rates was related to both Japan's invasion and the pattern of demand defined by China's import substitution industrialization and economic development in general.

Table 3.8   Geographical Composition of Imports of Main Chinese Ports, 1936–1939 (1,000 yuan)

	1936							
	UK		USA		Germany		Japan		Total
Tianjin	2,851	6%	3,927	5%	5,074	8%	11,992	18%	23,844
Jiaozhou	2,439	5%	3,778	2%	911	1%	11,617	17%	16,881
Hankou	2,951	6%	2,631	3%	1,027	2%	2,874	4%	9,483
Shanghai	30,082	62%	59,786	73%	47,522	71%	32,513	48%	169,903
Shantou	3,004	6%	683	1%	1,318	2%	788	1%	5,792
Guangzhou	1,452	3%	1,690	2%	2,613	4%	915	1%	6,670
Jiulong	2,611	5%	5,896	7%	2,603	4%	827	1%	11,937
Total	45,391	93%	76,526	93%	61,067	92%	61,526	91%	244,510
Other Ports	3,207	7%	5,586	7%	5,425	8%	6,337	9%	20,555
Grand Total	48598	100%	82,112	100%	66,492	100%	67,863	100%	265,065

	1937							
	UK		USA		Germany		Japan		Total
Tianjin	3,540	7%	4,329	5%	6,786	11%	12,718	19%	
Jiaozhou	1,143	2%	3,778	5%	2,147	3%	9,005	14%	16,072
Hankou	1,335	3%	3,648	4%	1,518	2%	2,765	4%	9,267
Shanghai	30,266	62%	51,187	62%	36,561	57%	33,096	50%	151,111
Shantou	3,570	7%	1,394	2%	1,440	2%	609	1%	7,013
Guangzhou	1,271	3%	2,631	3%	3,974	6%	904	1%	8,780
Jiulong	4,690	10%	8188	10%	7,004	11%	741	1%	20,624
Total	45,816	93%	75,155	90%	59,429	92%	59,839	91%	240,239
Other Ports	3,314	7%	7,920	10%	4,971	8%	6,259	9%	22,464
Grand Total	49,130	100%	83,075	100%	64,400	100%	66,098	100%	262,704

	1938							
	UK		USA		Germany		Japan		Total
Tianjin	3,539	11%	9,159	14%	5,826	12%	54,436	60%	72,960
Jiaozhou	368	1%	1,276	2%	882	2%	16,131	18%	18,658
Hankou	83	0%	549	1%	72	0%	35	0%	739
Shanghai	12,963	42%	26,523	40%	14,989	30%	16,154	18%	70,630
Shantou	3,707	12%	1,204	2%	1,946	4%	20	0%	6,876
Guangzhou	3060	10%	3,975	6%	5,139	10%	22	0%	12,196
Jiulong	3,738	12%	17,601	27%	16,278	33%	3	0%	37,620
Total	27,458	89%	60,285	91%	45,133	91%	86,802	96%	219,678
Other Ports	3,379	11%	5723	9%	4252	9%	3,679	4%	17,033
Grand Total	30,837	100%	66,008	100%	49,385	100%	90,481	100%	236,711

Table 3.8   Continued

	1939							
	UK		USA		Germany		Japan		Total
Tianjin	3,302	11%	15,657	18%	7,958	22%	5,991	46%	84,907
Jiaozhou	215	1%	3,290	4%	943	3%	28,501	23%	32,949
Hankou	6	0%	4	0%	1	0%	2	0%	14
Shanghai	16,069	51%	47,415	55%	18,773	53%	33,014	26%	115,271
Shantou	3,687	12%	2,079	2%	1,241	3%	2	0%	7,009
Guangzhou	140	0%	883	1%	177	0%	9	0%	1,208
Jiulong	397	1%	455	1%	140	0%	3	0%	995
Total	23,815	76%	69,784	81%	29,232	82%	119,522	94%	242,352
Other Ports	7,427	24%	16,466	19%	6,321	18%	7,034	6%	37,248
Grand Total	31,242	100%	86,250	100%	35,553	100%	126,556	100%	279,600

Source: China Maritime Customs, *The Trade of China*

Table 3.9   Geographical Composition of Imports of Machinery to Main Chinese Ports, 1937–1938 (1,000 yuan)

	1937							
	UK		USA		Germany		Japan		Total
Tianjin	287	5%	180	4%	1,034	15%	2,502	26%	4,243
Jiaozhou	115	2%	34	1%	168	2%	2,388	24%	2,725
Hankou	348	6%	232	6%	588	9%	101	1%	1,273
Shanghai	4,336	74%	2,669	66%	2,876	42%	4,507	46%	15,435
Shantou	4	0%	19	0%	26	0%	6	0%	64
Guangzhou	137	2%	225	6%	416	6%	23	0%	871
Jiulong	138	2%	223	6%	1,134	16%	17	0%	1,949
Other Ports	483	8%	467	12%	633	9%	230	2%	2,028
Total	5,850	100%	4,049	100%	6,876	100%	9,775	100%	28,588
	1938							
Tianjin	605	12%	225	11%	483	13%	5,456	44%	7,139
Jiaozhou	278	6%	41	2%	99	3%	5,446	44%	5,891
Hankou	3	0%	3	0%	2	0%	–	–	10
Shanghai	3,073	61%	1,188	58%	1,379	37%	1,468	12%	8,017
Shantou	6	0%	23	1%	12	0%	0	0%	44
Guangzhou	82	2%	138	7%	213	6%	0	0%	546
Jiulong	419	8%	253	12%	831	22%	0	0%	1,684
Other Ports	556	11%	180	9%	709	19%	137	1%	1,071
Total	5,021	100%	2,052	100%	3,727	100%	12,508	100%	24,403

Source and Note: Calculated from China Maritime Customs, *The Trade of China*, 1938, vol. I (Part 2). The figure for totals are from vol. II. The total of 'Other Ports' exceeds the sum of the four countries' totals but reasons are unknown.

Table 3.8 shows the composition of China's imports by port and by export destination. As seen in the tables, Japan's trade with China took place mainly through Shanghai until 1937. Needless to say, China needed to import manufactures as part of its import substitution industrialization. For example, imports of leading edge spinning machinery were desirable for the development of the cotton-spinning industry. Looking at the composition of China's machinery imports by port and export destination, Table 3.9 shows that imports of spinning machinery and other products from Japan occupied a non-negligible slot in machinery imports through Shanghai.[45]

For this reason, Sino-Japanese trade, in parallel with China's trade with European countries and the United States, represented a vital element of China's industrialization. Since 1938, in the composition of Japan's trade with China, there was a major shift from movements dominated by Shanghai to one led by ports in North China.[46] However, as long as trade flows quoted in the Chinese currency are concerned, Western countries' exports to China through two ports in North China also grew substantially. As Table 3.8 shows, despite Japan's advance, the share of North China in Western countries' exports to China, if anything, increased. Table 3.9 shows a dramatic shift in the ports through which China imported spinning machinery and other products from Shanghai to North China, whereas there was little change in imports of machinery from Western countries into North China in 1937–1938. Though the absolute value dropped slightly, the share of North China in China's machinery imports from Western countries rose substantially, with no indication of Western products being rapidly replaced by Japanese products in that area.[47] The situation is the same for imports from the United States and Britain alone, with Germany excluded. On the other hand, Japan's exports to China through Shanghai fell sharply, apparently reflecting the war. Despite this, the system of international division of labour did not break down in Shanghai, and the previous pattern of trade continued on a reduced scale through 1938–39.[48] Imports

---

[45]　See also Sugihara, *op. cit.*, p. 125, Tables 4–12.

[46]　From original statistics, the decline in China's trade from 1938 can be traced largely to a decrease in the number of maritime customs officers that could record statistics due to the occupation by Japanese troops, along with an actual drop in the amount of trade recorded at each customs office. Since trade in areas where trade statistics could no longer be taken did not halt immediately, Japan's trade with China is estimated to have lasted a little longer than shown in Tables 3.8 and 3.9. China Maritime Customs Service, *The Trade of China*, 1938, 'Introductory Survey,' pp. 31, 32 and 1939.

[47]　However, apart from trade that made its way into the tables, a large amount of illegal trade was also conducted during this period. Having said this, as illegal trade was nothing new, it is not easy to establish how much such trade increased in this period. See Toshiro Matsumoto, 'Heisei Kaikakuki no Nicchu Keizai Kankei: Jittai to Seisaku' [Japan–China Economic Relations during the Currency Reform Period: Reality and Policy], in Nozawa (ed.), *op. cit.*, pp. 308–12, and Takafusa Nakamura, *op. cit.*, pp. 213–19.

[48]　Kubo divides this period into two further periods – the war-torn period from August 1937 to February 1938 and the economic recovery period from March 1938 to December 1941 – and underscores the prosperity of the Shanghai economy in the latter period, calling it 'the prosperity of a solitary island'. Despite the political and military upheavals, Shanghai maintained diverse channels of distribution with foreign countries, and was able to withstand

of machinery from the West and Japan remained mutually complementary to some degree even after the outbreak of the Sino-Japanese war. It is not surprising, in a manner of speaking, that China required imports of a variety of machinery and parts in the process of import substitution industrialization. If it was thought previously that such complementarity had been entirely lost after 1937, that misconception must be corrected.[49]

Lastly, we briefly cover the fourth period (from April 1938 to 1939). In previous studies, it was understood that in China in the 1930s onward, the 'currency war' (or currency struggle) was waged between Japan and China. Basically, this 'war' is understood to have been a clash between the strategies to drive out the currency of the enemy and allow only the currency issued in areas under one's control to circulate, and to have been waged on a full scale in North China following the outbreak of the Sino-Japanese War in 1937. However, the 'currency war' is sometimes more broadly interpreted to include efforts such as stabilising prices by procuring material supplies from trade with enemy areas, and in some cases, using the enemy currency to create a situation serving its own interests.[50] If defined in this manner, the processes described in this section can also be understood in the context of the 'currency war' or as a preliminary skirmish toward that war. At any rate, in the 'war' between the yen-linked currency and the Chinese currency (legal tender), it was basically only after 1937, when Japan's Kwantung Army tried to separate North China in earnest, that the two currency camps came into full-fledged conflict. Despite this, the exchange rates between the yen and yuan remained stable while maintaining their links to the British pound, and this fact is the point emphasised by this chapter. This was the consequence of Japan's efforts

---

fluctuations of the currency's value, unlike other areas of China. Toru Kubo, 'Senji Shanhai no Busshi Ryutsu to Chugokujin-sho [Distribution of Goods in Wartime Shanghai and Chinese Merchants]', in Masanori Nakamura, Naosuke Takamura and Hideo Kobayashi (eds), *Senji Kachu no Busshi Doin to Gunpyo* [*Material Mobilisation in Wartime Central China and Military Currency*], (Tokyo: Taga Shuppan, 1994), pp. 310–17, 321–8.

[49]   Naosuke Takamura, in a book review (*Nihonshi Kenkyu*, 417, 1997) of my *Ajiakan Boeki no Keisei to Kozo*, in reference to my argument that the increased share of Japan in China's machinery imports in 1936–38 represented a new trend in trade in heavy and chemical industry goods, points out that 'it should not be considered as a natural course of events' because the Sino-Japanese War had already broken out in 1937. As shown in Table 3.9, his comment is basically correct. At the same time, however, in the context of the discussions in this chapter, it seems significant that the 'natural course of events' of East Asia's industrialization was not completely moribund despite the start of the Sino-Japanese War.

[50]   Teruhiko Iwatake, *Kindai Chugoku Tsuka Toitsushi: 15-nen Sensoki ni okeru Tsuka Toso* [*History of the Monetary Unification in Modern China: Currency Struggles during the Sino-Japanese War and After*], vol. I, (Tokyo: Misuzu Shobo, 1990), pp. 13–15. This chapter does not have leeway to extend its discussions to cover the Soviet currency and genealogy of the pienpi in North China. However, looking at subsequent developments up to 1950, the currency war can be seen mainly as antagonism among three actors – legal tender as the unified currency, the yen-linked currency and the currency linked to the Communist Party of China.

to extend its 'yen–yuan parity' policy worked out in Manchuria to North China. This also partly explains the continuance, to a certain extent, of the complementary trade relationship between Japan and Western countries in their trade with China, as described earlier.

The value of the yuan fell rapidly beginning in April 1938.[51] China's trade fell sharply when amounts of trade in Tables 3.8 and 3.9 are converted into pound or dollar terms. Also, while trade within the yen block continued to expand, the convertibility of the yen-linked currency in the Continent was subjected to a variety of restrictions. This is evidence that the yen could not maintain its position as a key currency in East Asia. Though the yen bloc was part of the sterling area, it cannot be denied that the significance of this fact changed after the convertibility of the yen-linked currency was restricted. It is true that the value of the yen-linked currency was well maintained relative to the value of the yuan. But neither the yen bloc nor the yuan bloc could still be described as part of the sterling area if the currency's inconvertibility into the pound became apparent. In the case of the monetary order in East Asia, it appears that this triggered the breakdown of the imperialistic international order and paved the way for Japan's strategy of desperation. Japan's 'yen–yuan parity' policy can be seen as one to stabilise the 'devaluation zone' in East Asia which had been engineered in this crisis situation. As previous studies rightly point out, many aspects of this policy were unrealistic and there was no chance that Japan would be able to incorporate the yuan into the yen bloc in this manner.[52] In other words, while East Asia's 'devaluation zone' did exist as part of the sterling area, there was no independent, self-reliant East Asian currency bloc either politically or as a currency bloc. Its emergence would have to wait until 1939 when Japan made a complete shift to the controlled economy.

(4) The Industrialization of East Asia and Acceptance by the Western Nations

Why did the Western powers tolerate the devaluation of East Asian currencies? As pointed out earlier, the devaluation of exchange rates has the effect of increasing exports and reducing imports, at least in the short run. It may also be possible to enjoy these benefits for a long period of time if the devaluation does not invite counter-devaluations by major trading partners. Such a situation is ideal for a country attempting to achieve export-led industrialization. Japan's exports

---

[51]   According to *Honpo Keizai Tokei* [*Economic Statistics of Japan*], one yuan was worth a little over one yen until March 1938, but then dropped to 0.97 yen in April, 0.93 yen in May, 0.84 yen in June, 0.78 yen in July, 0.66 yen in August and 0.65 yen in September, and no quotations were made from 27 September onward.

[52]   Takafusa Nakamura, *op. cit.*, pp. 147–57, 209–38. Yuzo Yamamoto, '"Manshukoku" o meguru Taigai Keizai Kankei no Tenkai: Kokusai Shushi Bunseki o Chushin toshite' [The Development of External Economic Relations surrounding 'Manchukuo': An Analysis of its Balance of Payments], in Yamamoto (ed.), *'Manshukoku' no Kenkyu* [*Studies in 'Manchukuo '*], (Kyoto: Institute for Research in Humanities, Kyoto University, 1993), pp. 224–32.

to Southeast and South Asia were denounced as dumping at the time, precisely because they brought out the effects of the devaluation in a superb way. The yuan's devaluation by China, though to a lesser extent than Japan, had an effect in facilitating Chinese exports to Southeast Asia.

However, as Britain had a great deal of assets in South and Southeast Asia, it was reluctant to devalue the currencies of countries there for fear of a depreciation of its assets. Its presence was of significance in such areas as services and shipping as well.[53] Furthermore, Britain wanted to contain the trend toward independence among its colonies and dominions by using its power to import primary products. However, to do so, it had to maintain the key currency status of the pound. Multilateral settlements were not uncommon. For example, the bulk of the income earned by Malaya from rubber exports to the United States might be used not to import machinery into Malaya from the United States, but might be remitted first to the home countries of Chinese and Indians overseas and used to pay for imports of machinery from the United States to those countries. In other words, trade relationships, as depicted by Figure 3.1, often relied on local multilateral trade settlement structures not captured by the Figure. In turn, local trade required a currency that made these settlements possible. Moreover, such settlements had to be conducted through the British pound, as the United States and France kept absorbing gold. In other words, Britain was performing the role of indirectly supporting industrialization in East Asia by providing international liquidity to support global trade as a whole.

Needless to say, the industrialization of Asia was also a problem for Britain, since the development of cotton spinning and other labour-intensive industries in India and competition from Japan were pushing Britain's 'old industries', such as the Lancashire textile industry, into dire straits. However, when the interests of industry and those of financial and services sectors led by the City clashed, Britain appeared, more likely than not, to favour the interests of the latter. The Netherlands, as it had assets to protect in the Dutch East Indies, also had the

---

[53]   Hiroyoshi Kano emphasised a major shift in Southeast Asia's trading partners to the Asia-Pacific region in the interwar period, a point missing in my discussion. While this is undoubtedly a theme worthy of consideration, it is also important to note, in the context of the history of international economic relations, that this shift did not immediately mean a decline of Britain's presence in Southeast Asia, especially when invisible trade balances and capital transactions, as well as the pivotal role of Singapore and Hong Kong, are taken into account. See Hiroyuki Kano, 'Kokusai Boeki karamita 20-seiki no Tonan Ajia Shokuminti Keizai: Ajia Taiheiyo Shijo eno Hosetsu' [Southeast Asian Colonial Economies in the 20th Century in an International Trade Perspective: Their Incorporation into the Asia-Pacific Market], *Rekishi Hyoron*, No. 539, March 1995, pp. 39–55, and Kaoru Sugihara, 'Kokusai Bungyo to Tonan Ajia Shokuminchi Keizai' [The International Division of Labour and the Colonial Economies of Southeast Asia], in Hiroyoshi Kano (ed.), *Iwanami Koza Tonan Ajia-shi, 6: Shokuminchi Keizai no Hanei to Choraku* [*Iwanami History of Southeast Asia 6: The Prosperity and Fall of Colonial Economies*], (Tokyo: Iwanami Shoten, 2001).

currency of its colony linked to that of the home country, which belonged to the gold bloc until 1936, to keep it overvalued.[54]

Meanwhile, East Asia received a relatively small amount of investment from European countries and the United States, meaning that losses for Western investors from the devaluation of East Asian currencies would be relatively small. Negotiations by the consortium of four great powers were a concerted attempt, though ultimately unsuccessful yet important in terms of diplomatic history, by the imperialistic countries of Japan, Britain, France and the United States to improve the investment climate in China, and also represented Britain's strong desire to secure 'structural power' in East Asia by some means or other.[55] Nevertheless, it seems likely that Britain tolerated the currency devaluation by East Asian countries not out of consideration for investment in China but because it maintained a world strategy that gave priority to the key currency status of the pound. Thus, within the international order led by the sterling area emerged a split between the 'devaluation zone' of East Asia and the high exchange rate zone of Southeast and South Asia.

It goes without saying that the trade relationship between these two regions in Asia was not determined by exchange rates alone. Tariff hikes following the Ottawa Agreements and the tendency of blocs to be formed through quantitative trade restrictions led to considerable drops in the amounts of imports from East Asia. Elsewhere I have argued that Japan's exports to India and the Dutch East Indies did not decline much even after the Indo-Japanese trade negotiations in 1933 and Japanese-Dutch trade negotiations in 1934. This was the result of a rough balance of the force toward blocs and the force for maintaining trade based on the openness of the sterling area.[56] Thus, despite the formation of blocs, the restructuring of the multilateral trade settlement mechanism was facilitated.

The countries of Continental Europe were preoccupied with the problem of war reparations, the return to the gold standard, high unemployment rates and other issues, and it was difficult for them to participate in international cooperation. Continental Europe and the United States did not have any programme to link disintegrated economic blocs and reorganise the multilateral trade settlement structure. The currency devaluations in East Asia did not invite counteractions from these countries, either, because for them, trade, investment and other relations with East Asia were not as important as trade among the Western nations,

---

[54] P.J. Cain and A.G. Hopkins, *British Imperialism 1688–2000* (Harlow: Pearson, 2001). Kaoru Sugihara, 'British Imperialism, the City of London and Global Industrialization', in Shigeru Akita (ed.), *Gentlemanly Capitalism, Imperialism and Global History* (Basingstoke: Palgrave Macmillan, 2002), pp. 185–204. Kagotani, *op. cit.*, Ch. 5.

[55] Taichiro Mitani, 'Kokusai Kinyu Shihon to Ajia no Senso: Shumatsuki ni okeru Taichugoku Yongoku Shakkandan' [International Financial Capital and Wars in Asia – The Four-Power Consortium in China at the Final Stage of its Existence], *Nenpo Kindai Nihon Kenkyu 2: Kindai Nihon to Higashiajia* [*Annals of Studies in Modern Japan, vol. 2, Modern Japan and East Asia*], (Tokyo: Yamakawa Shuppansha, 1980).

[56] Sugihara, *op. cit.*, Ch. 4.

and the impact of devaluations in East Asia on world prices was limited. At any rate, advanced technologies and machinery all flowed into East Asia from Europe and the United States, and for them, it must have been desirable to have the development of intra-Asian trade help countries in the region to boost their capacity to purchase manufactures as long as the enhanced purchasing power was not to be monopolised by Japan, since it would increase opportunities for Western countries to follow Japan and increase exports to the region without making massive investments there. Thus, the financial interests represented by the City of London supported an international trade order that pursued the gains from trade and tolerated the industrialization of East Asia without much debate, since there was no consensus among the advanced countries of the West on the global spread of industrialization or a new international division of labour among industries.

Previous studies examining the 1930s failed to fully address the significance of the restructuring of the world economy following the Great Depression, involving a transfer of the international leadership of labour-intensive industries from Europe and the United States to East Asia. In simple terms, the commonly accepted argument, summarised at the outset of this chapter, which traces the background of the 'collapse of world trade' purely to factors involving Western countries, is a one-sided way of looking at things. One of the fundamental issues for the international division of labour in the 1930s was whether Western countries, with high wages, could smoothly work out a system of division of labour with low wage-countries in the non-European world, particularly Asia. If Western countries had provided infrastructure, machinery and capital and Asia had supplied cheap mass consumption goods, it would have been possible to conceive of a new international division of labour on a global scale, quite different from the conventional division between manufactures and primary goods. This would have been a relationship where Western countries specialised in capital- and technology-intensive industries as well as financial and services interests and Asia specialised in labour-intensive industries. Generally speaking, little effort was put into establishing such a division of labour with the colonies. Nevertheless, the industrialization of East Asia in the 1930s undermined the Western monopolization of industrialization and subsequently led to the establishment of an international division of labour where Europe and the United States specialised in capital- and technology-intensive industries and East Asia specialised in labour-intensive industries. It heralded a fundamental structural change that defined the path of development of the world economy thereafter.

Conclusion

The shift to a managed currency system triggered by the British pound's departure from the gold standard in 1931 provided the foundation for the stable supply of local currencies in East Asia. The devaluation of East Asian currencies, which was carried out with relatively small gold reserves, enabled them to be linked to the key currency. The stability of regional currencies at low levels, increased international liquidity within the region, and exports of manufactures to Southeast and South Asia enabled by the currency devaluation, were consistent with the restructuring of the London-centred multilateral trade settlement mechanism and were a response to the requirements of the new system structured around the Anglo-American Group. More specifically, the industrialization-oriented monetary order in East Asia was formed based on reliance on and complementariness with the 'structural power' led by Britain and the United States. Needless to say, the devaluation of currencies brought a slowing or shrinkage of the share of East Asia in the world's GDP calculated in pounds or dollars. That must have led, at least temporarily, to a relative decline in the standard of living, and made it harder for the region's governing classes, who were accustomed to Western lifestyles, to sustain their standards of living. Despite that, the 'devaluation zone' of East Asia came into being and import substitution industrialization was facilitated in the region. This seems to suggest that in Asia at the time, the population of elites who sought cheap imports and employment by foreign capital was relatively small and that the political conditions were in place to make the above-described strategies feasible.[57]

After 1937, the 'devaluation zone' of East Asia gradually lost its convertibility into the British pound and began to move away from the sterling area. For Japan, the devaluation of the currency and expansion of the yen bloc were understood mainly in the context that the need to secure foreign currency settlements made the expansion of the yen bloc inevitable in many ways. However, in one sense it appears that Japan's invasion of China and the expansion of the yen bloc prompted the devaluation of the yuan, and as a consequence, the 'devaluation zone' was maintained. The devaluation of the yuan made it increasingly difficult for China to maintain economic relations with the West, giving Japan an edge over China in dealing with the Western powers. This was a convenient development for Japan as it weakened the Western presence in China and also reduced the West's ability to export machinery and other products to China.

Either way, the yen bloc did not necessarily envision 'autarky' (a self-contained and sufficient economy) from the outset. It is difficult to believe that there was any realistic prospect of applying Germany's idea of a broad economic bloc in Asia in the 1930s. It was only after World War II broke out in 1939 that the idea abruptly became a reality. With the outbreak of the war, the value of the British pound fell, and Japan effectively made a transformation to a full-fledged controlled economy. At the same time, Japan's invasion of Southeast Asia became a reality. Further, in the pursuit of a currency bloc that was not dependent on economic relations with Western countries, an attempt was launched to establish a multilateral

---

[57] There are countless cases where the currency devaluation strategy for industrialization was blocked by elements among the elites who sought cheap imports and employment by foreign capital. Recently, this tendency was discerned in the Asian currency crisis of 1997.

comprehensive settlement mechanism based on the yen exchange standard, with the Bank of Japan acting as the central settlement bank and in reference to Nazi Germany's idea of a broad economic bloc. This was the shape of the new financial order in Asia pursued under the 'Greater East Asian Financial Sphere' scheme.[58]

An examination of the process of revival of Asian trade in the postwar period shows that the sterling area played a major role until the 1950s. The international order in the 1950s was similar to that of the 1930s in the sense that the existence of the sterling area was instrumental in allowing East Asia's industrialization.[59] The countries that later grew into the newly industrializing economies (NIES) and the Association of Southeast Asian Nations (ASEAN) were able to gradually push ahead with industrialization in the period from the 1950s through the 1970s amidst the Cold War, supported by US assistance and the liberal international order. Despite the turmoil during the period of World War II, East Asia's industrialization in the 1930s had historical significance in that it set in motion changes to the international division of labour in the latter half of the twentieth century. The formation of the industrialization-oriented monetary order appears to have been one of the major factors that made it possible.

---

[58]   Hisaya Shimazaki, 'Bureton Uzzu Taisei Seiritsu-shi Zenshi no Yobiteki Kosatsu' [A Preliminary Discussion on the History of the Period Preceding the Establishment of the Bretton Woods System], *Keizaikei*, 123, 1980. Do., *En no Shinryaku Shi: En Kawase Honi Seido no Keisei Katei* [*A History of the Yen's Invasion – The Process of Formation of the Yen Exchange Standard*], (Tokyo: Nihon Keizai Hyoronsha, 1989). Yuzo Yamamoto, '"Daitoa Kinyuken" Ron [Discussion on "The Greater East Asian Financial Sphere"]', Institute for Research in Humanities, Kyoto University, *Jinbun Gakuho*, 79, 1997, pp. 1–26.

[59]   Kaoru Sugihara, 'International Circumstances surrounding the Postwar Japanese Cotton Textile Industry', in David Jeremy and Douglas Farnie (eds), *The Fibre that Changed the World: The Cotton Industry in International Perspective, 1600–1990s* (Oxford: Oxford University Press, 2004).

Chapter 4

The Korea-Centric Japanese Imperium and the Transformation of the International System from the 1930s to the 1950s

Bruce Cumings

The essential argument of this chapter is that Korea – first a colony, then (and still) a divided country, one mostly overlooked in the literature – became a site, and subsequently a highly unlikely fulcrum, for the transformation of the international system from one of rapidly declining British leadership in the early 1930s to a short period of regional Japanese hegemony in East and Southeast Asia, thence to a defining crisis in 1950–51 that became the global building block for American predominance in the international system ever since. Korea was Japan's most important colony and, later, a model for Manchukuo, and was the centrepiece of its regional political economy strategy in the interwar period. Later on, the Korean conflict ushered in a transformation of American power in the world, and in the 1960s became a key model for American-promoted export-led development as the remedy for underdevelopment in the 'Third World'.

This chapter will distinguish three aspects of this transformation: (1) a model of industrializing political economy that began under Japanese auspices in Northeast Asia in the 1930s, forming a regional bloc that deeply shaped the post-war political economy in the region; (2) the contribution of that regional formation to hastening British manufacturing decline (in the 1930s) and assisting American manufacturing advance (in the 1940s), which was one important aspect of the shift from British to American hegemony that characterized the 20 years from 1930 to 1950; (3) the civil war in Korea which provided in 1950–51 the fulcrum for building the military sinews of the American global position abroad and a national security state at home, both of which have now long outlasted their ostensible cause, namely, the Cold War that ensued from 1947 to 1989.

The Japanese empire in Northeast Asia embodied three countries that speak different languages, have different histories, different cultures (albeit all traditionally influenced by China), and, in Korea and Japan, two highly homogeneous but quite different ethnic constituencies. The dominant modes of inquiry in American economics, along with modernization theory, reinforced a tendency (at least since 1945) to view each country apart from the others and to examine single-country trajectories. Yet a country-by-country approach is incapable of accounting for the remarkably similar trajectories of Korea and Taiwan. Thus, specialists on Korea argue that its development success 'is unique in world history';[1] Taiwan specialists make similar claims. Both groups of specialists omit the essential Japanese context of Korean and Taiwanese development.

Conventional neo-classical economists attribute growth in Taiwan or Korea to specific attributes of each nation: factor endowments, human capital in the form of a reasonably educated workforce, comparative advantage in labour cost, and so on. Modernization theorists offer a diffuse menu of explanations for Taiwan or Korea, ranging from the discipline or 'rationality' of traditional Confucianism, through various cultural arguments, the passion for education, US aid and advice, the presumed 'natural' workings of the product cycle, and the diffusion of advanced education, science, and technology.[2] My position has been that an understanding of the Northeast Asian political economy can only emerge from an approach that posits the systemic interaction of each country with the others, and of the region with the world at large. Rapid upward mobility in the world economy has occurred, through the product cycle and other means, within the context of two hegemonic systems: the Japanese imperium to 1945, and intense, if diffuse, American hegemony since the late 1940s. Furthermore, only considerations of context can account for the similarities in the Taiwanese and South Korean political economies. Simultaneously, external hegemonic forces have interacted with different domestic societies in Korea and Taiwan to produce rather different political outcomes: this, too, has been characteristic throughout the century. Korea was more rebellious in 1910; it was more rebellious through much of the post-war period.

In the 1930s Japan largely withdrew from the world system and pursued, with its colonies, a self-reliant, go-it-alone path to development that not only generated remarkably high industrial growth rates but changed the face of Northeast Asia. In this decade what we might call the 'natural economy' of the region was created; although it was not natural, its rational division of labour and set of possibilities have skewed East Asian development ever since. Furthermore, during this period, Japan elaborated many of the features of the neo-mercantile state still seen today. One prescient writer in the mid 1930s speculated that Japan's heavy industrialization spurt was so impressive that 'if world trade were not restricted by tariff walls and import quotas ... Japan might become the largest exporter in the world – and in a very short time'. Guenther Stein saw in this spurt 'the beginning of a new epoch in the industrialization of the world'.[3] He was right on both counts. This is not the usual dating: the watershed years of 1945–50 are presumed to have remade Japan, but, as we shall see, they did not.

Furthermore we can find in the work of the best neo-classical economists an acknowledgement, however indirect, of the advantages of contiguity in this region.

---

[1]   L.L. Wade and B.S. Kim, *Economic Development of South Korea: The Political Economy of Success* (New York: Praeger, 1978), p. vi.

[2]   See, for example, Edward S. Mason et al., *The Economic and Social Modernization of the Republic of Korea* (Cambridge: Harvard University Press, 1980), Ch. 2.

[3]   Guenther Stein, *Made in Japan* (London: Methuen, 1935), pp. 181, 191.

In the middle of a highly technical article where he proposed to test all sorts of propositions about Taiwan's economic success, Simon Kuznets paused to note that:

> ... given the expected economic flows among market economies, particularly those in geographical and historical proximity to each other, the fact that some of them experience a rapid rate of growth in total and per capita product makes it easier to explain a similar experience in other countries of the group. Thus Japan's spectacular economic growth from the early 1950s to the early 1970s is a significant factor in the high growth rates of Japan's trading neighbours, including Taiwan; reciprocally, the high growth rate in Japan's trading neighbours contributes to Japan's growth. In that sense, the growth experience of any single country is a function of the growth of others...[4]

At a later point in his article Kuznets also cites 'the growth-stimulating effect' of 'the backlog of unexploited production opportunities' provided by 'the forward movement of technology and efficiency in other countries not affected by the conditions that retarded progress elsewhere'. This effect occurs 'even in LDCs':

> Though a backlog is presumably continuously present in them, even in some less developed countries per capita product may have grown in the past (as in Taiwan under Japanese occupation), a process that may have been interrupted by war preparations and war (again as in Taiwan since the early or middle 1930s). If, as noted above, Taiwan managed, even with Japanese dominance and constraints on domestic industrialization, to attain a growth rate of between 1 and 2 percent per capita per year before war preparations began, the interruption added to the effective backlog of production opportunities. Once the institutional and political conditions had changed, a much higher growth rate could be attained.[5]

This is an interesting example of the reasoning of American economists, particularly their supposition that language – in this case tortured English prose – is transparent and meaning is self-evident after a certain level of literacy. For example, what does 'historical proximity' mean beyond a redundancy for geographical proximity, since Japan, Korea and Taiwan have not moved any closer since their human settlement a few tens of thousands of years ago. This might, however, signify Kuznets' recognition of an 'historical proximity' known as Japanese imperialism, when Tokyo's Birnham Wood did indeed march to the hinterland's Dunsinane. Of course, these statements would seem to render impossible the scientific separation out and measurement of economic growth in Taiwan, Korea, and Japan, and instead would underline the influence of the

---

[4] Kuznets in Walter Galenson (ed.), *Economic Growth and Structural Change in Taiwan: The Postwar Experience of the Republic of China* (Ithaca: Cornell University Press, 1979), p. 49.

[5] Ibid., p. 53.

history of economic interaction and the Northeast Asian regional economic effort, whether in the 1960s, the 1930s or today.

The Level of the World

Since at least the turn of the last century, Japan has been acutely aware of its global position as a strong regional power, but a weak power *vis-à-vis* the hegemonic state. Thus in 1902 it allied with the reigning power of the time, Great Britain, with the United States as a kind of hidden partner in the Anglo-Japanese Alliance. After the Washington conference in 1922, the US became the senior partner in this three-way arrangement, one that lasted into the late 1930s. After it lost the Pacific War, Japan reengaged with the new global regime as the junior partner of the US, and remains so today – the second largest economy in the world, but with 100,000 American troops stationed in and around Japan. We can connote this longest-running position in the global system, and the preferences of Japan's leaders, with this metaphor: *Japan as Number Two*. Japan has prospered within a diffuse web of hegemony for the past century, with only one errant and disastrous attempt to escape.

Hegemony is a vexing term, no more so than now when neo-conservatives like William Kristol use it to connote a uni-polar and unilateral American role in the contemporary world. I mean something different by hegemony: the demarcation of outer limits in economics, politics, and international security relationships, the transgression of which carries grave risks for any non-hegemonic nation. In the post-war American case, hegemony meant the demarcation of a 'grand area'[6] within which nations oriented themselves toward Washington rather than Moscow; nations were enmeshed in a hierarchy of economic and political preferences whose ideal goal was free trade, open systems, and liberal democracy but which also encompassed neo-mercantile states and authoritarian politics; nations were dealt with by the United States through methods ranging from classic negotiations and trade-offs (in regard to nations sharing Western traditions or approximating American levels of political and economic development) to wars and interventions (in the periphery or Third World), to assure continuing orientation toward Washington.[7]

---

[6]   The 'grand area' was a concept used in Council on Foreign Relations planning in the early 1940s for the post-war period. See Laurence H. Shoup and William Minter, *Imperial Brain Trust: The Council on Foreign Relations and US Foreign Policy* (New York: Monthly Review Press, 1977), pp. 135–40.

[7]   Although I have been writing about hegemony for two decades, I found in Robert Latham's *The Liberal Moment: Modernity, Security, and the Making of the Postwar International Order* (New York: Columbia University Press, 1997) a particularly cogent analysis of post-war American hegemony. In particular, Dr. Latham emphasizes the simultaneous embrace of segregation at home (until the civil rights movement), various authoritarian allies abroad, and an 'external state' of American military bases, within a general conception of the 'free world' and liberal hegemony.

The hegemonic ideology, shared by most Americans but by few in the rest of the world, was the Tocquevillean or Hartzian ethos of liberalism and internationalism, assuming self-evident truths about human freedom generated in a born-free country that never knew serious (or European-style) class conflict. Not a colonial or neo-colonial imperialism, this was a new system of empire begun with Wilson and consummated by Roosevelt and Acheson. Its very breadth – its non-territoriality, its universalism, and its open systems (within the grand area) – made for a style of hegemony that was more open than previous imperialisms to competition from below. This form of hegemony establishes a hierarchy of nations, therefore, but not one that is frozen: it rendered obsolete the development of underdevelopment. Instead, far more than the German hegemony in Eastern Europe that Albert Hirschman analysed or Japanese unilateral, colonial hegemony in East Asia, it is open to rising talent from below and particularly to disparities of attention (what Burke, speaking of Britain and the American colonial revolution, called 'wise and salutary neglect') that give leverage and room for manoeuvre to dependencies. As Hirschman put it in a classic study, the dependent country 'is likely to up rise its escape from domination more actively and energetically than the dominant country will work on preventing this escape'.[8] Finally, this form of hegemony also fused security and economic considerations so inextricably that the United States has never been sure whether economic competition from its allies is good or bad for grand-area security. American post-war hegemony grew less out of specific human design (although Dean Acheson as architect would come close) than out of the long-term reaction of hegemonic interests to the flow of events.

In East Asia we can identify an abstract schema representing the workings of this system over the past century. This schema will satisfy no one except practitioners of shorthand, but for purposes of strict brevity this chapter will present the structure of a world system in which modern Japan has been an important, but almost always subordinate part. An abstraction of Japan in the past century's international system unearths the following timelines:

(A) 1900–1922: Japan in British-American hegemony
(B) 1922–1941: Japan in American-British hegemony
(C) 1941–1945: Japan as regional hegemon in East Asia
(D) 1945–1970: Japan in American hegemony
(E) 1970–2000s: Japan in American-European (or 'trilateral') hegemony

Highlighted is an interesting aspect of this structure: three of the periods (A, B, and E) are trilateral partnerships, and only one is colonial or necessarily imperial (C). A bilateral regime is predictable in the temporary phase of comprehensive predominance or hegemony (1945–70 for the US), whereas a trilateral regime is

---

[8]   Albert O. Hirschman, *National Power and the Structure of Foreign Trade* (1945; rpt. Berkeley: University of California Press, 1980), pp. ix–x; Burke is quoted in Hirschman.

predictable in the rising and falling phases of transitional hegemonies. Period C is perhaps the exception that proves the rule (at least for Japan).

This abstract pattern can be found readily in the *oeuvre* of the dean of diplomatic historians of East Asia, Akira Iriye, whose books dominate the field. Because Professor Iriye's work has dwelt in the realm of culture, ideas and imagery in international relations,[9] and perhaps because of his understated style, few recognize just how deeply revisionist his work is. Iriye has consistently argued through his career:

(1) That Japanese imperialism (conventionally dated from the Sino-Japanese War and the seizure of Taiwan in 1895) was subordinate to British imperialism, and coterminous with a similar American thrust toward formal empire in the 1890s, and no different in kind from the British or American variety;[10]

(2) That Japan pursued a 'cooperative' policy of integration with the international system at all times in the past century, except from the critical turning point of July 1941 and the resulting war;[11]

(3) That Japan got the empire the British and Americans wanted it to have, and only sought to organize an exclusive regional sphere when the other powers did the same, after the collapse of the world economy in the 1930s (and even then their attempt was half-hearted, and even then the development program was 'orthodoxly western');[12]

(4) That Japan's presumed neo-mercantilist political economy of protection at home and export to the free trade realm abroad, with corresponding trade surpluses, has been less important over the past century than an open market at home and a cooperative policy abroad.

---

[9] Especially in *Across the Pacific: An Inner History of American-East Asian Relations* (New York: Harcourt Brace, 1969), his most brilliant and original book; but see also *Pacific Estrangement: Japanese and American Expansion, 1897–1911* (Cambridge: Harvard University Press, 1972), *After Imperialism* (Cambridge: Harvard University Press, 1965), and the deeply revisionist *Power and Culture: The Japanese–American War, 1941–45* (Cambridge: Harvard University Press, 1981). All these books operate on the terrain of inter-cultural imagery and conflict.

[10] Iriye, *Pacific Estrangement*, pp. viii, 18–19, 26–7, 35–6. In fact the US was for the Japanese both 'a model and an object of their expansion'. Iriye has a remarkably benign view of both American and Japanese expansion, terming the former 'peaceful' and 'liberal' because it sought only commercial advantage – that is, what we call hegemony (see pp. 12–13, 36).

[11] *Power and Culture*, pp. 1–2; from the Meiji Restoration to 1941, he writes, Japan wanted to integrate itself with the regime of the great powers, which he connotes as a policy of 'international cooperation' or 'interdependence'.

[12] Ibid., pp. 3–4, 15, 20, 25–7. Iriye dates Japanese plans for an exclusive Northeast Asian regional hegemony from 1936, but according to him it still did not have a blueprint in 1939, and was still dependent on the core powers in the system until the middle of 1941.

Nor was Japan's singular attempt at regional hegemony without cause. In the midst of the world depression and shrunken world trade Japan's total exports more than doubled, 1932–37, and 'appeared to flood world markets'. Cotton yarn, woven goods, toys, iron and steel led the advance. Yet Japan registered a trade surplus only in 1935, when its exports were but three per cent of the world total, compared to America's ten per cent. Despite that, Japan's trade partners got obsessed about its exporting. The UK complained mightily about Japanese textile exports 'stealing our markets', and the American economist Miriam Farley explained the increasing trade conflict of the 1930s by saying Japan had merely 'picked the wrong century in which to industrialize', an observation as brilliant as it is correct. By 1936 every major nation had curtailed the influx of Japanese exports, yet Japanese business groups still 'tried to induce Americans to invest in Manchuria', even in the late 1930s. Meanwhile American textile concerns 'lobbied for restraints on exports to the US despite a massive trade surplus with Japan'. So it goes.

On the critical 1941–45 period, Iriye noted that until the Japanese military's 'turn South' in July 1941 (a decision deeply conditioned by Soviet power), Japan was still dependent on the United States, which he terms (in a nice summary of the dramatic change that came in the early 1920s) 'the key to post-war international relations ... its capital, technology, and commodities sustained the world economic system throughout the 1920s ... as the financial, business, and political centre of the world'. As conflict deepened in the late 1930s, the US deployed a series of 'slipknot' measures against Japanese expansion (to use Walter LaFeber's excellent metaphor[13]), finally invoking the outer limits of its hegemonic power by embargoing scrap iron and oil to Japan, which came as a tremendous psychological shock to Japan and made its leaders assume that the only alternative was war.

The US–Japan war moved quickly to its denouement, but even quicker was the American hand in pursuing Japan's restoration and its repositioning in the post-war international system. Within months of Pearl Harbor a small cadre of internationalists in the American State Department and in Japan began moving on remarkably parallel lines to reintegrate Japan into the post-war American hegemonic regime. According to Iriye, by early 1943 moderate Japanese and American leaders were coming back to 'the framework of 1920s internationalism'. In particular he cited a memo by Hugh Borton, a historian working for the State Department, which provided for 'a framework for long-range planning for US–Japanese relations' which would 'reintegrate [Japan] into the world community of economic interdependence'.[14]

---

[13] Walter LaFeber, *The Clash: A History of US–Japan Relations* (New York: W.W. Norton & Company, 1997), p. 182.

[14] Iriye, *Power and Culture*, pp. 148–50. What I would call hegemony Iriye calls 'Wilsonian internationalism'.

The Regional Level: Developmental Colonialism

Japan's industrialization has gone through three major phases: the first phase began in the 1880s, with textiles the leading sector, and lasted through Japan's rise to world power. In the mid 1930s Japan both perfected its position in the global textile regime by becoming the most efficient producer, and began the second phase of heavy industry based on steel, chemicals, armaments, and ultimately automobiles. This phase did not begin to end until the 1970s, and Japan remains competitive today in automobiles, chemicals, steel and ship-building. The third phase emphasized high-technology 'knowledge' industries such as electronics, communications, computers, and silicon-chip microprocessors. Within Japan each phase has been marked by strong state protection for nascent industries, adoption of foreign technologies, and comparative advantages deriving from cheap labour costs, technological innovation, and 'lateness' in world time. Each phase involved a bursting forth into the world market that always struck foreign observers as abrupt and unexpected, thus inspiring fear and loathing, awe and admiration.[15]

The definitive work by Kazushi Ohkawa and Henry Rosovsky saw two 'long swings' of Japanese industrial growth in the last century, one in the 1930s and the other in the post-1955 period; the first was only marginally less successful than the second. The development in the 1930s rested on the 'two sturdy legs' of cheap labour and 'a great inflow of technology', followed by massive state investments or subsides to *zaibatsu* investors. If exports were still mostly in light industries, mainly textiles, at home and in the imperium iron and steel, chemicals, hydroelectric power, aluminium, and infrastructure (transport and communications) grew markedly.[16] What is so often forgotten is that this growth spurt located new industries in the colonies as well.

For Japan the product cycle has not been mere theory; it has melded with conscious practice to make Japan the pre-eminent example of upward mobility in the world system through successive waves of industrial competition. In the 1930s Kaname Akamatsu elaborated his now-famous 'flying geese' model of industrial development in follower countries, predating Raymond Vernon's work by several decades, and providing a metaphor that became a virtual talisman of Japan's hopes for regional leadership in East Asia in the 1980s.[17] Akamatsu took time-series curves for given industries, showing the beginning, growth, apogee and

---

[15]   This section is drawn from various articles I have written on these themes, beginning in 1984 with 'The Origins and Development of the Northeast Asian Political Economy: Industrial Sectors, Product Cycles, and Political Consequences,' *International Organization* (winter 1984), pp. 1–40.

[16]   Kazushi Ohkawa and Henry Rosovsky, *Japanese Economic Growth: Trend Acceleration in the Twentieth Century* (Stanford, Ca.: Stanford University Press, 1973), pp. 180–83, 197.

[17]   Kiyoshi Kojima, *Japan and a New World Economic Order* (Boulder: Westview, 1977), pp. 150–51.

decline of given products, and superimposed them on each other: the result tended to form a pattern like wild geese flying in ranks. The cycle in given industries – textiles, steel, automobiles, light electronics has not simply been marked, but often mastered, in Japan; in each industrial life cycle there is also an appropriate jumping off place, that is, a point at which it pays to let others make the product or at least provide the labour. Taiwan and Korea (and Manchukuo before 1945) have historically been receptacles for declining Japanese industries. Adding agriculture produces a pattern in which in the first quarter of the twentieth century Korea and Taiwan substituted for the diminishing Japanese agricultural sector, exporting rice and sugar in great amounts to the mother country, soon providing 20 per cent of the food consumed in Japan. By the mid 1930s Japan had begun to export iron and steel, chemical, and electric-generation industries, although much more to Korea and Manchuria than to Taiwan. In the 1930s, and again in the 1960s and 1970s, both smaller countries received declining textile and consumer electronic industries from Japan (as well as from the United States), and in the 1980s some Japanese once again spoke of sending steel and automobiles in the same direction (and of course Japanese engines and other technologies were found in Korean-assembled vehicles from the 1950s down to the present).

Japan entered a period of economic stagnation in the 1920s and pursued free trade policies, and Westerners then and ever since lauded Japan for its liberal institutions. This period of '*Taisho* democracy' was for modernization theorists the progressive culmination of the Meiji success story, marred later by the aberration of the decade of militarism, 1936–45.[18] Japan girded its loins at home for trade competition, inaugurating tendencies in its political economy that remain prominent today; here was an early version of what is now termed 'export-led development'. Both Johnson and Fletcher date the origins of Japan's national industrial strategy and 'administrative guidance' from the mid- to late 1920s, and both the Americans and the British were most receptive to Japan's outward-turning political economy.[19]

Also visible at this early point was the developmental model of state-sponsored loans at preferential interests rates as a means to shape industrial development and take advantage of 'product cycle' advantages, yielding firms whose paid-in capital was often much less than their outstanding debt. Businessmen did not offer shares on a stock market, but went to state banks for their capital. Strategic investment decisions were in the hands of state bureaucrats, state banks, and state corporations (like the Oriental Development Company), meaning that policy could move 'swiftly and sequentially', and in ways that influenced South Korea in the 1960s and 1970s.

By the mid-1930s, this sort of financing had became a standard practice; the key institution at the nexus of this model was the Korean Industrial Bank (*Chōsen*

---

[18]   See John W. Dower's introductory essay in Dower (ed.), *Origins of the Modern Japanese State: Selected Writings of E.H. Norman* (New York: Pantheon, 1975).

[19]   Chalmers Johnson, *MITI and the Japanese Miracle* (Berkeley: University of California Press, 1982); William Miles Fletcher III, *The Japanese Business Community and National Trade Policy, 1920–1942* (Chapel Hill: University of North Carolina Press, 1989).

Shokusan Ginkō), the main source of capital for big Korean firms (by the end of the colonial period about half of its employees were Korean). Meanwhile, the Bank of Chōsen played the role of central bank and provisioned capital throughout the imperial realm in Northeast China. It had twenty branches in Manchukuo (the colony established in 1932), served as fiscal agent for Japan's Kwantung (Guandong) Army, and also had an office in New York to vacuum up American loans for colonial expansion. On the side, it 'trafficked in opium, silver and textile smuggling', and participated in the ill-famed Nishihara Loan, designed to buy off Chinese opposition to Japan's 'twenty-one demands' (most of which bit off pieces of Chinese sovereignty).[20] Most important for Korea, however, was the Industrial Bank's role under Ariga Mitsutoyo (1919–37) in 'jump-starting Korea's first industrial and commercial entrepreneurs', men such as Min T'ae-shik, Min Kyu-sik, Pak Hûng-sik, and Kim Yôn-su.[21]

In the 1930s a great scholar observed that Koreans were still 'poor merchants' and that Korea's cities still did not have a commercial bustle:

> The cities of Korea ... are largely centres of administrative activity ... Not a single city in Korea is busy and brisk like a trading centre of the Western world, or Tokyo or Shanghai; Seoul, the largest, has a population of less than 370,000, and even here everything seems at a standstill and quiet.[22]

The few seats of commerce were the new railway centres and rice-exporting seaports, and as they grew they slowly eroded the ancient hostility to commerce that had marked Korea. At first, Japan was determined to have Korea's commerce for itself. Colonial authorities passed laws in 1910 inhibiting the formation of Korean firms, with limits on how much paid-up capital could be Korean; this came at a time when Japanese capital was already quite predominant. Japanese-owned firms accounted for 70 per cent of the total, Japanese-Korean firms had 10.5 per cent, and purely Korean firms, only 18 per cent.

Massive Korean resistance that began on 1 March 1919 and continued throughout the country for months, however, convinced Japanese leaders to try and co-opt moderate Korean leaders and isolate radical ones. Under the new 'cultural policy', Korean commerce began to grow. One source argued for 'a tremendous increase in the number of Korean entrepreneurs', but by the end of the decade Koreans still held only about 3 per cent of total paid-up capital. Most Korean capitalists were still wholesalers, brokers and merchants dealing in grain or grain-based liquor transactions, with this activity mushrooming in the new ports.

[20]   Jung-en Woo, *Race to the Swift: State and Finance in the Industrialization of Korea* (New York: Columbia University Press, 1991), pp. 23–30.

[21]   Ibid., pp. 29–30.

[22]   Hoon K. Lee, *Land Utilization and Rural Economy in Korea* (Shanghai: Kelly & Walsh, 1936), p. 195.

The most important fruit of the cultural policy for Korean industry was the integral role it soon had in Japan's 'administrative guidance' of the entire Northeast Asian regional economy. Now Korea was to play a part in plans linking the metropole with hinterland economies, and it is from this point that we can date Japan's specific brand of architectonic capitalism that has influenced Northeast Asia down to the present.[23] Stefan Tanaka has argued that as Japan embarked on imperial conquests on the mainland, in the discourse of *tōyōshi* (Oriental or East Asian history, a kind of nativism) Korea and Manchuria became mere 'regions', often lumped together as *mansen* (Manshu and Chosen). If this had primarily a political-economic aspect until the Sino-Japanese War began, this concept soon changed into a 'metanational greater regionalism': for scholars like Hirano Yoshitarō, *tōyō* could extend beyond the East Asian nation states, but was still to be distinguished from imperialism, where 'the mother country is pitted against the colony'.[24]

Japan is among the very few imperial powers to have located modern heavy industry in its colonies: steel, chemicals, hydroelectric facilities in Korea and Manchuria, and automobile production for a time in the latter. According to Samuel Ho, by the end of the colonial period Taiwan 'had an industrial superstructure to provide a strong foundation for future industrialization', the main industries were hydroelectric, metallurgy (especially aluminium), chemicals, and an advanced transport system. By 1941, factory employment, including mining, stood at 181,000 in Taiwan. Manufacturing grew at an annual average rate of about 8 percent during the 1930s.[25]

Table 4.1   Industrial Companies, Japanese Empire, December 1937

	Number of companies	Average capital per enterprise
Korea	981	251,000 yen
Taiwan	335	572,000 yen
Kwantung (Guandong)	358	271,000 yen

Industrial development was much greater in Korea, perhaps because of the relative failure of agrarian growth compared to Taiwan but certainly because of Korea's closeness both to Japan and to the Chinese hinterland (see Tables 4.2 and 4.3).

---

[23]   Cumings, 'Origins and Development'.

[24]   Stefan Tanaka, *Japan's Orient*, pp. 247–57.

[25]   Samuel P. Ho, *The Economic Development of Taiwan, 1860–1970* (New Haven: Yale University Press, 1978), pp. 70–90; Lin Ching-yuan, *Industrialization in Taiwan, 1946–7: Trade and Import-Substitution Policies for Developing Countries* (New York: Praeger, 1973), pp. 19–22.

Table 4.2   Development of Taiwan's Industry, 1929–1939*
Gross Value of Production (million yen)

	1929	1935	1937	1939	% of total (1939)
Foodstuffs	190.0	212.0	261.0	353.0	70.6
Textiles	3.0	3.6	5.0	6.8	1.4
Metals	5.2	8.8	14.4	25.1	5.0
Machinery	5.3	6.7	8.6	14.9	3.0
Chemicals	23.1	27.2	33.8	47.6	9.5

Table 4.3   Gross Value of Industrial Production in Japan, Korea and Taiwan, 1929 and 1937–1938*

	Gross value, million yen			Per capita (yen)		
	1929	1937	1938	1929	1937	1938
Taiwan	263.8	360.1	386.4	58.0	64	67
Korea	280.5*	927.3	n.a.	14.0	41	n.a.
Japan	7716.8	16,412.5	19,667.2	122.5	230	272

*1930 figure

By 1940, 213,000 Koreans were working in industry, excluding miners, and not counting the hundreds of thousands of Koreans who migrated to factory or mine work in Japan proper and in Manchuria. Net value of mining and manufacturing grew by 266 per cent between 1929 and 1941.[26] By 1945, Korea had an industrial infrastructure that, although sharply skewed toward metropolitan interests, was among the best developed in the Third World. Furthermore, both Korea and Taiwan had begun to take on semi-peripheral characteristics. Korea's developing periphery was Manchuria, where it sent workers, merchants, soldiers, and bureaucrats who occupied a middle position between Japanese overlords and Chinese peasants; as Korean rice was shipped to Japan, millet was imported from Manchuria to feed Korean peasants in a classic core-semi-periphery-periphery relationship. As for Taiwan, its geographic proximity to Southeast Asia and South China made it 'a natural location for processing certain raw materials brought in from, and for producing some manufactured goods for export to, these areas'.[27]

We see the kernel of this logic in the Government-General's Industrial Commission of 1921, which for the first time called for supports to Korea's fledgling textile industry and for it to produce not just for the domestic market, but especially for exports to the Asian continent, where Korean goods would have

[26]   Mason et al., Economic and Social Modernization, pp. 76, 78.
[27]   Lin, Industrialization in Taiwan, p. 19.

a price advantage. This was by no means a purely 'top-down' exercise, either, for Koreans were part of the Commission and quickly called for state subsidies and hothouse 'protection' for Korean companies. The nurturing of a Korean business class was a necessity if Japan's new policy of 'gradualism' was to have any meaning, and this was in effect its birthday party – although a controversial one (three days before the Commission opened, two bombs were thrown into the Government-General building).[28] That Japan had much larger ideas in mind, however, is obvious in the proposal for 'General Industrial Policy' put before the 1921 conference:

> Since Korea is a part of the imperial domain, industrial plans for Korea should be in conformity with imperial industrial policy. Such a policy must provide for economic conditions in adjacent areas, based on [Korea's] geographical position amid Japan, China, and the Russian Far East.

One of the Japanese delegates explained that Korean industry would be integral to overall planning going on in Tokyo, and would require some protection if it were to accept its proper place in 'a single, coexistent, co prosperous Japanese-Korean unit.'[29]

Government-General subsidies to Korea's first large textile firm, Kyŏngbang Textile Company, began in 1924, amounting to 4 per cent of its capital, and continued every year thereafter until 1935 (except for the depression year of 1932–33), by which time they accounted for one-quarter of the firm's capital. Kyŏngbang's leader Kim Sŏng-su got loans from the Industrial Bank of ¥80,000 in 1920 and a loan triple that size in 1929, allowing a major expansion of his textile business. For the next decade Kyŏngbang got several million yen worth of loans from this bank, so that by 1945 its ¥22 million outstanding debt was more than twice the company's worth.[30] Kim Song-su and his industrialist brother Kim Yon-su founded Korea's first *chaebŏl* (conglomerate) that, with its extensive industrial, educational and publishing interests, developed a towering influence in Korea similar to that of William Randolph Hearst in the US, or the McCormicks of Chicago.

Japanese textiles had long been dominated by technology supplied by the famous Pratt Brothers in Britain, but by the mid-1930s Japan had become the most efficient textile producer in the world.[31] With Japan's new-found pre-eminence in textile machinery, however, a time came to find a buyer for obsolescent machinery:

[28] Carter J. Eckert, *Offspring of Empire: The Koch'ang Kims and the Origins of Korean Capitalism* (Seattle: University of Washington Press, 1991), pp. 44, 82–4.
[29] Quoted in Ibid., pp. 115, 128.
[30] Ibid., pp. 85–6.
[31] Bruce Cumings, 'Archaeology, Descent, Emergence: Japan in British–American Hegemony, 1900–1950,' in H.D. Harootunian and Masao Miyoshi (eds), *Japan in the World* (Durham, N.C.: Duke University Press, 1994).

why not find it in Japan's near reaches? Soon the giant firm C. Itoh was fobbing off its machines on Korean textile producers, who could match the older technology with lower labour costs and markets for cheap clothing in China, not to mention military uniforms (see for example the use of surplus Japanese machinery in a new yarn and cloth mill set up in Taejôn in 1942).[32] Thus began a product-cycle regime involving Japan and Korea that would continue down to the present.

In other fields, however, Japan remained dependent on the US and Britain. The Japanese allowed Americans to continue running lucrative Korean gold mines until 1939, because they needed American technology. Japan occupied 'an intermediate position' in mining, being an imperial power with mines, but requiring advanced technology it did not have to exploit them.[33] The Chōsen Oil Company set up a refinery in Wônsan, using American oil company 'blueprints and consultations', a reflection of American dominance in the world oil regime of the 1930s.[34] Kim Sông-su also invested in this refinery, considered 'the king of the peninsula's oil world' and of critical importance to Japan's war industry after American bombing of its home islands began, since the Wônsan plant produced high-quality lubricating oil.

The Japanese were and are great rail builders, as an integral part of their industrial architecture. To leave Tokyo station on a bullet train and whistle to Kyotō is still one of the great travel experiences in the world. Before 1939 you could board an express train in Pusan and travel all the way to Paris. Korea and Manchuria were stitched together by state-administered rail networks, webs drawn by colonial spiders on a determined Southeast (Japan) to Northwest (Asian mainland) axis, thus to shrink space and time and to pile up Korean rice and Manchurian soybeans all along the wharfs looking out to the East Sea (or Sea of Japan), then to bring back fruit-of-the-(Toyoda) loom cotton clothes onto the waiting backs of Koreans and Chinese. What the colonizers called 'a mighty trio' of railway, highway and sea transport drew the colonial peoples into new forms of exchange, not just with Japan but with the world market system. As much as any other Japanese institution, the railroad network provided the people of Korea and Manchuria with a harbinger of unprecedented change and a symbol of Japanese power. Villages like Taejôn became key railroad junctions, and remote outposts like Najin, near the Russian border, became entrepots of a large export trade. Najin grew from 500 people in 1927 to 26,000 a decade later; nearby Ch'ôngjin grew from 100 people in 1900 to 72,353 in 1938, making Ch'ôngjin by 1940 the leading port on the East Sea. Korea's traditional isolation was broken; now the majestic White Head mountains had black trains whistling through high tunnels on their way to China.

---

[32]   Eckert, *Offspring of Empire*, p. 118.

[33]   Foster Bain, 'Problems Fundamental to Mining Enterprises in the Far East', *Mining and Metallurgical Society of America*, 14/1 (Jan. 1921), pp. 1–34.

[34]   MacArthur Archives, Record Group 6, box 78, Allied Translator and Interpreter Service, Issue No. 23, 15 Feb. 1951, quoting original documents captured in Wônsan.

It was not the Harrimans and the Hills who built these railroads, but a state company, the South Manchurian Railway Company (SMRC), utilizing American locomotives and railway steel. Set up in 1906, it was the first of the great companies organized to promote Japanese interests on the continent. The big Japanese banks supplied its capital and the bureaucrats supplied everything else: to quote from an early SMRC handout,

> The traveller journeys in the company's cars and stops at the company's hotels, which are heated by coal from the company's own electric works. If unfortunate enough to fall sick on the way, [the traveller] is certain to be taken to one of the company's hospitals.[35]

After 1931 the SMRC took over Chinese and Russian rail lines and in 1933 the Korean rail lines (which had been run by a separate colonial company); within ten years it had doubled the rail lengths, to more than 10,000 kilometres in Manchukuo and over 6,000 in Korea. By contrast China, with a population about ten times larger than Korea's and whose rail lines were heavily concentrated in Manchuria, carried only about twice the number of total passengers per year as the Korean railroads in the 1940s. Meanwhile Vietnam had one rail line meandering from Hanoi down through Hue to Saigon. By 1945 Korea had the most developed rail system in Asia outside of Japan. In the early 1940s Korean rails carried almost 50 per cent as much traffic as in all of China.[36] By 1945 only the remote middling part of the East coast and the wild regions along the Sino-Korean border were untouched by the rails.

Along with the development of roads and ports this infrastructure put Korea quite a bit ahead of other developing countries in 1945 (something almost always forgotten in discussing economic development in North and South Korea in the post-Korean War era). The extensive transportation infrastructure also facilitated Japanese, and subsequently Korean, political control: the strength of the Southern infrastructure, including the strong central state, helps explain why Southern Korea (unlike Southern Vietnam) developed no strongly rooted insurgency in the late 1940s. Railroad and road length per square mile was much higher in Korea than in Vietnam or China. Until the twentieth century Korea was 'one of the most road-less countries in the world', but by 1945 it was estimated to have 53,000 kilometres of auto and country roads, compared to perhaps 100,000 kilometres of 'serviceable' roads in all of China.[37] In short, by 1945 Korea had a much better developed transport and communications infrastructure than any East Asian

---

[35] Japan Times, *Economic Development of Korea and Manchuria* (Tokyo: Japan Times Publishing Co., 1923), p. 250.

[36] Bruce Cumings, *Origins of the Korean War*, I (Princeton: Princeton University Press, 1981), p. 30.

[37] V.T. Zaichikov, *Geography of Korea*, trans. Albert Parry (New York: Institute of Pacific Relations, 1952), pp. 82–3.

country save Japan; this sets Korea off from China and Vietnam, and helps to explain the different fate of rural political movements in post-war Korea.

Although there was much skewing and distortion of this infrastructure to serve metropolitan needs, the fact remains that there is something hard and enduring about factories and railroads, leading in Korea to what we might call overdevelopment. That is, the infrastructure in 1945 bore little relationship to Korean society. During the 1930s and early 1940s Korean groups and classes were largely excluded from all the modernizing activity, except as labourers or low-level technicians and bureaucrats. Paid-up capital in the big enterprises was always 90 per cent or more Japanese. Developed in the interests of the core, the structure was located in a peripheral society that had not changed or developed at the same rate. Once the structure was wrenched from Japan, both North and South Korea had to invest much time and effort in developing the human resources necessary to turn the structure to their own uses.

Of course, it is possible to exaggerate how tightly integrated the Northeast Asian political economy was, or how cut off from the rest of the world economy: in a recent paper, Akita Shigeru noted that the previous complementarity between the British and Japanese economies declined in the 1930s, as Japan increasingly began to supply its own machinery, and to export machine tools and machinery to Manchuria and Korea in the 1930s. As a result, Japan came to be seen as a serious competitor with Britain. But at the same time, British India became Japan's largest trade partner in 1933, underselling British goods, especially in cotton textiles, rubber foot-ware, and sewing machines. Thus he concludes, 'We can identify in the 1930s a very unique complementary relationship between British economic interests and industrialization in Asia', involving export of British capital goods and Chinese and Indian industrialization, and mutual economic interdependence between Japan and the British Empire, in that Japan was exporting much of its production to India and British-influenced parts of China.[38] Likewise Haruo Iguchi demonstrates that until Pearl Harbor Manchukuo was more open to British and American investment than any simple assumption that Japan closed the 'open door' after the establishment of this puppet state.[39]

Data supporting the reality of the 'yen bloc' shows that exports from Japan to Manchukuo and China increased from 25 per cent of Japan's total exports in 1936 to over 40 per cent in the first half of 1938, and imports from those regions rose from 14 to 22 per cent in the same period. Still, the US remained Japan's most important trading partner, in 1938 supplying 460 million yen of Japan's total imports of 1,394,000,000 yen, mostly in petroleum, iron, machine tools, cotton, and internal combustion engines. By the time of Japan's 'move South', the reality

---

[38]   Akita Shigeru, 'British Economic Interests and International Order of Asia in the 1930s', prepared for the XIII Congress of the International Economic History Association (Buenos Aires, July 22–26, 2002), p. 1. See also Akita's chapter in this volume.

[39]   Haruo Iguchi, *Unfinished Business: Ayukawa Yoshisuke and US-Japan Relations, 1937–1953* (Cambridge: Harvard University Press, 2001).

was that Japan remained dependent upon 'Western economic resources, diplomacy and military vicissitudes'.[40]

After Japan took Manchuria in 1931 it also faced a strong anti-Japanese resistance in this less integrated colonial sphere, necessitating harsh counterinsurgency measures including village burning, 'collective hamlets' designed to separate people from insurgents, and large commitments of military force.[41] Koreans were the bulk of the insurgents and bore the brunt of the repression, and it was in this milieu that radicalized Koreans like Kim Il Sung and his allies turned to violent resistance. The repression had a refractory effect within Korea as well, and thousands of communists ended up in jail, many of them not to see the light of day until 15 August 1945. As Japan's war in China deepened in the late 1930s, the period of relaxation ended and Korea entered its last phase of intense colonial mobilization. Colonial police broke up moderate nationalist groups, closed their newspapers, and enforced a harsh Japanization on most Koreans. Radical intellectuals had their thoughts examined and reformed through the intense measures we have come to associate with Chinese Communism; they were then marched before the Korean people as exemplars of right thinking.

The period from 1935 to 1945 was when Korea's industrial revolution began, with most of the usual characteristics: uprooting of peasants from the land, the emergence of a working class, widespread population mobility, and urbanization. Because the Japanese accomplished industrialization from above, however, social change accompanying this revolution was greatest in the lower reaches of society. In other words Korean labour was what was needed, and the Japanese got it mostly in Korea's southern, rice-producing, populous provinces. Simply astonishing levels of population movement occurred within and without Korea in this period. Irene Taeuber estimated that by 1945 as much as 11.6 per cent of the Korean population was outside Korea, most of it in Japan and Manchukuo, and that fully 20 per cent of all Koreans were resident abroad or in a province other than their native one. This almost entirely owed to various colonial mobilization policies designed to serve industrialization or the war effort, and it deeply disordered a Korean society where inter-provincial and foreign population mobility had historically been very low. This was the period when Korean peasants were first uprooted from their villages and introduced to industry or urban life, or both, in Japan, Manchukuo, and Northern Korea. As mentioned earlier, much of this uprooted and aggrieved population returned to native homes after liberation, deeply disordering post-war politics.

Japan's closed door policy in the 1930s had clear Keynesian pump-priming goals – farm village relief, a military build-up and a 'big push' in heavy industries, thus to pull Japan and its colonies out of the depression. Ugaki Kazushige was Governor-General of Korea from 1931 to 1936; according to Eckart he was 'an

---

[40]   Iriye, *Power and Culture*, pp. 4–6, 15.

[41]   Chong-sik Lee, *Counterinsurgency in Manchuria: The Japanese Experience, 1931–1940* (Santa Monica, CA, The Rand Corporation, 1967).

ultra-nationalist, [who] deeply believed in the need for a Japanese imperium of economic autarky and industrial self-sufficiency'.[42] Korea, like Japan, was industrialized out of the depression, with growth rates in manufacturing averaging more than 10 per cent annually; unlike Japan, however, Korea was a 'capitalist paradise', with minimal business taxes and little regulation of working conditions and business practices. The *zaibatsu*, of course, got the best treatment of all; Mitsubishi, Mitsui, Nissan and Sumitomo were all heavily involved in Korea in this period, and by 1940 had become more important than the colonial state's companies, accounting for 75 per cent of total capital investment.

Perhaps the model *zaibatsu*, however, was Noguchi Jun's 'new' one, a very close model for post-war South Korea's *chaebôl*. Noguchi, who was known as the 'king of Korean industry', had his own little empire in the colony, accounting for more than one-third of Japan's total direct investment in Korea and including firms dealing in magnesium, coal, oil, explosives, aluminium, and zinc, in addition to his major firms in chemicals. He also built 90 per cent of Korea's electric resources, including the great Suiho dam on the Yalu River, second in the world only to Boulder Dam. Noguchi founded *Nippon Chisso*, the second-largest chemical complex in the world, which provided the starting point for North Korea's post-war chemicals industry (which was integral to its self-reliant industrial policy). Noguchi's main plant, the Chōsen Nitrogenous Fertilizer Company, was at Hûngnam; it made ammonium sulphates and phosphates, most of which went to Japan. In 1936 its production was one-eighth of that in the whole German empire – and Germany was the largest producer of chemicals in the world. Noguchi was able to build this huge complex because of nearby hydroelectric facilities which provided cheap energy, especially the Chōsin (Changjin) Reservoir.

In agriculture, Koreans were to eat millet from Manchuria while exporting rice to Japan, just as in textiles they were to make rough clothes for the Manchurians while Japan produced the fine silks and cottons preferred by metropolitan consumers. Meanwhile, wage rates were set such that even though their skills were the same, Japanese workers in Korea got over ¥2 per day in 1937, a Formosan worker 1 yen, and a Korean worker .66 yen. Rarely has the typically tri-partite segmentation of global capitalism into core, middling, and peripheral economies been so clear.[43]

These regional policies led to Japan's first burst of rapid growth in heavy industry, and to quick development in Korea and Taiwan. Japan's interwar annual growth rate of 4.5 percent doubled the rates of interwar Europe; colonial manufacturing growth in Korea, 1910–40, averaged 10 percent per annum, and overall GNP growth was also in the 4 percent range, as was Taiwan's. No nation's heavy-industrial growth rate was steeper than Japan's in the period 1931–40; furthermore in the textile sector, Japan's automation was ahead of Europe's. Yet, careful research suggests that both Korea and Taiwan experienced higher GDP growth rates than Japan between 1911 and 1938 (Japan, 3.36 per cent, Korea, 3.5

---

[42]   Eckart, *Offspring of Empire*, p. 119.

[43]   Cumings, *Origins*, I, p. 30.

per cent, Taiwan, 3.8 per cent).[44] W.W. Rostow argued that Manchuria experienced 'a regional take-off' in the mid and late 1930s; if in the early 1930s its per capita product was about 16 per cent higher than that of China, by the 1940s, the gap was 74 per cent. The rate of gross investment in fixed capital went from 9 per cent in 1924, to 17 per cent in 1934, and to 23 per cent in 1939. By 1953, the Northeast provinces (Manchuria), with 9 per cent of the population, contributed 14 per cent to China's national product, and almost a third to national manufacturing output.[45]

Manchukuo was established on 1 March 1932, the date chosen precisely to stick in the Korean craw. Modelled on the Korean colony, the new puppet state was not going to have anything as disagreeable as another March First Movement. Instead Manchuria got something far worse, a skeleton of modernized cities and new industries, and an interior that became a quagmire of revolt and violence for the Japanese army. As historian Ienaga Saburo was among the first to point out,[46] it was the army's failure to pacify Manchuria and (subsequently) North China that deeply influenced the military's critical July 1941 decisions to turn South and, four months later, to attack Pearl Harbor.

Manchuria was also an arena of opportunity for Koreans, however, as the Chōsen Business Club knew when it held a celebration of the new Manchukuo regime in Seoul in May 1932, with many important Korean business leaders attending.[47] Manchukuo was a frontier for Korean rice farmers, bureaucrats, soldiers and businessmen. Nearly one and a half million Koreans were there by 1940, including a large population just across the Yalu River that was deeply hostile to Japanese imperialism, but also the thousands of Korean families that the Japanese settled there because, so they thought, they were better rice farmers than the Chinese (apparently true in many cases). Koreans also served in the Japanese police and military organizations in the puppet state, and many of the most important civil servants in post-war South Korea also served there, for example Ch'oe Kyu-ha (interim president in 1980–81). Kyôngbang Textiles even opened a spanking new subsidiary in Manchuria in 1944, just in time to lose it to incoming Soviet forces, who carted off $45 million worth of spindles and looms.[48]

---

[44]   G.C. Allen, *Japan's Economic Policy* (London: Macmillan, 1980), p. 1; see also Ohkawa and Rosovsky, *Japanese Economic Growth*, pp. 74, 82–3. For the comparisons of growth rates with Korea and Taiwan see Mataji Umemura and Toshiyoki Mizoguchi (eds), *Quantitative Studies on Economic History of Japan Empire [sic], 1890–1940* (Tokyo: Hitotsubashi University, 1981), p. 64.

[45]   W.W. Rostow, *The World Economy: History and Prospect* (Austin: University of Texas Press, 1978), p. 525.

[46]   Saburō Ienaga, *The Pacific War: World War II and the Japanese, 1931–1945*, trans. Frank Baldwin (New York: Pantheon Books, 1978).

[47]   Eckert, *Offspring of Empire*, p. 169.

[48]   Cumings, *Origins*, I, p. 55; Eckert, *Offspring of Empire*, pp. 162, 178–9.

Of course, it would be wrong to link Japanese strategies in Manchuria only to goals of economic growth. Ienaga Saburo wrote that the war in North China after 1937 was partially caused by Japanese leaders who were 'deeply anxious over the loss of markets due to tariff barriers', but that ideologues like Ishiwara Kanji preferred an essentially racial division of labour in Northeast Asia, and also saw Manchuria as a base for moving North against the Soviet Union.[49]

Within Korea, by 1936 heavy industry accounted for 28 per cent of total industrial production, and more than half a million Koreans were employed in industry, a figure that had tripled by 1945. Industry expanded in Korea at double or triple the rate in Taiwan. By 1943, furthermore, the production ratio between Korea's heavy and light industry had become equal. Nor is it really the case that Northern Korea had all the heavies and the South only light industry; the South surpassed the North in machine building, electric machinery, heavy vehicles, mining tools, and the like.[50] Thus Korea's industrial revolution began in earnest during the last 15 years of Japanese rule.

One observant scholar was much impressed by the rapid development of Korea in the late 1930s. Here was an 'obvious, indeed astonishing success', even if the development was 'oriented toward the needs of the empire'. This, combined with a succession of excellent harvests in 1936–38, yielded the idea of a 'Korean boom': with 'the rapid development of all of Korea's economic capacity ... a certain amount of prosperity is beginning to enter even the farmer's huts'.[51] The Northeast corner of Korea, long backward, was 'experiencing an upswing unlike any other part of Korea', mainly because of its incorporation into Manchukuo trading networks.[52]

The social and regional conflicts that racked Korea in the 1945–53 period have their origins in the immense population shifts, agrarian disruptions, and industrial dynamism of the final phase of the Japanese imperium. This was truly a decade-long pressure cooker, and the lifting of the lid in 1945 deeply affected Korea.[53] Meanwhile Taiwan was both less disrupted and less disruptive than Korea: only 35,000 Taiwanese were in Japan when the war ended, compared to 2 million Koreans, and nothing like the 1 March Movement or the guerrilla activities in Manchuria and Northern Korea occurred. This pattern holds even for Japan's state-sponsored religion. By 1940 there were 368 Shinto shrines in Korea, 137 shrines in Manchuria, but only 18 in Taiwan – yet Taiwan was colonized 36 years

---

[49]   Ienaga, *The Pacific War*, pp. 69, 70–72. Ishiwara said in 1930 that the Japanese would supply 'political leadership and large industry'; the Chinese, 'labour and small industry; Koreans, rice; and Manchus, animal husbandry'.

[50]   Woo, *Race to the Swift*, pp. 31, 34–6, 41.

[51]   Hermann Lautensach, *Korea: A Geography Based on the Author's Travels and Literature*, trans. Katherine and Eckart Dege (Berlin: Springer-Verlag, 1945, 1988, pp. 383, 386–7.

[52]   Ibid., pp. 204–7.

[53]   Cumings, *Origins*, I, Ch. 1–2.

before Manchuria. Furthermore, problems regarding these shrines 'arose several times in Korea, while Taiwan and mainland China were more quiescent'.[54]

Japan, Korea and Manchukuo thus formed a 'Northeast corner' in the world economy, one that was growing dynamically in the 1930s, and which returned to rapid growth after two devastating wars (1937–45, and 1950–53). When we factor in North Korea's rapid industrial growth in the 1950s and 1960s, and the dramatic regional skewing of China's industrial growth toward the Northeast in the same period, we uncover one of the truly weighty regional economic engines of the twentieth century, obscured by the lines drawn through warfare, both hot and cold.

The Great Crescent and the Kennan Restoration

The definition of Japan and Korea's place in the post-war world occurred in the period 1947 to 1951, and still governs the situation today. It was in that period that the tectonic plates of the international structure found their resting place after the earthquake of World War II. Dean Acheson, George Kennan, and John Foster Dulles – to take three of the most important American planners – wished to situate Japan structurally in a global system shaped by the United States, so that Japan would do what it should without having to be told – by remote control, as it were. In so doing they placed distinct outer limits on Japan's behaviour, and these limits persist today.[55]

Japan was demilitarized and democratized during the early Occupation years, if with less thoroughness than the proponents of the policy had hoped for. It is thus proper to view the years 1945–47 as an exception to the general thrust of American policy toward Japan in the post-war period, a policy elaborated during the war years by Japanophiles in the State Department who looked forward to reforms that would quickly restore Japan's position in the world economy, and that would not penalize Japan's industrial leaders for their support of the war. It is also important to remember, however, that the twin goals of democratization and demilitarization were not antithetical to the subsequent strategy,[56] but in fact represent the extraordinary reach of American hegemony in the late 1940s:

---

[54]   Helen Hardacre, *Shintō and the State, 1868–1988* (Princeton: Princeton University Press, 1989), p. 95.

[55]   At the time the leader of the small 'Japan Lobby,' Harry Kern, said of the US–Japan relationship, "remote control' is best.' Harry Kern, 'American Policy toward Japan,' 1948, a privately-circulated paper, in Pratt Papers, box 2. Kern's quotation marks on 'remote control' refer to George Sansom's use of the term.

[56]   The exception would be industrial reparations policy, which was a key element in the early development of the Cold War in Europe, but which was rejected outright in East Asia by late 1946 because it would benefit Japan's communist or communizing neighbours at the expense of democratizing Japan.

restructuring both the world system and the internal political economies of major industrial competitors Japan and Germany (something that Britain tried but failed to do in regard to Germany after World War I).

The United States was the one great power with the central economic, financial and technical force to restore the health of the world economy. Although hegemony usually connotes 'relative dominance' within the group of core states, by 1947 it was apparent that the US would have to exercise unilateral dominance for some time, given the gross asymmetry between the robust American industrial system, then producing half of the entire world's output, and the poverty of nearly all the others. It was this critical problem of industrial revival, spanning Western Europe and Japan, that detonated basic shifts in 1947; the so-called 'reverse course' in Japan was thus an outcome of global policy. The new goal was the reconstitution and flourishing of the German and Japanese industrial economies, but in ways that would not threaten hegemonic interests.[57] The revival of Axis industry also spelled out a new regional policy.

Soviet-American conflict in central Europe had erected barriers to almost any exchange, a great divide known to Americans after Churchill's 1946 speech in Missouri as the 'Iron Curtain'. This curtain sliced up marketing and exchange patterns that had underpinned important regional economies. The bulwarks dropped across the central front in Europe and the developing Cold War in Asia cut the Western European and Japanese economies off from peripheral or colonial sources of food, markets, raw materials, and labour – in Eastern Europe, grain from Poland and Hungary, meat and potatoes from Poland, oil and coal from Rumania and Silesia; in East Asia, rice and minerals from Korea, sugar from Taiwan, coking coal and soybeans from Manchuria, tungsten from South China. With the European recovery so sluggish, Japan still dormant, and communist parties threatening in Italy and France, China and Korea, this structural problem was newly perceived and demanded action in 1947. The East Asian expression of this policy had an elegant metaphor.

By the time of the famous 'fifteen weeks' in early 1947 George Kennan had elaborated plans for Japan's industrial revival, plans that called for a modified restoration of Japan's former colonial position in Northeast Asia. But the foundation of 'containment' in East Asia was a world economy logic, captured by Under-Secretary of State Dean Acheson's notion of a 'great crescent' stretching from Japan through Southeast Asia and around India, ultimately to the oil fields of the Persian Gulf. Although containment was thought to be pre-eminently a

---

[57]   William S. Borden, *The Pacific Alliance: United States Foreign Economic Policy and Japanese Trade Recovery, 1947–1955* (Madison: University of Wisconsin Press, 1984). Borden and Schaller have completed original work on the 'great crescent' programme (Acheson and the State Department used the term several times in 1949–50). See Michael Schaller, *The American Occupation of Japan: The Origins of the Cold War in Asia* (New York: Oxford University Press, 1985). I have set out my ideas here at greater length in *Origins*, II, Chs 2–5.

security strategy against communist expansion, in East Asia it mingled power and plenty inextricably. To complement and to achieve their security goals, American planners envisioned a regional economy driven by revived Japanese industry, with assured continental access to markets and raw materials for its exports. This would kill several birds with one stone: it would link together nations threatened by socialist state-controlled economies (containment), make Japan self-supporting (not incontinent), weave sinews of economic interdependence with Japan and the US (plenty), and help draw down the European colonies by getting a Japanese and American foot in the door of the pound and franc blocs in Asia (power and plenty). Peter Booth Wiley aptly summarized these changes as follows: 'Japan, having emulated Perry in its first military expedition to the Asian mainland in 1876, was being invited to build a new economic empire under the guns of the modern equivalent of the black ships'; he referred to the Occupation as 'the second opening of Japan'.[58]

In South Korea, the 'reverse course' started immediately, as the US sought to contain both a strong left-wing within the South, and North Korea, which was ruled by Kim Il Sung and his allies essentially from February 1946 onward. From 1945 to into the 1980s the leading officers of the South Korean military came largely form those individuals who, in the 1940s, were trained in Manchurian and Japanese military academies.[59] The big central bureaucracy in Seoul not only was carried over virtually intact after 1945, but American Occupation authorities usually required that Koreans have experience in the colonial apparatus before employing them.[60] Such agencies as the Oriental Development Company simply had their names changed (in this case to the New Korea Company), and Americans found that they had to use Japanese systems of recruitment to staff the bureaucracy.

After the victory of the Chinese revolution, the search for Japan's Asian hinterland came to mean mostly Southeast Asia, but in 1947–48 Korea, Manchuria and North China were all targets of potential reintegration with Japan. In a stunning intervention at the beginning of the famous 'fifteen weeks' that inaugurated the Truman Doctrine and the Marshall Plan, Secretary of State George Marshall himself scribbled a note to Acheson that said, 'Please have plan drafted of policy to organize a definite government of So. Korea and connect up [sic] its economy with that of Japan', a pearl that cannot be brought to the surface and examined

---

[58] Peter Booth Wiley, *Yankees in the Land of the Gods: Commodore Perry and the Opening of Japan* (New York: Penguin Books, 1991), pp. 60, 492. The 1876 reference is to Japan's unequal treaty with Korea, enforced by gunboats anchored off Inchon Harbour. Others, of course, have made the same point about the late 1940s as Japan's 'second opening'.

[59] Chonsa p'yonch'an wiwonhoe, *Han'guk chonjaeng-sa* [*History of the Korean War*] I, *Haebang kwa kon'gun* [*Liberation and the establishment of the army*] (Seoul, Kukpang-bu, 1967), pp. 247–303.

[60] Cumings, *Origins*, I, Ch. 5.

without demolishing much of the diplomatic history on Korea in this period.[61] It captures with pith and foresight the future direction of US policy toward Korea from 1947 through to the normalization with Japan in 1965, and the emergence of rapid export-led growth.

The irony, of course, is that Japan never really developed markets or intimate core-periphery linkages in East and Southeast Asia until the 1960s. It was the Korean War and its manifold procurements, not the 'great crescent', that pushed Japan forward along its march toward world-beating industrial prowess (indeed, Chalmers Johnson has called the Korean War procurements 'Japan's Marshall Plan'). A war that killed three million Koreans was described by Prime Minister Yoshida as 'a gift of the Gods',[62] giving the critical boost to Japan's economy; the Tokyo stock market fluctuated for three years according to 'peace scares' in Korea. Yet the logic of an Asian hinterland persisted through the Korean War; it is remarkable to see how vexed the Eisenhower administration still was with 'the restoration of Japan's lost colonial empire'.[63] Ultimately this logic explains the deep re-involvement of Japanese economic influence in Korea and Taiwan from the 1960s onward.

Security and economic considerations were inextricably mixed. A revived Japan was both a bulwark against the Soviets and a critical element in a reformed and revived world economy. What is surprising, in the multitude of formerly classified American documents now available on early post-war Asian policy, is how powerful the economic voices were. In particular, a cluster of bankers and free traders, dubbed the 'Japan Crowd', were instrumental in the ending of the post-war reforms in Japan and the revival of the regional political economy that persists today.[64] Economics bulked so large because, as Charles Maier points out, the defeated Axis powers (Japan and West Germany) were to become world

---

[61]   National Archives, 740.0019 Control (Korea) file, box 3827, Marshall's note to Acheson of 29 January 1947 attached to Vincent to Acheson, 27 January 1947.

[62]   Dower, *Empire and Aftermath: Yoshida Shigeru and the Japanese Experience, 1878–1954* (Cambridge, Mass: Council on East Asian Studies, Harvard University, 1979), p. 316. Japan lost about two million people during the entire Pacific War.

[63]   At the 139th meeting of the NSC, 8 April 1953, 'The President expressed the belief that there was no future for Japan unless access were provided for it to the markets and raw materials of Manchuria and North China.' Secretary of the Treasury Humphrey wanted the US to be 'aggressive' in providing Japan and West Germany with a secure position where they could 'thrive, and have scope for their virile populations.' In some respects, it seemed to him, 'we had licked the two wrong nations in the last war.' Whereupon, 'Mr. Cutler [Special Assistant to the President] inquired whether the Council wished to go further than this and adopt a policy which would look to the restoration of Japan's lost colonial empire.' Eisenhower said no, probably not. (Eisenhower Presidential Library, Eisenhower Papers [Whitman file], National Security Council Series, box 4.)

[64]   John G. Roberts, 'The "Japan Crowd" and the Zaibatsu Restoration', *Japan Interpretor* 12 (Summer 1979), pp. 384–415.

centres of capital accumulation and growth, not of political or military power.[65] Thus Japan's economy was reinforced, while its political and military power (beyond its borders) was shorn. The result is that in the post-war world economy Japan resembles a sector as much as a nation-state.

As thinking about a revived Japan evolved in 1948–50, two problems emerged: first, how could Japan's vital but second-rate status be assured; second, how could a pre-war political economy that got raw materials and labour from the Northeast Asian periphery survive in the post-war world without a hinterland? George Kennan raised these problems in a 1949 Policy Planning Staff meeting:

> You have the terrific problem of how the Japanese are going to get along unless they again reopen some sort of empire toward the South.

> If we really in the Western would could work out controls ... foolproof enough and cleverly enough exercised really to have power over what Japan imports in the way of oil and other things ... we could have veto power over what she does.[66]

Thus, once the decision to revive Japan was made, two questions predominated: the hegemonic problem and the hinterland problem. The CIA in May 1948 suggested Northeast Asia as the new (old) hinterland: as in the past, Japan for normal economic functioning on an industrial basis, should have access to the Northeast Asiatic areas – notably, North China, Manchuria, and Korea-now under direct, indirect, or potential control of the USSR.[67] A high official in the Economic Cooperation Administration, a few months later, suggested the same hinterland, and a drastic method of recovering it. Without North China and Manchuria, he argued, Japan would have 'no hope of achieving a viable economy', it (and Korea) would be 'doomed to military and industrial impotence except on Russian terms'. Therefore, 'Our first concern must be the liberation of Manchuria and North China from communist domination'.[68] This rollback option, however, was delayed; the victory of Mao's forces throughout China and the possibility in 1949 that Washington might be able to split Moscow and Peking (Acheson's policy) combined to suggest a hinterland for Japan in Southeast Asia.

[65] Charles S. Maier, 'The Politics of Productivity: Foundations of American International Economic Policy after World War II', in Peter Katzenstein (ed.), *Between Power and Plenty: Foreign Economic Policies of Advanced Industrial States* (Madison: University of Wisconsin Press, 1978), p. 45.

[66] See Kennan's remarks in 'Transcript of Roundtable Discussion', US Department of State, 6, 7, and 8 October, 1949, pp. 25, 47, in Carrollton Press *Declassified Documents Series*, 1977, 316B.

[67] US Central Intelligence Agency, ORE 43–8, 24 May, 1948, in HST/PSF file, Memos 1945–49, box 255, Harry S. Truman Library, Independence, Missouri.

[68] Economic Cooperation Administration, unsigned memorandum of 3 November 1948, in Dean Acheson Papers, box 27, Harry S. Truman Library.

In July 1949, the CIA asserted that the United States had 'an important interest' in 'retaining access to Southeast Asia, for its own convenience and because of the great economic importance of that area to Western Europe and Japan'. It argued that 'the basic problem with respect to Japan is to recreate a viable economy. This in turn requires a stabilization of the situation in Southeast Asia and a *modus vivendi* with Communist China'. The latter requirement might be satisfied if China could be drawn away from 'vassalage toward the USSR'.[69] Southeast Asia was the preferred candidate for Japan's hinterland. It would provide markets for Japan's textile and light industrial exports, in exchange for raw materials Japan badly needed. The problem was that France and Britain sought to hold the countries in the region exclusively, and nationalist movements resisted both the Europeans and a reintroduction of the Japanese. Thus, 'Anglo-American consensus over Japan dissolved' as the United States played the hinterland option. Japan was a threat to sterling bloc trade and currency systems, and was 'perforce in the dollar bloc'; the United States wanted Japan to earn dollars in the sterling bloc, which would have the dual virtue of supporting Japan's revival while encouraging Britain's retreat from empire.[70]

Particularly important is the triangular structure of this arrangement, a structure clearly articulated in the deliberations leading up to the adoption of NSC 48/1 in late December 1949, a document so important that it might be called the NSC 68 for Asia. With this the United States made the decision to send military aid to the French and the Bao Dai regime in Vietnam, not after the Korean War began. The first draft argued the virtues of a 'triangular' trade between the United States, Japan, and Southeast Asia, giving 'certain advantages in production costs of various commodities' – that is, comparative advantage in the product cycle. It also called for a positive policy toward Communist-held territory in East Asia: the goal was 'to commence the rollback of Soviet control and influence in the area'. The final document changed this phrase to read, 'to contain and where feasible to reduce the power and influence of the USSR in Asia'.[71] The roll-back contingency expressed both the fear of continuing communist encroachment, what with the fall of China in 1949, and the search for a Japanese hinterland.

Acheson came to understand Great Britain's inability to defend Greece and Turkey (and by implication, the Middle East) as the final death wriggle of British global leadership; after receiving the UK Foreign Office's famous 'blue note' in February, 1947, he walked off to lunch with a friend, remarking that 'there are only two powers in the world now', the US and the Soviet Union. In a short five years since Roosevelt reached for global leadership after Pearl Harbor, events had

---

[69]   Central Intelligence Agency, ORE 69–49, 'Relative US Security Interest in the European-Mediterranean Area and the Far East', 14 July 1949, in HST/PSF file, Memos 1945–49, box 249, Harry S. Truman Library.

[70]   David P. Calleo, *America and the World Political Economy* (Bloomington: Indiana University Press, 1973), pp. 198–202.

[71]   Draft paper, NSC 48, 26 October 1949, in NSC materials, box 207, Harry S. Truman Library.

delivered it into the American lap. It was also in those fifteen weeks that Acheson told a Senate committee in secret testimony that the US had 'drawn the line' in Korea, and sought funding for a major program to turn back communism there on the model of 'Truman Doctrine' aid to Greece and Turkey.

Thus decisions taken in early 1947 foreshadowed the American decision to enter the Korean War in June 1950; the initial decision was simply to defend South Korea, but by late August Truman and Acheson had decided to attempt a 'roll-back' of the North Korean regime (in the language of National Security Council document 81). Chinese and North Korean forces dealt a catastrophic defeat to American and South Korean soldiers in the depths of that frigid winter, but later on Secretary of State Dean Acheson remarked that 'Korea came along and saved us', because it finally convinced Congress to fork over the massive defence budget that he and Paul Nitze had called for in the most important American Cold War strategy paper, National Security Council document number 68 (approved but not funded in April 1950). US defence spending was pegged at $13.5 billion in June 1950, and nearly $55 billion six months later (or more than $500 billion in current dollars, a high point never reached again).[72]

Two June visits symbolize both the abrupt change, and the desires for continuity, that the Korean War occasioned. A Toyota representative landed in San Francisco on a mission to interest Americans in his products. The war began during this visit, however, and he immediately returned to Japan – as Toyota's fortunes took off, selling trucks and other vehicles to the US in Korea. That same month, the veteran industrialist Pak Hûng-sik showed up in Japan and gave an interview to *The Oriental Economist*, published the day before the war began. Described as an advisor to the Korean Economic Mission (that is Korea's Marshall Plan organization), he was also said to have 'a circle of friends and acquaintances among the Japanese' (a bit of an understatement). In the years after Liberation a lot of anti-Japanese feeling had welled up in Korea, Pak said, owing to the return of 'numerous revolutionists and nationalists'. Today, however, 'there is hardly any trace of it'. Instead, the Republic of Korea 'is acting as a bulwark of peace' at the 38th parallel, and 'the central figures in charge of national defence are mostly graduates of the former Military College of Japan'. Korea and Japan 'are destined to go hand in hand, to live and let live,' and thus bad feelings should be 'cast overboard'.

The Japanese should buy Korean raw materials, he said, of which there was an 'almost inexhaustible supply', including tungsten and graphite; the Koreans will then buy 'as much as possible' of Japanese merchandise and machinery. They will also invite Japanese technical help with Korea's textile, glass, chemical, and machine industries. Pak himself owned a company that was an agent for Ford Motors: 'we are scheduled to start producing cars jointly in Korea before

---

[72] For an excellent summary of the transformation in the US position in the world from 1947 to 1951, see Thomas J. McCormick, *America's Half-Century: United States Foreign Policy in the Cold War and After* (Baltimore: Johns Hopkins University Press, 1995), Ch. 5.

long'. The problem today, Pak said, was the unfortunate one that 'an economic unity is lacking whereas in pre-war days Japan, Manchuria, Korea and Formosa economically combined to make an organic whole'.[73] If Karl Polanyi was right to call the Rothschilds the microcosm of the internationalist vision, Pak Hûng-sik was the embodiment of the Japanese colonial idea – having been born a Korean his only unfortunate, but not insurmountable, fate.

After the crisis of 1950–51, American elites came to agree on a bipartisan strategy of containment, putting 'liberation' or 'rollback' on the back burner of covert action thereafter – useful only against new regimes or small countries that appeared to be going communist, like Cuba. But containment was very expensive, necessitating that building of military and economic bulwarks at various choke points around the Soviet–Chinese perimeter. American expeditionary forces remained in Korea and garrisoned Japan, keeping it on twin outer-limit dependencies: resources, primarily oil shipped from the Middle East along lines policed by the US Navy; and a defence dependency that rendered Japan a semi-sovereign state ever since. All this happened quickly, coterminous with the emergence of the Cold War and the hot war in Korea, and it deepened as Japan benefited from America's wars to lock in an Asian hinterland, first in Korea and later in Vietnam. This dual structure of international relations and regional political economy remains in place today.

---

[73]   *The Oriental Economist* (Tokyo), 24 June 1950.

Chapter 5

Sterling, Hong Kong and China in the 1930s and 1950s

Catherine R. Schenk

At first glance there appears to be little continuity between the 1930s and the 1950s in international monetary policy. These decades were certainly very different eras for sterling and for international financial and monetary relations generally. For sterling, the financial crisis of September 1931 marked the end of the inter-war gold standard of fixed exchange rates and ushered in the first general experiment with floating the pound. This was followed by a reversal of Britain's traditional free trade policy with the unprecedented increase in tariffs in 1932. Throughout the 1930s the international financial and monetary system suffered a series of crises associated with competitive devaluation, economic nationalism and protectionism. After the interruption of the Second World War, the new international monetary system formalised at Bretton Woods in 1944 was specifically designed to avoid the interwar crisis associated with floating exchange rates. It established pegged (although adjustable) exchange rates, and an agenda to reduce trade barriers to promote multilateral trade and payments. However, the combination of fixed exchange rates and the post-war dollar shortage meant that in common with most currencies, sterling remained officially inconvertible at a fixed exchange rate until the end of 1958.

Nevertheless, there are continuities in the British approach to creating complementary monetary and trade blocs focussed on the Empire and Commonwealth. In both the 1930s and the 1950s there was an attempt by the British to establish a complementary system composed mainly of members of the Empire. In each case this was a response to the crises rocking the international monetary and trade systems in these decades. In the 1930s the depression, collapsing primary product prices, rising protectionism and capital flight prompted defensive action such as the Sterling Bloc and Imperial Preference. In the 1940s and early 1950s, the dollar shortage and chronic British balance of payments fragility made the continuation of wartime controls necessary. This led to the formalisation of the sterling area within which relatively free trade and payments were supported by strict trade and exchange controls against the rest of the world.

A second aspect of continuity was that the special positions of Hong Kong and China in the international monetary system in the 1930s were repeated in the post-war period with important implications for their relationship with Britain and for the international monetary system as a whole. After the establishment of the People's Republic of China (PRC) ended China's economic relationship with the

USA, sterling emerged as an important element in China's international links. The global environment of the 1950s created opportunities for Hong Kong that arose out of Britain's decision in 1941 to take Hong Kong into the sterling area while still allowing a parallel floating exchange rate to operate. After the Communist victory in China in 1949, political necessity and practical considerations combined to allow this situation to continue, even though the trade entrepot role of Hong Kong was undermined by the US and United Nations embargoes. This left the Hong Kong dollar in a unique position in the international monetary system with convertibility to sterling and other sterling area currencies but also convertibility to the US dollar at a floating exchange rate. Moreover, the embargo did not end Hong Kong's entrepot role, partly due to the competitive advantage that the free market delivered in terms of price. As political regimes changed across East and Southeast Asia, Hong Kong's colonial political stability, lax regulation of the financial sector, and the free exchange market proved unrivalled attractions for Asian capital as well as capitalists. These regional relations were the foundation of Hong Kong's emergence as an international financial centre in the post-war period. This paper addresses the foundation of Hong Kong's special monetary status in the 1930s and 1950s and the implications of this for its relations with China and the rest of the world.

Sterling in Asia in the 1930s

After the devaluation of sterling in September 1931 several countries, mainly in the Empire and Commonwealth, but also Scandinavia, maintained their pegged exchange rate to sterling. It made sense for those countries that traded mostly with the UK to avoid destabilising exchange rate fluctuations. As sterling became more stable and confidence was restored, more countries also chose to peg their currencies to sterling.[1] This suited Britain because it created an area of exchange rate stability that it was hoped would facilitate trade in an otherwise volatile world. Moreover, the devaluation of sterling up until 1933 gave British exports a considerable competitive advantage within the sterling bloc. Thirdly, the overseas members of the Sterling Bloc were mainly primary producers that were able to supply British industry with essential raw materials relatively cheaply.[2]

For those countries that had not been on the gold standard, the situation in the 1930s was very different. In the late 1920s, the monetary systems of China and Hong Kong were crippled by the falling price of silver on which their currencies were based. The emerging crisis led the British government to investigate the

---

[1]   I.M. Drummond, *The Floating Pound and the Sterling Area: 1931–39* (Cambridge University Press, 1981).

[2]   The National Archives, Kew, London (hereafter TNA), CAB 58/169, Report on Sterling Policy reprinted in S. Howson and D. Winch, *The Economic Advisory Council 1930–39* (Cambridge University Press, 1977), pp. 254–63.

functioning of the currency systems of Hong Kong in 1930 that established the principle that the Hong Kong currency must be linked to or at least have the same basis as the Chinese currency.[3] This was not so much because of the entrepot activity of Hong Kong, narrowly defined as the physical shipment and transhipment activity in the port. Rather, it was argued that introducing barriers between the Hong Kong and Chinese currencies would critically undermine the international financial services offered in Hong Kong. These services included financing trade and receipt of remittances, on which Hong Kong's prosperity depended. While the Chinese currency was linked to silver, there was no capacity to cover forward contracts in Hong Kong dollars if the latter currency were based on gold or sterling. This reflected the recognition by Britain that Hong Kong was monetarily closer to China than to Britain. In the post-1945 Cold War era that was to follow, it was the persistence of this economic reality that over-rode political factors and pushed Hong Kong into a unique position in the international monetary system.

The report on Hong Kong currency was completed in May 1931 but was quickly overtaken by events as Britain itself went off the gold standard in September and started a controlled float of the pound. The recommendations of the report to establish a paper legal tender and a currency board in the colony were, therefore, postponed. From 1933 the monetary system in China began to deteriorate due to regional political difficulties and the poor trade environment due to the global depression.[4] Clumsy British and American attempts to support the world price of silver led to wide fluctuations in the sterling–Hong Kong dollar–Chinese exchange rate and silver began to be exported in unsustainable amounts. As the collapse of the Chinese currency prompted capital flight, the Hong Kong dollar climbed to a premium of 45 per cent.

In response to the emerging crisis, the British became involved in the reform of the Chinese currency. In 1935, Leith-Ross, chief economic adviser to the government, was sent out to advise the Chinese on currency reform. He suggested the introduction of a sterling exchange standard facilitated by a loan of £10 million, a sum eventually doubled by negotiations finally concluded in 1937.[5] However, the collapse of the Chinese monetary system ran ahead of Leith-Ross's negotiations and the Chinese government chose another interim route. Since it seemed likely that the USA could provide aid to the beleaguered Chinese government, China opted to keep its political and monetary allegiances balanced between the USA and the UK. In November 1935, the Central Bank of China abandoned the silver standard and introduced the convertible fapi that was pegged to both the US dollar and to

---

[3]   *British Parliamentary Papers* (1930/31) Cmd. 3932. For a fuller discussion see C.F. Joseph Tom, *Monetary Problems of an Entrepot: the Hong Kong experience* (New York: Peter Lang, 1989).

[4]   See the chapter by Tomoko Shiroyama in this volume.

[5]   In the end the Japanese invasion meant that the £20 million loan did not materialise. S.L. Endicott, 'British Financial Diplomacy in China; the Leith-Ross Mission, 1935–37', *Pacific Affairs*, 46 (4), 1973, pp. 481–501.

sterling. The rate to sterling, however, was kept fixed while the US dollar rate was allowed to adjust until September 1936.[6] From this time the pound–US dollar rate began to fluctuate, forcing the Bank of China to accommodate these fluctuations by widening the spread. For the next year the target was stability against the two currencies until the opening of the Sino-Japanese War in the summer of 1937. For almost a year during 1936, however, China was essentially on a sterling standard and this allowed Hong Kong also to be placed on a sterling standard.

The 1935 Currency Ordinance of Hong Kong established an Exchange Fund that held sterling against the issue of paper currency by three main Western banks in the colony.[7] Because the Chinese currency was linked to both the US dollar and sterling, the Exchange Fund was legally allowed to back the currency issue with a variety of assets, but in practice it operated almost exclusively in sterling.[8] In December 1935 the exchange rate of the Hong Kong dollar was successfully stabilised at the prevailing rate of 1s 3d 3/8, while the Chinese Yuan was stabilized at 1s 2d 3/8.

In the case of China, Britain's interest in promoting sterling as the base for the currency was to stabilise the economy, to support current and future British business interests there, and also to restore an effective fiscal system that would allow the repayment of China's considerable external debt. The goal in Britain's Hong Kong policy was to stabilise the Hong Kong currency but to keep it in line with the Chinese monetary system in accordance with the position established in the 1931 report. These motives led Britain to support China's currency first through the Sino-British Stabilization Fund of March 1939 (made up of banks) and then by the US–UK–China Stabilisation Board of 1941 (directed by governments). In June 1939 the Fund was forced to relax its support of the fapi under pressure of speculation, and the currency depreciated to 3 1/4d by August.[9] A month later, the operations of the Hong Kong Exchange Fund were made public and the Hong Kong dollar exchange rate was stabilised at only a slightly depreciated rate with a spread of 1s 2d 13/16–1s 3d. The strength of the Hong Kong dollar compared to the Chinese currency prompted currency substitution in China that would be a recurring theme in the 1940s with important implications for political and economic relations between China and Hong Kong.[10]

---

[6]   S.H. Chou, *The Chinese Inflation 1937–1949* (New York: Columbia University Press, 1963), pp. 116–17.

[7]   The Hongkong and Shanghai Banking Corporation, the Mercantile Bank and the Chartered Bank.

[8]   F.H.H. King, *Money in British East Asia* (London: HMSO, 1957), p. 108.

[9]   Chou, *Chinese Inflation*, p. 122. King details the continued operations of the Stabilisation Board and its successor, F.H.H. King, *The Hongkong Bank Between the Wars and the Bank Interned, 1919–1949: Return from Grandeur* (Cambridge University Press, 1988), pp. 424–43.

[10]   The Hong Kong dollar circulated widely throughout South China from 1941–50 as the *de facto* transactions currency. C.R. Schenk, 'Another Asian Financial Crisis: monetary

Hong Kong in the Post-War Sterling Area

In August 1949 the Treasury boldly declared in a telegram to the British embassy in Tamsui that 'Sterling has been in the past and will be, we believe in the future, the currency most generally used for trade throughout the Far East and Southeast Asia. In this connection the close proximity of the great sterling entrepot of Hong Kong has considerable relevance'.[11] The reality was much more complex.

During the 1930s, it was shown that the role of sterling in Asia was different than in other parts of the sterling bloc. Although a British colony, it was recognised that Hong Kong's monetary links were closest with China and this precluded bringing Hong Kong onto a sterling standard until 1935. The complex political and economic relationship between Hong Kong, China and Britain after 1945 also left Hong Kong in a special category in its monetary relations.

During the war Britain imposed new exchange controls that formalised and narrowed the inter-war Sterling Bloc. Members of the sterling area agreed to maintain their foreign exchange reserves in sterling (thus pooling their other exchange earnings in central reserves in London). They also operated a strict common exchange control to contain the convertibility of sterling, while allowing relatively unrestricted exchange among themselves. This created a large (although closed) area of sterling transferability. The members of the sterling area that emerged from these controls at the end of the war were the Commonwealth (except for Canada with its strong links to the US dollar), all the British colonies and a few others (mainly in the Middle East).[12]

As a colony, Hong Kong's natural political place was as a member of the sterling area, and in August 1941 it was brought into the sterling area to complement the blocking of Chinese sterling balances and the currency stabilisation. This relationship was sustained through the chaos immediately after the Japanese surrender in 1945. Given the new post-war international monetary system based on fixed exchange rates and very limited convertibility, however, there soon emerged considerable debate between the Bank of England and the Treasury over whether Hong Kong should be excluded from the sterling area.

Because of the pre-war pattern of Asian trade, Hong Kong operated a free market in US dollars against the Hong Kong dollar and therefore also against sterling so long as the colony remained in the sterling area. As in 1930, it was accepted that in order to maintain its entrepot competitiveness, Hong Kong needed to have a

---

links between Hong Kong and China 1945–50', *Modern Asian Studies*, 34 (3), 2000, pp. 739–64.

[11]   Bank of England Archives, Threadneedle Street, London [hereafter BoE], OV 104/45, telegram from Her Majesty's Treasury (HMT) to Tamsui, 10 August 1949. It was believed that Taiwan preferred US dollars to pounds at this time and this was to be discouraged.

[12]   C.R. Schenk, *Britain and the Sterling Area: From Devaluation to Convertibility in the 1950s* (London and New York: Routledge, 1994).

floating exchange market so long as China and other East Asian ports had them.[13] The question, therefore, was whether the political damage that would ensue from ejection from the sterling area outweighed the possible monetary damage to sterling if the Hong Kong dollar remained convertible to both sterling and the US dollar. If Hong Kong were excluded, strict exchange controls would have to be imposed on relations between Britain and Hong Kong and it would be the only colony not linked to the benefits of the sterling area. A further issue was the possibility that the Chinese would dump the Hong Kong dollars that they had accumulated during the war if they thought that convertibility to sterling might be suspended, with serious consequences for the colony.[14] In November 1947 J.S. Beale of the Bank of England noted that 'Hong Kong currency circulates in South China and therefore, from a financial and monetary point of view – particularly in the foreign exchange field – Hong Kong should be considered as a part of China rather than a part of the sterling area'.[15] This, however, was not practical politics during the 1940s.

In 1948, Portsmore was sent from the Bank of England to investigate, and on his advice the Bank of England recommended that Hong Kong should remain in the sterling area, although some extra restrictions were imposed to isolate Hong Kong's US dollar market from sterling. He recommended that the free market should be against US dollars only, local banks should confirm that the purpose for which sterling was sold was legitimate, there should be a dedicated Exchange Controller and staff rather than a secondment from the Hongkong and Shanghai Banking Corporation (HSBC), and legislation should be introduced to control the activity of local small banks.[16] Portsmore reported that 'the most important bankers and traders in Hong Kong are unanimous in regarding exclusion (from the sterling area) as a disaster for Hong Kong'.[17] Some in the Treasury (N.E. Young in particular), however, wanted to keep open the option of excluding Hong Kong in the future.[18]

After considerable debate, the Bank of England view was put to the Chancellor of the Exchequer and in August 1948 local 'authorised' banks were designated to ensure that sterling debits were for legitimate purposes and not for cheap sterling deals.[19] The authorised banks could not engage directly in the free exchange market, although in June 1949 Portsmore noted that Chinese compradores of these banks dealt in the free market for their customers 'in all cases'.[20] The delegation

---

[13]   C.R. Schenk, 'Closing the Hong Kong Gap: Hong Kong and the free dollar market in the 1950s', *Economic History Review*, XLVII (2), 1994, pp. 335–53.

[14]   Schenk, 'Another Asian Financial Crisis'.

[15]   BoE, OV 104/87, memorandum by J.S. Beale, 11 November 1947.

[16]   BoE, OV 14/3, Bank of England Report, 3 May 1948.

[17]   Ibid., Portsmore to Beale, 4 June 1948.

[18]   Ibid., H. Wilson Smith to Governor Cobbold (Bank of England), 12 May 1948.

[19]   For a discussion of the structure of the Hong Kong banking system in this period see, C.R. Schenk, 'Banking Groups in Hong Kong 1945–65', *Asia Pacific Business Review*, 7 (2), 2000, pp. 131–54.

[20]   BoE, OV 14/4, Portsmore's report of his trip to Hong Kong, 27 June 1949.

of exchange control to the authorised banks, however, did not close the matter and the expulsion of Hong Kong from the sterling area was reconsidered periodically throughout the 1950s.

In August 1949, a year after this first decision was taken (and as the People's Republic of China was about to be established) the Chancellor of the Exchequer asked for an update on the situation in Hong Kong and was told that the free market had been effectively limited to the US dollar (although it later traded in a wide range of currencies). Furthermore, Hong Kong's drawings on the central reserves were small and their hard currency expenditure was below the colonial ceiling set by London.[21] Indeed Hong Kong's entrepot trade soon generated a surplus of hard currency for the central reserves. There was still the danger, however, that the free market would attract speculation and arbitrage, that is that sterling area residents would buy US dollars in the Hong Kong free market at a premium or that non-sterling area residents would buy sterling at a discount on the official exchange rate.[22]

More generally, the government believed that the rates quoted on the free exchange market in Hong Kong undermined confidence in the official sterling fixed exchange rate. Hong Kong had the largest free market in Asia, and markets in China, Bangkok, Taiwan and elsewhere in East Asia followed the discounted Hong Kong cross rate, which seemed to confirm the impression that sterling was overvalued (sterling was subsequently devalued in September 1949). In Japan, the Supreme Commander Allied Powers (SCAP) administration came under considerable American criticism for signing a payments arrangement with the sterling area based on the overvalued official rate. Also, as the volume of China's trade fell, the rationale of keeping the free exchange market in order to allow this trade to continue was no longer as convincing. The report noted, however, that there was considerable unrecorded trade with China that depended on the free market, and also there were substantial remittances from overseas Chinese through the market. Together, these allowed Hong Kong to pay for its US dollar imports without recourse to the central reserves in London. For this reason, and because it would be impossible to police the closure effectively, the option of closing the free market was again dismissed.[23]

On the prospect of excluding Hong Kong from the sterling area instead, by 1949 the political obstacles were deemed to have increased since 1945 because of the civil war in China. Any loosening of Hong Kong's links to Britain would be viewed abroad as a first step towards giving up the Colony. This would also have the perverse effect of increasing cheap sterling deals once the control of the

---

[21] Ibid., Report to the Chancellor of the Exchequer on the Currency and Exchange position in Hong Kong, 27 August 1949.

[22] The amount of traffic was difficult to determine, but the Bank of England noted one transaction of £15,000 in legal fees due in London by a resident of Canada and paid for in cheap sterling bought in Hong Kong.

[23] Schenk, 'Closing the Hong Kong Gap'.

authorised banks was lifted.[24] The Bank of England and Treasury agreed that with hindsight it would have been wiser to exclude Hong Kong from the sterling area directly after the war. The Bank of England advised that:

> financially and technically it was probably wrong to include Hong Kong in the sterling area at the time of the re-occupation of the Colony, and the position which has developed there is such that Hong Kong should by rights be excluded from the area now, but the political considerations against this appear so strong that action on these lines does not appear a practical possibility at the present time.[25]

They suggested that the government should only allow British banks in Hong Kong to be 'authorised' in order to tighten up the existing controls. They also advocated the introduction of a dual account system. Sterling accounts at authorised banks would be 'No. 1' accounts and would be controlled by the local exchange controller. All sterling accounts at non-authorised banks would be designated 'No. 2' accounts and debits subject to control by the Bank of England unless they involved a transfer to a 'No. 1' account.

These proposals were put to the Chancellor of the Exchequer in August 1949.[26] However, the devaluation of sterling a few weeks later and the advance of the Communists through China in the weeks that followed rather changed the complexion of the problem. Instead, the Governor of Hong Kong was instructed to close the free market immediately since the gap between the official and free market sterling rates was likely to be reduced now that sterling was no longer overvalued. Chinese remitters were expected to prefer Hong Kong's superior facilities and stability 'rather than fiddle around in the jungles of Macao, Bangkok or elsewhere for a slightly better rate'.[27] Grantham protested that the transit trade with the USA was still large (HK$44 million per month), that the China trade was not dwindling, and that if the free market were suspended this amount of US dollars would have to come out of the central reserves in London.[28] The Bank of England agreed with Grantham.[29] In the end, the establishment of the PRC a few months later precluded closing the free market since it was such a politically sensitive time for Hong Kong. Again, politics intervened to preserve Hong Kong's unique position in the international monetary system.

---

[24] BoE, OV 14/4, Report to the Chancellor of the Exchequer on the Currency and Exchange position in Hong Kong, 27 August 1949.

[25] Ibid., Fisher on behalf of the Bank of England to Treasury, 9 July 1949.

[26] Ibid., Report to the Chancellor of the Exchequer on the Currency and Exchange position in Hong Kong, 27 August 1949.

[27] Ibid., telegram from Secretary of State for the Colonies to Sir A Grantham, Hong Kong, 16 September 1949.

[28] Ibid., telegram from Grantham to Secretary of State for Colonies, 9 October 1949.

[29] Ibid., letters from Portsmore to Treasury, 31 October 1949.

The Chancellor of the Exchequer (Stafford Cripps), however, continued to have serious misgivings. At the beginning of 1950 he wrote that:

> The free market in Hong Kong, a British Colony and part of the sterling area, is as you know a matter of deep concern to me particularly because the persistence since devaluation of cheap sterling transactions is one of the most serious of all our financial anxieties. In view of the harm which is undoubtedly being done to sterling by the free market in Hong Kong – both direct and by reason of the encouragement and excuse which the free market gives other Far Eastern free markets, I have felt great doubt whether HMG [His Majesty's Government] ought not to press for the immediate closure of this, the only free market within the sterling area.[30]

He only resisted because of the immediate political situation, but warned that this was a temporary reprieve that would be reconsidered in the future. Instead Grantham was instructed to introduce the dual account system and to restrict the number of authorised banks.[31] Grantham managed to delay the introduction of these exchange controls for a further four months, for fear that they might be interpreted as a loss of political commitment by the UK to Hong Kong. He believed that new controls might generate a flight from sterling in Hong Kong and Asia, especially when the British were planning to withdraw a Ghurkha brigade from Hong Kong to Malaya.[32] Eventually, however, Grantham had to accede to the British pressure at the beginning of June 1950.

The new restrictions in Hong Kong were accompanied by controls on China's use of sterling. At the end of 1949 it was decided that since Chinese sterling balances had been used illegally for cheap sterling transactions, all transfers from Chinese accounts in London should be subject to approval. Chinese sterling was apparently on offer in New York at a substantial discount and was being used, for example, by American importers of furs from South Africa. This prompted new controls requiring that spending sterling for legitimate imports from the sterling area and usual remittances would be allowed, but selling sterling cheaply to buy other currencies would be blocked. The goal was to maximise the usefulness of sterling for China's imports but to reduce the pool of cheap sterling on the global market.[33]

---

[30]   BoE, OV 14/5, letter sent by Chancellor of Exchequer to Secretary of State for the Colonies, 14 January 1950.

[31]   Ibid., telegram from Secretary of State for the Colonies to Grantham, 6 February 1950.

[32]   Ibid., telegrams from Grantham, 12 and 28 February 1950. The Treasury believed Grantham was merely procrastinating. Grantham was told to set the date for the new controls on 29 March 1950. TNA, T 236/5112, N.E. Young to H. Brittain, 10 March 1950.

[33]   TNA, FO 371/92273, Treasury note of 11 January 1950. As of February 1949 Chinese sterling balances in London amounted to £13 million. TNA, T 236/1813, B. Granger-Taylor to P.D. Coates (Foreign Office), 7 February 1949.

The position of Hong Kong in the sterling area continued to be reviewed periodically throughout the 1950s as part of general efforts to prop up the sterling exchange control system. The political obstacles remained persuasive, however. In May 1953, R.H. Turner of the Bank of England noted that 'the burden of any future defence of Hong Kong's position in the sterling area would, I think, have to rest on the political arguments'.[34] The continued presence of Hong Kong in the sterling area during the 1950s had profound implications for its relations with Britain, its relations with China, and its importance in the international monetary system that will be discussed in the following sections.

Sterling and Hong Kong's relations with China

Sterling's role in Asian trade owed much to the different policies adopted by the USA and the UK to the PRC. One of the greatest challenges to Britain's policy in the Far East was the American embargo on trade with China begun in 1949. The Americans sought to gather Britain into their embargo, which would involve trade controls on British trade with Hong Kong.[35] Like the Americans, the British pursued a policy of exploiting economic relations to achieve political goals, but their assessment of the most likely way to achieve their ends was completely opposite to that of the Americans. In 1949 the Foreign Secretary asserted that:

> at the moment we are concerned only with the survival of our business interests in China. If they do not survive, then we shall have lost the trading machinery with the aid of which we hope, in due course, to convince Mao Tse Teng (sic.) and his boys that there is some advantage in playing with the West. We should also lose all our contacts with China, and the Communists would recede still further into the arms of Moscow.[36]

For these reasons, the Foreign Office resisted US pressure on Britain to join its embargo in 1949–50.

The use of business and economic relations as a tool of policy seemed to be at the forefront of the minds of the Foreign Office. Elsewhere, however, more practical objections held sway. The Treasury, Bank of England and the Governor of Hong Kong all agreed that a trade embargo could not be made completely effective since smuggling would occur either through Hong Kong or, if this were somehow closed off, through Macao and Southeast Asian ports. In the words of

---

[34]   BoE, OV 14/9, R.H. Turner to P.L. Hogg, 1 May 1953.

[35]   For a fuller analysis of the British attitude to the embargo see C.R. Schenk, *Hong Kong as an International Financial Centre: Emergence and Development, 1945–65* (London and New York: Routledge, 2001), pp. 35–42.

[36]   TNA, FO 371/75857, Memo by Dening (Foreign Office), 11 August 1949. Agreed by Secretary of State, 12 August 1949.

Graffety-Smith of the Bank of England, 'any economic blockade would be fairly useless in view of the long coastline, the neighbouring countries and the innate qualities of the smuggler which are present in every Chinese'.[37]

China's trade was also disrupted briefly by the Nationalist blockade of the port of Shanghai in 1949–50 that resulted in considerable congestion in the port of Hong Kong and required the extension of letters of credit, squeezing many merchants in Hong Kong and China.[38] In August 1949 the Hong Kong government temporarily refused to allow further shipments of bulky items such as cotton, wool or paper to be offloaded.[39] By January 1950 Hong Kong godown companies decided that they could no longer accept cargo destined for Shanghai.[40] The British Chamber of Commerce suggested that those who could get their letters of credit amended should ship their goods to a Northern port such as Tianjin via Hong Kong and try to arrange for the onward journey to Shanghai from there.[41] Banks in Hong Kong nursed their customers through the crisis and the congestion soon cleared as the blockade receded.

In May 1951, after the United Nations embargo on strategic trade with China drew the rest of the world along with American policy, the British Cabinet considered whether financial controls should be applied to back up the trade embargo. Both the Bank of England and the Treasury advised against increasing exchange control against China's use of sterling. First, it broke a principle that exchange control should not be used for non-financial purposes. Second, it would undermine the reputation of sterling but could not stop smuggling anyway. Hong Kong would always be a loophole in any embargo.[42] The Bank noted that the UN embargo did not include India, Burma or Ceylon, who would be using sterling for their trade with China. More exchange controls would merely shift this trade from sterling to some other currency, which contradicted the British policy of increasing the use of sterling as an international currency.[43] The Chancellor of the Exchequer eventually agreed that no further financial controls on China's use of sterling were advisable.[44]

---

[37]   BoE, OV 104/89, note from Graffety-Smith to Heasman, 8 December 1950.

[38]   For a fuller account of the blockade see, Schenk, *Hong Kong as an International Financial Centre*, Ch. 2; see also C.R. Schenk, 'Hong Kong's Economic Relations with China, 1949–55: blockade, embargo and financial controls' in Lee Pui-tak (ed.), *Between Hong Kong and Modern China: History of Hong Kong in the National Context* (Hong Kong: Hong Kong University Press, 2005).

[39]   HSBC Group Archives (hereafter HSBC), SHG711, Message to British Chamber of Commerce from H.K. Collar (Hong Kong) via ICI to Shanghai, 5 August 1949.

[40]   Ibid., telegram from Far Eastern Freight Conference (London) sent by British Chamber of Commerce to all members, 21 February 1950.

[41]   Ibid., British Chamber of Commerce circular, 1 March 1950.

[42]   BoE, OV 104/89, A.J. Phelps (HMT) to Serpell (HMT), 22 May 1951.

[43]   Ibid., H.A. Siepmann to H. Brittain (HMT), 23 May 1951.

[44]   Ibid., Memo by Heasman, 15 June 1951.

The different political attitudes of the British and the Americans toward the PRC promoted the use of sterling in China's trade. A considerable amount of China's trade was denominated in sterling because of the danger of using the US dollar given the American antipathy to the new regime. In September 1950 the Bank of China expressed its desire to increase trade with the sterling area. For example, ICI in China was known to have large orders for British exports, but it was hampered by the need to put up a 100 per cent margin on such imports. Hence, the British multinational asked the HSBC for short-term credit facilities.[45] The Bank of England refused to allow the HSBC to offer credit and instead preferred to take up China's offer to sell US$1 million in London to boost its sterling liquidity since this would be more beneficial for British foreign exchange reserves.[46] Chinese fears about using US dollars were justified at the end of 1950 when the US Treasury issued a freezing order on all China-related US dollar balances and accounts outstanding. This seriously disrupted China's trade with the rest of the world and was an important factor in pushing China toward an autarkic trading system and relying on barter. The embargo, the blockade, and the freezing order all meant that financial institutions in Hong Kong remained vital to China's trade and payments.

In the early 1950s the relationship between the HSBC and the Bank of China branch in Hong Kong was very cordial.[47] Indeed the Bank of China (Hong Kong)'s letters of guarantee for international trade were considered more reliable than those of the London branch.[48] They also had good relations with other Chinese banks. HSBC remarked in August 1951 that, 'We have always found the Sin Hua Trust reliable and do not think they would telegraph for TT (Telegraphic Transfer) reimbursement stating that documents conformed to the credit unless such were the case. The National Industrial Bank (of China) are also reliable and conservative.'[49] This confidence allowed the recognition of letters of credit that kept the sterling area trade with China going despite the requirements for imports to arrive in China before payment was made (thus exporters needed letters of credit to guarantee that the money could be paid). In the first eight months of 1950, the London office of the HSBC opened 149 letters of credit with its branches in China (about 5 per cent of the bank's global total), of which £963,178 (US$2.7 million) were in sterling and US$211,576 were in US dollars.[50] Other foreign banks' letters of

---

[45]   HSBC, SHG760.5, W.T. Yoxall (Shanghai) to Gray (London), 1 September 1950.

[46]   Ibid., Gray to Yoxall, 12 September 1950.

[47]   HSBC, SHG741.8, Turner (London) to Yoxall (Shanghai), 8 March 1951. Turner also noted that HSBC freely converted sterling to Hong Kong dollars for the Bank of China in Hong Kong.

[48]   HSBC, GHO170, letter from R.P. Moodie (Hong Kong) to Mourtrie (Hamburg), 7 December 1954.

[49]   HSBC, SHG760.5, Yoxall (Shanghai) to Wallace (London), 10 August 1951.

[50]   The official exchange rate was US$2.80 to the pound.

credit advised to HSBC in China totalled 322 of which £2.2 million (US$6.2m) was in sterling and US$2.6 million in US dollars.[51]

Sterling was also the currency used for the trade between Japan and China through Hong Kong. By June 1950 Hong Kong was selling considerable amounts of Kailan coal to Japan, totalling about £5–6 million and denominated in sterling.[52] At the end of 1952 the Shanghai branch of the Bank of China opened a sterling account with the HSBC head office in Hong Kong to make payments to Japan and the sterling area.[53] This was unusual since the Bank of China had its own branch in Hong Kong. The Shanghai manager of the HSBC remarked that the Bank of China (Shanghai) seemed very reluctant to deal with its own Hong Kong office.[54] The Bank of China (Shanghai) claimed to want to link with the HSBC because the latter handled most of Hong Kong's trade with Japan and had considerable experience as well as branches in Japan that would expedite the business.[55] The Bank of China (Hong Kong) did, however, finance Chinese exports to Europe in sterling and in December 1954 the HSBC was permitted by its head office to do the same.[56]

Of course the activities of foreign banks in China were restricted by the communist nationalisation of commerce and political campaigns during the early 1950s. Several Hong Kong banks, however, continued to operate in China including the Bank of East Asia and the Chiyu Bank. The Shanghai office of the HSBC tried to close but was prevented by the Chinese government unless they would honour pre-war liabilities.[57] The Bank of China periodically promised to divert some foreign exchange business to the HSBC in the early 1950s but Head Office refused to let them do any business until their disagreement with the Bank of China over pre-war liabilities was resolved and the branch successfully closed. The Shanghai branch of the HSBC ceased business in March 1952 but the Chinese government refused to allow the bank to close completely. In 1953, the Bank of China urged the Shanghai branch of the HSBC to resume its trade finance, especially with Japan.[58] This was not completely out of the question since the HSBC wanted to replace its debt-ridden branch with an agency to finance

---

[51]   HSBC, SHG 760.5, S.A. Gray (London) to A. Morse (Hong Kong), September/ October 1950.

[52]   TNA, FO371/83359, B. Granger-Taylor (HMT) to D. Kelvin Stark (Colonial Office), 21 June 1950.

[53]   HSBC, SHG741.9, Yoxall (Shanghai) to Moodie (Hong Kong), 27 December 1952.

[54]   Ibid., Yoxall to Moodie, 10 September 1952.

[55]   Ibid., Yoxall (Shanghai) to Moodie (Hong Kong), 13 August 1952.

[56]   HSBC, GHO170, letter from R.P. Moodie (Hong Kong) to Mourtrie (Hamburg), 7 December 1954.

[57]   See correspondence in HSBC, SHG651.2.

[58]   Ibid., correspondence between Yoxall (Shanghai) and Turner (Hong Kong) in July 1953.

trade with the sterling area.[59] Given that the government required China's traders to get payment in advance of export, overseas importers of Chinese goods often preferred a well-known foreign bank to handle the documents and send telegraphic confirmation that they were in order.[60] Meanwhile, the sterling trade of China was financed through Hong Kong, amounting to an estimate of about £2 million per month, often for shipments from Europe.

In May and June 1955, after the transfer of outstanding liabilities to the Da Hua Bank, the HSBC resumed new trade business for first class clients like ICI and Shell.[61] The Chartered Bank was also operating in Shanghai again by this time, although in 1956 the local HSBC manager noted that, 'I drop into his office 2 or 3 times a week on a snooping visit but have never seen any of his staff doing anything more than routine work'. In September 1956, the Chartered Bank increased its business to letters of credit and bills, mainly for blue chip companies like ICI and Verders Ltd (the latter was a large Chinese firm). This news led to similar instructions for the HSBC.[62] The Shanghai office of the Chartered Bank recovered gradually to show a slight profit of RMB90,000 by 1958.[63] The HSBC's business also began to grow. The increase in outward bills business required the Shanghai office of the HSBC to increase its sterling overdraft in London from £100,000 in 1958 to £400,000 in March 1966.[64]

Hong Kong remained a strategically important market for China throughout the 1950s despite the PRC's nationalisation of trade, move to autarky and leaning towards the Soviet Union. In the run-up to the UN embargo on trade with China in May 1951, Hong Kong's re-exports to China soared, generating a substantial trade surplus. This was quickly reversed as recorded exports to China plummeted due to the embargo. However, Hong Kong continued to import substantial amounts of food from China, generating a large and growing deficit in its balance of trade with China. The deficit grew from about HK$300 million per annum in 1952–54 to about HK$1000 million per annum for the years 1956–60. Because of Hong Kong's position in the sterling area and the location of the free market, this surplus of foreign exchange was particularly valuable for China since it was readily convertible into sterling or any other currency. Given the controls on China's use of US dollars, sterling became an especially important currency for settlement of China's international trade. The HSBC increased its sales of sterling to China from £35 million per annum in 1955 to almost £133 million per annum ten years later, as China's trade surpluses with Hong Kong increased. The HSBC's purchases of

---

[59]   Ibid., Turner to Yoxall, 17 February 1954.

[60]   Ibid., Yoxall to Turner, 18 May 1954.

[61]   HSBC, SHG651.3, Yoxall to Stacey, 10 May 1955.

[62]   HSBC, GHO154, A.M. Mack (Hong Kong) to R.G.L. Oliphant, 10 September 1956.

[63]   HSBC, GHO170, G.O.W. Stewart to S.W.P. Perry-Aldworth (London), 23 May 1958. HSBC was rather left behind at this time.

[64]   HSBC, GHO 170.

sterling in New York to meet the demand from the Bank of China were enough to support the exchange rate of security sterling in New York at the official rate in the 1960s.[65] Hong Kong was therefore a vital pivot in China's external economic relations throughout the post-war period.

Hong Kong and Regional Trade and Payments

Since the rationale for Hong Kong's economic existence was as an entrepot in East Asia there was no exchange control imposed on transactions with its traditional trading partners; Macao, China, Taiwan and South Korea. A variety of other controls, however, tried (not very effectively) to restrict the transferability of sterling by countries such as Thailand, Indonesia and Indo-china that were subject to exchange control from Britain.

Thailand was a major source of US dollars for the free market in Hong Kong. This was mainly due to the export of gold from Hong Kong to Bangkok in the years leading up to the establishment of a legal gold market in Bangkok in 1952.[66] About half of the dollar supply in Hong Kong was believed to come from Thailand at this time.[67] Bangkok operated its own free exchange market and traded in certain grades of rice in US dollars, but the exchange rate of the US dollar consistently traded at a lower premium than the Hong Kong market, making it more profitable to sell US dollars in Hong Kong. In 1950 the IMF wanted Thailand to close its free market but it protested that the existence of the Hong Kong market made it impossible to peg the bhat at the official cross rate.[68] The Hong Kong market was also a competitive target for other holders of US dollars in Asia. In the second half of 1952, for example, the Tokyo rate for US dollars was about 5 per cent below the Hong Kong rate because of the disposal of surplus US dollars by the Japanese. As a result, arbitrageurs operated between the Hong Kong and Tokyo market, generally increasing the supply of US dollar notes in Hong Kong.[69]

Hong Kong's regional role included being a vital early link for the recovery of Japan's international trade. From March 1948, Hong Kong operated a two-way account system with Japan aimed at balanced bilateral trade. Hong Kong was not, therefore, part of the overall sterling area payments agreement with SCAP. Outstanding balances between Hong Kong and Japan were converted to US dollars on a six-monthly basis. The general pattern of the trade was that Hong Kong re-exported Chinese goods to Japan in exchange for non-essential Japanese

---

[65]   Schenk, *Hong Kong as an International Financial Centre*, pp. 85–8.

[66]   C.R. Schenk, 'The Hong Kong Gold Market and the Southeast Asian Gold Trade in the 1950s', *Modern Asian Studies*, 29, 2, 1995, pp. 387–402.

[67]   TNA, T 231/705, Brief for UK representatives for IMF consultations, 29 November 1952.

[68]   BoE, OV 25/11, Telegram from Washington to Foreign Office, 10 March 1950.

[69]   *Far Eastern Economic Review*, 16 October 1952, p. 511.

products. This arrangement was particularly valuable for Japan in the late 1940s and early 1950s when Japan was very short of foreign exchange. Most of Japan's trading partners would only import essential goods, but this was not the case for Hong Kong. As a result, Hong Kong provided Japan with an opportunity to import essential raw materials in return for 'exports of gastronomical delicacies and bazaar goods which no other country will take; and it pays her to buy at higher prices through Hong Kong commodities which she could get cheaper from the country which produces them'.[70]

The two-way account was renegotiated annually and the UK tried to insist that the account should be denominated and settled in sterling or Hong Kong dollars rather than US dollars. By 1950, Japan had substantial sterling balances that Britain was keen to see spent on sterling-area goods. The British representative at the negotiations at the beginning of 1950 noted, however, that 'in SCAP, as in many American organisations, there naturally exists quite a strong anglophobe element; this element sees every attempt to expand the use of sterling as an attack on the Almighty Dollar'.[71] Soon, however, Hong Kong became an irritant to the Japanese since the free market allowed Hong Kong to re-export Japanese goods at cheaper prices than Japan could directly.[72] In September 1953, for example, Hong Kong's re-exports of Japanese goods to Thailand and Indonesia was running at a rate of £250,000 and £900,000 per month respectively.[73]

Other Asian sterling area countries also had access to the market in Hong Kong. In April 1950 the Secretary of State wrote to the colonial territories in Southeast Asia asking them to restrict imports of hard currency goods from Hong Kong merchants who used the free market to get their foreign exchange.[74] This was to stop overseas sterling area demand from increasing the demand for US dollars on the free market and so depressing the Hong Kong dollar rate and therefore the sterling cross rate. All the colonies initially agreed, except for Singapore. The Bank of England advised that since 'a fair case could be made for applying to Singapore nearly all the various concessions made to Hong Kong' enforcing the new restrictions on Singapore might be impossible. In the end Malaya/Singapore was allowed to buy American and Canadian goods through Hong Kong as long as the level did not exceed that of 1950, which amounted to about £8 million per year in 1952 and 1953.

---

[70]   BoE, OV 14/5, 'Report of Negotiations in Tokyo' by K.M.A. Barnett, 11 February 1950.

[71]   Ibid.

[72]   TNA, T 236/5113, M.T. Flett to Brittain, 27 October 1952.

[73]   BoE, OV14/9, Telegram from Chandler (Exchange Controller in Hong Kong), 12 September 1953.

[74]   BoE, OV14/6, Telegram from Secretary of State to Singapore, Malaya, North Borneo, Sarawak, Hong Kong, 8 April 1950.

Hong Kong and Asian Capital Flows

As well as acting as a trade entrepot, the unique role of Hong Kong in the international monetary system made it a target for regional capital flows. A major advantage Hong Kong had over its neighbours was relative political stability. Although the future of Hong Kong was uncertain in the long term, the immediate commitment of the UK and the USA to the continued Western control of Hong Kong was assured after the spread of the Cold War to East Asia. The threat that China would invade Hong Kong in this period was not a serious one, and the prospect that Hong Kong would return to China in 30–40 years was well outweighed by the benefits the colony offered in the present. This was reinforced by the economic and political turmoil that plagued most other territories in East Asia during this period. Japan was a notable exception to political instability in the region, but its banking system was tightly regulated.

In the late 1940s, most flight capital came from China, and in particular from wealthy Shanghai business families. Increasing taxation, unprofitable manufacturing, political and legal uncertainty, and police harassment all contributed to the flow. The escape of capital from the Nationalist regime generated considerable political as well as economic friction between the Guomindang, the Hong Kong government and the British government in London.[75] Hong Kong was also the traditional conduit for remittances from overseas Chinese to China. The rate of overseas remittances increased during the Korean War period to peak at over £100m per annum in 1953 but then gradually declined through the rest of the decade to a low of £34m in 1959.[76]

In the 1950s decolonisation in Southeast Asia, the Korean War, Indonesia's 'confrontation' with The Netherlands, and the communist take-over of North Vietnam further destabilised the region. Chinese businesses and bankers, who dominated financial and commercial sectors in many Southeast Asian economies, found themselves increasingly under threat from nationalist regimes seeking to restore economic power to indigenous populations. In many Asian countries indigenous interests were promoted over international interests (sometimes through nationalisation). Additionally, there were curbs on the activities of the immigrant Chinese populations.[77] Usually these policies were enforced by the establishment of a strongly interventionist central bank, and generally on the principle that international finance was incompatible with domestic economic development. Corruption was another factor that raised transactions costs in many

---

[75] C.R. Schenk, 'Commercial Rivalry between Shanghai and Hong Kong during the Collapse of the Nationalist Regime in China, 1945–49', *International History Review*, XX (1) March 1998, pp. 68–88.

[76] F-H. Mah, *The Foreign Trade of Mainland China* (Edinburgh: University of Edinburgh Press, 1972), pp. 238–45.

[77] Y.L. Wu and C.H. Wu, *Economic Development in Southeast Asia: the Chinese Dimension* (Stanford: Hoover Institution Press, 1980), pp. 173–9.

countries, especially in the Philippines and Thailand. These threats encouraged wealthy Chinese to collect assets in the relatively secure haven of Hong Kong where the economic dominance of the Chinese population was never threatened and there was free convertibility should the money need to be repatriated.[78] Estimates suggest that the capital inflow from Overseas Chinese amounted to about HK$6.3 billion between 1950–65, or about US$1 billion.[79] There is little doubt that this had important implications both for Hong Kong's financial system and its economic development in this decade.

Conclusions

The one main element of continuity between 1930 and the 1940s and 1950s is that the monetary system of Hong Kong continued to be heavily influenced by that of China and vice versa. Unlike the usual account of the PRC's economic policy, this chapter has argued that in the 1950s the inconvertibility of China's currency and the economic sanctions imposed on China did not eliminate its close financial relationship with Hong Kong. In particular, the banks of Hong Kong continued to play a role in the financing of China's trade. Britain's acceptance of Hong Kong's free foreign exchange market as an economic necessity, and the political requirement to keep the colony also within the sterling area, provided Hong Kong with an enhanced importance in the post-war period as a 'gap' in the Bretton Woods system of exchange control. This unique position was due to the combination of the legacy of the interwar Asian regional economic system, the Cold War in Asia that caused the USA to withdraw its direct economic contact with China, and the new international monetary system based on fixed exchange rates and inconvertible currencies. As a result, Hong Kong provided unrivalled opportunities for China and other regional Asian economies.

I have argued elsewhere that in the late 1940s flight capital, currency substitution and smuggling between Hong Kong and China had important implications for the political as well as economic relations of China, Hong Kong, and Britain.[80] In the 1950s, the trade surplus earned by the PRC from Hong Kong provided much needed and (crucially) convertible foreign exchange. Hong Kong also provided opportunities for other East and Southeast Asian countries to acquire dollar goods without spending dollars, as well as providing a safe haven for Chinese capital during the decades of uncertainty in the 1950s and 1960s. This formed the basis for Hong Kong's rise to prominence as an international financial centre in the

---

[78]   J.J. Cowperthwaite (Hong Kong's Financial Secretary) apparently refused to join the Hong Kong Club because it did not admit Asians. BoE OV 14/22, *Personal Report*, J. Tomkins, 9 May 1962.

[79]   Wu and Wu, *Economic Development*, p. 95.

[80]   Schenk, 'Commercial Rivalry'.

decades that followed and the renewal of Hong Kong's role as financial and trade entrepot for China in the 1980s.

Chapter 6

Malaya and the Sterling Area Reconsidered: Continuity and Change in the 1950s[1]

Nicholas J. White

Introduction

The central importance of Malaya[2] for the post-war sterling area has become an article of faith in the historiography of British decolonisation.[3] Reconstructed after the Japanese occupation, the 'twin pillars' of the Malayan economy, rubber and tin, re-established massive export markets in the US and, in repetition of the late-1930s, Malaya topped the list of the empire's dollar earners. Post-war Britain's most important export industry was to be found some 8,000 nautical miles from the British Isles because Malaya's rubber production alone earned more dollars for the hard currency pool in London than all of metropolitan Britain's combined exports to the US. Malaya's vast dollar earnings, and the accumulation of huge sterling

[1] The author would like to thank the British Academy for an Overseas Conference Grant. This made possible his attendance at the XIII Congress of the International Economic History Association in Buenos Aires in July 2002 where an earlier version of this chapter was presented at a panel organised by Professor Akita Shigeru and Professor Kagotani Naoto. He is also most grateful to the Japan Society for the Promotion of Science and Professor Akita for making it possible to discuss this paper further in Osaka and Tokyo. The chapter has also benefited from the comments of Professor A.J. Stockwell.

[2] Given the economic interconnections of mainland and island into contemporary times, the term 'Malaya' is here taken to include the Federation of Malaya (which became independent in 1957) with the island of Singapore (which joined Malaya, Sarawak and Sabah [North Borneo] in the Federation of Malaysia in 1963 but left to become a separate republic in 1965).

[3] See, for example, Martin Rudner, 'Financial Policies in Post-War Malaya: the Fiscal and Monetary Measures of Liberation and Reconstruction', *Journal of Imperial and Commonwealth History*, 3, 3 (1975), pp. 327–8; A.J. Stockwell, 'British Imperial Policy and Decolonization in Malaya, 1942–52', *Journal of Imperial and Commonwealth History*, 13, 1 (1984), p. 78; R.F. Holland, *European Decolonization: An Introductory Survey*, Basingstoke: Macmillan, 1985, pp. 108–9; John Darwin, *Britain and Decolonisation: the Retreat from Empire in the Post-war World* (Basingstoke: Macmillan, 1988), pp. 108, 136, 138, 156–7; P.J. Cain and A.G. Hopkins, *British Imperialism: Crisis and Deconstruction, 1914–1990* (Harlow: Longman, 1993), pp. 279–80.

balances, underpinned British economic recovery after 1945, and Malayan exports continued to shore up the exchange value of sterling throughout the 1950s.

Yet, from this potentially 'Eurocentric' perspective there is a danger of exaggerating and over-emphasising the importance of the sterling area in Malaya's economic history. Malaya was important for the sterling area, but how important exactly was the sterling area for Malaya? As this chapter points out, a number of modifications were made to the operation of the sterling regime in Southeast Asia during the 1950s, allowing the imperial economic bloc to metamorphose into a less ferocious beast by the end of that decade. Moreover, Malaya's continued adherence to empire-Commonwealth exchange controls and commercial preferences did not exclude the region from engagement with the revival and expansion of intra-Asian trade and investment flows. In this, a number of continuities can be identified with the 'international order' of the 1930s, and the sterling area system in Asia exhibited a degree of 'openness' which is often overlooked.[4]

The Imperial Economic System Maintained

Between the 1930s and the 1960s, the key to Malaya's crucial position in the imperial economic system lay not in invisible earnings from City investments or in markets for ailing provincial manufacturers, but in the ability of the peninsula's tin mines and rubber plantations to earn hard currency. Malaya's largest source of imports, making up between one-fifth and one-quarter of the total in the 1940s and 1950s, was the UK. The rest of the sterling area accounted for a further quarter of the total. Before the war, the US supplied no more than 3 per cent of Malaya's total imports. It accounted for about one-tenth of the total in 1947–48, having made substantial gains as a source of cotton textiles and machinery. However, exchange controls reduced imports from dollar sources so that in the 1950s, the US share of Malaya's imports dropped down to 5–6 per cent. As for exports, Britain took approximately 15 per cent of Malayan produce after the war. About 18 per cent went to the rest of the sterling area. In contrast, the US received nearer to 30 per cent of Malayan exports. Although less pronounced than in the 1930s, the massive and consistent balance of trade surplus with the dollar area gave Malaya a key role in the post-war international payments system. In addition, Malaya earned a significant hard

---

[4]   On the pre-Pacific War international order of Asia and the open nature of the sterling bloc see Akita Shigeru and Kagotani Naoto, 'The International Order of Asia in the 1930s' in Akita Shigeru (ed.), *Gentlemanly Capitalism, Imperialism and Global History* (Basingstoke: Palgrave, 2002). For a critique see Antony Best, 'Economic Appeasement or Economic Nationalism? A Political Perspective on the British Empire, Japan and the Rise of Intra-Asian Trade, 1933–37', *Journal of Imperial and Commonwealth History*, 30, 2 (May 2002): 77–101.

currency surplus through its export trade with Western Europe, representing 18 per cent of Malayan exports in 1950 against just 6 per cent of imports.[5]

The boom in rubber and tin prices during the Korean War served to further enlarge the Malayan area's surplus with the dollar area, and it still stood at over £70 million in 1952. Despite the decline in commodity prices at the end of the Northeast Asian conflict, Malaya's dollar surplus in 1956 was in excess of £50 million (see Table 6.1). In 1958, Malaya continued to maintain a favourable balance of trade with the dollar area of M$356 million (approximately £42 million).[6] As was recognised in Whitehall, 'Malaya pulls a great weight for her size in the sterling area'. The Federation delegation at the London Constitutional Conference in early 1956 calculated that, between 1950 and 1954, Malaya earned *surpluses* of about £400 million with the dollar area and £240 million with the OEEC (Organisation for European Economic Cooperation) countries. These were hard currency surpluses far greater than any other member of the sterling area and contrasted drastically with UK *deficits* of £1,525 million and £860 million. Malaya achieved such a surplus in its overseas transactions that the region's sterling balances grew by £110 million between 1950 and 1955 alone.[7] By 1958, one-quarter of total sterling area balances were attributed to the Malayan area.[8]

Table 6.1   Malaya (including Singapore, North Borneo, Sarawak and Brunei): Net Current Balance, 1950–1956 (£ million)

	1950	1951	1952	1953	1954	1955	1956
Dollar Area			+71	+43	+37	+68	+51
Other Non-Sterling Area			+6	-2	-6	-1	+1
Sterling Area	-59	-29	-58	-58	-37	-24	-42
Total All Areas	+91	+122	+19	-17	-6	+43	+10

Source: Bank of England Archives, London (hereafter BoE), OV 65/5, Copy of D.O. Henley, Office of the Commissioner-General for the UK in Southeast Asia, Singapore to S.T. Charles, Treasury, 19 November 1957 enclosing 'Draft Note on Malaya and Sterling Area'.

---

[5] *The Sterling Area: An American Analysis*, London: US Economic Cooperation Administration Special Mission to the UK, 1951, pp. 371–6, 386–8.

[6] *FMS Chamber of Commerce Yearbook, 1958*, Kuala Lumpur, 1959, President's Address, 29 April 1959, p. 13.

[7] The National Archives (formerly the Public Record Office), London (hereafter TNA), CO 1030/72, 'Federation of Malaya talks: finance': Colonial Office Far Eastern Department Note, January 1956 reproduced in A.J. Stockwell (ed.), *Malaya* (London: HMSO, 1995), Part III, Doc. 396, p. 245.

[8] Catherine R. Schenk, *Britain and the Sterling Area: From Devaluation to Convertibility in the 1950s* (London: Routledge, 1994), p. 25.

Hence, US economic hegemony in Commonwealth Southeast Asia was hardly instantaneous at the end of the Pacific War. Indeed, in the Federation and Singapore, US commercial and financial influence was still marginal in the 1950s. American direct investments in the decolonisation era were discouraged by the operation of sterling-area exchange controls, and colonial governments placed restrictions on the repatriation of profits from US investments.[9] A substantial flow of American private capital only began in 1961, following the signing of a US investment guarantee in Kuala Lumpur.[10]

Even then, financial and monetary continuities persisted. When the Federation of Malaya became fully self-governing in August 1957, the conservative Alliance government chose to remain inside the Commonwealth economic bloc.[11] This meant that the Federation's surplus on its dollar balance of payments continued to be offset by a deficit on its sterling equivalent. Malaya's spatial pattern of trade did not suddenly shift after 1957, and the governments in Kuala Lumpur and Singapore continued to convert their dollar surpluses into sterling in order to buy the goods required from empire-Commonwealth sources.[12] Despite the creation of a central bank in Kuala Lumpur in 1959, the time-honoured allegiance to the pound was retained, as was the adherence to the neo-Gladstonian fiscal and monetary policies which had prevailed under colonial rule. The link to sterling was reinforced by perseverance with a common currency for Malaya, Singapore and the Borneo territories. A currency board, and not the Federation's central bank, managed the 'Greater Malaysia' monetary system, while the Malayan dollar continued to be pegged at 2s. 4d. to the pound until November 1967.[13] Notwithstanding the 14 per cent devaluation of sterling in that month, as well as the development of separate currencies after Singapore's exit from Malaysia, it was only in June 1972, following the decision of Her Majesty's Government (HMG) to allow sterling to float on world currency markets, that the Malaysian and Singaporean governments took up the US dollar as the instrumental currency which would regulate the movements of their currencies.[14]

The system of preferences accorded by Malaya to products of Commonwealth countries also survived political decolonisation, and it was only in August 1966 that the Malaysian government abolished most of the residual advantages granted

---

[9]   White, *Business, Government, and the End of Empire*, p. 54.

[10]   The agreement was extended to the whole of Malaysia (including Singapore) in June 1965. TNA, DEFE 25/212, Copy of Telegram from High Commission, Kuala Lumpur to Commonwealth Relations Office (CRO), 6 July 1965.

[11]   Singapore remained a British colony, achieving internal self-government in 1959.

[12]   BoE, OV 65/5, 'Draft Note on Malaya and the Sterling Area'.

[13]   Catherine R. Schenk, 'The Origins of a Central Bank in Malaya and the Transition to Independence, 1954–59', *Journal of Imperial and Commonwealth History*, 21 (1993), pp. 409–31.

[14]   BoE, EC 5/543, Memorandum enclosed in John Wilson, Chartered Bank, London to Douglas Stone, Bank of England, 30 October 1972.

to British goods. This adherence to sterling and Commonwealth trade, combined with the minimal restrictions placed on the flow of capital to and from the UK, helped British firms retain control of the commanding heights of the post-colonial Malayan economies.[15] 'Economic decolonisation', it would appear, 'was a much slower process than the transfer of political power. In 1958, 25 per cent of Malaya's imports were from the UK, in 1963, 21 per cent. In 1970, 65 per cent of foreign capital in Malaysia was British'.[16]

A desire in London to maintain these sterling area benefits may well have played a significant part in 'making Malaya safe for decolonisation' – firstly, through defeating communist insurgency and, secondly, through accelerating the transfer of power during the 1950s in favour of the alliance of communal parties, led by Malay aristocrats and overseas Chinese and Indian business leaders.[17] Admittedly, the attraction of Tunku Abdul Rahman's Alliance lay principally in its geo-political orientation – that is, its pro-Western, anti-communism against the backdrop of France's scuttle from Indo-China.[18] But, clearly, the commitment of the anglophile alliance to the sterling area served to further bolster the respectability of its leadership in British eyes.[19] After political independence in

---

[15]   Another factor which tended to mitigate against investment from outside the sterling area was the operation of blocked account procedures in Malaysia until July 1967 – before that time, proceeds from the sale of investments in Malaysia by non-sterling area residents could not be remitted home. *Bulletin of the Malaysia-Singapore Commercial Association*, 51, December 1967, p. 5.

[16]   T.N. Harper, *The End of Empire and the Making of Malaya* (Cambridge: Cambridge University Press, 2000), p. 363.

[17]   The phrase is from Holland, *European Decolonization*, p. 103. The general argument that the preservation of sterling's world role was the key element in decolonisation can be found in Cain and Hopkins, *Crisis and Deconstruction*, pp. 285–91. See also Gerold Krozewski, *Money and the End of Empire: British International Economic Policy and the Colonies, 1947–58* (Basingstoke: Palgrave, 2001) which argues that the colonial empire became antithetical to British financial interests by the late-1950s.

[18]   Stockwell (ed.), *Malaya*, Part I, pp. lxxiii–iv.

[19]   White, *Business, Government, and the End of Empire*, p. 146. The financial orthodoxy of H.S. Lee – the Federation's Finance Minister after 1956 – was all the more attractive given that there were many in the decolonisation era who advocated Malaya's withdrawal from the sterling area. In October 1955, the Governor of Singapore, Sir Robert Black, had written to London regarding the 'feeling that Malaya is being exploited. [amongst] ... the mercantile and producing middle-classes': 'The danger is that the question of Malaya severing itself from the sterling area might become a political issue'. And, in Singapore, at least, Black noticed that a US dollar based economy was being advocated to allow the entrepot to 'enjoy the same freedom as its rival Hong Kong'. Cited in Greg Poulgrain, *The Genesis of Konfrontasi: Malaysia, Brunei, Indonesia, 1945–65* (London: Hurst, 1998), p. 72. Even British officials and commercials 'on the spot' were suggesting that Malaya should divorce itself from sterling. During the tour of Malaya by the Bank of England's W.J. Jackson in 1951, H.A.L. Luckham in the economic secretariat revealed that

1957, as senior expatriate officers retired and more nationalist-minded elements in Malaya searched for ways of asserting economic *merdeka* [freedom], there were pressures on the government to join the dollar area, thus linking Malaya's economy to the strongest and most stable currency in the world and attracting US venture capital. Yet, senior ministers in Kuala Lumpur appear to have accepted the strenuous arguments of the Bank of England against such moves:

> [If the Federation] left the Sterling Area, it would cut itself off to a large extent from the supplies of UK capital and credit on which its economy has been built up and largely depends. ... [A]ll its current trade with the Area would be subject to exchange restrictions, UK bank credit would be less freely available, private capital investment from the UK would be severely restricted, and borrowing in the UK capital market would not be possible. This could disrupt the whole economy and there is no reason to think that any other country, for example, the US, would fill the gap left by the UK, even if the Federation held substantial amounts of US dollars.[20]

So it would seem that the sterling area, and the British financial and commercial connections which accompanied it, were the crucial determinants of Malayan economic activity in the 1950s. However, the remaining sections of this paper are devoted to revealing the cracks which were opening up in the imperial economic edifice during the decolonisation and immediate post-colonial years. These developments looked forward to the exponential growth of the Asia-Pacific

---

he wished to end the Malayan dollar's parity with sterling and maintain Malaya's own US dollar reserves, controlling them through a central bank. E.M.F. Fergusson, the Singapore legislative councillor and industrialist, also believed that Malaya should retain its dollar earnings. BoE, OV 44/79, Report of Malayan Visit, 27 February–30 March 1951.

[20]   BoE, OV 65/5, 'The Federation of Malaya and the Sterling Area'. Draft Note by the Overseas Department, July 1958. Bank officials could pinpoint only one apparent advantage in Malaya leaving the sterling area: if it ever built up its reserves entirely in US dollars, the Federation could protect itself against a sterling devaluation. Yet, even then, Malaya would not be fully protected since the US dollar had been devalued in the past. To get full protection, the Federation would have to hold gold. At prevailing rates of interest this would cost Malaya about 5 per cent per annum – in just five years, for example, the Federation could lose as much in interest corresponding to a 20 per cent devaluation of the currency in which its reserves were held. Schenk points to the maintenance of foreign-investor confidence as the principal reason for Commonwealth countries choosing to remain in the sterling area after independence. *Britain and the Sterling Area*, p. 42. The available evidence from Malaysia confirms this – in 1967, Finance Minister Tan Siew Sin, publicly justified his government's continued policy of free capital transfers within the sterling area on the grounds that 'the surest way to trigger off a flight of capital is to impose restrictions on capital outflow'. TNA, FCO 24/162, Speech to Alliance Youth reported in British High Commission, Kuala Lumpur to the Commonwealth Office, London, 26 May 1967.

trading and investment realm during the 1970s and 1980s, but, at the same time, resurrected and revitalised aspects of the Asian regional economy of the 1930s.

The Changing Sterling Area

The tightly controlled sterling bloc of the early-1950s was a shadow of its former self by the end of the decade. For one, political change *did* impact upon the operation of the sterling area in Malaya. Even before independence, the Federation government spent dollars virtually as it chose. The Malayan delegation at the London constitutional talks of January–February 1956 had sought concessions in recognition of Malaya's exemplary service to the dollar pool in London.[21] As a prelude to political *merdeka*, therefore, the Malayans won 'self-determination' in dollar expenditure, and a new Ministry of Finance was established. HMG was now informed about Kuala Lumpur's proposed dollar import programme and might comment on it – for example, as regards possible alternative sterling sources for particular items – but had effectively surrendered the right to approve it. By independence, the Federation was in the same position as any other independent Commonwealth country: in framing its dollar import policy, Malaya was expected to take account of its obligations as a member of the sterling area in the light of the information received periodically from Britain's central bankers in Threadneedle Street about the state of the reserves and other things. But, ultimately, Federation ministers and civil servants, and not Bank of England exchange controllers, managed the expenditure of Malayan hard currency on imports from the dollar area.[22] In other words, the successful functioning of the sterling area in Southeast Asia now rested upon Malayan consent and not British coercion.

It should also be noted that British, metropolitan-led financial and commercial liberalisation after 1955 resulted in the progressive relaxation of import restrictions on dollar goods throughout the sterling area, with the goal of full convertibility.[23] The chairman of the Malayan Exchange Banks Association observed that the large dismantling of exchange controls on an international scale, beginning from early 1959, produced a much freer movement of funds across exchanges. A wide relaxation of import controls, especially over goods from the dollar area, accompanied the new freedom from exchange control – so much so, that Singapore importers could now do substantial business directly with North America where formerly dollar goods had been supplied via Hong Kong.[24]

---

[21]   TNA, CO 1030/72, 'Federation of Malaya talks: finance' reproduced in Stockwell (ed.), *Malaya*, Part III, p. 246.

[22]   BoE, OV 65/5, Copy of D.O. Henley, Office of the Commissioner-General for the UK in Southeast Asia, Singapore to S.T. Charles, Treasury, 19 November 1957 enclosing 'Draft Note on Malaya and the Sterling Area'.

[23]   Schenk, *Sterling Area*, Ch. 5

[24]   *Singapore Chamber of Commerce Annual Report for 1959*, Singapore, 1960, p. 32.

These liberalisations corresponded with a growing disenchantment with the sterling area in influential circles in Britain, on top of a specific scepticism regarding Malaya's future wealth potential, burdened as the area was with an enduring dependence on two commodities which were highly vulnerable in the face of global technological advance. With the massive re-activation of the synthetic rubber industry in the US during the Korean War, Malaya's rubber export markets became more diversified and Britain, with about 20 per cent of the market, emerged as Malaya's main buyer of plantation rubber by 1958.[25] The result was a sharp downturn in Malaya's dollar earnings by the 1960s.[26] Moreover, during 1958, a synthetic rubber plant came on stream in the UK, encouraged by the Treasury and the Board of Trade.[27] In addition, the Board promoted the full liberalisation of dollar-area synthetic rubber imports into the UK to permit British manufacturers access to the best and cheapest raw materials and so help them compete in hard-currency markets.[28] This policy was pursued despite warnings from the High Commissioner in the Federation and the Commonwealth Relations Office that such moves might prejudice Malaya's continued membership of the sterling area, as well as the position of UK business interests in the peninsula.[29] 1958 would also prove a watershed year in terms of economic developments in Malaya itself, marking the beginnings of a breakdown in the old economic complementarities between metropole and periphery. The 'openness' of the colonial export economy was eroded by the introduction of pioneer industry legislation and protective tariffs designed to encourage import substitution (similar state initiatives soon followed in decolonising Singapore). The development of a synthetic rubber industry and the liberalisation of raw material imports in Britain, as well as the encouragement of manufacturing in Malaya, were the Anglo-Malayan manifestations of a trend towards the marginalisation of the sterling area, 'in the wake of changing priorities both in Britain and in the overseas sterling area as countries increasingly focused

---

[25]   TNA, DO 35/9759, 'Brief for the Secretary of State's Visit to Malaya. Rubber', c. January 1959. The US was still the main buyer of Malayan tin but conservation, reclamation and replacement strategies by American consumers greatly reduced the peninsula's percentage share from pre-war. The British agency houses had diversified into oil palm but as Sir Norman Kipping, Director-General of the Federation of British Industry, discovered in early 1958, the crop 'may increasingly suffer from the wider use of synthetic detergents'. Confederation of British Industry Records, Modern Records Centre, University of Warwick, Mss. 200/F/3/D3/6/75, D/5528. 'Report on the Federation of Malaya'.

[26]   For example see TNA, CAB 148/7, DO (O) (64) 59, 'British Policy Towards South-East Asia'. Memorandum by the Foreign Office, 22 September 1964.

[27]   White, *Business, Government, and the End of Empire*, pp. 190–94.

[28]   TNA, BT 258/76, Minute by J.C. Burgh for Miss Hix, 24 November 1958; BT 258/991, Minute by A.L. Burgess, 20 October 1959; DO 35/9905, Copy of G.H. Andrew, Board of Trade to Sir Henry Lintott, Commonwealth Relations Office (CRO), 28 January 1958.

[29]   TNA, DO 35/9905, Memorandum by the UK High Commissioner, 3 January 1958; Copy of H.A.F. Rumbold, CRO to Andrew, 3 February 1958.

on their own development and trade links independently of their sterling area relations'.[30]

Malaya and the Intra-Asian Economy: the 'Official Market'

China

Even without a declining UK economic interest in Malaya, the survival of the sterling area in Asia, throughout the 1950s, did not preclude the revival and expansion of intra-Asian trade. Indeed, by the end of 1956, British merchants in Penang had noticed the increased volume of trade between India, Japan, Indonesia, Burma, China and Malaya to the detriment of UK sales. British industry was unable to compete for reasons of distance and cost, and the effect of such competition had already been felt in some markets – for example, Japan was threatening to supersede the UK as the peninsula's main supplier of cement.[31] The Federation's Trade Commissioner to the UK re-assured the UK agency houses that his government had no plans to enter into restrictive trade agreements with other Asian countries, but Malaya's emerging political and business leaders were certainly seeking to intensify these non-Western economic links. Under the Federation's semi-independent regime, a trade mission was assembled to visit China and Japan. The adviser to the mission was the Melaka business politician, Tan Siew Sin, later Minister of Commerce and Industry and then Minister of Finance in the post-colonial Federation. The mission was strictly non-official in character, but had the blessing of the Federation's Chief Minister (and later Prime Minister), Tunku Abdul Rahman.[32] For Tan Siew Sin, 'Red China' offered an alternative, long-term trade strategy to reliance on Western markets. As he explained to T.H. Tan, a fellow Chinese business leader (*towkay*) and also Chief Executive Secretary of the Malayan Chinese Association, in June 1956:

> ... [T]he USA may be heading for a general economic recession. If this is so, it might well lead to a general trade recession throughout the entire non-communist world, and it is at such times that rubber sales to the Communist bloc may give us some help in arresting the inevitable collapse of rubber prices on world markets.[33]

---

[30] Schenk, *Britain and Sterling Area*, p. 128.

[31] Arkib Negara Malaysia, Kuala Lumpur (hereafter ANM), AE 99/M, Penang Chamber of Commerce Confidential Minutes, November 1946–July 1958, 'Notes of a Meeting between members of the Chambers Committee and J.N. Davies, Trade Commissioner for Malaya in the UK, 22 November 1956'; Confidential Minutes, 9 February 1954.

[32] ANM, Tan Siew Sin Papers, SP 45/897, T.H. Tan to Tan Siew Sin, 20 June 1956; 'Rules of the Trade Mission to China and Japan', April 1956.

[33] Ibid., Tan Siew Sin to T.H. Tan, 28 June 1956.

Pre-war, a flourishing trade between Malaya and China had been facilitated by the Malayan Chinese community. China supplied traditional goods and foodstuffs but increasingly textiles, and by the end of the 1930s, China controlled 4 per cent of the total volume of imports into British Malaya. China's export trade to Malaya was far less marked than the UK's or the US's but, as Nie Dening points out, it was on a par with Australia and the countries of Western Europe. In return, China took a share of Malaya's primary products – some 40 per cent of China's rubber was shipped from Malayan ports by 1936. In addition, overseas Chinese remittances from the Straits Settlements and the Malay States were running at approximately 100 million yuan (about £12.5 million) by the end of the 1930s.[34]

There was a vast growth in Sino-Malayan trade after the Second World War – the total volume of trade worth about US$63 million in 1950 was two and a half times that of 1940. Strategic controls on trade with Communist China were introduced in May 1951 as a consequence of Beijing's intervention in the Korean War. These were lifted, however, in mid-1956, and the People's Republic began to purchase rubber from Malaya in increasing quantities. In the first three-quarters of 1958, a figure of 64,000 tons was attained, and mainland China was now the sixth largest purchaser of Malayan rubber. In return, Malayan imports from China for the first nine months of 1958 were worth M$120 million (as against M$100 million for the whole of 1957). The principal trade was in cotton textiles plus other light industrial goods. Jimmy Donald, the chairman of the British-dominated Singapore Chamber of Commerce and manager of the Borneo Company Ltd (BCL) in the island colony, reported to London that these manufactures from the People's Republic were 15–20 per cent cheaper than from Western sources and even slightly cheaper than those arriving from Japan.[35] As in the 1930s, an indispensable institution, the Bank of China, underpinned the China-Malaya trades. Its branches in Singapore, Kuala Lumpur and Penang provided user-friendly exchange services, particularly export and import purchase bills.[36]

Yet, for both economic and geo-political reasons, the government in Kuala Lumpur grew increasingly wary of mainland China's influence in Southeast Asia. In the autumn of 1958, the Alliance government banned Communist China's textile imports. The Federation also amended its banking legislation to proscribe

---

[34]   Nie Dening, 'Changes in the Trading Ties Between China and Malaya, Prewar to Postwar', *Journal of the Malaysian Branch of the Royal Asiatic Society*, LXXII, 1 (1999), pp. 101, 104, 108.

[35]   TNA, DO 35/9759, 'Brief for Lord Home's Visit to Malaya. Economic Relations with China', c. January 1959; Inchcape Archives, Guildhall Library, London (hereafter IA), Ms. 27259/5, Donald to Malcolm, 20 October 1958 enclosing copy of letter to W.C.S. Corry, Malayan Commercial Association of Great Britain, 20 October 1958; Nie, 'China and Malaya', pp. 100, 102, 104. In the course of 1958, the Singapore Plywood Company Ltd – part of the BCL's industrial and commercial empire – discovered its local markets 'flooded with cheap imports' from China (and Japan). BCL, *Annual Report and Accounts 1958*.

[36]   Nie, 'China and Malaya', pp. 110–11.

any bank whose control was vested in a foreign government; an action which had the effect of closing down the Bank of China because of suspected financial links to the Malayan Communist Party. At the same time, Beijing was barred from organising trade fairs in the Federation, culminating in embargoes on trade between Malaya and China. As such, Malaysian–Chinese economic links would not fully revive until the beginning of the 1970s.[37] But, the important point here is that without anti-communist exigencies, and irrespective of the continued existence of the sterling area, Malaya's trade with the People's Republic might well have expanded dramatically from the end of the 1950s.

Japan

In the meantime, however, Japan's anti-communism made it an ideal Asian trading partner for Malaya, and the Federation (and Singaporean) trade delegation of 1956 would prove ultimately more successful in Tokyo and Osaka. Informal meetings with Japanese political and business figures paved the way for a number of top-level Malayo-Japanese meetings, which culminated in the Japan-Federation trade agreement of 1960, and the Singapore-Japan Tax Convention of 1961.[38] British officials were relieved that the trade deal between Tokyo and Kuala Lumpur expressly excluded Japan from the system of Commonwealth preference, while the Federation's 'rights and obligations' as a member of the sterling area were not affected. But, significantly, the Malayo-Japanese pact was Kuala Lumpur's first most-favoured-nation commercial agreement outside the Commonwealth.[39]

From the early 1950s onwards, Japanese general trading companies (*sogo shosha*) and individual entrepreneurs had rejuvenated Japan's commercial links with sterling area Southeast Asia. Although less marked than in other parts of the region, by the late 1950s, Japanese economic penetration of Malaya was causing alarm in British official and commercial circles. On his visit to Southeast Asia in November 1957, Japan's Prime Minister, Kishi Nobusuke, complained that the government of the autonomous Federation continued to maintain a virtual ban on long-term visits for Japanese businessmen. Yet, the commercial attaché in the UK High Commission in Kuala Lumpur noted that 'Japanese goods are already making noticeable headway in several fields' and he had also learnt that the Japanese delegation to an upcoming meeting of the Economic Cooperation

---

[37]   TNA, DO 35/9759, 'Economic Relations with China'; BoE, OV 65/6, copy of telegram from High Commissioner, Kuala Lumpur to CRO, 30 October 1958; Nie, 'China and Malaya'. Tan Siew Sin's pro-China economic policy seems to have been overturned by the Minister of Finance, H.S. Lee. Lee's antipathy towards Beijing stemmed from his pre-war and wartime links to the Guomindang.

[38]   Tomaru Junko, *The Postwar Rapprochement of Malaya and Japan, 1945–61: the Roles of Britain and Japan in South-East Asia* (Basingstoke: Macmillan, 2000), Ch. 6.

[39]   TNA, DO 35/9974, Woodruff to Phillips, 19 May 1960, Enclosure III: Note by McKelvie, 19 May 1960.

Administration in the Far East (ECAFE) in the federal capital would be supported by a trade mission and by additional official delegates 'whose chief objective will be to "push the Japanese co-prosperity line"'.[40] In terms of total value, Japan was now second to Britain as a supplier of imports to the Federation of Malaya. The period of the early-1930s, when the low value of the yen had permitted Japan a growing share of the Malayan industrial goods market, appeared to be repeating itself. Between 1931 and 1933, the UK's share of Malaya's imports of manufactures was maintained at around 20 per cent, but Japan's proportion more than doubled from 6.4 per cent to 13.6 per cent, and even after the imposition of import quotas, Japan still supplied nearly one-fifth of Malaya's textiles in 1938.[41]

The resurrection of Japanese trade with Malaya after the war was a slow process, and it was not fully complete by the end of the 1950s. As late as 1961, Japan's percentage share of the Federation's imports was still outstripped more than two and half times by the UK (see Table 6.2).

Table 6.2   Imports into the Federation of Malaya by Britain and its Principal Industrial Competitors, 1961

	M\$ million	Percentage of total
United Kingdom	503	22.6
Japan	182	8.2
US	112	5.0
Australia	95	4.3
Hong Kong	84	3.7
West Germany	83	3.7

Source: TNA, DO 189/219, 'Britain's Trade with Malaya'. Note by the CRO, c. January 1962.

But, while there was little significant expansion in total Japanese exports to Malaya during the latter half of the 1950s, a qualitative and far-reaching shift in the nature of that trade did occur. Sales of Japanese textiles in Malaya declined as newer industrialising countries in Asia, such as China and India (along with the Federation and Singapore themselves) started to compete. On the other hand, sales of Japanese radios, photographic equipment and consumer durables showed spectacular growth – for example, by 1960, Japan could claim over 70 per cent

---

[40]   TNA, DO 35/9972, L. Bevan to R.C. Wright, Board of Trade, 17 December 1957.

[41]   ANM, BMA (Intelligence) 506/31, 'Memorandum on the Entrepot Trade of Singapore', 25 November 1944, p. 6; Yuen Choy Leng, 'Japanese Penetration of Pre-war Malaya' in K.S. Jomo (ed.), *The Sun Also Sets: Lessons in 'Looking East'* (Kuala Lumpur: INSAN, 1983).

of the pan-Malayan market in battery radios.[42] In January 1958, the leading Malayan daily, the *Straits Times*, hailed an '[i]nflux of Japanese made electrical goods'. This followed the prediction of the Dutch firm, Hagemeyer Trading, that Japan 'would eventually rank among the world's foremost electrical goods manufacturers'. The demand in Malaya for low-priced, high-quality Japanese electricals was so apparent to Hagemeyer's Singapore branch that its managing director secured the local agency for the products of the Osaka-based Matsushita Electric Industrial Company throughout the region.[43] Despite the enduring system of imperial preference, British industry was proving increasingly uncompetitive in the supply of 'high-tech' goods to Southeast Asia.[44] Hence, we can clearly discern the emergence of trends during the 1950s which would culminate in Japan becoming Malaysia's major trading partner by 1965–66.

Concurrently, Japan was beginning to supply private development capital for Malaya's first phase of industrialisation through import substitution. In 1960, the manager of the Maruzen Toyo Oil Company, the Japanese firm establishing an oil refinery in Singapore, prophesised that capital investment rather than the export of goods would prove the major form of Japanese economic penetration of Malaya in the future. In the Federation, Japanese manufacturers had already helped establish companies to build a sugar refinery, refrigeration and processing plants for tuna-fishing, an asbestos plant, a factory manufacturing galvanised iron sheets, and another unit producing toothpaste. More ambitious plans were afoot for a tin-smelter, an oil refinery and a steel plant. Admittedly, the level of Japanese industrial investment in the Federation's pioneer industries was slight when compared with the funds channelled by the alliance of British transnationals and agency houses to defend long-established markets, and eased into Malaya by the continued functioning of the sterling area. Much of the industrial capital raised in the Federation and Singapore also represented the recycling of profits from the

---

[42]   Unless otherwise indicated, the following six paragraphs are primarily based upon TNA, DO 35/9974, copy of H.W. Woodruff, UK Trade Commissioner, Kuala Lumpur to E.L. Phillips, Board of Trade, 19 May 1960 and enclosures.

[43]   *Straits Times*, 17 January 1958.

[44]   Catherine Schenk argues that imperial preference did not necessarily 'feather-bed' British manufactures in the decolonising empire. 'Decolonization and European Economic Integration: the Free Trade Area Negotiations, 1956–8', *Journal of Imperial and Commonwealth History*, 24, 3 (1996). Indeed, in Singapore, British goods enjoyed no preferences and in the Federation less than one-third of British exports by value were covered by Commonwealth trade advantages. The only sector in which there was a clear UK advantage was in the motorcar market where British manufacturers were protected by Commonwealth preferences on the payment of registration tax. The real problem facing Britain in the competitive struggle with Japan was that UK industry had 'earned itself a bad reputation in the Far East and Southeast Asia for haphazard deliveries, lackadaisical salesmanship and an off-hand manner'. TNA, DO 189/359, Sir Stephen Luke, Senior Crown Agent to Sir Alexander Clutterbuck, CRO, 22 December 1960 enclosing note by Luke, 4 May 1960.

British agency houses, direct investments by British-owned industrial companies, and the raising of loans from the local branches of the British exchange banks. Additionally, the majority of funds from the tax-haven territories of the West Indies, plus the White Commonwealth, were likely to have been controlled by British-based multinationals. Hence, British domination of Federation manufacturing was probably far more overbearing than Table 6.3 suggests, and as late as 1969, Japan ranked a mere fifth among foreign countries with investments in Malaysia.[45]

Table 6.3   Sources of Called-up Capital for Pioneer Industries in the Federation of Malaya, 1958 to June 1962

	M$ million	Percentage of total
Singapore	19.6	28.4
United Kingdom	16.0	23.2
Federation of Malaya	13.0	18.9
The Bahamas	5.0	7.3
Hong Kong	4.3	6.2
USA	3.6	5.2
Australia	2.7	3.9
Canada	1.8	2.6
Japan	1.3	1.9
Other	1.7	2.5

Source: E.L. Wheelwright, *Industrialization in Malaysia* (Melbourne: Melbourne University Press, 1965), pp. 47–8.

Yet, the Japanese factories were typically joint ventures with politically well-connected Malayan *towkay* – for example, T.H. Tan, who as Secretary-General of the Alliance and a close personal friend of the Tunku was 'one of the most powerful men in the country'.[46] A branch of the Bank of Tokyo was set up in Kuala

---

[45]   Mehmet Sami Denker, 'The Evolution of Japanese Investment in Malaysia' in K.S. Jomo (ed.), *Japan and Malaysian Development* (London: Routledge, 1994).

[46]   Desmond Tate, *Power Builds the Nation: The National Electricity Board of the States of Malaya and its Predecessors*. Volume II: Transition and Fulfilment (Kuala Lumpur: Tenaga Nasional Berhad, 1991), p. 63. Links between Chinese entrepreneurs and Japanese firms in Malaya were nothing new. As Rajeswary Brown has shown, the vast growth of Malayan Chinese rubber business during the 1930s was due to connections to the *sogo shosha*. See *Capital and Entrepreneurship in South-East Asia* (Basingstoke: Macmillan, 1994), pp. 117–22. Robert Kuok began his phenomenal business expansion in the late-1950s through a joint venture in sugar refining with the leading trading company, Mitsui Bussan Kaisha, and the Nissin Sugar Refining Co. – the latter supplied the 'know how'

Lumpur towards the end of 1959 with the express intention of providing loans for joint Japanese-Malayan ventures. It may be, therefore, that the above figures significantly underplay Japanese participation in Malaya's nascent manufacturing industry. By the end of 1961, interestingly, the UK's Board of Trade regarded new Japanese investment in the peninsula as 'impressive' and already running 'second to ours'.[47] The scene was being set for the explosion of Japanese industrial investment in Malaysia from the 1970s.

After 1955, meanwhile, Malaya became the largest supplier of iron ore to Japan. In 1960, almost all of the 5.5 million tons of iron ore shipped from the peninsula was destined for Japanese steel plants, and the Hongkong and Shanghai Banking Corporation discovered that 'the projected future of the Japanese steel industry was based on a certain amount of ore being brought from Malaya'.[48] Before the Pacific War, the East-coast mines had been developed by Japanese enterprises, and in 1937 the states of Johor, Kelantan and Terengganu produced 2.5 million tons or about half of Japan's iron ore imports.[49] Although the colonial authorities were insistent that Japanese businesses should not be allowed absolute financial or managerial control in the post-war iron industry, many of the Malayan mining companies relied on Japanese capital, equipment and mining technicians, and a leading Japanese industrial and trading concern, Mitsubishi Shobi Kaisha, established a mining department in Singapore to provide prospecting services for the Federation's iron industry.

Additionally, Japanese economic influence expanded into Malaya through the provision of experts and technical aid. In the late-1950s, arrangements were made for two engineers from the Federation's Department of Telecommunications to receive training in Japan. The Japanese also supplied rice-planting experts to mainland Malaya under the provisions of the Colombo Plan.[50] Meanwhile, a Japanese

---

and the former provided the plant. Kuok's father, interestingly, had been active in the rice trade with Mitsubishi during the Japanese Occupation. Although Brown is critical of the intra-Asian trade thesis, she still finds that, in addition to close links with Southeast Asia's political elites, Chinese business success from the 1940s was built on ties with the *sogo shosha*. *Chinese Big Business and the Wealth of Asian Nations* (Basingstoke: Palgrave, 2000), pp. 36–7, 83, 277–8, 284–5. See also Akita and Kagotani, 'International Order', pp. 162–3, as well as the essay by Kagotani in this volume.

[47]   TNA, DO 189/151, Copy of Draft Note for the President by Commercial Relations and Export Department, 17 November 1961.

[48]   *FMSCC Yearbook 1960*, Kuala Lumpur, 1961, President's Address, 14 March 1961, p. 10; HSBC Archive, London, Chief Manager's Private File: Singapore (Personal & S/O OUT.), Jan. 1957–Dec. 1960, enclosure in G.O.W. Stewart, Hong Kong to I.J.O. Cruickshank, Singapore, 1 February 1960.

[49]   Yuen Choy Leng, 'Japanese Rubber and Iron Investments in Malaya, 1900–41', *Journal of Southeast Asian Studies*, 5, 1 (1974), pp. 18–36; *idem.*, 'Japanese Penetration', pp. 222–3.

[50]   Although originally Commonwealth-dominated, Japan was admitted to membership of this scheme for the economic development of South and Southeast Asia in 1954. Tomaru,

industrial advice bureau was established in Kuala Lumpur to offer assistance to Malay entrepreneurs who wished to found industrial ventures in partnership with Japanese investors. On a more populist level, Japan's industrial might was on display at the Kuala Lumpur trade fair of February 1960, and during the autumn of that year an industrial floating fair visited Port Swettenham as well as Singapore.

Indeed, a similar pattern of Japanese economic penetration prevailed in the island colony: the remarkably popular trade fair of 1958 had been preceded by the establishment of an inter-connected cluster of branches of Japanese shipping firms, the *sogo shosha*, banks and insurance companies. In the manufacturing sector, the Bridgestone Tyre Company began operations in October 1956 while a subsidiary of the Onoda Cement Company was registered on the island in June 1958.[51] The trade fairs in Malaya were organised by the government-backed JETRO (the Japan External Trade Organisation), which established an office in Singapore as the successor to the pre-war Commercial Museum.[52]

As with economic ties between China and Malaya, there clearly were continuities between the 1930s and the 1950s in Japan's commercial connections with the Federation and Singapore – not least, because many of the Japanese firms in 1950s Malaya were reincarnations of pre-war businesses. For example, Japan's premier shipping line, Nippon Yusen Kaisha, re-established its services to Singapore in mid-1952; the Bank of Tokyo was the virtual successor to the pre-1945 Yokohama Specie Bank; while, the first Japanese trading company to set up in 1950s Singapore, the Dai-ichi Bussan, was an off-shoot of the reconstructed Mitsui group.[53] Given recent negative memories of the Japanese occupation and lingering 'blood-debt' claims amongst the Malayan Chinese communities, it might seem distinctly odd that Malayans should welcome economic links with Japan during the 1950s. Yet, engagement with the burgeoning Japanese economy proved an important means of stressing an Asian identity as colonialism crumbled. Many of those Malays who held high office in the post-colonial era had received their wartime education in the Japanese *koa kunrenjo* [youth training schools].[54] Even the moderate Malay nationalist politician, Dato Onn Jaafar, reflected after the war:

Postwar Rapprochement, pp. 137–50.

[51]   Shimizu Hiroshi and Hirakawa Hitoshi, *Japan and Singapore in the World Economy: Japan's Economic Advance into Singapore, 1870–1965* (London: Routledge, 1999), pp. 164, 166–77. By 1964, Japanese companies, supported by government loans from Japan, were the leading investors in Singapore's pioneer industries. Wheelwright, *Industrialization*, pp. 59–61.

[52]   W.G. Huff, *The Economic Growth of Singapore: Trade and Development in the Twentieth Century* (Cambridge: Cambridge University Press, 1994), p. 284.

[53]   Nicholas J. White, 'Britain and the Return of Japanese Economic Interests to South East Asia after the Second World War', *South East Asia Research*, 6, 3 (1998), pp. 284–5, 289, 297.

[54]   Akashi Yoji, 'Watanabe Wataru, the Architect of the Malay [sic.] Military Administration, December 1941–March 1943', paper presented to the Second International

'Under the Japanese I learnt that an Asian is just as good as a European. [The Japanese] were brutal, true, but they inspired us with a new idea of what Asia might become'.[55]

The Cambridge-educated Tunku Abdul Rahman remained more at home in London than in Tokyo, but the Federation's Commonwealth-oriented Prime Minister could still see considerable advantages in expanding economic links with Japan. During the Tunku's visit to the Asian Games in Tokyo in June 1958, means of boosting trade with Japan and increasing co-operation in the field of industrial development were discussed. In subsequent press conferences, the Tunku stressed that the economies of Japan and the Federation were complementary. His Minister of Commerce and Industry, Tan Siew Sin, pressed for increased purchases of iron ore, tin and rubber, considered amending GATT restrictions on the import of Japanese manufactured goods, and sought Japanese capital for the development of Malayan industries. The Tunku had two particular pet projects which would involve Japan – the first, to gain assistance in the development of small-scale cottage industries as a means of providing employment for rural Malays and, the second, to establish a large Japanese department store in Kuala Lumpur as a means of bringing down Malaya's cost of living. Notwithstanding the objections of local business leaders who feared exclusion from development opportunities, the Alliance government increasingly wooed Japanese industrial capital. Rather than pan-Asian sentimentality, Federation ministers were here influenced by more hardheaded and immediate concerns: namely, the looming danger of Malayan unemployment amongst a rapidly growing working population (which had doubled since 1947 to reach four million ten years later). With little or no expansion possible in the labour forces of the staple primary industries, the development of factory-based manufacturing offered a solution to the unemployment problem. As Sir Geofroy Tory, Britain's High Commissioner in Kuala Lumpur appreciated in June 1958: 'the Tunku and his Minister of Commerce and Industry appear to be determined to bring industry to Malaya from whatever sources may offer it, and if necessary *without regard to traditional trading patterns*' (my emphasis).[56] Japanese industrial capital was thus assigned a crucial role in stabilising Malayan society and polity. After 1955 in Singapore too, the emergent political

---

Malaysian Studies Conference, University of Malaya, Kuala Lumpur, Malaysia, 2–4 August 1999, p. 13.

[55]   Cited in John Keay, *Last Post: the End of Empire in the Far East* (London: John Murray, 1997), p. 230. In October 1945, Esler Dening, political adviser to Lord Mountbatten, the Supreme Allied Commander in Southeast Asia, appreciated that the Japanese had not been entirely unsuccessful in their occupation of Southeast Asia during the Pacific War: 'what could offer better prospects for the future than a series of embryo States in the Far East opposed in principle to the West yet incapable of self development without the aid of some greater force [which the Japanese would hope ultimately to supply again themselves]'. Cited in Nicholas Tarling, *Britain, Southeast Asia and the Onset of the Cold War, 1945–50* (Cambridge: Cambridge University Press, 1998), pp. 94–5.

[56]   TNA, DO 35/9974, Confidential Despatch to Lord Home, 18 June 1958.

leaders regarded the development of manufacturing industries with Japanese capital as a means of anaesthetising the communist undertow with prosperity.[57]

There also existed a broad degree of British official support for the economic revival of Japan in Southeast Asia.[58] Ignoring howls of protest emanating from British manufacturers in Lancashire and Staffordshire, as well as from the agency houses in Malaya, the UK Commissioner-General's Office in Singapore supported the American Cold War design to build up Japan as a counterweight to Communist China. In this, Southeast Asia's markets for textiles and light industrial goods, in exchange for badly needed raw materials and food supplies, would be critical to Japanese economic survival and prosperity. Japan would atone for the war, not through crippling reparations payments, but through increased trade, capital investment, and technical assistance to Southeast Asia. Moreover, from the early 1950s, British officialdom permitted Japanese trade and capital a key role in making up the Malayan development deficit and thus winning Malaya's domestic Cold War. This was particularly pressing as supplies of capital from the City of London became increasingly scarce. For example, during talks with Prime Minister Kishi in November 1957, Singapore's British Governor, Sir Robert Black, supported Japanese involvement in Singapore's industrialisation as a means of countering communist influence in the region.[59]

Indeed, the desperate desire to encourage economic development to win Malayan 'hearts and minds', and so aid the political management of decolonisation, came to over-ride the strict enforcement of sterling-area rules. In the re-development of the peninsula's iron mines, the Treasury disliked Japan's 'objectionable' barter deals and bilateral trading methods. Pahang's deposits, for example, were to be exploited by the Eastern Mining and Metals Company (EMMCO) via indirect payments for Japanese steel supplies in the form of deductions from the proceeds of the ore sales to Japan. For the protection of metropolitan interests, the Treasury, and the Board of Trade, would have preferred to see sterling-area equipment and finance more fully utilised.[60] But, the views of the Federation's assertive expatriate Member for Economics, Oscar Spencer, won the argument:

[T]he over-riding requirement is the rapid development of Malaya on a sound economic basis; providing this is achieved we consider we must be prepared to compromise, if necessary, by accepting foreign plant and machinery to a greater extent than we would really like ... We recognise of course that there is a foreign

57   Shimizu and Hirakawa, *Japan and Singapore*, p. 161.
58   White, 'Japanese Economic Interests'.
59   Shimizu and Hirakawa, *Japan and Singapore*, p. 161.
60   TNA, CO 1030/184, Dalton, Treasury to MacKintosh, Colonial Office (CO), July 1954; Dalton to Harding, CO, 3 September 1954; telegram from Colonial Secretary to Kuala Lumpur, 13 September 1954.

exchange aspect to be considered, and that it is an important one ... [B]ut this objective should be secondary to the really important issue of development.[61]

As the Bank of England finally conceded in the summer of 1954:

> If the company [EMMCO] is convinced that the proposed scheme is necessary and it of advantage, particularly from the point of view of securing a footing on the Japanese market ... the Federation Government ... could hardly be expected to hold things up simply out of our dislike of Japanese bilateral trading methods.[62]

Besides the dash for development, it was also appreciated in both London and in Malaya that there was a complementarity between the recovery of Japan and the prosperity of the sterling area.[63] As Yokoi has argued, in the negotiation of the various Sterling Payments Agreements with Japan from 1951–57, London-based policy-makers appreciated 'Japan's potential role for stimulating intra-Asian trade as the regional "workshop", and in the process, revitalising sterling as the trading currency of choice' throughout Eastern Asia.[64] Moreover, at the end of 1953, the UK Treasury argued for a general liberalisation of Japanese trade with the colonial empire to boost sterling-area dollar receipts. After all, the sterling area, *not* the dollar area, had proved Japan's main international market before the Pacific War, and the Treasury and the Board of Trade both hoped that Japan could be persuaded to use its dollar resources for increased purchases from the colonies.[65] Indeed, as Japanese domestic industry began exceeding pre-war levels of production, and Malaya's exports to the US declined, Japan emerged as a major consumer of Malayan commodities. By 1958, for example, Japan was the second most important destination for the peninsula's tin, and the 'overwhelming proportion' of tin supplies for Japanese industry now came from Malaya.[66] Japanese factories increased their

---

[61]   Letter to CO, 26 June 1953 cited in Tomaru, *Post-war Rapprochement*, p. 108.

[62]   TNA, CO 1030/184, Copy of Ryan, Bank of England to Dalton, Treasury, 31 August 1954.

[63]   Again, there is a parallel with the 1930s. See Akita and Kagotani, 'International Order', pp. 147–8.

[64]   Noriko Yokoi, *Japan's Postwar Economic Recovery and Anglo-Japanese Relations, 1948–62* (London: Routledge, Curzon, 2003), pp. 3–4.

[65]   TNA, CAB 134/846, EA 31 (53) 1 reproduced in David Goldsworthy (ed.) *The Conservative government and the end of empire, 1951–1957*, Part III (London: HMSO, 1994), doc. 377, pp. 69–72.

[66]   See BT 258/739, Copy of telegram from British Embassy, Tokyo to Foreign Office, 7 October 1958. Hence, Malayan mining entrepreneurs – both British and local Chinese – set great store on Japan joining the UN's International Tin Agreement (ITA) as a consumer member, especially as a possible switch to unregulated Russian tin supplies by the Japanese steel companies threatened a collapse of Straits tin prices. See also *Financial Times*, 12 September 1958. Japan finally signed up to the ITA in 1961.

consumption of rubber (both natural and synthetic) by nearly six times between 1950 and 1962 to reach 294,000 tons, and, despite an expanding synthetic capacity in Japan, 57 per cent of this rubber was derived from Malayan plantations.[67] In Kuala Lumpur, Oscar Spencer shrewdly observed in the summer of 1953 that to deny the Japanese supplies of iron ore from Malaya, 'would lay us open to a charge of discrimination; this in turn would stop us from pressing the Japanese to accord more favourable treatment to our own rubber and tin exports'.[68]

Hong Kong

The relatively 'open' nature of the sterling-area system in Asia can be further illustrated through an examination of the economic relations between Malaya and Hong Kong during the 1950s. The Malayan territories were permitted to take advantage of the so-called 'Hong Kong gap' whereby, combined with the normal colonial dollar programme procedure, the Federation and Singapore benefited from special arrangements for the import of dollar goods through Hong Kong's free market (albeit incurring a 5–6 per cent commission). Because of the opportunities for abuse – outlined in the next section – the guardians of sterling in Threadneedle Street were far from happy about Singapore's import of hard currency goods via Hong Kong. The Treasury in London, meanwhile, regarded the intra-Asian dollar trade as difficult to defend in the IMF and discriminatory within the sterling area since other colonies and dominions were not permitted purchasing rights in Hong Kong. Yet, as with the issue of Malayan iron-ore development by Japan, the Colonial Office argued successfully in favour of local interests: the colonial administration believed that the Hong Kong dollar trade was vital to Singapore's intra-Southeast Asian trade – particularly since North American goods could be bartered for Indonesian rubber which was subsequently processed and sold on by Singapore Chinese merchants for US dollars.[69] It was also pointed out that Malaya's need of anti-inflationary goods was met partly from the Hong Kong

---

[67] Guildhall Library, London, Rubber Growers' Association Council Minutes, Ms. 24863/72, 7 October 1963, 'Report on Visit Overseas, 6 April–15 June 1963 by Leslie Bateman [Controller of Rubber Research, Federation of Malaya]'.

[68] Cited in White, 'Japanese Economic Interests', p. 296. A growing awareness of the need to appease Japan economically to ensure the prosperity of the sterling area was another factor in permitting the re-establishment of Japanese commercial banks in Malaya from the mid-1950s. Ibid., p. 298.

[69] Indeed, Singapore was not an exclusively Malayan port. Indonesian trade, both legal and illegal, was probably more significant than pan-Malayan trade for the British entrepot during the 1950s. See, Huff, *Economic Growth*, pp. 279–81. Indonesia's contribution to Singapore's position as the world's largest rubber market was acknowledged through an inter-governmental agreement whereby Jakarta received US dollars for rubber sent to the British port. This is another example of the flexible, open nature of the sterling-area system in Southeast Asia.

trade and if this was stopped an even more substantial increase than that already allowed in Malaya's dollar ceiling would be required. Hence, in 1951, it was agreed within Whitehall that Malayan purchases through Hong Kong should be allowed to continue (although subject to certain 'safeguards'). Attempts were made to draw attention to sterling-area sources of supply, particularly from the UK, to lessen the attraction of this trade to Malayan importers.[70] But, the practice remained widespread to the late-1950s, and this concession in the dollar trade proved an important factor in official tolerance of the sterling area in the post-colonial Federation. As Minister of Commerce and Industry Tan pointed out in the Malayan legislature at the end of 1957, the independent Federation would remain in the sterling area for the foreseeable future and an immediate increase in direct imports of dollar consumer goods was unlikely since that market was already well supplied indirectly through Hong Kong.[71]

Strictly speaking, the Hong Kong-Malaya trade in US and Canadian goods was intra-Pacific rather than intra-Asian. Yet, these exchanges were fuelling the intra-Asian economy, not least through consolidating links between Hong Kong Chinese and Malayan Chinese merchants. Indeed, on top of supplying dollar goods, Hong Kong proved a significant supplier of capital for Malaya's import-substitution industrialisation in the late-1950s and early-1960s – with 6 per cent of the capital share, Hong Kong was the fifth largest industrial investor in the Federation (see Table 6.3). Here, links between Hong Kong and Malayan Chinese entrepreneurs were crucial in the development of the Federation's textile production. The M$2 million weaving and dyeing mill at Scudai, Johor started operations during 1958 with a production capacity of 15 million yards of cloth per annum for the domestic market. The Singapore industrialist, David Lee, with capital and technicians from Britain's East Asian colony, promoted this pioneer industry.[72] Moreover, in the aftermath of the official ending of direct trade with Communist China in the later 1950s, it was through overseas Chinese commercial networks that Chinese products continued to find their way into Malaya via Hong Kong.[73]

---

[70] BoE, OV 44/79, Note by Payton for O'Brien, 15 May 1951.

[71] Reported in TNA, DO 35/9972, Bevan, British High Commission, Kuala Lumpur to Wright, Board of Trade, 17 December 1957. Indeed, once the removal of virtually all restrictions on the importation of US goods eventuated at the end of the decade, British merchants in Singapore did not anticipate a surge of American exports since 'For several years … anything of US origin capable of finding a market in this area was being imported by exploitation of the Hong Kong open-market facility'. Since 1956 this added not more than 1/40th to landed costs and 'Few things are so marginal that a surcharge of 2.5 per cent will totally exclude them from our markets'. IA, Ms. 27298, W.K. Young, BCL deputy general manager, Singapore to K.H. Simpson, managing director, London, 26 July 1960.

[72] *Straits Times*, 2 January 1958.

[73] Nie, 'China and Malaya', pp. 103, 109.

Malaya and the Intra-Asian Economy: the 'Unofficial Market'

In addition to the tolerance, and indeed encouragement, of a degree of regulated intra-Asian trade and investment, British officials in Singapore, Kuala Lumpur and Penang encountered great difficulty in imposing sterling-area dictates upon Malaya's commercial community. There was massive evasion of controls and wide-scale smuggling which produced an intra-Asian 'black market'. This was part of a long tradition of Southeast Asian 'passive resistance' to European economic designs in the region. There existed, for example, a huge illegal barter trade between the Netherlands East Indies and British-controlled Singapore during the inter-war years, as well as the Japanese occupation, while smuggling back and forth across the Straits of Melaka by ethnic Chinese entrepreneurs proved crucial in the financing of the Indonesian revolution after 1945.[74] Smuggling across the Thai border, meanwhile, and also between the peninsula and the archipelago, had seriously undermined the rubber restriction schemes of the 1920s and 1930s.[75] The British Military Administration of post-war Malaya became known as the 'Black Market Association', illustrating what Harper has called 'the resilience of local economic life to attempts by the state to control it'.[76] Meanwhile, rubber was illegally shipped over the Thai border to take advantage of Bangkok's free exchange market. This trade proved so large that it contributed to the decline of hard currency earnings from Malayan rubber during the first nine months of 1949, culminating in the sterling crisis and devaluation of that year.[77]

W.J. Jackson of the Overseas and Foreign Office of the Bank of England paid an unofficial visit to the Federation and Singapore in February and March 1951. Although laced with colonial racism and stereotypical views of ethnic Chinese business practice, Jackson's reports for his seniors in London provide a fascinating first-hand account of the 'large seamy side' to Malaya's economy. '[T]he whole area appears riddled with graft, vice, rackets of all kinds, smuggling and so on', reported Threadneedle Street's envoy in June 1951.[78] Perhaps recalling wartime Britain, Jackson declared that 'controls breed rackets'. Official command over the

---

[74]   Twang Peck Yang, *The Chinese Business Elite and the Transition to Independence in Indonesia, 1940–50* (Kuala Lumpur: Oxford University Press, 1998).

[75]   D.J.M. Tate, *The RGA History of the Plantation Industry in the Malay Peninsula* (Kuala Lumpur: Oxford University Press, 1996), pp. 357–8, 379; Derek Mackay, *Eastern Customs: The Customs Service in British Malaya and the Opium Trade* (London: The Radcliffe Press, 2005), p. 36.

[76]   Harper, *Making of Malaya*, p. 43.

[77]   TNA, BT 64/4000, 'Draft Note on Rubber for Inclusion in the Report of the Working Party on Raw Material Prices by A.E. Lee, 4 August 1949'; see also Mackay, *Eastern Customs*, pp. 89–92.

[78]   BoE, OV 44/79, 'Note for O'Brien, 28 June 1951'. Unless otherwise indicated, the following paragraphs are largely based upon this extensive note as well as Jackson's letter of 20 April 1951 to O'Brien.

movement of currency notes was illusory: there was a street in Singapore known locally as 'Change Alley' where 'every currency under the sun can be obtained without difficulty'. Travellers to Bangkok smuggled Malayan notes out, and in the Thai capital they were bought by Thai traffickers and subsequently smuggled back into Malaya. There was additionally widespread trafficking and commodity deals in notes between Malaya, Thailand and Indonesia and within Malaya itself. Indeed, the banking habit was tending to decline since physical currency provided a useful means of evading the income taxes in the Federation and Singapore (first introduced in 1948).

Moreover, Jackson discovered that it was 'common knowledge' that Malayan Chinese merchants were 'salting away funds' in the US. A widespread practice was to under-invoice rubber – that is, to export top-quality rubber (Grade 1) as the low-quality commodity (Grade 4). Singapore was a busy free port and examination by customs officials could not be relied upon. As long as the weight of the rubber agreed with the declaration made by the exporter no further examination of the bales was ordinarily undertaken. The agent in New York made payment for Grade 1, but the exporter in due course would only surrender the dollar proceeds of Grade 4.

Singapore's Exchange Controller, Eric Himsworth, discovered that this rubber 'racket' further fuelled intra-Asian trade, particularly between Hong Kong and Singapore. The Singapore Chinese owners of the non-surrendered US dollars profited by selling them in Hong Kong for local currency. These Hong Kong dollars were either used by the Singapore Chinese rubber exporters themselves or sold to importers who were subsequently able to buy US goods under licence from Britain's East Asian entrepot. From the perspective of the Bank of England, therefore, the Hong Kong free market was being severely misused and represented a major loss of dollars for the hard-currency pool. But, worse still, Jackson found that offers of American goods – ranging from cars to cameras – against payment in sterling were then being sold on from Singapore to other parts of the sterling area, and as far away as Southern Rhodesia. This practice prevailed despite the supposed condition of 1950 that Singapore's purchases through the Hong Kong free market would be tolerated only so long as goods imported under this arrangement were not subsequently offered to other sterling area territories. The argument of Andrew Gilmour, Singapore's Economic Secretary, that the Hong Kong trade was an essential anti-inflationary device, as well as an inducement to Indonesia and Thailand for rubber, was seriously flawed in the Bank of England's view.

In all this, Jackson was particularly mistrustful of the rubber multi-millionaire, Lee Kong Chian, who, with a network of agents and branches throughout East and Southeast Asia, had many opportunities 'to get up to his tricks'. In the imaginings of British officialdom, Lee's suspected links with the Malayan communists provided a political edge to his allegedly illicit commercial activities. Furthermore, one intra-Asian trade, which was almost completely beyond sterling-area control, was 'Yunnan' opium which, in the 1950s, reached the local Chinese dealers at Singapore's Boat Quay by sea, land and air principally from Communist China, but also from Laos, Burma and Thailand.[79] Narcotics trafficking proved so rife and so unmanageable that some Europeans in Malaya felt that the government should legalise the trade as a lucrative source of revenue. Indeed, one former expatriate customs officer has confessed that, 'The abrupt imposition of a total ban on the drug [that is opium, in 1946] provided the traffickers with a dazzling opportunity to replace the government as suppliers to a large and long-established market'. There were probably about 85,000 regular opium smokers in the Federation of Malaya alone in the mid-1950s, consuming in total at least half a ton of *chandu* (opium prepared for smoking) per day.[80] Overseas Chinese networks also facilitated the clandestine trade in gold, another illegal set of intra-Asian transactions stimulated by a desire to avoid exchange controls. After 1952, Singapore became the major market for gold smuggled from Hong Kong. As with opium, the Bank of England discovered that Singapore acted as the redistribution centre for gold up-country to the Federation, and indeed for the whole of Southeast Asia.[81]

For all these reasons, Jackson was wholly opposed to the suggestions that Malaya should have an entirely free hand in US dollar spending because 'the area would become a sink'. It is impossible, of course, to calculate the importance of the illicit, non-sterling trades for Malaya during the 1950s, but their prevalence and economic importance cannot be doubted. As an indication, Huff has noted that the illegal barter trade between Singapore and Indonesia was 'larger than the legal', that it fed off Indonesian controls, and that it contributed significantly to the economic growth of the British port:

> ... Indonesian traders could obtain more manufactured goods if rubber and produce were bartered in Singapore than marketed legally, and could sell these manufactures at a large profit in Indonesia. Thus, Indonesian regulation set up a 'virtuous' circle for both the Singapore economy and Indonesians in contact with the port: high 1950s world rubber prices stimulated Outer Province smallholder

---

[79] As Iranian supplies of opium declined, the 'Yunnan' zone became Malaya's principal source of the drug, accounting for just less than one-quarter of the customs service's seizures in 1954 but over two-thirds of official hauls three years later. Mackay, *Eastern Customs*, p. 156. It was claimed by the Nationalist Chinese regime in Taipei that the communist guerrillas controlled Malaya's opium trade. Yet, as British officials discovered, the dealers in Singapore, if they were politically affiliated, tended to support the Guomindang. Singapore National Archives, MF 096 (Chief Secretary's Office 972/53), Telegram from CO to Singapore, 3 March 1953 and reply of 12 March.

[80] Mackay, *Eastern Customs*, p. 152.

[81] Catherine R. Schenk, 'The Hong Kong Gold Market and the Southeast Asian Gold Trade in the 1950s', *Modern Asian Studies*, 29, 2 (1995), pp. 387–402; Mackay, *Eastern Customs*, p. 212. It should be stressed, however, that in the evasion of sterling-area controls to profit from intra-Asian trade, Europeans were not beyond reproach. In 1951, a major Danish trading house was under suspicion regarding the shipment of rice from Thailand to Singapore. There were also doubts about how the British exchange controllers obtained their whisky and cigars.

production; Singapore Chinese traders provided the means for Indonesians to realize these prices; and Singapore's trade in rubber and the shipment of manufactures expanded accordingly, with further important benefits for the island's remilling industry ...[82]

Conclusion

This chapter has stressed the enduring value of Malaya for the sterling area throughout the 1950s. The desire to maintain Malaya's dollar earnings and manage its sterling balances was clearly a central, though not exclusive, tenet of Britain's controlled decolonisation strategy for maritime Southeast Asia. Even so, the liberalisation of the sterling area after 1955, combined with Malayan political devolution, produced a number of significant changes in the functioning of the imperial economic system in the region. At the same time, the examples of Japanese participation in the Federation's iron-ore industry and the Malayan dollar trade via Hong Kong, illustrate that the Colonial Office and the colonial administrations in Malaya were able to temper the more hard-line, sterling-minded tendencies of the Bank of England and the Treasury.

Perhaps, therefore, a more important, longer-term continuity in Malaya's international economic history, linking the 1930s to the 1950s and beyond, was the existence of the sterling area alongside large and burgeoning intra-Asian trade and investment flows. Some of these economic exchanges and practices, such as opium trafficking and the under-invoicing of rubber, were unregulated and defied imperial controls, and they point both to the limits of British economic imperialism in Southeast Asia during the 1950s and to the inherent flexibility of the Asian commercial community, particularly in Singapore. As such, a considerable volume of intra-Asian trade is hidden from the official statistics. Threadneedle Street's W.J. Jackson sardonically concluded in 1951 that, 'a huge dollar surplus covers a multitude of sins'.[83] We can, however, be more certain of Malaya's re-engagement with, and growing incorporation into, the regulated Asia-Pacific economy. Returning from a visit to Malaya at the end of 1957, it was already obvious to

---

[82] Huff, *Economic Growth*, pp. 280–81. A lucrative smuggling business along the West coast of Johor proved to be Sumatran tobacco leaf because until 1956 'locally grown' tobacco carried no excise duty in the Federation. Moreover, European goods, such as liquors and cigarettes, were frequently re-exported to Riau and Sumatra from Singapore and Penang without incurring duty, and subsequently within a couple of days these luxury items were 'run back'. Mackay, *Eastern Customs*, pp. 180–81, 201, 206. The smuggling trade with Singapore was further stimulated during the Sumatra rebellion of 1957–58. See J.A.C. Mackie, *Konfrontasi: the Indonesia–Malaysia Dispute, 1963–1966* (Kuala Lumpur: Oxford University Press, 1974), p. 30.

[83] BoE, OV 44/79, Copy of Jackson to O'Brien, 20 April 1951, p. 2.

the Liverpool shipping baron, Sir John Nicholson, that 'European exports to Asia must be supplanted to an increasing extent by Japan and later China'.[84]

---

[84] Merseyside Maritime Museum, Liverpool, Ocean Transport and Trading Plc Archives, 2107, handwritten letter to Sir John Hobhouse, 20 November 1957. Nicholson had just become the senior executive in the largest British Far Eastern shipping line, the Ocean Steamship Company or Blue Funnel/Alfred Holt group. He would later become a member of the Shipping Advisory Panel which met monthly from July 1962 with ministers and officials in the Ministry of Transport, concerned with the erosion of the UK's world shipping share.

PART 2
The International Order of Asia and Asian Regional Economies

Chapter 7

Japan's Commercial Penetration of South and Southeast Asia and the Cotton Trade Negotiations in the 1930s: Maintaining Relations between Japan, British India and the Dutch East Indies

Naoto Kagotani

Introduction: Was Japan isolated from the world economy in the 1930s?

The purpose of this chapter is to analyse Anglo-Japanese relations during the 1930s, focusing on the problem of international rivalry between the cotton industries of Britain and Japan in the Asian market. The major trade friction between Britain and Japan was over cotton textile markets as a result of bitter commercial rivalry between the Lancashire and Osaka cotton industries. The nature of Anglo-Japanese relations in the 1930s is closely linked to the historical assessment of the course of Japanese expansion, both politically and economically.

In Japanese political historiography, many studies aim to show a basic continuity from the Manchurian Incident of 1931 through the second Sino-Japanese War, which started in 1937, to Pearl Harbor in 1941. Historical studies of Japan's foreign policy have tried to trace these processes as the inevitable road to Anglo-Japanese confrontation. As an outline of Japanese imperialism, these explanations hold good. But the emphasis on the continuity of Japanese imperialism during 15 years, from 1931 to 1945, tends to ignore the economic aspects, and the fact that there could have been alternative courses in the first half of the 1930s. Such alternative courses might have reduced antagonisms between some of the imperialist states (even if this possibility was very small).

Anglo-Japanese relations in the 1930s, especially the commercial aspect, are likely to give us a valuable case for inquiring into the possibilities of alternative courses. In the first half of the 1930s, Japan was able to take advantage of its proximity to South and Southeast Asian markets, including those in the British and Dutch colonies, to compete successfully with European goods. The main factor behind the increase in exports of Japanese cotton textiles was their low price, which had come about through the rationalization of the Japanese cotton industry from the mid-1920s and the drastic devaluation of the Japanese exchange rate in

1932.[1] As a result of the rationalization movement, which was stimulated by the Japanese government's policy of deflation to return to the gold standard in 1929, the process of concentration was intensified, especially in the spinning mills, and capital productivity increased. In the early-1930s, rings were replaced almost entirely by high draft rings.

After abandoning the gold standard in December 1931 and devaluing the yen, Japan decided to link its currency to sterling in 1932. Although it continued its efforts to expand the 'yen bloc' on the Asian continent, the majority of Japanese trade in the first half of the 1930s was conducted with countries outside this yen bloc.[2] The fact that the yen was linked to sterling at a heavily devalued rate, enabled Japan to shift its exports from East to South and Southeast Asia. The fact that the Indian rupee was obliged to link to sterling at a high level, at 1s 6d from 1925 to 1947, while the Dutch East Indies' florin remained linked to the Dutch guilder, and, hence, to the French-led 'gold bloc' until mid-1936, also supported the increase in exports of Japanese goods to these European colonies. On the other hand, in the industrial aspect, the fact that after sterling's departure from gold and prior to the yen's devaluation, the Japanese cotton mills had bought up vast quantities of raw cotton at the old currency rate, and these raw materials were utilized cheaply, was to prove one of Japan's major assets in the promotion of its exports in the early-1930s.[3]

The increase in exports of Japanese textiles became a central source of conflict in both Anglo- and Dutch-Japanese commercial relations, and prompted Japan to hold trade negotiations with the government of India in 1933, and with the government of the Dutch East Indies in 1934, both under the *de facto* control of their 'home' countries.[4] In the existing Japanese historiography, most scholars see these trade negotiations as part of the process of 'ironing out' the differences in industrial interests between the European and Japanese cotton industry.[5] Thus, they

---

[1]   Kaoru Sugihara, 'Japan's Industrial Recovery, 1931–1936' in Ian Brown (ed.), *The Economies of Africa and Asia during the Interwar Depression* (Routledge, London, 1989); Alex J. Robertson 'Lancashire and the Rise of Japan', in Mary B. Rose (ed.), *International Competition and Strategic Response in the Textile Industries since 1890* (Frank Cass, London, 1991).

[2]   Kaoru Sugihara, 'Intra-Asian Trade and East Asia's Industrialization, 1919–1939', in Gareth Austin (ed.), *Industrial Growth in the Third World, c. 1870–c. 1990: Depressions, Intra-regional Trade, and Ethnic Networks*, LSE Working Papers in Economic History, 44/98, London School of Economics and Political Science, London, 1998.

[3]   Naoto Kagotani, *Ajia Kokusai Tsusho Chitujyo to Kindai Nihon* [*The Asian International Trading Order and Modern Japan*] (Nagoya Daigaku Shuppankai: Nagoya, 2000), Ch. 6.

[4]   Osamu Ishii, 'Rivalries over Cotton Goods Markets, 1930–36', in Ian Nish and Yoichi Kibata (eds), *The History of Anglo-Japanese Relations, 1600–2000, Vol. 2: The Political-Diplomatic Dimension, 1931–2000* (Macmillan, London, 2000).

[5]   Osamu Ishii, *Cotton-textile diplomacy: Japan, Great Britain and the United States, 1930–1936* (Ann Arbor, Mich., 1977).

emphasize that each country's diplomatic policies toward the trade negotiations were formulated to serve the interests of each country's cotton textile industry, that is, to secure markets abroad. Some have even suggested that the Asian-Pacific War was brought about partly by the tendency of the Japanese cotton industry to expand rapidly into Asian markets, most of which were under European political control in the 1930s.[6] These authors claim that the increase in exports of Japanese cotton textiles in the first half of the 1930s to the European colonies in Asia made the European powers intensify their protectionist policies, thus isolating Japan from the world economy. The common understanding is that Japan's isolation was intensified after the Dutch–Japanese trade negotiations, which were suspended in December 1934. Japanese historiography has further supposed that the negotiations with the European colonial governments 'were broken off',[7] and that Japan abandoned its co-operation with industrial Europe. This body of scholarship concludes that Japan's diplomatic policy toward Europe in the 1930s was formulated to serve the interests of its cotton textile industry, and by the middle of the decade did not maintain the *status quo*. For Japanese historians, this has entailed a focus on Japan's aggressive policy to secure raw materials and export markets in China after 1937. In other words, Japanese historians argue that Japan's economic isolation from the world economy in the first half of the 1930s turned into political aggression in China after 1937.

It is argued that the European nations blocked Japanese goods to protect their respective home textile industries. The Europeans did this by setting up 'tariff barriers' and 'quota systems' in those trade negotiations. In other words, 'bloc' economies were created to preserve markets for the home textile industries by giving preference to goods produced within the European empires. But, if we look at the figures from *The Cotton Statistics' Yearbooks*, edited by the Japan Cotton Spinners' Association (JCSA) in Osaka, this argument does not hold. That is, the trade statistics do not correspond with the notion that Japan was forced into isolation from the world economy. The quantity of Japanese cotton textile exports to British India was 478 million yards in 1936, compared with 357 million yards in 1928. In the case of the Dutch East Indies, Japanese cotton textile exports amounted to 350 million yards in 1936, compared with 172 million yards in 1928.[8] These statistics alone show that Japanese cotton exports were maintained at the same level, even after the two rounds of trade negotiations.

---

[6]   Hiroshi Nishikawa, *Nihon Teikoku Shugi to Mengyo* [*Japanese Imperialism and the Cotton Industry*] (Mineruva shobo, 1987).

[7]   Ishii, *Cotton-textile diplomacy*. See also Shinya Sugiyama, 'The Expansion of Japan's Cotton Textile Exports into South-East Asia' in Shinya Sugiyama and Ian Brown (eds), *International Rivalry in South-East in the Interwar Period* (Yale University Press, 1995).

[8]   JCSA (ed.), *Statistics of the Cotton Trade, 1919–1936*. These statistics are held in the JCSA library, Osaka.

European Financial Interests and Japan's Trade Penetration into the European Colonies

The idea of 'gentlemanly capitalism' put forward by P.J. Cain and A.G. Hopkins offers an alternative interpretation regarding the motivation behind British policy in Asia.[9] Not only were the colonies expected to serve as markets for European goods, but they also had to pay interest on government loans, dividends on investments, and the 'political costs' of the home government. The political costs were, for example, the 'Home Charges' for British India, and pension payments for the Netherlands East Indies. British India was not only the largest single market for British goods, but the subcontinent was also a large debtor. This argument is based on the notion that the main concern of the British authorities after World War I was to restore the flow of overseas investment and re-establish London's position as the world's leading financial services centre. If this is the case, this perspective implies that the concerns of the City of London as the centre of finance were of greater significance to the prosperity of Britain than the interests of Manchester, Birmingham or Glasgow, and that the City of London had an enormous influence on overseas and domestic policy. The economic relations between Britain and its empire, say Cain and Hopkins, were viewed from this financial perspective. Thus, the interests of the manufacturing sector were sometimes sacrificed for the sake of financial considerations.

Figure 7.1 shows that three types of economic policy were needed to enable the British colonies to pay such interest, dividends, and political costs to the metropole on a regular basis. The first policy required that the colonial government should balance its own budget in order to assist the public credibility of sterling. In the case of British India, the government's revenues declined from Rs 1,584 million in 1929–30 to Rs 1,389 million in 1930–31; customs receipts dropped from Rs 513 million in 1929–30 to Rs 468 million in 1930–31. The government required a substantial additional source of revenue to avoid confidence in the rupee sliding. In order to balance the budget, the government of India tried to raise the duties on cotton in the early 1930s.[10] The increase in import duties not only protected the Indian industry, but also maintained confidence in the rupee by balancing the budget. It was clear to the government of India that Japanese goods were much more dutiable than Lancashire goods in the 1930s.

And, it was also a problem for the Dutch East Indies that an extraordinary decline in revenues had occurred since 1929; not least, because a great deal of the colonial government's expenditure was fixed in character, such as in pensions both in Holland and its colonies.[11] It was a serious problem for The Netherlands that

---

[9]   P.J. Cain and A.G. Hopkins, *British Imperialism, 1688–2000* (Second Edition, Longman: London, 2001), Chs 20, 23 and 25.

[10]   Basudev Chatterji, *Trade, Tariffs and Empire: Lancashire and British Policy in India 1919–1939* (Oxford University Press, 1992), Ch. 7.

[11]   Treasury to Cobbold (Bank of England), 5 February 1934, The National Archives, Kew, London (formerly Public Record Office, hereafter TNA), FO 371/18567, w 1491.

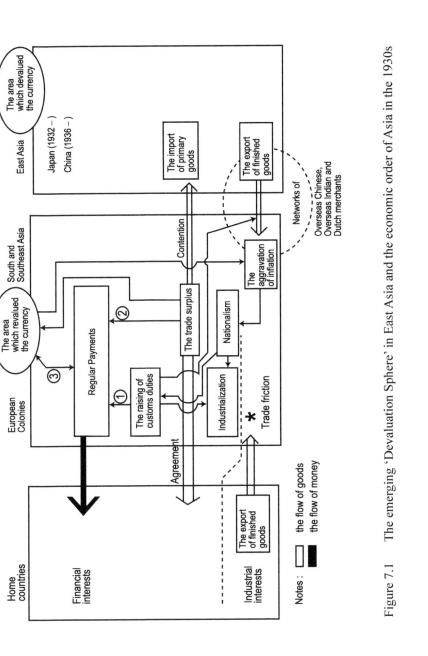

Figure 7.1   The emerging 'Devaluation Sphere' in East Asia and the economic order of Asia in the 1930s

Dutch capital invested in the Dutch East Indies could bring in little or no return after the Great Depression.

The second policy on the part of both the British and the Dutch was to maintain an export surplus in the balance of payments of the colonies, which was necessary for payment of their debts to Europe. British India's ability to service its debts had been severely affected by the collapse of its export trade after the Great Depression. Hence, the colonies were encouraged to promote exports of primary products, such as raw cotton, to the industrial countries.[12] But, exports from the colonies faced a difficult situation, because, as described later, the colonial territories were obliged to maintain relatively high exchange rates.[13] In British India, the level of the rupee was fixed at 1s 6d against sterling from 1925 onwards, while Indian industrialists attempted to decrease the level to 1s 4d in the hope of stimulating their exports. Therefore, the metropolitan country had to encourage an increase in colonial exports through political and largely artificial arrangements. This is why Britain was prepared to open its home market to the Dominions and colonies through the Ottawa Agreements in the 1930s. In the Great Depression, the Dominions and the colonies suffered such a reduction in income from the export of primary goods that Britain had to expand empire-Commonwealth incomes by offering to buy more products from the colonies and Dominions, for which Britain had a large demand. In return, Britain required tariff preference for its industrial goods. In actual fact, 'preferential arrangements' in the Ottawa Agreements led to a far more rapid rise in colonial imports into Britain than British exports to the colonies.[14] Without securing a significant slice of the British market, the Dominions and the colonies could not have re-paid their debts to Britain.

But those goods for which Britain had only limited demand required other foreign markets, and a search for alternative export markets was encouraged by the diplomatic policies of the 1930s. In particular, the government of India expected to increase exports of raw cotton to Japan. The Indo-Japanese negotiations were completed in early January 1934. The agreement was on a barter basis. Japan was allowed to export 400 million yards of cotton textiles to India, provided that it imported 1.5 million bales of Indian raw cotton in return. This implied that the Japanese market was also necessary for British India in order to secure an export surplus from the point of view of maintaining the stability of the rupee at 1s 6d and, hence, London's financial position.[15]

It is believed that these types of relationship also existed between Holland and its colonies. The Dutch East Indies was encouraged to increase exports of primary products to the industrial countries, especially to Germany, the United States and Japan. The latter was a particularly attractive market, both geographically and economically,

---

[12]   Kagotani, *Ajia Kokusai Tsusho Chitujyo to Kindai Nihon*, Ch. 5.

[13]   Dietmar Rothermund, *India in the Great Depression, 1929–1939* (Manohar, New Delhi, 1992), Ch. 2.

[14]   Ragnar Nurkse, *International Currency Experience: Lessons of the Inter-War Period* (Geneva, 1944), Ch. 3.

[15]   Kagotani (2000), *Ajia Kokusai Tsusho Chitujyo to Kindai Nihon*, Chs 6–7.

because its recovery from the Great Depression was very rapid after the second half of 1932, thanks to the 'reflationary policy' of Finance Minister Korekiyo Takahashi.[16]

The third policy on the part of the Europeans was, as mentioned above, to require the colonies in Asia to establish relatively high rates of exchange, since exchange rate fluctuations were not desirable from the point of view of regular debt payments. The stabilisation of the rupee at 1s 6d suited British financial interests. The economic experts in British India insisted that 'the budget be balanced, that the 1s 6d exchange rate be maintained and that [there] be no difficulties in transferring money to London'.[17] Additionally, British industrialists and exporters had an interest in the maintenance of India's exchange rate at 1s 6d. During the interwar period, the British government continued to discourage India's industrialisation by keeping the value of the rupee consistently high.

On the other hand, this relatively high exchange rate aggravated deflation in British colonies and subsequently stimulated Indian anti-colonial nationalism.[18] This deflationary situation induced very strong criticism of import restrictions and of the currency system, forced upon India by the metropolitan power. Because the purchasing power of consumers in the colonies was weakened in the 1930s, it was necessary for the colonies to import cheap Japanese goods.

While South and Southeast Asian territories set their exchange rates relatively high, East Asian countries devalued their currencies and linked to sterling at a heavily devalued rate – for example, Japan after 1932 and China after 1935.[19] This meant that East Asia formed a 'devaluation sphere' against South and Southeast Asia. Moreover, it is important to note, that it was Chinese merchants,[20] and particularly in the 1930s Indian merchants as well,[21] who took advantage of this 'devaluation sphere' by promoting the export of Japanese goods to South and Southeast Asia.

---

[16]   Jyuro Hashimoto, *Dai kyoko ka no Nihon Shihonn-shugi* [*Japanese Capitalism under the Great Depression*] (Tokyo, Daigaku Shuppankai, 1984), Ch. 3.

[17]   Basudev Chatterji, *Trade, Tariffs and Empire*, p. 333.

[18]   B.R. Tomlinson, *The Political Economy of the Raj, 1914–1947: The Economics of Decolonization in India* (Macmillan, 1979), Ch. 3. For the Netherlands East Indies see Ann Booth, 'The Evolution of Fiscal Policy and the Role of Government in the Colonial Economy' in Ann Booth, W.J. O'Malley and Ann Weidemann (eds), *Indonesian Economic History in the Dutch Colonial Era* (Yale University Southeast Asian Studies, 1990) and Ian Brown, *Economic Change in South-East Asia, c. 1830–1980* (Oxford University Press, 1997), Ch. 13.

[19]   Sugihara, 'Japan's Industrial Recovery'.

[20]   Peter Post, 'Chinese Business Networks and Japanese Capital in South-East Asia, 1880–1940', in Rajeswary Ampalavanar Brown (ed.), *Chinese Business Enterprise in Asia* (Routledge, London, 1995). Hiroshi Shimizu and Hitoshi Hirakawa, *Japan and Singapore in the World Economy: Japan's Economic Advance into Singapore, 1870–1965* (Routledge, 1999), p. 87.

[21]   Rajeswary Ampalavanar Brown, *Capital and Entrepreneurship in South-East Asia* (St. Martin's Press, London, 1994), Ch. 10; Claude Markovits, *The Global World of Indian Merchants, 1750–1947: Traders of Sind from Bukhara to Panama* (Cambridge University Press, 2000), Ch. 4.

In the case of British Malaya, where 'the goods imported can not all go into consumption unless the Chinese distribute a part of them',[22] Chinese merchants attempted to implement a boycott of Japanese goods in protest at the Manchurian Incident of September 1931. But, it proved impossible for the leading Chinese merchants in the Circular Road area of Singapore, who had remained loyal to British piece goods in the 1920s,[23] to ignore the fact that their boycott had largely become futile. Chinese merchants outside of Circular Road bought Japanese goods from Indian, Japanese and Arab importers and beyond Singapore, the smaller Chinese dealers stocked Japanese goods and Chinese consumers were buying them. The Chinese merchants' patriotism could not prevail over their trading instincts, given the fact that 100 Straits dollars purchased 131.75 yen in May 1932, and 170 yen just three months later.[24]

Table 7.1 is based upon the annual reports of *Nanyo Kyokai* (the Japanese Southeast Association in Singapore), which attempted to document the results of the quota system, announced by the British government in May 1934, on cotton goods imports into the British colonies from all foreign countries. The quotas were to be based on average imports between 1927 and 1931, which was the period before the rapid increase in Japanese trade was felt. This indicates that, in the case of imports into Singapore of Japanese cotton textiles from June to December 1934, Chinese importers handled 38.4 per cent, Japanese importers 30 per cent, and Indian importers 26.3 per cent. The relative position of Japanese importers was not as overwhelming as might be assumed, meaning that imports into Southeast Asia depended on Chinese and Indian merchant networks, notwithstanding the imposition of the quota system after June 1934. Table 7.2 shows that the main descriptions of textiles imported by European importers from the West (4) were similar to textiles imported by the Chinese from Japan (1), such as W. cotton, D. cotton, Print cotton and G. cotton, while the Japanese imported W. shirtings, Print poplin, G.T. cotton and India imported Rayon, Print poplin and C. poplin from Japan. This suggests that Chinese importers sought to deal in Japanese textiles which were similar to those imported from the West, and that the Chinese directly competed with European merchants in Singapore during the 1930s. Therefore, the competitive advance of Japanese textiles was not only supported by the drastic devaluation of the Japanese yen in 1932, but also depended upon Chinese merchant networks. It was crucial for the success of Japanese goods that Chinese merchants preferred Japanese products to European ones. The fact that Chinese merchants had a tendency to deal with Japanese goods, despite the way in which the European powers intensified their protectionist policies to secure markets abroad in the interests of domestic textile

---

[22]   Trade Commissioner, Singapore to the Comptroller-General, Department of Overseas Trade, 30 May 1932, TNA, CO 273/583/13.

[23]   W.G. Huff, *The Economic Growth of Singapore: Trade and Development in the Twentieth Century* (Cambridge University Press, 1994), p. 268.

[24]   Memorandum about the boycott of Japanese goods by Chinese in Malaya by H.M. Trade Commissioner in Singapore, 20 October 1932, TNA, CO 273/583/13; see also Consul-General in Saigon to H.M. Secretary of State for Foreign Affairs, Foreign Office, 22 June 1934, TNA, FO 371/18173,f 4471, p. 27.

Table 7.1   Imports of Cotton Textiles into Singapore from Main Countries and by Main Merchants

(A) (June to December 1934)

(thousand yards)

Imports from / by	Japanese	Chinese	Indian	European	Total Imports
Total Imports	15,841	25,608	14,416	13,821	69,688

(% by yards)

	Japanese	Chinese	Indian	European	Total Imports
Japan	30.0%	38.4%	26.3%	5.3%	100%
China	0.3%	94.9%	0.0%	4.7%	100%
Britain	0.0%	9.7%	4.5%	85.8%	100%
Total Imports	22.7%	36.7%	20.7%	19.8%	100%

(number of firms)

	Japanese	Chinese	Indian	European	Total Imports
Total Imports	15	105	64	53	237

(% by number of firms)

	Japanese	Chinese	Indian	European	Total Imports
Japan	13.6%	31.1%	37.9%	17.5%	100%
China	2.7%	91.9%	2.7%	2.7%	100%
Britain	0.0%	40.2%	24.7%	35.1%	100%
Total Imports	6.3%	44.3%	27.0%	22.4%	100%

(B) (January to December 1937)

(% by yards)

(thousand yardage)	Japanese	Chinese	Indian	European	Total Imports
Japan (34,208)	28.9%	27.4%	38.9%	4.8%	100%
China (10,287)	0.0%	99.1%	0.3%	0.6%	100%
Dutch East Indies (2,945)	0.0%	42.9%	52.0%	0.1%	100%
Netherlands (1,239)	0.0%	0.0%	0.0%	100%	100%

(% by number of licences)

	Japanese	Chinese	Indian	European	Total Imports
Japan	11.9%	24.8%	48.6%	14.7%	100%
China	0.0%	78.8%	18.2%	3.0%	100%
Dutch East Indies	0.0%	30.4%	67.4%	2.2%	100%
Netherlands	0.0%	0.0%	0.0%	100%	100%

Sources: (A) is based upon Nanyo Kyokai [The Japanese Southeast Asia Association in Singapore]; *Eiryo-Maraya ni okeru Menpu* [*Cotton Textiles in British Malaya*], November 1935. And (B) on Straits Settlements, *Annual Report on the Administration of the Quota System Regulating the Importation of Cotton and Artificial Silk during January to December 1938*, p. 4, CO852/224/3, p. 4, TNA, CO 852/224/3

Note: British merchants were not included in the data for European merchants in 1938.

Table 7.2   The Principal Types of Textile Goods Imported by the Principal Ethnic Groups of Merchants in Singapore, June to December 1934 (thousand yards)

	Japanese			Chinese			Indian			European		
1	W.Shirtings	2,824	J5	D.cotton	4,888	E2	Rayon	2,337		W.cotton	3,446	C2
2	Print.Poplin	1,649	J2	W.cotton	3,941	E1	Print.Poplin	1,250	J2	D.cotton	1,886	C1
3	G.T.cotton	1,199		Print.cotton	2,894	E3	C.Poplin	1,045	C6	Print.cotton	1,415	C3
4	D.Poplin	973		B.cotton	1,720	E5	Print.Shirtings	1,037		G.cotton	1,227	
5	G.Shirting	954	I6	C.cotton	910		W.Shirtings	902	J1	B.cotton	594	C4
6	B.Shirtings	812		C.Poplin	846	I3	G.Shirting	691	J5	Str.Poplin	575	
Totals		8,411			15,199			7,262			9,143	

Source: As in Table 7.1.

Note: E=European; C=Chinese; I=Indian; J=Japanese.

industries, indicates that bloc economies in Asia were not always successful.[25] G.N. Carey, a British Commercial Agent in Batavia (Jakarta), pointed out the necessity of dealing with the Chinese merchant networks in Southeast Asia, indicating that 'British exporters should not overlook sales possibilities through certain well-established Chinese import concerns of good financial standing, who are willing to purchase direct, and pay cash against documents f.o.b. [full on board] English port'.[26]

On the other hand, Table 7.2 also shows that the main types of textiles imported by Indian merchants from Japan were similar to textiles imported by Japanese firms, such as Print poplin, W. shirtings, G. shirtings and B. shirtings. But this does not indicate direct competition between Japanese and Indian importers. Rather, here was a phenomenon related to the Chinese boycotts of Japanese products in 1928 and from October 1931 to mid-1932. During these periods, Chinese importers were extremely hesitant to distribute textile goods known to have Japanese origins, and their boycotts created a major opening for Indian importers. By 1933, Indian, along with Arab dealers, were responsible for the distribution of Japanese goods in the local markets in Southeast Asia, which Japanese dealers could not easily penetrate due to Chinese boycotts of their products.[27]

---

[25]   After the second Sino-Japanese war broke out in July 1937, however, Chinese attitudes changed in comparison with the Indian importers in British Malaya. The former instigated a far more effective boycott of Japanese goods on account of the Far Eastern situation. During 1937, the licences for Japanese textiles in Malaya, which had been issued by the colonial government from June 1934, were divided among the different communities of importers in the following approximate proportions: Indian and Arabs 38.9 per cent, Japanese 28.9 per cent, Chinese 27.4 per cent and Europeans 4.8 per cent (see Table 7.1). While the overall imports of regulated textiles from Japan did not show any diminutions, there had been a definite transfer of licences from one community to another. Chinese importers, who held licences for 27 per cent of the total quota, transferred a large proportion of their licences to Indian importers from September 1937: the Indian sellers of Japanese textiles increased their yardage to nearly 50 per cent of the total quantity imported (W.B. Willmot [Trade Commissioner, Singapore] to the Comptroller-General, Department of Overseas Trade, 23 October 1934, TNA, CO 852/109/120).

[26]   G.N. Carey (Batavia) to John Simon, 5 January 1934, TNA, FO 371/18571.

[27]   Given the tendency for Indian merchants to increasingly deal in Japanese goods after 1932, 'Indian Commercial Associations' were formed by Indian merchants in Osaka in November 1934 for the purpose of increasing the volume of exports of Japanese goods to South and Southeast Asia (Oswald White [Osaka] to Robert Clive [Tokyo], 22 November 1934, TNA, FO 371/19349, f 37). The Indian community in Kobe, mostly from Bombay, Sind and Punjab, was also a large one. Kobe's Muslim mosque was opened through the efforts of local Indian Muslims (*The Japan Chronicle*, 12 October 1935, TNA, FO 371/19349, f 7227). Mian Abdul Aziz, former President of the All-India Muslim League, was invited to the ceremony to celebrate the completion of this mosque in October 1935. It was estimated that some 90 per cent of the Indians in Kobe could be classified as 'revolutionary and anti-British'. This was equally true of Hindus as it was of Muslims, given the free intermingling of both communities owing to the interconnections of business and political interests. This was not the case with the Parsees, however. (I.M. Stephens [Home Department, Government of India] to H. MacGregor [India Office], 9 April 1934,

Furthermore, as low-priced Japanese exports increased their market penetration, European importers, which were financed by European investors and therefore had to pay dividends to them, began to show an interest in handling potentially profitable Japanese goods. As such, large-scale European importing houses began to regard the restrictions placed on Japanese products as disadvantageous.[28] In particular, a number of important Dutch concerns, taking advantage of the higher purchasing power of their guilder, and of low yen freight rates, opened a buying office in Kobe. This consortium bought on cash terms, transported by Japanese ships, and sold through its organization in the Dutch East Indies.[29]

There was clearly a sense of complementary between European financial/ commercial interests and Japanese exporters to Asian markets through the stimulation of merchant's networks (including European ones). The interests of the Western manufacturing sector during the 1930s were also sacrificed so long as Japanese goods were dutiable for colonial governments and profitable for Asian and European importers.[30]

The nature of the First Indo-Japanese cotton trade negotiations, 1933–1934

Reflecting European financial interests, the governments of India and the Dutch East Indies tried to co-operate with third-country foreign markets, especially with Japan, in order to export food and raw materials and so secure smooth payments to the metropolitan country. Thus the following two points became the focus of each round of trade negotiations from 1933 to 1934:[31]

1. What quantities of primary products, such as raw cotton and sugar, was Japan willing to buy from the European colonies annually, to enable the colonies to secure an export surplus?
2. What quantities of Japanese cotton textile goods would Japan be regularly permitted to import into the European colonies, to enable the colonial governments to collect sufficient duties?
3. Additionally, in the specific case of the Dutch East Indies, what proportion of Japanese cotton textile goods would Japanese importers grant Dutch

---

TNA, FO 371/18185, f 4022, p. 57; Memorandum by G.H. Phippe [Consulate in Kobe], 10 October 1934, TNA, FO 371/18185, f 7156, p. 130).

[28]   The Governor-General in Batavia to H.M. Secretary of State for Foreign Affairs, 23 December 1935, TNA, FO 371/20504, w 5, p. 9.

[29]   G.N.Carey (the Comptroller-General of the Department of Overseas Trade) to Foreign Office, 24 February 1934, TNA, FO 371/18571, w 1916.

[30]   Kagotani, *Ajia Kokusai Tsusho Chitujyo to Kindai Nihon*, Ch. 5.

[31]   Hiroshi Shimizu, 'A Study of Japan's Commercial Expansion into the Netherlands Indies from 1914 to 1941', *Nagoya Shoka Daigaku Ronshu* [*The Journal of Nagoya Commercial University*], vol. 34, No. 2, 1990.

importers, so that the latter might benefit from dealing with Japanese goods and would be able to regularly pay dividends to The Netherlands?

The Indo-Japanese cotton trade negotiations commenced in September 1933, following the announcement by the Indian government in April that the Indo-Japanese commercial treaty of 1904 would be abrogated, and its denunciation would take effect from November. In June 1933, through the British government, New Delhi also announced an increase in the duty on foreign cotton goods from 50 to 75 per cent, as compared with a 25 per cent duty levied on imports from Britain. The Japanese cotton industrialists were convinced that Lancashire and the British government were behind the trade convention's denunciation. But the abrogation of the Indo-Japanese commercial treaty was actually spontaneously planned and decided upon by the government of India. Following New Delhi's adoption of import tariffs to differentiate between British and non-British goods in early 1930, the gap widened with each further tariff increase introduced by the government. By early 1933, although tariff preferences had been introduced for the import of cotton goods which exceeded the provisions of the Ottawa agreement, demands from Lancashire for increased preference were met by counter-demands for its abolition from Indian nationalists.[32] Only the abrogation of the 1904 Indo-Japanese commercial treaty, which would allow for the suspension of the most-favoured-nation clause, would permit further discrimination solely against Japanese goods. The British government approved India's denunciation of the commercial treaty, which was accompanied by an invitation for trade negotiations with the government of India. The regime in New Delhi expected to avoid both Indian and Lancastrian resentment through consolidating the preferential gap between British and non-British goods in the new Indo-Japanese commercial treaty.

As Table 7.3 shows, there were four main points which were discussed in the Indo-Japanese cotton trade negotiations:

1. the quantity of Japanese cotton textiles to be imported into British India per year;
2. the quantity of Indian raw cotton to be exported to Japan per year, that is a 'linking' of Japan's export of cotton goods to India with Japan's purchase of a fixed amount of Indian raw cotton;
3. an allocation of Japanese textiles among the various categories, such as plain greys, bordered greys, bleached goods and coloured (printed, dyed and woven) goods;
4. the rate of import tariffs on non-British goods, in particular on Japanese goods, which was as high as 75 per cent by June 1933.

Amongst these points, it is notable that the agreement reduced the level of duty to 50 per cent (point 4) in the early stage of the negotiations, and that the Indian delegation granted Japan 'most-favoured-nation' status in exchange for Japan's

---

[32]   Basudev Chatterji, *Trade, Tariffs and Empire*, pp. 377–81.

Table 7.3   The Main Course of the First and Second Indo-Japanese Cotton Trade Negotiations

Day/Month/Year	① Import of Japanese cotton goods into India (million yards)	② Export of Indian raw cotton to Japan (million bales)	②/① ×1000 (bales / thousand yards)	③ Allocation of ① Japanese cotton goods imported into India						④ Import tariff on non-British goods	
				Greys (%)	Bordered greys (%)	Bleached (%)	Prints (%)	Coloured (%)	Woven (%)	Greys (%)	others (%)
17 Oct. 1933	*300–350*	*1.25–1.50*	*4.28*	*45*	*13*	*8*	*15*	*9*	*10*	*50*	*50*
23 Oct.	578	1.25	2.16							50	50
9 Nov.	325–400	1.00–1.37	3.43	45–60		20–35		35–50		50	50
15 Nov.	*325–400*	*1.00–1.50*	*3.75*	*45–50*	*13–14*	*8*		*34–37*		*50*	*50*
21 Nov.	325–400	1.00–1.50	3.75	45–55	13–23	8–18		34–44		50	50
5 Jan. 1934	325–400	1.00–1.50	3.75	45–50	13–16	8–10		34–37		50	50
30 Jul. 1936	325–400	1.00–1.50	3.75	40–48		20–24		40–48		40	40
20–27 Aug.	*275–350*	*1.00–1.50*	*4.29*	*40*	*13*	*10*	*20*	*17*		*50*	*50*
15 Sep.	325–425	1.00–1.50	3.53	45–54		15–18		40–48		45	45
3 Oct.	325–364	1.00–1.26	3.46	35–39	13–16	12–14		40–44		45	45
9 Nov.	300–360	1.00–1.40	3.89	40	13	10		37		45	45
19 Feb. 1937	283–358	0.93–1.43	3.99	40–44	13–16	10–12	28–37	9–11			
27 Feb.	*325–400*	*n.a.*		*40–44*	*13–14*	*10–11*	*20–21*	*17–18*			
6 Mar.	283–358	1.00–1.50	4.19	40–44	13–16	10–12	25–28	12–13			
20 Mar.	*283–358*	*1.00–1.50*	*4.19*	*40–44*	*13–16*	*10–12*	*20–22*	*17–19*			
late Mar. 1937	283–358	1.00–1.50	4.19	40–44	13–16	10–12	20–22	17–19		50	50

Source and Note: Naoto Kagotani, *Ajia Kokusai Tsusho Titsujyo to Kindai Nihon* [*The International Trading Orders of Asia and Modern Japan 1880–1940*] (Nagoya Daigaku Shuppan kai, 2000), pp. 271, 312–13. Italics mean the proposals offered by the Indian delegation. Others mean the Japanese.

concurrent recognition of voluntary control over her exports to British India (point 1). Japanese delegations, represented by Sawada Setsuzo, who was nominated as an ambassador plenipotentiary from the Ministry of Foreign Affairs due to his role as secretary of the Japanese delegation to the League of Nations in 1931, did not indicate in negotiations that they would retaliate against the Indian measures (although the resentment of Japanese industrialists over tariff discrimination had aroused a boycott of Indian raw cotton in June 1933).

It was fully recognised that high rates of duty resulted in a serious loss of customs revenue from Japanese goods and that if the rates had not been prohibitive Japan's share of Indian imports would not have declined. Both sides believed that a level of 50 per cent was reasonable. Sir George Sansom, as Commercial Counsellor in Tokyo, was informed by Saburo Kurusu, Director of the Commercial Affairs Bureau of the Ministry of Foreign Affairs, that Koki Hirota, the Minister of Foreign Affairs, 'had hitherto hoped that some system of export control and quotas could solve the main difficulties caused by the competition of low-priced exports from Japan'. After acknowledging Japan's co-operative attitude, Sansom journeyed to British India to advise the Indian delegation on Japan's diplomacy.[33] Therefore, the problems of an import tariff barrier (point 4) and restrictions on Japan's exports (point 1) were not as serious issues as might be assumed.

The crucial issue was whether or not Japan could countenance the quantity of Indian raw cotton imports, which the Indian delegation proposed (point 3). Although the Japanese delegation agreed to the importation of raw cotton on a regular basis, it was the JCSA, whose members controlled 97 per cent of all the spindles and nearly half of the mechanical looms in Japan at that time, which had adopted a resolution of non-importation of Indian raw cotton in June, following the government of India announcement of an increase in duty on foreign cotton goods to 75 per cent (as compared with the 25 per cent duty levied on UK imports). Japanese mill-owners anticipated that because the Japanese market for Indian raw cotton was larger than Britain's, their boycott would do substantial harm to the Indian cotton growers and this drastic measure would significantly increase Japan's bargaining power *vis-à-vis* India. The Indian delegation was actually in a most unenviable position, since harvest time for raw cotton was usually in October. With the prospect of ongoing Japanese boycotts, the Indian delegation was inclined to meet the Japanese demand that an allocation of 20 per cent of all Japanese cotton goods be bleached ones. It was the trade in bleached goods in which Lancashire took a particular interest, and where Japan was increasing its exports, while the Indian cotton industry found it difficult to compete.

When the Indian delegation made a series of concessions to the Japanese, the British government felt obliged to interfere in the negotiations in order to deprive the Japanese of their chief weapon, the boycott of Indian raw cotton. The British government declared its readiness 'to replace Japan as the buyer of not more than 1.25 million bales by guaranteeing the Government of India against

---

[33]   Memorandum by G.B. Sansom, 8 June 1933, TNA, FO 371/17160.

loss on purchases'.[34] The Treasury's guarantee enabled the Indian delegation to resist Japanese pressure. Thus, the agreement, finally concluded at the beginning of 1934, limited Japan's exports to India to 400 million square yards (point 1), as against 552 million in 1932, and divided all Japanese cotton goods into four categories. Moreover, Japanese exports were made dependent on the purchase of Indian raw cotton. The Japanese could export the full quota of 400 million square yards only if they bought at least 1.5 million bales of cotton annually (point 2). Furthermore, the ratio of the 400 million square yards for the four categories – plain greys, bordered greys, bleached goods and coloured goods – were 45, 13, 8 and 34 per cent respectively (point 3). This meant that the Indian delegation, fortified by a financial guarantee from the British government, did not accept the terms previously put forward by the Japanese in November 1933, notably a demand that 18–20 per cent of all Japanese goods be bleached goods (see Table 7.3). The Japanese Government persuaded the industrialists in Osaka to accept the final terms and to lift the boycott on Indian raw cotton. A new trade agreement was thence formally agreed in early January 1934. On 19 April, the new Indo-Japanese cotton trade agreement was initiated, effective until 31 March 1937.

Most studies view the Indo-Japanese trade negotiations as a process that reveals Lancashire's huge influence over Indian commercial policy, since the government of India insisted on its proposed percentages for the four categories in which Lancashire had particular interests, supported by a financial guarantee from the UK government. But it was also an important issue for the government of India to 'to protect [its] exchange position', following the US's embargo on gold exports in April 1933.[35] Figure 7.2 shows that the depreciation of the US dollar during 1933 and 1934 had been a new and most important background factor during the India-Japan trade negotiations. Indeed, the British government was anxious that Japanese industrialists 'were able, owing to the depreciation of the dollar, to find an alternative and cheaper source of supply in America'.[36] The Japanese cotton mills adapted easily to using American raw cotton, as a result of rationalisation from the mid-1920s. This changeover from Indian to US cotton was a serious problem for the government of India, causing potential havoc for the Indian balance of payments with a consequent weakening of the exchange rate. If the devaluation of the dollar resulted in serious losses in India's overseas markets for raw cotton exports, the additional loss of the Japanese market as a consequence of the breakdown of trade negotiations and a subsequent 'tariff war' with Japan might well have created 'a disaster of the first magnitude in this country'.[37] Neville Chamberlain, the Chancellor of the Exchequer, also declared to the Cabinet Committee on Indian Cotton that it 'ought to envisage the worst eventuality. Japan might determine upon a permanent boycott of Indian cotton,

---

[34]   N. Chamberlain to Samuel Hoare, 1 December 1933, TNA, CAB 27/556, p. 20.

[35]   Viceroy to H.M. Secretary of State for India, 3 December 1933, Ibid., p. 42.

[36]   First meeting of the Cabinet Committee, 28 November 1933, Ibid., p. 6.

[37]   Viceroy to H.M. Secretary of State for India, 24 November 1933, Ibid., p. 65.

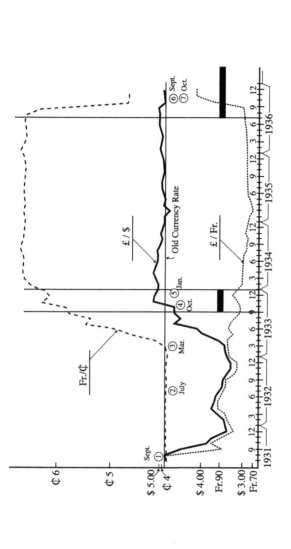

Figure 7.2   Nominal Exchange Rate, July 1931–December 1936

Source: Yokohama Shokin Ginko [Yokohama Species Bank], *Geppo* [*A Monthly Report*].

Notes : Old Currency Rate is as follows;

£1=$4.866
£1=Fr.124.21
Fr.1=￠3.9174

■ : Indo-Japanese Cotton Negotiations.
① : Britain's suspension of convertibility, departure from the Gold Standard.
② : Start of British Exchange Equalisation Account
③ : U.S. departure from the Gold Standard.
④ : U.S. Purchases of Gold.
⑤ : Devaluation of the U.S. dollar.
⑥ : Tripartite Agreement between France, U.S. and U.K..
⑦ : France's departure from the Gold Standard.

might convert the machinery in her mills, and [might] purchase all her supplies from [the] United States. We should then be faced with the permanent problem of disposing of the Indian cotton crop'. [38] This was the reason why the Treasury decided to give a guarantee to the India Office.

The Japanese delegation accepted the Indian proposal: Japan would import 3.75 bales of Indian raw cotton for every thousand yards of Japanese cotton goods exported (point 2/1 in Table 7.3). Thus, the Indian government as a means of protecting the rupee required a new trade agreement, which would enable Japan to purchase Indian raw cotton regularly. It meant that the British Government could avoid full financial responsibility in future. The decisive factor in the changing trend in the trade negotiations was not so much Lancashire's interests in securing the market, as protection of India's exchange position by maintaining Japan's regular purchase of raw cotton. The government of India argued that it was no longer its function to preserve Lancashire's interests. Instead, its aim was to take any action that would 'make this serious loss of trade by Lancashire as gradual a process as possible, to enable the necessary readjustment to be made'.[39] If there were very serious losses of customs revenue from Japanese piece goods due to high rates of duty, for example 75 per cent, the government of India hoped to 'to recoup its losses by imposing further duties on the products of Lancashire'.[40] Lancashire's influence on Indian tariff policy was indeed limited:[41] Lancashire's interests were almost completely ignored by New Delhi.

By the same token, Osaka's influence on the Japanese delegation was also of a limited nature. The formal Japanese delegation in the Indo-Japanese trade negotiations, and also in the Netherlands-Japanese trade negotiations, did not include a member of the cotton textile industry. The documents of the JCSA show that the representatives of this Association voluntarily went to British India and the Dutch East Indies to report back to the Association in Osaka.[42] This means that the interests of the private manufacturing sector, especially the Japanese cotton industry, were not reflected in these negotiations and that there was a discrepancy in the interests of the representatives of the Japanese government and private sector representatives.

---

[38]   1 December, 1933, TNA, CAB27/556, p. 14.

[39]   Thomas M. Ainscough (Senior Trade Commissioner in India) to A. Edgcumbe (Department of Overseas Trade), 27 October 1933, TNA, FO 371/17164, f 7065, p. 166.

[40]   Ibid., p. 18.

[41]   John Sharkey, 'Economic Diplomacy in Anglo-Japanese relations, 1931–41' in Ian Nish and Yoichi Kibata (eds), *The History of Anglo-Japanese Relations, 1600–2000, Vol.2: The Political-Diplomatic Dimension, 1931–2000* (Macmillan: London, 2000), pp. 84–5.

[42]   Keizo Kurata, *Nichi-In Kaisho ni Kansuru Denpo Ofuku Hikae* [*The File of all telegrams for the Indo-Japanese Cotton Trade Negotiations*], (JCSA, April 1934); Yasuo Tawa, *Nichi-Ran Kaisho no Keika* [*The Process of Dutch-Japanese Cotton Trade Negotiations, 1934*] (The Japan Cotton Spinners Association, March 1935). These documents can be found in the library of The JCSA (Osaka).

In the case of the Indo-Japanese trade negotiations, as mentioned above, the JCSA boycotted Indian raw cotton imports from July to December 1933. But the government never acquiesced in this aggressive act by this private body. Instead, the representatives of the Japanese government were prepared to purchase raw cotton regularly without seeking approval from the cotton spinners (although the Japanese delegation was prepared to exploit the boycott movement as a lever to improve the terms of the Indo-Japanese cotton treaty in Japan's favour). As Keizo Kurata, a leader of the boycott and an executive of Dai Nippon Boseki Kabushiki Kaisha (The Japan Cotton Spinning Co. Ltd, one of the 'Big Five' cotton spinning companies of the pre-war period), pointed out, their boycott was not fully in effect by December 1933, because European and Indian merchants began to buy Indian raw cotton in the inner district of Osaka, while the Japanese trading companies maintained a policy of not purchasing raw cotton.[43] When the representatives of the Japanese government realised that the boycott, led by a private body, was no longer in effect, and that the British government was prepared to replace Japan as the buyer of 1.25 million bales of Indian raw cotton, the Japanese delegation immediately concluded the trade agreement in December 1933, and, in so doing, conceded ground to the Indian delegation (see Table 7.3).

The real aim of the Japanese government in the 1930s was to gain European recognition of Japan's political expansion in Asia through demonstrating its willingness to co-operate on commercial matters. Koki Hirota expected to establish a link between Anglo-Japanese trade co-operation, British concessions in China, and the recognition of Manchukuo (the Japanese puppet regime in Manchuria). Clare Lees, a former president of the Manchester Chamber of Commerce, was inclined to give Japan a freer hand in China, so long as Japan restricted its competition with UK interests within the British Empire, since Lancashire's position would be helped by concessions to Japan in the China market and the recognition of Manchukuo. But the British government had never been prepared to accept Japan's foreign policy goals, although the approach of the 'Treasury Group' was not necessarily illogical – to try and gain political concessions through economic understanding.

The Nature of the Second Indo-Japanese Cotton Trade Negotiations, 1936–37

The second Indo-Japanese cotton negotiations were held from July 1936 to March 1937, before the expiry of the first Indo-Japanese cotton trade conventions. The second set of negotiations were expected to be concluded smoothly with the minimum of revision, since both Japanese and Indian delegations hoped to maintain the existing trade conventions and the exchange rate of the US dollar against sterling remained stable (see Figure 7.2). The Japanese delegation was small compared to the forty individuals who made up the 1933–34 party. Kikuji

---

[43]   Kurata to Osaka, 30 December 1933 in Kurata, *Nichi-In Kaisho ni Kansuru Denpo Ofuku Hikae*; Kagotani, *Ajia Kokusai Tsusho Chitujyo to Kindai Nihon*, Chs 4, 6–7.

Ishizawa, a Consul General in Calcutta, was appointed as the head of the Japanese delegation. Ishizawa did not view his task as a mission of first-class political importance as Sawada had back in 1933. But the second set of negotiations were more prolonged than might have been expected, taking eight months, compared to the four months for the first set of negotiations (see Table 7.3). This was due mainly to a change in Japan's foreign policy and also to the fact that the Burma-Japanese cotton trade negotiations were being held at the same time because of Burma's separation from India in 1935.

This prolongation of the second set of negotiations was clearly related to Japan's foreign policy objectives in Northern China, which changed in August 1936. After the currency reform of 1935 in China, partially influenced by Sir Frederick Leith-Ross,[44] the Japanese military sought to destabilise the new currency because it threatened to bring about the economic unification of China, while Japan was seeking to create an exclusive sphere of interest in the North of the country. After the 26 February Incident in 1936,[45] Japan's foreign policy was increasingly under military direction and Tokyo sought to create a Japanese sphere of influence in Northern China, which would provide material resources for Japan, such as raw cotton. Moreover, Japan would no longer allow Britain to interfere with the expansion of its influence in East Asia. It was important for the Japanese delegation in India that new raw cotton cultivated in northern China could now be substituted for US raw cotton. In asking for concessions from the government of India, the Japanese delegation pointed out that the Japanese cotton industry was no longer dependent upon supplies of Indian raw cotton.

But Japan's bullish attitude drastically changed due to China's increasing tendency towards political unity after the Xi'an Incident of December 1936.[46] In early 1937, the Foreign Ministry, Finance Ministry and the War Ministry in Tokyo demanded a joint economic development plan and political co-operation also with Britain in Northern China. Additionally, the Japanese ministries strongly advised the Japanese delegation in India to make concessions in Burma, as well as in the Indo-Japanese trade negotiations. Table 7.3 indicates that the Japanese delegations dramatically made their concessions from February 1937, accepting an import tariff of 50 per cent (point 4) and agreed to the importation of 4.19 bales of Indian raw cotton for every thousand yards of Japanese cotton goods exported to India. This

---

[44]   See the chapter in this volume by Tomoko Shiroyama.

[45]   The coup attempt in Tokyo on 26 February 1936 by army officers associated with the extremist *kodo* faction involved the assassination of prominent politicians, including Finance Minister Takahashi. The suppression of this rebellion confirmed the ascendancy of the more moderate *tosei* wing of the armed forces, and, in turn, led to burgeoning military influence within the Japanese government.

[46]   At Xi'an in Shaanxi province, Chiang Kai-shek was temporarily taken prisoner by his own troops from Manchuria. As a condition of his release, the Generalissimo agreed to shift the course of his policies, and, in focusing upon the enemy without rather than within, particularly re-think the necessity of the Guomindang's military campaign against the Chinese communists.

compared with 3.75 bales in the first agreement (point 2/1), and was very much in compliance with the Japanese government's requirement of Anglo-Japanese co-operation after the Xi'an Incident had provided a boost to Chinese patriotism. Hence, Japan's diplomacy exhibited a new co-operative attitude towards Britain's colonies at a time when the Japanese government no longer had confidence that 'Japan alone should act as a stabilizing power in East Asia'.

The Nature of the Dutch-Japanese Cotton Trade Negotiations of 1934

The standard understanding has been that Western reactions to the influx of Japanese industrial goods in the European colonial empires weakened Japanese foreign trade. Most studies emphasise that the Dutch-Japanese cotton trade negotiations were not completely successful since the negotiations were suspended in June 1936 when the French-led 'gold bloc' began to show its readiness to depart from the Gold Standard and to devalue its currencies.[47] After the negotiations were suspended, the government of the Dutch East Indies continued to impose restrictions on Japanese textile goods. This is why the negotiations are believed to have been 'broken off' in existing Japanese studies. This body of work has also suggested that the government of the Dutch East Indies imposed restrictions on imports in order to give the Dutch cotton textile industry a chance to secure an overseas market. Indeed, the restrictive provisions did include a quota for Dutch goods.

But it can be argued that in the case of the Dutch East Indies, where (with the exception of the local sarong industry) the modern cotton industry was smaller than in British India, the colonial government recognised that continuing to import cheap Japanese goods was necessary in two respects. One reason arose from social policy: native consumers needed cheap Japanese goods at a time when their purchasing power was being weakened. The Netherlands was in the French-led 'gold bloc' until September 1936. The British and American purchases of gold put pressure on the 'gold bloc', forcing the member countries to revalue their currencies. The fact that quite a large proportion of the public debt of the Dutch East Indies was held by comparatively small investors in Holland precluded any un-pegging of the colony's currency from that of the metropole. Thus, the high exchange rates of the 'gold bloc' against the rest of the world aggravated deflation in the Dutch East Indies and stimulated nationalism. Dr. Hendrikus Colijn, the prime minister of The Netherlands, emphasised that 'this was … [because] the purchasing power of the native[s] had dropped to such an extent that the Government was bound to take into account the low prices, at which Japan could supply the native with certain indispensable requirements'.[48]

The second reason for continuing to welcome cheap Japanese imports related to the interests of the Dutch importers. In particular, the government of the Dutch East

---

[47]   Ishii, *Cotton-textile diplomacy*; Shimizu 'Japan's Commercial Expansion into the Netherlands Indies'; Sugiyama, 'Expansion of Japan's Cotton Textile Exports'.

[48]   H. Montgomery, 21 April 1934, TNA, FO 371/18566, p. 237.

Indies considered that restrictive measures were called for, not so much against the import of cheap goods of Japanese origin, but to rein back the operations of Japanese importers, whose selling methods were undermining the existing system dominated by Dutch importers.[49] Hence, the colonial government introduced an import quota system, and not a series of import tariffs as in British India. These quotas were aimed at limiting imports of Japanese cotton textile goods based on the levels of 1933, when the quantity of Japanese goods entering Indonesia was particularly high. If it had wanted to strictly limit Japanese imports, the colonial regime in Batavia would have chosen the levels of 1932. Moreover, there was a strong inclination amongst the Dutch delegation that it would be unreasonable to push the level of Japanese imports back to those pertaining in the 1927–31 period, and there was also a sense that European interests were too inclined to look on the colony's textile market solely from the producers' point of view in metropolitan Holland.

During the Dutch–Japanese negotiations, both sides attempted to make compromises in the following two areas:

1. The Japanese government 'advised' the Japanese business circles concerned that they should give preference to the Dutch East Indies in its raw sugar purchases.
2. Japanese trading firms in the Dutch East Indies were to handle 25 per cent of all imports from Japan on the basis of the 1933 figures; this measure being designed to protect the Dutch wholesale merchants established in Indonesia.

The Dutch East Indies suffered in the Great Depression, an economic downturn which was further aggravated by the determination of The Hague government to maintain the gold standard. As was the case with most of the great producers of raw materials, the Dutch East Indies had been handicapped in the world's markets by this crushing disadvantage. It is not an exaggeration to say that colonial opinion was behind the influences that were pressing devaluation upon a stubborn government in The Hague. The result of Java's inability to compete in the sugar markets had been to lose the Indonesian island many customers, especially in British India. The condition of the Javanese sugar industry showed no improvement in the 1930s in contrast to rubber prices which were influenced favourably by the international scheme for the control of rubber production, which came into force in May 1934, while tin and tea too benefited from international arrangements to control production. It seemed quite possible that over the long-term Java would not be able to sell the quantities of sugar that she had done only a few years previously. The body responsible for the marketing of Dutch East Indies sugar, known as Ned. Ind. Vereeniging voor den Afzet van Suiker (NIVAS), had not given satisfaction to the sugar-growing interests. The whole question of the position of the sugar industry

---

[49]   G.N. Carey (Assistant to Commercial Agent) to John Simon, 2 July 1934, TNA, FO 371/18571, w 7348.

had for some time been attracting the attention of the government. The visible trade of the Dutch East Indies with Japan was very much in the latter's favour, the ratio being probably 1 to 4. It was the intention of the Dutch government, therefore, to try and get Japan to buy a greater quantity of sugar.

Item [2] in the Dutch–Japanese trade negotiations was the question of the apportionment of imports into Indonesia among the trading houses. The Dutch importers were financed by European investors, and therefore had to pay dividends to them, and they had previously purchased profitable Japanese goods through their own branches in Kobe and Osaka, and transported them to Indonesia on Japanese ships. But the Dutch outfits found themselves undercut and boycotted by the Japanese distributors, as well as the stores controlled by the Japanese trading companies both in Japan and the Dutch East Indies. The margin of the Dutch importers' profits was either non-existent or too low to compete with the Japanese enterprises. Therefore, the most crucial problem was how the share of Japanese goods handled by Dutch importers might be increased. Japanese importers had handled 38 per cent of the total imports in 1933, and in item [2] the distribution of 13 per cent of total Japanese imports on the basis of the 1933 figures was conceded to Dutch importers, such as N.V. Internationale Crediet-enHandels-Vereeniging 'Rotterdam', Borneo-Sumatra Maatschappij, Jacobson & van den Berg, and Geo Wehry & Co.[50] The Dutch merchants expected that 'as far as they are free to buy outside Holland [to] make up the rest of their business mainly with cheap Japanese imports, that will, with the price increases anticipated, give them big profits to compensate for handling Dutch goods at little profit'.[51] The Dutch delegation was not prepared to move from its position in these matters, unless the Japanese met their views in regard to the purchase of sugar and other products from the Dutch East Indies. Some members of the Dutch delegation believed that, in the absence of any development of a sugar offer in Europe, a 'sugar-cotton bargain' might be very useful. Both Messrs. van Gelderen and Hart (the latter specifically representing sugar interests) were of this opinion.[52]

In the early stages of the negotiations, in September 1934, the Japanese delegation conceded the principle of Dutch liberty of action with regard to the implementation of further quota restrictions.[53] The Japanese delegation displayed a co-operative attitude, recognizing the Dutch right to protect their trading firms established in the Dutch East Indies. Furthermore, the Japanese government agreed to item [2] without consulting the JCSA or the Japanese trading companies dealing with Japanese cotton textile goods. The Japanese government negotiated on the

---

[50] Kagotani, *Ajia Kokusai Tsusho Chitujyo to Kindai Nihon*, Ch. 8. G.C. Allen and Audrey G. Donnithorne, *Western Enterprise in Indonesia and Malaya* (George Allen & Unwin, 1957), Ch. 14.

[51] H. Fitzmaurice to H.M. Secretary of State for Foreign Affairs, 13 March 1934, TNA, FO 371/18566, p. 229.

[52] Fitzmaurice to C.C. Farrer, 24 July 1934, TNA, FO 371/18567, p. 304.

[53] R.V. Laming (Commercial Secretary) to H. Montgomery, 1 November 1934, TNA, FO 371/18572, w 9829, p. 155.

basis of wanting to co-operate with Holland and the Dutch East Indies, and did not necessarily take into account the interests of the Japanese cotton industry.[54]

In the case of the Dutch–Japanese trade negotiations, Seizaburo Nakayama, an employee of Mitsui Bussan dealing with Javanese sugar, was the only representative of the private sector in the formal delegation. Japan's Foreign Ministry required Nakayama for discussion of item [1] during the negotiations. If Japan were to give preference to the Dutch East Indies in its raw sugar purchases, then Japan's Foreign Ministry would need to deal with a conflict of interest that would arise between the Javanese and Taiwanese sugar industries.[55]

Indeed, the negotiations were suspended due to antagonisms on the Japanese side concerning item [1]. The potential increase in imports of Javanese sugar would affect the competitive position of Taiwanese sugar in East Asia. The Dutch delegation's offer was the purchase by Japan of 500,000 tons per year of Indonesian sugar cane from 1935 onward, with the condition that none of this be re-exported to Asia. The result of this purchase would have been a *de facto* restriction on the cultivation of sugar in Taiwan. Japanese officials were faced with the prospect of having to call on the Taiwanese sugar industry to make a huge sacrifice by way of restricted production in order to please sugar interests in the Dutch East Indies.[56] Hence, Japan's Foreign Ministry decided not to sign a formal agreement with the government of the Dutch East Indies since the Governor-General of Taiwan opposed item [1]. Thus, the negotiations on Indonesian sugar could only result in a 'gentleman's agreement': that is, the Japanese government vaguely recommended to the business circles concerned that they show a preference for the Dutch East Indies in their raw sugar purchases. It could be argued, therefore, that the negotiations were formally broken off and Japan once again began to cease co-operation with industrial Europe.

But, it is important to note that the interdependence between Japan and the Dutch East Indies was maintained in two important respects. Figure 7.3 indicates that Japan increased its imports of Javanese sugar after 1934. Japan took 14 per cent of the total exports of Javanese sugar in 1933 and 25 per cent in 1935, an increase in line with the fall in Javanese exports to British India. This was because Aiichiro Fujiyama, a representative of the Japanese sugar industry, organised business interests in Japan to purchase Javanese sugar according to Hirota's instructions following the 'breakdown' of formal negotiations.

And, as Table 7.4 shows, the Dutch merchants' share of imports of Japanese cotton textile goods also increased. They took 20 per cent of all cotton imports from Japan to the Dutch East Indies in 1932 and 33 per cent in 1935. The Japan Association of Exporters of Cotton Textiles, composed of exporters and controlled by the government, was also disposed to meet the Dutch demand for greater

---

[54]   Tawa, *Nichi-Ran Kaisho no Keika*, p. 126.

[55]   Ibid., Ch. 8.

[56]   H. Fitzmaurice (Consul-General in Batavia) to H.M. Secretary of State for Foreign Affairs, 25 June 1934, TNA, FO 371/18571, 6623).

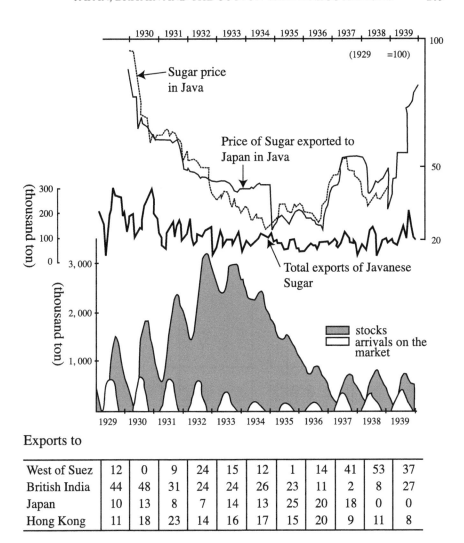

Exports to

	1929	1930	1931	1932	1933	1934	1935	1936	1937	1938	1939
West of Suez	12	0	9	24	15	12	1	14	41	53	37
British India	44	48	31	24	24	26	23	11	2	8	27
Japan	10	13	8	7	14	13	25	20	18	0	0
Hong Kong	11	18	23	14	16	17	15	20	9	11	8

Figure 7.3   Price fluctuations, export and stock of Javanese sugar, 1929–1939

Source: Nihon Sato Kyokai [Japan Sugar Association], *Sato Nenkan* [*The Yearbook of Sugar*] (Tokyo, 1929–1939).

Table 7.4   The Imports of Japanese Cotton Goods into the Dutch East Indies by the Principal Ethnic Groups of Merchants 1932–1935 (thousand yards)

Ethnic Groups	1932				1935				
	Greys	Bleached	Coloured	Totals ①	Greys	Bleached	Coloured	Totals ②	② − ①
European	4,137	9,532	63,153	76,823	20,589	16,805	108,446	145,841	69,018
Japanese	57,272	49,045	180,138	286,456	57,674	35,939	171,069	264,684	-21,772
Indian	301	1,376	14,388	16,066	167	1,367	23,014	24,549	8,482
Chinese	277	374	11,028	11,680	761	1,340	5,086	7,187	-4,492
Totals	61,989	60,328	268,709	391,027	79,192	55,503	306,053	440,749	49,722

Ethnic Groups	1932				1935			
	Greys	Bleached	Coloured	Totals ①	Greys	Bleached	Coloured	Totals ②
European	5%	12%	82%	100%	14%	12%	74%	100%
Japanese	20%	17%	63%	100%	22%	14%	65%	100%
Indian	2%	9%	90%	100%	1%	6%	94%	100%
Chinese	2%	3%	94%	100%	11%	19%	71%	100%
Totals	16%	15%	69%	100%	18%	13%	69%	100%

Ethnic Groups	1932				1935			
	Greys	Bleached	Coloured	Totals ①	Greys	Bleached	Coloured	Totals ②
European	7%	16%	24%	20%	26%	30%	35%	33%
Japanese	92%	81%	67%	73%	73%	65%	56%	60%
Indian	0%	2%	5%	4%	0%	2%	8%	6%
Chinese	0%	1%	4%	3%	1%	2%	2%	2%
Totals	100%	100%	100%	100%	100%	100%	100%	100%

Source: Naoto Kagotani, Ajia Kokusai Tsusho Titsujyo to Kindai Nihon [The International Trading Orders of Asia and Modern Japan 1880–1940] (Nagoya Daigaku Shuppan kai, 2000), Ch. 8

security for Dutch firms in Japan against measures to hamper their participation in the export of Japanese cotton goods.[57] Dutch merchants in Kobe almost exclusively handled the increase of Japanese cotton goods by 49.7 million yards from 1932 to 1935, while Toyo Menka, the largest Japanese importer, reinforced its connection with Dutch trading houses in the Netherlands East Indies.[58] Professor Van Gelderen, one of the Dutch representatives in the Japanese-Netherlands negotiations, regarded the regulation of imports from Japan 'as a problem that had been solved' by late-1936, and indicated that this arrangement 'had at the same time safeguarded the essential European trade and had not prevented the native[s], who could buy only poor quality goods, from getting as much of these poor quality goods as they wanted'.[59]

Conclusion

In June 1937, the Manchester Chamber of Commerce sent a memorandum, calling for 'a more effective policy by the Government', to the Board of Trade, which was copied to the India Office, the Foreign Office and the Dominions Office. It was critical of a lack of government action to assist the expansion of UK exports to the Empire-Commonwealth. The Manchester memorandum pointed out that the British government was 'not exploiting to the full the bargaining power conferred on us [Britain] by the dependence of other countries on access to the United Kingdom market for their exports' and that, if so, 'those countries, which refuse to accede to our [Manchester's] demands, should be threatened with curtailment or forfeiture of ... [British] import facilities – i.e. presumably with deprivation of their most-favoured-nation right, to be followed by discriminatory action against their exports.'

But the Board of Trade reacted calmly, suggesting that 'the United Kingdom is a creditor country, and it is the natural corollary of this position that we should have an unfavourable balance of visible trade with many countries, which are suppliers of essential raw materials. Attempts to eliminate this balance would in any case be likely to lead to a default by the countries concerned on their financial obligations to this country'.[60] Although the Board of Trade had frequently stated that the British government was not prepared to continue to afford favourable import facilities to the products of countries which did not treat British exports fairly, they considered that maintaining the export surplus of Empire-Commonwealth

---

[57]   Fitzmaurice to H.M. Secretary of State for Foreign Affairs, 18 December 1936, TNA, FO 371/21022,f 39, p. 88.

[58]   Kagotani, *Ajia Kokusai Tsusho Chitujyo to Kindai Nihon*, Ch. 8.

[59]   'The Dutch Attitude toward Japanese Economic Penetration; Note of a Conversation with Professor Van Gelderen' by Eastwood, 15 December 1936, TNA, CO 852/62/7.

[60]   'Brief on Memorandum submitted by the Manchester Chamber of Commerce for "a more effective policy" by H.M. Government in their dealings with Empire and Foreign countries from the point of view of the well-being of the Cotton Export Trade' by Commercial Relations and Treaties Department, Board of Trade, June 1934, TNA, CO 852/107/11.

countries was important for imperial politics to avoid default by the countries concerned and to stabilise the pound sterling as the world's key currency.

If so, Japan's economic diplomacy, which focused on purchasing raw materials from the European colonies on a regular basis from 1934 to 1939, was conciliatory towards European financial interests in Asia. But this Japanese amenability 'seemed to betoken a desire to conciliate European countries generally in order to concentrate on measures directly against one'.[61] In other words, the Japanese government hoped that its amenable attitude towards Europe's colonial empires in Asia would lead to European recognition of Japanese political expansion in China. But, here was a fundamental miscalculation, since the British government, at least, was never prepared to accept Japan's foreign policy goals.

Even so, until 1937, Japan was able to maintain a certain level of interdependence with British India and the Dutch East Indies, linking the Japanese yen to sterling at a devalued rate, and so long as Japanese goods were dutiable for the colonial governments and profitable for Asian and European importers. Japan's diplomatic policy toward Europe in the 1930s was formulated primarily by considering the financial interests of European countries and their colonial possessions, not by taking into account the interests of the Japanese cotton textiles industry. In this regard, and to the first half of the 1930s, at least, Japan was never isolated from the European-dominated world economy.

Figure 7.4   The Indo-Japan Cotton Trade Negotiations of 1933: The first official visit of the Japanese delegation to Joseph Bhore, head of the Government of India delegation, 22 September 1933, Simla, India. (Second from left: Setsuzo Sawada, the head of the Japanese delegation; second from right: Joseph Bhore, the head of the Government of India delegation.) © Asahi Photo Archive, 'Nichi-In Kaishou [Indo-Japan Trade Negotiations'(No. 065345), *The Asahi Shimbun*, Tokyo.

---

[61]   G.N. Carey to H.M. Secretary of State for Foreign Affairs, 16 October 1937, TNA, FO371/21023, p. 289.

Chapter 8

China's Relations with the International Monetary System in the 20th Century: Historical Analysis and Contemporary Implication

Tomoko Shiroyama

Introduction

The first half of the 1930s, the years following the Great Depression, marked a major shift in the Chinese economy in terms of China's position in the international monetary system. Until November 1935, China was virtually the only country in the international monetary system still adhering to the silver standard. Fluctuations in the international price of silver in the 1930s destabilized its economy. Establishing a new monetary system, the foreign exchange standard, required committed government intervention, and ultimately, the process of economic recovery and monetary change politicised the entire Chinese economy.

Investigating China's relationship with the international monetary system, this chapter seeks to offer critical insights into China's position in the East Asian economy. Although there existed significant economic interdependence between East Asian countries, at the same time, political conflicts were tense over territory (for example in Manchuria, and also over foreign concessions in rump China), naval force, trade, and so on.[1] Given this complexity in the region's international relations, one question is how politicians perceived economic circumstances to formulate policies. Taking China's currency reform in 1935 as a case, this chapter will investigate this problem.

Previous scholarship shows that in competing for dominance over the Chinese economy, foreign powers in East Asia, namely Britain, the United States, and Japan, had a keen interest in currency reform.[2] However, a question remains: how did the

---

[1] On economic interdependence and the international order of 1930s East Asia see Shigeru Akita and Naoto Kagotani (eds), *1930-nendai Ajia Kokusai Chitsujo* [*The International Order of Asia in the 1930s*] (Hiroshima: Keisuisha, 2000).

[2] On the international conditions surrounding China's currency reform, the classic work is Yutaka Nozawa (ed.) *Chūgoku no heiseikaikaku to kokusai kankei* [*China's currency reform and international relations*] (Tokyo: Tokyo Daigaku shuppan kai, 1981).

Chinese government perceive the international circumstances surrounding reform? Using Chinese archives previously unavailable, this chapter focuses on policy formation surrounding currency reform within the Chinese government. Why was the monetary system to be altered in the middle of the Great Depression? How did the Chinese government pursue its goal under pressure from the foreign powers? What were the impacts of the monetary reform on China's economy and politics? Exploring these questions, this chapter demonstrates China's close link with the international monetary system and its influence on Chinese political economy.

The chapter has four sections. Section 1 provides background information on the silver standard in China. Section 2 discusses how the policies taken by other countries to get out of the Great Depression influenced the silver standard Chinese economy. Section 2 also analyses the impact of the US Silver Purchase Act, which raised the international price of silver and critically destabilized the Chinese financial market. Section 3 investigates the formation and execution of the currency reform in November 1935, focusing on the Chinese government's economic diplomacy with foreign institutions. Section 4 examines the effects of the reform. The conclusion evaluates China's link with the international financial system and its influence on Chinese economic policies from a historical perspective.

China on the Silver Standard

From the late-nineteenth century, the Chinese government sought to change its monetary system. As the international monetary system was on the gold standard, fluctuations in the price of silver in terms of the gold-standard currencies were disturbing for the Chinese government, given its heavy reliance on foreign loans.[3] Nonetheless, it was not until November 1935 that the government left the silver standard, linking its currency to foreign exchange. To understand why this path was taken, it is necessary to understand that fluctuations in the international price of silver during the Great Depression of the 1930s had an immediate and massive impact on China.

In the early-twentieth century, being on the silver standard, China possessed a unique position in the international monetary system dominated by the gold standard. Only in China was silver the legal standard of value. The domestic supply of money was directly related to the supply of silver.[4] Little silver, however, was

---

[3]   Takshi Hamashita, 'Chūgoku heisei kaikaku to gaikoku ginkō [China's currency reform and foreign banks]' *Gendai chūgoku* vol. 58 (April 1984).

[4]   Edwin Kemmerer, a leading American scholar of monetary policy, who investigated China's monetary and banking situation in 1929 as foreign advisor to the Nationalist government, described the specifics of China's silver standard. See Commission of Financial Experts, *Project of Law for the Gradual Introduction of a Gold-Standard Currency* (1930), p. 47. Wei-Ying Lin, a member of the National Economic Council and an acting chief of the Research Department of the Bank of China, also noted that China was on the silver standard, even though various kinds of currencies coexisted. See *The New Monetary*

mined in China. China had to import silver. Produced principally in North and South America and absorbed chiefly by China and India, silver moved around the globe. There were four leading world silver centres, London, New York, Shanghai, and Bombay. London had long been a leading silver market. New York was a trading centre for silver bullion mined in North America. The chief receiving port for silver was Shanghai, followed by Bombay. China's silver business was cleared through Shanghai, or, with occasional exceptions, through Hong Kong.[5]

Exchanges between gold-standard countries were based on a fixed par of exchange, which was the ratio of the gold content of the two coins concerned. Actual exchange rates fluctuated around this between the narrow limits of the gold shipping points, which were determined by the cost of shipping coin or bullion. In exchanges between China, on a silver standard, and gold-standard countries, there was no fixed par of exchange. However, given a particular price of silver in London (in terms of shillings per ounce), for example, one can calculate the value of silver per unit of Shanghai silver currency in terms of London gold currency (in terms of shillings per *teal* or *yuan*). This was taken as the parity for that particular silver price; as the price of silver in London varied, the parity varied, but always proportionately. On the one hand, if the exchange rate in Shanghai was quoted above parity drawn from the price of bullion, it meant the value of silver was higher in Shanghai. Thus, this scenario induced the purchase of silver in London and the sale in Shanghai. On the other hand, if below parity, this situation favoured the purchase of silver in Shanghai and the sale in London. It was necessary to add charges (shipping, insurance, and so on) and interest, both subject to changes, to parity to see whether importing or exporting silver was profitable. These rates were called import and export points, and these ruled silver transactions.[6]

China was the major purchaser of silver, and the country's demand might affect the international silver market. Nonetheless, the international price of silver tended to be influenced by supply and demand factors, irrespective of what was going on in China. As a number of countries shifted their monetary systems from the silver to the gold standard, the demand for silver considerably decreased. Consequently, from 1873 to 1931, the value of silver continued to depreciate against gold, encouraging the import of silver into China.[7] The imported silver

---

System of China: A Personal Interpretation (1936), p. 5. Miyashita Tadao, an economist at Tōa dōbun shoin in Shanghai, echoed Kemmerer's and Lin's views. Miyashita reviewed discussions over China's currency standard in *Shina kahei seido ron* [*A study of the Chinese monetary system*] (Osaka: Hōbunkan, 1943), pp. 142–6.

[5]   Herbert Bratter, *The Silver Market* (Washington DC: Government Printing Office, 1932), pp. 1–19.

[6]   Dickson Leavens, 'A Chart of Silver and Exchange Parities', *Chinese Economic Journal* 3 (August 1928): 394–8.

[7]   Between 1890 and 1930, China recorded fifteen years of excess silver exports (1890–92, 1901–1908, 1914–17) and twenty-six years of excess silver imports (1893–1900, 1909–13, 1918–30).

bullion went mostly into monetary uses, entailing a mild level of inflation. Between 1911 and 1926, wholesale prices in Shanghai rose 33 per cent.[8] Many factors influenced commodity prices, but the increased silver supply was one of the major reasons for this rise.[9]

Until the early 1930s, the downward trend in the price of silver and its consequent inflation conditioned in the Chinese economy. During the prolonged years of inflation, Chinese industrialists, financiers, and farmers tended to take it for granted that the inflationary trend would last for the long-term. Their belief, however, proved to be unfounded.

The Impact of the Great Depression on the Chinese Monetary System

The world economy fell into the unprecedented slump of October 1929. Most of the countries suffered from the severe depression. It was only China that avoided the dire effects of the first two years of the crisis because silver depreciated considerably against gold and other commodities, and large amounts of silver flooded into China. However, in September 1931, when Britain left the gold standard, the downward tilt in the exchange rate of Chinese currency in relation to foreign currencies began to reverse. In Shanghai, the exchange rates for countries in the sterling bloc rose in accordance with the depreciation of the pound sterling. One country after another – India, the Straits Settlements and the Malay States, Japan, and so on – depreciated its currency. The appreciation of China's silver currency had a profound impact on the country's economy in terms of import and export prices, the current of international trade, and the balance of international payments.

In order to make up for deficiencies in its international trade balance, China was forced to export silver. China recorded net exports of silver valued at 7,346,000 *yuan* in 1932 for the first time since 1918.[10] Following the slump in import and export prices and reflecting the deflationary consequences of the appreciating silver exchange rate, Chinese wholesale prices experienced a serious decline at the end of 1931. The average annual percentage change in wholesale prices for the six principal cities in China was about 5 per cent in 1932, while Shanghai saw a further drop of 11.3 per cent.[11]

---

[8]   Edward Kann, *The Currencies of China: An investigation of Silver and Gold Transactions Affecting China* (Shanghai: Kelly and Walsh, 1927), p. 87. Zhongguo kexueyuan Shanghai jingji yanjiusuo and Shanghai shehui kexueyuan jingji yanjiusuo (eds), *Shanghai jiefang qianhou wujia ziliao huibian* [*The collection of price data in Shanghai prior to and after the liberation*] (Shanghai: Shanghai renmin chubanshe, 1958), p. 4.

[9]   Fukusaburo Hisashige, 'Bukka yori mita shina keizai no ichimen [An analysis of the Chinese economy with special attention to commodity prices]', *Shinakenkyū* 36 (March 1935): 105–12.

[10]   Lin, *New Monetary System*, p. 29.

[11]   *An Annual Report of Shanghai Commodity Prices*, 1934, p. 117.

The US's suspension of the gold standard in March 1933 had a decisive impact on China's exchange rate for dollars. China's trade deficit was at its largest ever, 733,739,000 *yuan*. The condition of the Chinese economy worsened. The movement of treasure resulted in a net export of 189.4 million dollars in gold and 14.2 million dollars in silver. Wholesale prices continued to fall, 9.4 per cent on average in the six largest cities and 7.7 per cent in Shanghai.[12]

The end of the gold-standard monetary system critically influenced the silver standard Chinese economy. When a number of countries depreciated their currencies to recover from the depression, the Chinese economy sank into severe crisis. China, however, could not control the trend of international silver prices.

It was the US Silver Purchase Act, approved in June 1934, which fatally destabilized the Chinese silver-standard monetary system. US motives for the policy were mainly domestic. The US was one of the major producers of silver. As the price of silver considerably declined after the end of the First World War, especially after 1930, the American Silver Producers' Association and senators from silver-producing states had required the government to 'do something about silver.' Although nothing was done during the administration of President Herbert Hoover, President Franklin D. Roosevelt, who took office in March 1933, addressed the issue of silver as part of his measure to stimulate a US economy severely harmed by the world depression.[13] President Roosevelt at first was reported to oppose the legislation designed to raise the dollar price of silver.[14] However, after numerous meetings with the advocates of silver, Roosevelt finally recommended a compromise bill in his message to Congress on 22 May 1934.

The Silver Purchase Act of 1934, approved on 19 June, declared it to be the policy of the US to increase its stock of silver with the ultimate objective of making it one quarter of the total monetary stocks of silver and gold. The act provided that the Secretary of the Treasury should purchase silver to this end at such times, and upon such terms and conditions, as he might deem reasonable and most advantageous to the public interest. No silver was to be purchased at a price in excess of the monetary value, 1.29 dollars per ounce, nor was any silver, situated in the continental US on 1 May 1934, to be purchased at over 50 cents per ounce.[15] The act gave no authority to the Treasury to sell silver, except when the stock exceeded 25 per cent of the total monetary stocks or when the market price of silver exceeded its monetary value. For China, the key issue in the Silver

---

[12]   Ibid.

[13]   Dickson Leavens, *Silver Money* (Bloomington: Principia Press, 1939), pp. 244–5.

[14]   Dorothy Borg, *The United States and the Far Eastern Crisis of 1933–1938: From the Manchurian Incident through the Initial Stage of the Undeclared Sino-Japanese War* (Cambridge: Harvard University Press, 1964), p. 121.

[15]   The calculation is as follows: the monetary value of silver was $1.2929 per fine ounce. Deducting 61.32 per cent thereof for seigniorage, brassage, coinage, and other mint charges, the equivalent of a net price per fine ounce was 50.01 cents.

Purchase Act was that the limit of 50 cents per ounce applied only to silver in the US on 1 May, so that the real limit was $1.29 per ounce.

The price of silver in the US rose steadily, from 46.3 cents per ounce in June to 49.5 cents in August, which was slightly below the nationalization price of 50.01 cents per fine ounce (equivalent to 49.96 cents per ounce, 0.999 fine). The market price during August and September remained around 50 cents per ounce, which was suitable for buying up the silver. But, in October, it rose to over 55 cents per ounce and fluctuated between 53 and 56 cents per ounce during November and December. The price on the London silver market, where the US government also purchased silver, followed the upward trend of the US silver price, rising 6.7 per cent from September to December, from 21s 13/16d to 24s 1/2d.[16]

Although the US Silver Purchase Act itself did not target China, the sudden and massive rise in the international price of silver caused by the heavy US purchases upset the silver-standard Chinese economy. In the first half of 1934, Chinese silver imports and exports were minimal. But, in June, silver valued at 12,936 *yuan* was exported. Compared to net silver exports in the whole of 1933 of 14,122 *yuan*, this amount in one month was obviously unusual. The outward movement of silver became even more conspicuous thereafter, rising to 24,308 *yuan* in July 1934, 79,094 *yuan* in August, and 48,140 *yuan* in September.[17]

Although being alarmed by the massive outflow of silver, the Nationalist government could not take immediate and effective action against it. Large exports increased fears that the government would have to take action to depreciate the value of the Chinese currency and further increase silver exports before it was too late. The possibility of an embargo on silver and the disparity in the value of silver between China and abroad provided a rationale for further exports.

Finally, in October 1934, the government found itself with only two remaining options: either to prohibit the free trade of silver or to devalue its currency. On 14 October 1934, the Minister of Finance, Kong Xiangxi, announced a duty of 10 per cent (less 2.25 per cent in the case of silver dollars and minted bars, which already had paid the amount in seigniorage) together with an equalization charge, on the export of silver. The equalization charge would be adjusted daily so that, with the duty, it would make up for any discount in the exchange rate below parity, and render the export of silver unprofitable.[18]

Soon after the announcement of the equalization charge, the exchange rate dropped over 10 per cent in a few days.[19] Thereafter, it fluctuated around 19 per cent below parity with New York silver prices.[20] The imposition of duty and equalization charges caused recorded exports of silver to fall off sharply, from 57 million *yuan* in October to around 12 million *yuan* per month in November

---

[16] *An Annual Report of Shanghai Commodity Prices*, 1934, Table IX, p. 19.

[17] Ibid., Table XII, p. 22.

[18] Leavens, *Silver Money*, pp. 299–301.

[19] *Finance and Commerce* (hereafter *FC*) 24, 17 (24 October 1934): 458.

[20] *An Annual Report of Shanghai Commodity Prices*, 1934, Table XII, p. 23.

and December. Beginning in 1935, recorded exports of silver practically ceased. However, the estimated amount of silver smuggled out of China was calculated to be as large as the amount legally exported in 1934.[21] The disparity between the exchange rate in Shanghai, namely the price of silver in terms of foreign currencies and the export parity of silver estimated from the price of silver quoted in the international markets, remained and increased significantly after April 1935, and this the export duty and equalization failed to offset. As long as the large difference between the price of silver abroad and the price in China existed, it remained profitable to export silver.

The silver drain ushered in a struggle for liquidity. Falling prices further curtailed credit, which in turn put more pressure on business enterprises. Foreign banks began to restrict and later to refuse any collateral loans, which put native banks in a serious management crisis.[22] They served as money brokers to foreign and Chinese banks, although their own financial backing was usually weak, borrowing call loans from the latter two institutions and extending these loans to commercial and industrial enterprises. As foreign and modern Chinese banks tightened credit, native banks suffered a liquidity crisis.

Under this deflationary cycle, Shanghai wholesale prices gradually declined from February until September 1935, when they were 6.4 per cent below the level of a year before.[23] However, the downward movement suddenly turned upward in October. Uncertainty about the future of the Chinese economy, particularly the recurrent rumours of government devaluation of the *yuan*, spurred people to change their cash into foreign exchange or commodities. Transactions in foreign exchange and gold bars, along with basic commodities like cotton, wheat, and bean oil, became feverish in October 1935. As the rumour of devaluation prevailed, the rates of exchange dropped by 17 per cent while the price of commodities traded on the official exchange advanced by nearly 15 per cent in the last two weeks of October.[24] Chinese currency was overwhelmed by the distrust by the market toward the end of October 1935.

China revealed itself extremely vulnerable to changes in the international silver price. It did not have control over fluctuations in the price of silver nor over exports of silver. Once large amounts of silver drained out of China, a credit

---

[21]   Leavens, *Silver Money*, Table 18, p. 303. Based upon reports by the Bank of China for 1934 and 1935, Leavens estimated the net export of silver from China in 1934 totaled 280 million *yuan* (211 million fine ounces), out of which 260 million *yuan* was officially recorded, only 20 million *yuan* was smuggled. In 1935, the recorded amount decreased to 59 million *yuan* but 230 million *yuan*-worth of silver was estimated to have been smuggled out of China. The total net export thus amounted to 289 million *yuan* (218 million ounces.)

[22]   Zhongguo renmin yinhang Shanghaishi fenhang (ed.), *Shanghai qianzhuang ziliao* [*Materials on Shanghai native banks*] (Shanghai: Shanghai renmin chubanshe, 1960), p. 253.

[23]   An Annual Report of Shanghai Commodity Prices, 1935, p. 27.

[24]   Lin, *New Monetary System*, pp. 76–7.

crunch followed. At this point the government was supposed to cope with the currency and banking crisis by transforming the existing systems.

The Chinese Government's Diplomacy over the Currency Reform

Until the mid-1930s, the government did not take the lead in regulating the Chinese monetary and banking system. Note issuance was not restricted to the Central Bank. The Central Bank did claim to be the 'State Bank', but it did not occupy the special position of central banks in other countries. It shared the right to issue notes with other banks and it was not obliged to keep legal reserves for the management of the domestic banks. At the same time, there was no control over the movement of silver inside and outside of the country. The turbulence of the price of silver in the world market destabilized the silver standard Chinese economy. In search of a way out of the crisis, the government for the first time was expected to play a key role in controlling the money supply.

Going off the silver standard in the mid-1930s, the Chinese government had to balance the divergent interests of several powers in East Asia, namely Great Britain, the US, and Japan. When a number of countries left the gold standard, the international monetary system was divided into several groups, such as the US dollar bloc, the British pound-sterling bloc, and the Japanese yen bloc. Although China's currency reform itself was a monetary issue, it had profound political implications in the context of international circumstances prevailing at the time. If a country committed to China's currency reform, other countries would be suspicious of its ambition to dominate the Chinese economy. It should be noted that the Chinese government was well aware of the powers' interest in its monetary reform. If China's currency was to be linked to any foreign currencies like the US dollar or the pound sterling, then the Chinese government would have to prepare sufficient reserves other than silver. In search of the necessary funds, the Chinese government sought to make the best of foreign competition surrounding its monetary reform.

Japanese Claims Over the Chinese Economy

Japan had claimed special privileges in China's economy. Japan's diplomacy under Foreign Minister Koki Hirota pursued several contradictory aims. After the Manchurian Incident in 1931, Japan had a constrained relationship with China. On the one hand, Japan tried to strengthen its control over Manchuria. On the other hand, it did not aim to confront China's Nationalist government. The Japanese government tried to avoid international isolation, but it rejected any foreign intervention in Chinese domestic issues. Especially in the case of China's currency reform, the Japanese government refused to cooperate with China, while also insisting that other foreign governments should not support China's reform on the grounds that the Chinese government would lack the ability to carry out the project.[25] Japan, in particular, opposed any intervention by Western countries in the Chinese economy.

In April 1934, Eiji Amou, a spokesman for the Japanese Foreign Office, had explained the position of the Japanese government regarding foreign aid to China. The so-called Amou Doctrine proclaimed that Japan had a special responsibility for the maintenance of peace in East Asia and therefore did not always agree with the views of other nations in respect to China. While Japan hoped to see the Chinese preserve their national integrity, restore order, and achieve unification, such objectives should be attained through China's own independent effort. Japan would thus oppose any foreign intervention in the name of technical and financial assistance and any projects such as appointing military instructors or military advisers to China or supplying the Chinese with warplanes.[26]

Japan's proclamation forced the British and US governments to make difficult decisions. The UK and the US wished for the success of China's currency reform, hopefully with their support, but were reluctant to take the risk of antagonizing Japan. Given the complicated relationships between these countries, China sought to secure funds from the US and the UK.

China's Unsuccessful First Approach to the US

As the US Silver Purchase Act raised the international price of silver and severely disturbed the Chinese monetary system, the Chinese government first approached the US government for its assistance in coping with the crisis. Inside the US government, there were two different views concerning Chinese monetary issues. The Department of State, headed by Cordell Hull, regarded the multilateral approach as indispensable in handling China's monetary crisis. At the same time, the Department of State was suspicious of the Chinese government's ability to reform the monetary system. On the other hand, the Department of the Treasury, headed by Henry Morgenthau, opposed the Department of State. As the modification of the Silver Purchase Act itself would not be politically feasible, Morgenthau suggested that the US government should make efforts to help China reorganize its monetary system. Depending on which side President Roosevelt took, US policies fluctuated.[27]

Given this confrontation between departments in the US government, it was natural that in September 1934, Hull refused Kong's proposal to exchange gold

---

[25]   Hideo Kobayashi, 'Heisei Kaikaku wo meguru nihon to chūgoku [Sino-Japanese relations in terms of China's currency reform]' in Nozawa, *China's Currency Reform*, pp. 233–64; Sumio Hatano, 'Heisei kaikaku he no ugoki to nihon no taich seisaku [The currency reform and Japanese policies toward China]' in Nozawa, *China's Currency Reform*, pp. 265–98.

[26]   Borg, *The United States and the Far Eastern Crisis*, pp. 75–6.

[27]   Kenji Takita, 'Roosevelt Seiken to beichū kyōtei [Roosevelt administration and US – China agreement]' in Nozawa, *Chinese Currency Reform*, pp. 165–98.

for silver with China to enable China to gradually introduce a gold-based currency in the future. Hull noted that China should acquire gold in world markets, such as London.[28]

Since the US refused to directly purchase silver from China, the Chinese government subsequently asked the American government to stabilize the price of silver at a lower level. In December 1934, Kong Xiangxi sent a message to the US government through the Chinese ambassador in Washington, Shi Zhaoqi, pointing out that the rising price of silver drained silver out of China and that China could not bear exchange rates as high as parity. Kong suggested a maximum US purchase price of 0.45 dollars an ounce, based on a US exchange rate of one Chinese *yuan* to 0.34 US dollars.

The Department of the Treasury reasoned that silver buying would proceed, even though it would put China off the silver standard. The price per ounce was to be kept at 0.55 dollars.[29] Kong claimed that China could not accept this price since it would cause disastrous deflation, a negative balance of trade, and ultimately, the collapse of the Chinese currency system. As a compromise, Kong suggested 0.50 dollars per ounce, equivalent to 0.37 dollars per Chinese *yuan*, the rate at which China could abolish its tax on silver and regain the people's trust in the currency.[30] On 19 January 1935, he sent another proposal suggesting that the US purchase silver only if it had been newly mined, had been declared under the London agreement in 1933, or could be delivered in a relatively short period, perhaps two weeks, at New York or London markets. These restrictions, Kong noted, would reduce the smuggling of silver out of China.[31] The response from the US was negative; the Silver Purchase Act possessed legal power and could neither be altered in a short period nor circumvented.[32]

After all, even a rate of 0.55 dollars turned out to be politically unsustainable in the US. The silver senators continued to oppose the proposal, and Morgenthau, the Secretary of the Treasury, had little choice but to cancel it immediately. The price of silver rose to a peak of 0.81 dollars in April and fluctuated around 0.65 dollars until November 1935.[33]

Because of the confrontation inside the US government, China could neither sell silver to the US nor make the international silver price low enough for China to bear.

---

[28]   United States Department of State, *Foreign Relations of the United States: Diplomatic Papers, 1933–1934* (hereafter *FRUS*) vol. III, pp. 443–4.

[29]   Arthur Young, *China's Nation-Building Effort, 1927–1937: The Financial and Economic Record* (Stanford: Hoover Institution Press, Stanford University, 1971), p. 224.

[30]   Zhongguo renmin yinhang zonghang canshishi (ed.) *Zhonghua minguo huobishi ziliao dierji, 1927–1937* [*Materials on the monetary history of Republican China, second series, 1927–1937*] (hereafter *Huobishi* 2) (Shanghai: Shanghai renmin chubanshe, 1991), pp. 125–6.

[31]   *Huobishi* 2, p. 130.

[32]   *FRUS 1935*, vol. III, p. 529.

[33]   Young, *China's Nation-building Effort*, p. 225.

By early 1935, government authorities had come to regard departing from the silver standard as inevitable.[34] The details of the reform plan, however, were unclear.

Chinese high-ranking officials were most concerned about Japanese intervention in the vacuum left by the Western powers. Kong Xiangxi noted that Japan unofficially hinted at an offer of a large loan to China to cope with the crisis. He sensed that the loan would be part of large-scale economic cooperation, leading to strong Japanese control over the Chinese economy, particularly in the Northern part of China. At the same time, Japan suggested that China and Japan should unite to protest against US silver purchasing policies. Although the Chinese government refused this Japanese suggestion, it was afraid that Japan would take advantage of the Chinese crisis to increase its influence over the Chinese economy. Kong reasoned that Japan was trying to prevent the Western powers from offering any substantial assistance, so that China could not avoid asking for Japanese help. Kong lamented that, 'The Western powers would not oppose Japan in this circumstance, as they had never taken a risk to rescue China.'[35]

The fear of Japanese intervention was shared by the key policy-makers, such as Song Ziwen, president of the Bank of China, who had expressed his concern over Japanese dominance of the Chinese monetary system in conversation with A.S. Henchman, the manager of the Shanghai branch of the Hongkong and Shanghai Banking Corporation (HSBC).[36] Finally, on 31 January, Song Ziwen sent a message to the US government claiming that China's currency system was expected to collapse some time before June, and that this would put China under Japan's economic control. In order to prevent an international crisis, China was asking the US to offer loans. If it agreed, China would peg its currency to the US dollar and provide silver for American needs.[37] According to an unofficial memorandum submitted by China's ambassador in the US, China would offer 200 million ounces of silver for the first year in order to secure a loan of at least $100 million.

With their different positions regarding domestic silver purchase policies, as well as towards international relations in East Asia, there was no reason to suppose that the Department of State and the Department of the Treasury would agree with each other; the former was against the US purchase of Chinese silver, while the latter supported the idea. At the meeting with staff from the Division of Far Eastern Affairs of the Department of State on 14 February 1935, Secretary of the Treasury Morgenthau criticized the Department of State's opinion that the loan to China should be supplied under international cooperation.[38] Although Morgenthau

---

[34]   'Appointment of a Monetary Advisory Committee', *FC* 25, 6 (6 February 1935): 142.

[35]   *Huobishi* 2, pp. 160–61.

[36]   Mentioning that Japan went into Manchuria following a collapse of its currency, Henchman recalled that Song Ziwen had already predicted that a similar thing might happen in Shanghai. HSBC archive, Hong Kong, GHO 12. 14, 23 January 1935.

[37]   *Huobishi* 2, p. 133.

[38]   *FRUS 1935*, vol. III, pp. 535–7.

sensed that the President was on his side, in the end, Secretary of State Hull rejected the Chinese proposal: the US alone could not commit to China's scheme given the unstable international situation.

With the dim prospect of US assistance, the Chinese government had to seek another way to secure necessary funds for the currency reform. On 17 February 1935 Kong ordered Ambassador Shi to secretly tell the US government that the Chinese government would be ready to talk with an international consortium over loans. Hull accepted China's proposal, saying that 'If a group of other countries agree to support China's plan, the United States would possibly support China.'[39] At this point, the role of the British government became important.

Negotiations with Leith-Ross

Britain initiated the drawing up a plan for collective aid to China involving the US, the UK, France, and Japan.[40] On 8 March, the British government notified the Chinese government that Great Britain was willing to help China as long as the plan would contribute to the establishment of peaceful relations between China and Japan. The British proposed that the four countries send their financial representatives to Shanghai for discussions. On 18 March, the Chinese government agreed to the British government's proposal, sending this message to the British ambassador in Nanjing:

> The National Government of the Republic of China has given careful consideration to the contents of the Aide-Memoire of 8 March 1935, and appreciates the friendly spirit therein manifested by His Majesty's Government in the United Kingdom. The Chinese government shares the view of His Majesty's Government in the United Kingdom that a lasting and satisfactory solution of China's economic monetary difficulties can only be found with the friendly co-operation and assistance of the interested foreign governments chiefly concerned. The Chinese Government also shares the view that a détente in the Far East is essential to the successful realization of any plan to meet these difficulties in which China is involved, and is desirous on its part to contribute its best efforts to this end. The Chinese Government therefore warmly welcomes the action of His Majesty's Government in the United Kingdom in opening discussions with China and the Governments of the U. S. A., France, and Japan, holds itself ready to participate in discussions with the interested Governments chiefly concerned, and will be glad to be informed of the views of His Majesty's Government in the United Kingdom as how best to facilitate preliminary discussions.[41]

---

[39]   Ibid., p. 539.

[40]   *Huobishi* 2, p. 162.

[41]   Ibid.; Young, *China's Nation-Building Effort*, p. 228.

Despite its official statement, the Chinese government, in fact, was not happy with the multilateral scheme proposed by the British government. As long as it took the multilateral approach, the British government would share with the governments of the other three countries any information regarding Chinese monetary reform. Any news about the possible monetary reform would seriously disturb the Chinese financial market. The Chinese government decided not to consult the British government on any detailed plans about the currency reform, while asking it to urge the other three governments to send their envoys as soon as possible. The scenario drawn up by the Chinese government was that China at best would agree the details with the specialists from the four countries, even if the four governments would not be totally satisfied by the solution.[42] However, the US, Japan, and France did not promptly respond to the British proposal. As a consequence, the British government did not appoint an expert pending other powers' similar action.

While waiting for foreign specialists, in order to facilitate changing the monetary system, China consulted the British government about floating bonds in Shanghai which would be opened to both British and other foreign governments. The British government retained its answer to this scheme on the ground that it should confirm the other governments' commitment to multilateral cooperation. By the beginning of May 1935, the Chinese government became irritated at the slow progress in the powers' scheme over China's monetary issues.[43]

After all, Japan expressed its disagreement with the British plan. The US also backed out, concerned that American delegates to China would be criticized for the US Silver Purchase Act.[44] France would not participate in the British plan without the cooperation of the other two countries. In the end, only Britain announced in June that it would send Sir Frederick W. Leith-Ross, its financial representative, to China.[45] The proposed visit aroused rumours in China, including expectations of loans from Britain and of the pegging of the Chinese *yuan* to the pound-sterling, despite repeated announcements that the mission was merely exploratory.[46] For example, Zhejiang Industrial Bank contributed an article entitled 'Analysing Sir Leith-Ross's mission to China' to *Dongfang zazhi*, one of the leading magazines in China:

> The main purpose of Sir Leith-Ross's [sic.] visit to China is to strengthen its central position in the Chinese economy. British power in China has visibly declined in the face of harsh competition with the U. S. and Japan ... Japan, in particular, has increased its political influence over China, while Great Britain

---

[42]   *Huobishi* 2, pp. 162–3.

[43]   Ibid., p. 164.

[44]   Ibid., p. 166.

[45]   For Britain's domestic politics surrounding the Leith-Ross mission, see Stephan Lyon Endicott, *Diplomacy and Enterprise: British China Policy 1933–1937* (Manchester: Manchester University Press, 1975).

[46]   Leavens, *Silver Money*, p. 311.

concentrated her attention on Europe. When Great Britain realized that Japan had increased her influence over the Chinese economy as well as Chinese politics, it was too late to force Japan back. But, Great Britain was not ready to abandon her superior position. Under the circumstances, any strategies that Great Britain should take to reserve its position in the Chinese economy both in terms of trade and of investment should avoid confronting Japanese interests ... According to my analysis, the ideal policy for Great Britain will be to seize rights over the monetary system of our country .... The scheme to peg the *yuan* to the pound-sterling would be extremely advantageous for British businesses in China. At the same time, as the financial crisis daily deepens in China, the Chinese side may also may take the scheme seriously. In addition, as Great Britain makes a number of concessions to Japan, the Japanese government may accept the British plan.[47]

In fact, Leith-Ross, who arrived in China in September 1935, aimed to reach a Sino-Japanese détente through Japanese collaboration on the loan. The Japanese government, however, refused to cooperate with the British, claiming that such loans would not be of use to the current Chinese government without stable domestic support.

Even after the Japanese refusal, Leith-Ross stayed in China. Hoping that his visit would result in financial support from the UK, the Chinese government consulted Leith-Ross about the currency reform scheme. Even though the Chinese officials thought the reserve for currency reform would be mainly secured from the sale of silver to the US, China needed funds to improve government finances. Thus, the government officials discussed with Leith-Ross not only the reforms themselves but also various issues regarding the improvement of the Chinese government budget. They shared the view that balancing the budget was essential for the success of the currency reform as well. In particular, reducing internal and external debt arrears was most crucial.[48] The Chinese government claimed that the establishment of a substantial balance between current income and expenditure was needed in order to place the finances of the government in a stable position, and to create confidence in the reform of the currency.[49] Song Ziwen, the general manager of the Bank of China, explained that if currency reform was initiated without foreign help it would mean a forced conversion or prolongation of domestic debts, and further restriction of payments for foreign debts. Song said that he wanted to avoid the 'shock to credit that this would cause.'[50]

---

[47]   Shanghai Zhejiang shiye yinhang, 'Luosi jueshi laihua shiming zhi fenxi' cited in *Huobishi* 2, pp. 172–5, originally printed in *Dongfang zazhi*, 32, 20 (1 October 1935).

[48]   Leith-Ross Papers, The National Archives, Kew, London (formerly Public Record Office, hereafter TNA), T 188/118, p. 27.

[49]   Ibid., p. 79.

[50]   Ibid., p. 16.

Although the British government was 'most anxious not to appear to be putting pressure on China to adopt a sterling basis', Leith-Ross warned Song that loans were only allowed for countries in the sterling bloc if the Chinese government wanted a loan in London. Song Ziwen, however, noted that he originally regarded sterling as most appropriate when China put the *yuan* on a foreign currency basis. He pointed out that sterling was the currency of the world's most important trading area and the London market was the best place for raising money and holding reserves. Moreover, as Song added, the Japanese currency was more or less linked with sterling.[51] In answer to Leith-Ross's concerns about the US's view on the stabilization of the *yuan* on a sterling basis, Song said that he thought it might be possible to put the *yuan* on something like the same basis as the Japanese *yen*; namely, to keep it approximately at the same value in sterling without definitely linking it to sterling.

Song Ziwen also expressed his concerns to Leith-Ross regarding Japan's attitude to China's currency reform; Song said that he therefore would like to get on as quickly as possible with the programme so as to present Japan with a fait accompli.[52] Song reasoned that Japan would try to prevent a British loan for the reform, but that if they found that the British were going to issue one, the Japanese banks would come in rather than be left out.[53]

After all this, the British government did not offer a loan to China for the currency reform. Even if the Chinese government authorities consulted Leith-Ross about the reform, they had written up the outline of the programme before he arrived; they just deferred its announcement pending Leith-Ross's arrival. Nonetheless, Leith-Ross's influence should not be underestimated. He not only provided the moral support for currency reform but also shared his knowledge with Chinese officials on sound fiscal management. And, most importantly, Leith-Ross's presence in China put pressure on the US government, and the Chinese took advantage of this during negotiations on the sale of silver.

The Sale of Silver to the US

Although having failed to sell silver to the US from late 1934 to early 1935, the Chinese government deemed that large silver sales to the US were the only solution to securing foreign reserves for currency reform. While discussing with

---

[51]   According to China's foreign trade in 1934 classified in relation to currencies, the trade with countries using sterling, or basing their currencies thereon, shared 22.7 per cent of China's imports and 18.7 per cent of the country's exports. The share of Japan, Korea, and Guandong (Kwantung) was 13.6 per cent in imports and 21.5 per cent in exports. Trade with the US, Canada, and the Philippines accounted for 28.5 per cent of imports, and 19.3 per cent of exports. See Arthur Young, 'Outline of a Program of Financial Reform for China: A Report Presented to His Excellency Dr. H.H. Kung' (September 1935).

[52]   TNA, T 188/118, p. 145.

[53]   Ibid., p. 172.

the British government about its reception of British, American, Japanese, and French specialists, the Chinese government proposed to the US government that it should sell its silver not through diplomatic but through commercial channels in April 1935. In May, Kong Xiangxi, the Minister of Finance, instructed ambassador Shi to tell the US government that the Chinese government hoped to gain US support, particularly in the form of the purchase of silver by the Department of the Treasury.[54]

During the first half of 1935, the US government was reluctant to purchase a large amount of silver from China; if it showed support for China's currency reform, the so-called silver senators would accuse the government of helping China to abandon silver. In the latter half of 1935, however, the attitude of the US government gradually changed. Inside the country, the influence of the 'silver senators' waned. Internationally, the US, as well as Japan, remained suspicious of the Leith-Ross mission, the outcome of which might result in the new Chinese currency being pegged to the British pound sterling.[55] The Chinese government did warn the US that Japan would dominate China's economy should its monetary and financial systems collapse under the pressure of the high price of silver. Under these circumstances, President Roosevelt's position shifted towards the Department of the Treasury, which was willing to support China's currency reform by purchasing silver.[56]

The Chinese government might have sensed the US government's support before the end of September 1935. Asked by Leith-Ross whether he had approached the US on its possible purchase of silver, Kong Xiangxi answered that the Chinese government had asked the US Treasury whether it would constitute China as its purchasing agent for silver. According to Kong, the US Treasury answered that it could not confine its operations to purchases of silver from China because it also had to operate in the world market. Nevertheless, the US Treasury disclosed that it was anxious to help China and would be prepared to purchase any silver which China could release.[57] Confirming Kong's statement, Song Ziwen, the general manager of the Bank of China, told Leith-Ross that the sale of silver to the US would provide ample cover for currency reform.[58] Song was 'proceeding with preparations on the assumption that matters could be fixed up with America', and, if so, the scheme could be launched by the end of October or during the first fortnight of November.[59]

Finally, on 26 October 1935, Ambassador Shi Zhaoqi was instructed to offer the US 50 million ounces of silver at 0.65 US dollars an ounce for delivery within two months, plus 50 million more ounces within the next four months, and to ask for an

---

[54]   *Huobishi* 2, pp. 163–4.
[55]   Ibid., p. 167; Young, *China's Nation-Building Effort*, p. 235.
[56]   Ibid.
[57]   TNA, T 188/118, p. 24.
[58]   Ibid., p. 28.
[59]   Ibid., p. 145.

option of another 100 million during the following six months. The proceeds were to be used for exchange stabilization. Given the competition among the foreign powers over their dominance of the Chinese economy, Secretary of the Treasury Morgenthau was receptive to China's plea for US support, as he commented to President Roosevelt, 'It is very amusing to have the Chinese come to us with Leith-Ross sitting in China'.[60] Still, Morgenthau required further information from the Chinese government on the new financial and currency programme and on how funds were to be used.[61]

On 29 October, Song Ziwen told Leith-Ross that 'action' would be taken in the following week, confirming this on the next day to the HSBC. The scheme was kept a secret only from Japan. In the hope of confirming US consent over the purchase of silver, on 1 November, Kong ordered Ambassador Shi to tell Morgenthau that China was going to launch currency reform, probably that weekend. Besides providing an outline of the programme, Shi was instructed to refer to the possible sale of Chinese government bonds on the London market, explaining that if this issue eventuated China's currency would be linked to sterling, not to another currency or to gold.[62] When Shi met Morgenthau on 2 November, the latter agreed to purchase 100 million ounces of silver with President Roosevelt's approval. The offer was based upon several conditions: (1) that the proceeds would be used only for currency stabilization; (2) that the Chinese government would establish a currency stabilization committee that included American bankers, and (3) that the new currency would be linked to the dollar and China would agree to make it convertible at a level of America's own choosing. The US government's decision was not final, as issues such as currency pegging were still to be resolved. Still, from Morgenthau's attitude, the Chinese government regarded it as fairly certain that a sale could be arranged.[63] By the beginning of November, the Chinese government had managed to secure funds, as well as British and US support, indispensable for the currency reform. However, whether the reform would be successful was not clear.

The Currency Reform of 4 November 1935 and Its Impact

On 3 November 1935, the Minister of Finance, Kong Xiangxi issued decrees establishing the currency reform that would be in force on the following day. The purpose of the reform was 'to conserve the currency reserves of the country and effect a stable monetary and banking reform' and 'to prevent a financial catastrophe.' The nature of the reform and its procedures were described in six articles:

---

[60] John Blum, *From the Morgenthau Diaries: Years of Crisis, 1928–1938* (Boston: Houghton Mifflin, 1959), p. 211.

[61] Young, *China's Nation-Building Effort*, p. 234.

[62] *Huobishi* 2, p. 168.

[63] Young, *China's Nation-Building Effort*, p. 235.

1. [The Abandonment of the Silver Standard] As from 4 November 1935, banknotes issued by the Central Bank, the Bank of China, and the Bank of Communications shall be full legal tender. Payment of taxes and discharge of all public and private obligations shall be effected by legal tender notes. No use of silver dollars or bullion for currency purposes shall be permitted; and in order to prevent smuggling of silver, any contravention of this provision shall be punishable by confiscation of the whole amount of silver seized. Any individual found in illegal possession of silver with intention to smuggle it shall be punishable in accordance with the law governing acts of treason against the State.

2. [Bank Notes] Banknotes of issuing banks, other than the Central Bank, the Bank of China and the Bank of Communications, whose issue had been previously authorized by the Ministry of Finance, shall remain in circulation, but each bank's total outstanding banknotes shall not exceed the amount in circulation on 3 November 1935. The outstanding banknotes of these banks shall gradually be retired and exchanged for Central Bank banknotes within a period to be determined by the Ministry of Finance. All reserves held against the outstanding banknotes, together with all un-issued or retired notes from these banks, shall be handed over at once to the Currency Reserve Board. Notes previously authorized and in the process of being printed shall also be handed over to the said Board upon delivery.

3. [Reserves] A Currency Reserve Board shall be formed to control the issuance and retirement of legal tender banknotes and to keep custody of reserves against outstanding banknotes. Regulations governing the said Board shall be separately enacted and promulgated.

4. [Handover of Silver] As from 4 November 1935, banks, firms and all private and public institutions and individuals holding standard dollars, other silver dollars, or silver bullion shall hand over the same to the Currency Reserve Board or banks designated by the Board in exchange for legal tender notes, at face value in the case of standard silver dollars, and in accordance with the net silver content in the case of other silver dollars or silver bullion.

5. [Conversion of Silver to Dollars] All contractual obligations expressed in terms of silver shall be discharged by the payment of legal tender notes in the nominal amount due.

6. [Exchange Rate] For the purpose of keeping the exchange value of the Chinese dollar stable at its present level, The Central Bank, The Bank of China, and The Bank of Communications shall buy and sell foreign exchange in unlimited quantities.

Following these articles, the declaration referred to several important issues related to currency and banking. The first concerned the reorganization of the Central Bank. The reorganized Central Bank was intended to function as a bankers' bank. As the liquidity crisis of the summer of 1934 revealed, when reserves were scattered among financial institutions, no one institution could control the money supply. A strengthened Central Bank would increase liquidity to the commercial banks under sound conditions, allotting them the resources necessary to finance the legitimate requirements of trade and industry.

The second issue was credit. Credit secured by real estate had been particularly important to the Chinese capital market. The decree stated that a special institution would be created to deal with the mortgage business and that steps would be taken to amend the present legal code affecting real estate mortgages to make real estate a more acceptable form of security for loans.

Third, the decree promised sound government fiscal policy. In proposing the reform programmes, the government took into account how its decisions would look in the eyes of the public. There was a strong feeling against inflation, rooted in the fear that the Central Bank would become a government cash machine. The government concluded the declaration with the reassurance that, 'plans for financial readjustment have been made whereby the National Budget will be balanced. Also with the centralization of note issuance, the provision of adequate reserves against legal tender, and a system of rigorous supervision, confidence in the currency will be strengthened.'

In the Direction of the New Currency System, made public on 18 November, the government guaranteed that the system would not lead to inflation. By way of 'answering people suspicious of the new currency system', the government emphasized four important aspects of the reforms. The first concerned stabilizing the exchange rate. Referring to those who 'doubt the feasibility of the exchange stabilization', the Direction would guarantee a stable exchange rate, since the three government banks would intervene if the exchange rate varied widely. Second, the government warned of temporary fluctuations in commodity prices but predicted that they would be stabilized within a short period, preferably at a slightly inflated level. The third and fourth points concerned the circulation of silver. The government rejected the position that people accustomed to using silver would not accept notes (Article 3), asserting that notes backed with enough reserves would have no problem circulating (Article 4).[64]

The Direction of the New Currency System illuminates the international (foreign reserves and exchange rates) and domestic (note issuance and inflation) problems in implementing the reform. Both problems were closely related. The currency reform presented a particular difficulty since the government had to deal with mass confidence in the currency. The public, which customarily used silver as a means of

---

[64]   Zhuo Zun (ed.), *Kanzhanqian shinian huobishi ziliao* (1) [*Materials on the historical decade prior to the Sino-Japanese War*] (Taipei: Guoshiguan, 1985), pp. 213–14. Hereafter cited as *Kanzhanqian*.

exchange, might not readily accept notes instead. Despite the government concern, the issue of notes steadily increased after the reform (see Table 8.1).

Table 8.1   Note Issue of Government Banks, November 1935–June 1937 (1,000 yuan)

Month/ Year	Central Bank	Bank of China	Bank of Communications	Farmers Bank of China	Total
1935					
Nov.	152,221	248,636	143,432	29,847	574,136
Dec.	176,065	286,245	176,245	29,771	668,326
1936					
Mar.	252,349	310,151	186,698	34,777	859,447
Jun.	300,099	351,773	204,912	92,035	948,819
Sept.	314,353	377,768	217,110	108,503	1,017,734
Dec.	326,510	459,310	295,045	162,014	1,242,879
1937					
Mar.	361,835	501,404	308,577	200,053	1,371,869
Jun.	375,640	509,863	313,548	207,951	1,407,002

Source: Frank Tamagna, *Banking and Finance in China* (New York: Institute of Pacific Relations, 1942), p. 144.

Note: The new currency regulations of 1935 did not make any provision regarding the status of notes issued by the Farmers Bank of China. In February 1936, the government granted a status of legal tender for that bank's notes. See *Huobishi 2*, p. 200.

Why did people accept banknotes as legitimate currency? As Chen Guangfu, the general manager of Shanghai Commercial and Savings Bank, recalled, 'the most important function of a managed currency is to enable one to exchange a legal tender note for either cash or foreign exchange'.[65] In order to sustain the credibility of the currency, it was crucial for the government to keep the open market rate close to the official rate declared in November 1935. The task was not easy.

Even after the currency reform, the Chinese government did not control foreign exchange transactions. The restriction itself would damage the credibility of the currency, which would incur immediate massive capital flight only to ruin the new monetary system. Shi Demao, the chief of the management office of the Central Bank, opposed to the government's control of foreign exchange transactions, noted that:

---

[65]   Chen Guangfu, 'Reminissance of Ch'en Kuang-fu' (Rare Book and Manuscript Library, Columbia University, New York), p. 79.

The obvious reason is that when restrictions are enforced in a country, there would be an entire cessation of inflow of capital outside only except that part of favourable balances, whereas in China the balance of payments has been adverse for some years. It is vital to our country that the inflow of capital continues in the form of overseas remittances, investments of foreign capital here and the repatriation of our own capital ... [r]estriction of any kind would also tend to impede restoration of confidence. The chief cause of the success of our new monetary reform is due to the fact that the scheme has inspired confidence in that our new currency is freely convertible into foreign exchange and vice versa. When the political situation clears up, the repatriation of our capital would take place again. However, speculators would start to unload their overbought position, thus rendering the market more stable.[66]

Recognizing the vital importance of the flow of foreign capital to the Chinese economy, government officials did not close the Chinese financial market from abroad. Therefore, the government's commitment to exchange rate stabilization, and ultimately, to the new monetary system could be tested on the financial market. From the end of 1935 to the middle of 1937, the government banks faced three large-scale sales of *yuan*: in December 1935 (the beginning of the new monetary system), in May 1936 (the political crisis in Southern China), and in December 1936 (the Xi'an incident). With foreign reserves mainly obtained from the sale of silver to the US, the Chinese government could protect its currency.[67] In each case, the government banks met all demands for foreign exchange at the official rate, which enhanced the public's confidence in the currency.[68]

The supporting policies for the stabilization of the exchange rate included the limited supply of notes and a tendency to refrain from excessive budgetary expansion. If the government conducted these policies, the value of *yuan* in terms of foreign currencies would drop. Despite the popular concern prior to the reform that the government would increase the money supply to make up for its budgetary deficits, the government refrained from budgetary expansion.[69] Since military

---

[66] 'Memorandum to his Excellency Dr. H.H. Kung on the study of Mr. T. Chen's Memorandum Regarding the Restriction of Foreign Exchange, 8 July 1936' in Arthur Young Archives (Hoover Institute of War, Revolution, and Peace, Stanford, California), Box 42.

[67] In addition to the initial sale of 50 million ounces, China continued to sell silver to the US. Altogether, China's prewar sales of silver to the US after currency reform amounted to 187 million ounces. In total, the Chinese government's silver sales provided a reserve of about 100 million dollars to support its currency reform. Young, *China's Nation-Building Effort*, pp. 242–4.

[68] Tamagna, *Banking and Finance in China*, p. 148.

[69] There are many articles in contemporary magazines and newspapers, expressing such concerns. See, for example, Hou Shutong, 'Ping zaibu bizhi xinling' *Dagongbao* (16 November 1935) reprinted in *Kanzhanqian* 3: Fabi zhengce, pp. 247–64 and Huang Yuanbin, 'Xin huobi zhengce chenggong guanjian' *Yinhang zhoubao* 20, 15 (April 1936)

expenditure could not be easily reduced, the government consolidated domestic debts as well as restricted the new issuance of bonds.[70]

The problem was even more complicated because the value of the Chinese *yuan* had to be stable in terms of both the British pound sterling and the US dollar. As we have seen in the Chinese government's negotiation with the British and the US government during 1934 and 1935, the officials were well aware of the Western powers' keen interest in China's monetary issues. As Kong Xiangxi noted, 'It would cause jealousy and suspicion on the part of countries whose currency was not selected as a basis for China's currency, and therefore tend to make more difficult China's international position. In this connection it may be added that it has been indicated to the Government that the American, British and Japanese Governments would each be glad to have China's currency linked to its particular currency'.[71] The Chinese government thus avoided choosing either the US dollar or the pound sterling to peg the *yuan*, but decided to keep the declared rates of each currency. The US government at first required the linking of the *yuan* and the US dollar as a condition for its purchase of silver from China. The Chinese government, however, did not accede to the US requirement. Chinese Ambassador Shi warned the US government of possible difficulties which would be caused by the pegging of the *yuan*. For example, if the *yuan* was tied to the dollar and something went wrong in China, the US would be blamed. American intransigence would drive the Chinese into the arms of the British or even the Japanese. At last, the Department of the Treasury, as well as the Department of State, came to regard a link as unnecessary.[72]

The rates initially announced after the reform, 14 3/8d and US$0.29 for selling, and 14 5/8d and US$0.30 for buying, reflected a cross rate for fluctuating sterling of about US$4.92, the approximate rate at the time of the reform. China could retain the position of the *yuan*, as long as the cross exchange rate between New York and London fluctuated within narrow limits.[73] However, it became difficult

---

reproduced in *Kanzhanqian* 3, pp. 336–58. Gu Qigao observed that some bankers opposed the currency reform because of their distrust of the government. Gu Qigao, 'Zhongguo xinhuobi zhengce yu guoji jingji junheng' *Jingjixue qikan* 7, 1 (June 1936), reprinted in *Kanzhanqian* 3, pp. 373–4.

[70]   'Guomin zhengfu zhun zhongzheng hui heding 1936 niandu guojia putong yusuan xunling', Zhongguo dier lishi danganguan (ed.), *Zhonghua minguoshi dangan ziliao huibian* 5–1 caizheng jingji (1) (Archives of Republican China 5–1 finance (1))(Nanjing: Jiangsu guji chubanshe, 1994), pp. 548–9.

[71]   Letter to Chen Guanfu from Kong Xiangxi, 14 March 1936 in Mr. K.P. Chen's Private Papers, Silver Mission 1936, A1 Diaries (Rare Book and Manuscript Library, Columbia University, New York).

[72]   Blum, *Morgenthau Diaries*, pp. 212–13.

[73]   In this regard, the Tripartite Monetary Agreement which the US, Great Britain, and France established in October 1936 to stabilize the exchange rates made Chinese management of the exchange rate easier. On the Tripartite Monetary Agreement, see Barry

to keep the currency stable in terms of two currencies when the dollar-sterling rate rose to over US$5.05. In order to prohibit arbitrage transactions, the Central Bank widened the spread between selling and buying for both currencies to 14 1/4 – -14 3/4d and US$0.29 1/2 – -30 1/2, respectively. In this way, the Chinese government did not have to change the official rates prior to the outbreak of the Sino-Japanese war in 1937.[74]

With the 20 to 25 per cent devalued exchange rates, China's international trade, exports in particular, improved. Foreign trade in December 1936 easily established record figures for the year: trade increased in 1936 by 10.1 per cent compared with 1935, an increase comprising gains of 2.4 per cent in imports and 22.5 per cent in exports. Exports of agricultural products were most promising. It was estimated that the annual farm income from the sale of wheat, rice, cotton, millet, kaolin, and tobacco averaged 3,900 million dollars in the years from 1933 to 1935, but in 1936 it reached 5,600 million dollars, an increase of 1,700 million dollars, or nearly 44 per cent. When silk, tea, wool, groundnuts, and other minor agricultural products were included, the increase amounted to almost 2,000 million dollars. The beneficial effects of China's new currency system were also apparent in the general rise in wholesale prices, which in Shanghai had advanced from 90.5 during the deflationary period of mid-1935, to 103.3 in November 1935, and to 118.8 in December 1936.[75] Since wholesale prices apply mainly to primary agricultural products, an increase in prices entailed greater purchasing power for producers.

Altogether, as Chen Guangfu, the general manager of the Shanghai Commercial and Savings Bank, recalled, '[I] would say that the years 1936 and 1937 up to the outbreak of war were banner years'.[76] If the excellent crops throughout the country were a great boon, 'coming as they did at a time when the exchange had just been fixed at a reasonably low level, and when the demand for China's produce was improving', the reform of the monetary system was the major factor in the Chinese economy's recovery from the depression.[77]

Conclusion

During the Great Depression, the Chinese currency endured wide fluctuations in exchange rates caused by changes in the international price of silver. The initial

---

Eichengreen, *Golden Fetters: The Gold Standard and the Great Depression, 1919–1939* (Oxford: Oxford University Press, 1992), pp. 378–81.

[74]   Young, *China's Nation-Building Effort*, p. 250.

[75]   It should be noted that wholesale price levels were not necessarily inflationary, rather they were reflationary, since they were almost equivalent to those prevailing in 1931, just before the exchange rate started to rise.

[76]   Chen Guangfu, 'Reminiscence of Ch'en Kuang-fu', p. 87.

[77]   Zhang Gongquan (Chang Kia-Ngau), *Inflationary Spiral: The Experience in China, 1939–1950* (New York: John Wiley and Sons, 1958), pp. 98–100.

drop of the silver price from 1929 to 1931 caused a boom in the Chinese economy which only deepened the economic crisis after the price turned upward in 1931. The end of the gold-standard monetary system had a huge impact on the silver standard Chinese economy. When a number of countries left the gold standard and devalued their currencies in order to recover from the Great Depression, China's silver-standard currency in turn was appreciated in terms of foreign currencies, over which China did not have any means of control. In particular, when the US Silver Purchase Act of 1934 raised the silver price even higher, the Chinese economy descended into severe deflation. To eliminate the negative effects of the fluctuating international silver price, China had to leave the silver standard.

The Chinese government took the lead in reforming the monetary system through its economic diplomacy with Britain and the US. As the gold standard ended in 1931, the international monetary system became segmented into several groups. Thus, the powers in East Asia, like Britain, the US, and Japan, were very much interested in China's monetary reform. Japan's insistence on a paramount position in the Chinese economy complicated the policies of other governments towards China. Sending Frederick Leith-Ross, a high-ranking Treasury official, the British government tried to lead international cooperation in lending money to China to support currency reform. Ultimately, the British government tried to increase its influence over the Chinese economy through this support. And, it also wished to see Japanese participation in the loan scheme, as a means of easing tension between China and Japan, leading also to the resolution of the sovereignty dispute in Manchuria. In the end, British aspirations proved unattainable.

Inside the US government, there were two opposite policies toward China. During the course of China's currency reform, the US government led by the Department of State first hesitated to commit to the reform, but later under the initiative of the Department of the Treasury the US bought silver from China, which was crucial for raising the foreign reserve.

It should not be overlooked that the Chinese government was well aware of the foreign competition surrounding Chinese monetary issues. Moreover, as this chapter demonstrates, to secure the funds indispensable for the reform, the Chinese government took advantage of conflicts amongst the foreign powers, for example, the British and the US governments' concerns about Japanese dominance in China, or the competition between Britain and the US regarding which currency the *yuan* should be pegged to. The Chinese government noted that the reserve to sustain the new monetary system could be secured only through the large-scale sale of silver to the US. Even so, it continued to consult the British government about monetary issues in order to balance US and Japanese influence, as well as to draw British capital to China.

The transition from the silver standard to a managed foreign exchange system in November 1935 marked a major shift in Chinese political economy. Under the silver standard, domestic trust in the currency rested on its convertibility with silver. China was exposed to the fluctuation of silver prices in the world market but was relatively free of government intervention in monetary affairs.

Under the new monetary system, the government's management of the monetary system became much more important. There was a danger of the government's arbitration of the monetary system to finance its budgetary deficits. In recognizing the Chinese economy's close integration with the world economy in terms of trade and capital flows, the government, nonetheless, found it necessary to cultivate mass confidence in the currency by keeping the Chinese *yuan* convertible and by stabilizing its exchange rate. For that purpose, the government had to refrain from excessive note issuance or budgetary expansion.

The now-stabilized exchange rate following the currency reform was one of the major factors that contributed to the expansion in business and trade after 1935. China's case echoes Kaoru Sugihara's observations on the role of the pound sterling in the East Asian economy; as a result of the region's linkage with the pound sterling during the 1930s, intra-Asian trade flourished; the devaluation of East Asian currencies in terms of the pound sterling helped import-substitution industrialization in the area by discouraging imports from Western countries.[78]

The outbreak of the Sino-Japanese war in July 1937 terminated the prospect for the further improvement of the Chinese economy. But, still, we should not overlook the fact that currency convertibility was regarded as most significant well into late-1938.[79] Fearing that the vast drop of the exchange rate would create a panic among the public, the government supported the exchange rate of the currency through continued supply of foreign exchange to the Shanghai market during the early war years. This action not only mitigated the wartime inflation but also bolstered general confidence in the currency, although this was at the cost of a large leakage of foreign exchange.

The relationship between the state and the public over exchange stability and fiscal policies deteriorated, after retreating to the interior province of Sichuan in October 1938, with insufficient foreign reserves, the Nationalist government was unable to sustain the exchange rate. Meanwhile, military expenditure increased in 1940, and the share of government outlays financed through monetary expansion rose steadily. The Chinese economy gave way to inflationary pressure.

The Communist regime, which established the People's Republic in October 1949, tackled the hyperinflation inherited from the Nationalist regime by channelling the circulation of money into tightly controlled paths. Gold, silver, and foreign exchange were barred from circulation. The handling of all foreign trade was placed in the hands of state-operated companies (after March 1950) and trade was conducted only in foreign currencies, not in Chinese currency, *ren min bi.* In this way, free from the influence of the international market, the government effectively tightened its control over the domestic circulation of *ren min bi* from then on.[80]

---

[78] Kaoru Sugihara, 'The Formation of an Industrialization-oriented Monetary Order in East Asia' in this volume.

[79] Zhang, *Inflationary Spiral*, pp. 95–6. *Huobishi* 2, pp. 284–5.

[80] Dwight Perkins, *Market Control and Planning in Communist China* (Cambridge: Harvard University Press, 1966), p. 11.

Separated from the international monetary system, the Chinese economy in the 1950s looked quite different from that of the 1930s, which was significantly open to the world economy. However, the wide shift in the nature of the Chinese economy illuminates the influence of China's linkage with the international monetary system on policy options for the Chinese government. As long as the Chinese financial market was open to the global economy, the government was not free to formulate monetary and fiscal policies because of its commitment to currency convertibility and exchange stability. On the other hand, once the Chinese government decided to abandon foreign capital flows into China, it gained tight control over the domestic economy. Although the paths taken by the regimes in the 1930s and the 1950s might be different, China's linkage with the international monetary system continued to regulate government policies from the mid-1930s onwards.

Chapter 9

China's Economic Development and the International Order of Asia, 1930s–1950s

Toru Kubo

Introduction

China is one of the most important players in the international order of Asia, while China's economy itself is also strongly influenced by the Asian regional economic situation. This is not only true in the twenty-first century, but was also the case from the 1930s to the 1950s, and suggests that we should pay special attention to China's economy and its relationship with Asia. This chapter focuses on the various strategies and policies pursued to promote China's economic development from the 1930s to the 1950s, and examines their effects on China's foreign trade, and especially on China's trade with Asian countries.

The Pre-War Period, c. 1928–1938

As a result of the Nationalist Revolution from 1924 to 1928, a new National Government, characterized by the firm assertion of national interests, was established in Nanjing. It was necessary for the new government to promote positive financial-economic policies designed to build a modern national economy. We can identify four key individuals who designed and carried out such financial-economic policies within the National Government in Nanjing.[1]

Kong Xiangxi, who worked as the Minister of Industry from 1928–30 and as the Minister of Finance from 1933–44, proposed in 1928 that the government should build eight categories of state-operated factories. Although the intentions behind this plan are an important means of gauging how the government viewed its own role in economic development, the plan was never realized because of financial shortages.

---

[1]   Kubo Toru, 'Kokumin Seifu no Seiji Taisei to Keizaiseisaku [The Political System and Economic Policy of the Nationalist Government]', in Ikeda Makoto et al. (eds), *20Seiki Chugoku to Nihon, Gekan* [*Twentieth Century China and Japan, vol. 2*], Chugoku Kindaika no *Rekishi to Tenbou* [*History and Prospect of China's Modernization*] (Kyoto: Law and Culture Publishing, 1996).

Meanwhile, Song Ziwen (T.V. Soong), who worked as the Minister of Finance from 1928–33, as the Vice-President of the National Economic Council from 1933–44 and as the Deputy Prime Minister from 1945–47, made energetic efforts to build infrastructure and to particularly develop the private sector of the modern economy. He was able to gain Western economic aid for some of his projects. His tariff policy, which promoted a strategy of import-substitution industrialization, and currency reform, which stabilized the rate of Chinese foreign exchange, obtained remarkable results.[2]

Of course, the significance of the protective tariff policy for economic development should not be exaggerated. In sectors such as the cotton-spinning and cotton-weaving industry and the cigarette-manufacturing industry a considerable degree of self-sufficiency based on domestic production had already been achieved, while powerful foreign capital enterprises had also been established in China. As a result, even though a high rate of import duty was set, this had hardly any effect in terms of protection and the nurturing of Chinese capital. There were different stories in other sectors of modern industry. For example, the match-manufacturing industry was affected by many internal problems, including a proneness to excessive competition. As for the mechanized flour-milling industry, products manufactured by the traditional sector were of great importance and demand dropped dramatically with the fall in purchasing power of the masses caused by the recession. In this case, even if exports decreased due to high tariffs, domestic industry was not necessarily able to get normal development under way. In this sense, there was a limit to what could be achieved by a protective tariff policy.

However, there certainly were sectors of production, such as the cement industry, the rayon-weaving industry and the cotton cloth processing industry, for which the decline in volume of imports, following the raising of import duties, helped to create conditions advantageous to domestic production, and Chinese capital enterprises were able to develop. Overall, the protective tariff policy pursued by the Nationalist government caused a dramatic decline in imports, especially light industrial goods, and promoted the development of China's domestic industry, including enterprises that had been established by Chinese capital.[3]

On the other hand, Chen Gongbo, who worked as the Minister of Industry from 1931–35, aimed for a strategy of export-oriented industrialization. In his view, China should develop light industry. He frankly wrote in his memoirs:

> If we discuss our national basic policy, there is no question that we must attach importance to heavy industry. If we consider China's economic conditions, however, I'd like to say that we should simultaneously start from light industry. Why? The reasons are as follows. (1) There is not enough technology or skilled

---

[2]   Kubo Toru, *Senkanki Chugoku Jiritsu e no Mosaku − Kanzei Tsuuka Seisaku to Keizai Hatten* [*China's Quest for Sovereignty in the Inter-war Period, Tariff Policy and Economic Development*] (Tokyo: University of Tokyo Press, 1999).

[3]   Kubo, *China's Quest for Sovereignty*, Ch. 6.

workers to develop heavy industry in China, while China has good fundamentals in light industry. (2) It is not so easy for the Chinese people to invest in heavy industry, while they have already successfully invested in light industry. (3) Foreign governments support heavy industries such as the shipyard industry, the steel industry etc., but the Chinese government has not enough money to do so.[4]

At the same time, Chen insisted in his paper published in *Zhonghua Yuebao* [*China Monthly*] that China should promote the export trade. 'The balance of foreign trade often has an important influence on the total national economy ... China's imports are not so large, while her exports are too small. Needless to say when compared with European countries, China's imports are less than any other Asian country's every year ... So according to my observation, we must promote exports and need not make haste to constrain imports'.[5] Pointing out the importance of the Southeast Asian markets where a multitude of Overseas Chinese resided, Chen visited Southeast Asian countries and encouraged the Chinese export trade, which he believed would help to develop new manufacturing industries (such as rayon weaving, celluloid processing, electric-bulb manufacturing, amongst others) in Shanghai. But his policies faced great difficulties due to the overall depression in the world economy in the 1930s and hostilities with Japan.[6] After the outbreak of the Sino-Japanese War, exports from Shanghai to Southeast Asian countries developed under special conditions (see below).

The last key personality was Weng Wenhao, who worked as the head of the National Resources Commission from 1935–49 and as the Minister of Economy (formerly the Minister of Industry) from 1938–46. He and his colleagues, including Qian Chanzhao and Sun Yueqi, believed that the most important task for the war economy, after the beginning of hostilities with Japan, was to construct a munitions industry based on heavy industry in the interior.[7] Weng wrote as follows: 'If there is no economic centre in the inland area, we are going to be poor by developing during peacetime and to be controlled by the enemy during wartime. So we could say that constructing the inland means constructing our China. As long as we have a self-supporting inland, we can defend ourselves and gradually try to make a counterattack'.[8]

Moreover Weng's proposals included distinctive methods and an original development strategy. Weng insisted in another paper that: 'As everything is under-developed in China, there are a lot of construction projects to pursue. But the national finances are limited and the responsible persons have not enough time to

---

[4] Chen Gongpo, *Sinian Congzhenglu* [*Documents and Memoirs of Four Years Engaged in Politics*] (Shanghai: Commercial Press, 1936), p. 91.

[5] Chen, *Documents and Memoirs*, pp. 232–3.

[6] Kubo, *China's Quest for Sovereignty*, pp. 141–9.

[7] William C. Kirby, *Germany and Republican China* (Stanford: Stanford University Press, 1984).

[8] Weng Wenhao. 'Zenyang Jianshe Neidi [How to Reconstruct the Inland Economy]', *Duli Pinglun* [*Independent Critique*], No. 124, 28 Oct. 1934.

acquire experience. All of these factors suggest that the Government doesn't need to proceed on everything simultaneously, but it must decide the order of proceeding on constructive projects'.[9] From this we can see that Weng and his colleagues attached great importance to a controlled economy and they promoted a planned economy to pursue the strategy of munitions industrialization. Such strategies and policies, as we will see later, were pursued extensively during the Sino-Japanese War.

China's foreign trade clearly reflected the various development strategies and economic policies mentioned above. According to the statistics of the China Maritime Customs, China's most important trading partners were the USA, Britain, Germany, Japan, and the Southeast Asian countries (including the intermediate trade of Hong Kong) (see Table 9.1). Due to the pursuit of import-substitution industrialization under the protective tariff policy, the figures for imports into China from the powers fell dramatically, especially those for light industrial goods.

However, the changes in the import trade varied greatly from country to country. In the case of the United States and Germany, which exported only small amounts of light industrial goods to China, the reduction in the figure for imports of light industrial goods was not so great. Taking the USA as the example, the decline in exports of light industrial goods between 1926 and 1936 amounted to no more than 30 million yuan (see Table 9.2). By contrast, in the case of countries with large exports of light industrial goods to China, the reduction in these exports was very marked. For Japan, in particular, the 188 million yuan reduction in exports of light industrial goods between 1926 and 1936 was six times the US figure (see Table 9.3).

On the other hand, China could export her light industrial goods to Southeast Asian countries. The intermediate trade of Hong Kong is included in this category of exports to Southeast Asian countries, since most of the exports from China to Hong Kong were re-exported to Southeast Asian countries. In 1936, China's total trade balances with Hong Kong (HK) and Southeast Asian (SEA) countries went into the black (see Table 9.1). Meanwhile, China's trade balances with Britain, Japan, and Germany reached tremendous import surpluses in the same year. No doubt, these trade phenomena encouraged the pursuance of a strategy of export-orientated industrialization.

The Period of War, 1938–1945

After the outbreak of the Sino-Japanese War in 1937, the Japanese Army occupied China's coastal plain, while the Chinese Army continued to resist in the inland area. Due to such a military situation, China's national economy was divided into several areas and the economic strategies and policies pursued in each area exhibited clear differences.

---

[9]   Weng Wenhao, 'Jingji Jianshe zhong Jige Zhongyao Wenti [Several Important Problems of Economic Reconstruction]', *Duli Pinglun* [*Independent Critique*] No. 69, 24 Sept. 1933.

Table 9.1   China's Foreign Trade by Countries, 1933–1937 (Value in 1,000 US $)

Imports	Year	Total (val.)	USA (%)	Gt. Br. (%)	Jpn (%)	Ger. (%)	USSR (%)	HK (%)	SEA (%)
	1933	354,517	22.11	11.45	9.84	8.03	1.63	3.59	20.00
	1934	347,893	26.39	12.11	12.32	9.07	0.83	2.88	15.58
	1935	333,150	19.03	10.69	15.19	11.25	0.84	2.21	16.95
	1936	279,752	19.70	11.74	16.31	15.96	0.13	1.89	12.97
	1937	279,935	19.75	11.68	15.71	15.31	0.04	2.00	15.18
Exports	Year	Total (val.)	USA (%)	Gt. Br. (%)	Jpn (%)	Ger. (%)	USSR (%)	HK (%)	SEA (%)
	1933	161,321	18.48	7.96	15.65	3.40	0.97	19.75	5.75
	1934	181,008	17.63	9.30	15.16	3.58	1.05	18.85	6.65
	1935	208,868	23.67	8.58	14.24	5.02	0.74	16.47	4.71
	1936	210,002	26.36	9.18	14.48	5.54	0.60	15.07	4.86
	1937	245,802	27.59	9.58	10.05	8.64	0.58	19.42	5.59
Balances	Year	Total (val.)	USA (val.)	Gt. Br. (val.)	Jpn (val.)	Ger. (val.)	USSR (val.)	HK (val.)	SEA (val.)
	1933	-193,196	-48,563	-27,737	-9,628	-22,980	-4,229	19,146	-61,614
	1934	-166,885	-59,903	-25,287	-15,425	-25,080	-980	24,111	-42,175
	1935	-124,282	-13,961	-17,675	-20,852	-26,986	-1,255	27,013	-46,637
	1936	-69,750	240	-13,553	-15,216	-32,999	881	26,370	-26,088
	1937	-34,134	12,535	-9,143	-19,286	-21,622	1,305	42,149	-28,760

Source: Computed from Appendices.

Table 9.2   Commodity Group Composition of Chinese Imports from the United States, 1926–1936 Million Yuan (%)

Year	Primary products	Heavy industry goods	Light industry goods	Others	Total
1926	109 (57.9)	39 (20.9)	35 (18.8)	4 (2.4)	188 (100.0)
1930	142 (61.1)	56 (24.0)	31 (13.5)	3 (1.4)	232 (100.0)
1933	93 (60.8)	44 (29.2)	15 (9.6)	1 (0.5)	152 (100.0)
1936	27 (32.7)	37 (45.4)	5 (6.6)	12 (15.2)	82 (100.0)

Source: Kubo, *China's Quest for Sovereignty*, p. 171, Tables 6–9.

Table 9.3   Commodity Group Composition of Chinese Imports from Japan, 1926–1936 Million Yuan (%)

Year	Primary products	Heavy industry goods	Light industry goods	Others	Total
1926	76 (22.6)	49 (14.6)	205 (60.9)	7 (2.0)	337 (100.0)
1930	52 (15.9)	90 (27.6)	177 (54.1)	8 (2.4)	327 (100.0)
1933	10 (14.2)	24 (34.9)	32 (48.0)	2 (2.9)	68 (100.0)
1936	11 (15.5)	38 (55.9)	17 (25.7)	2 (2.9)	68 (100.0)

Source: Kubo, *China's Quest for Sovereignty*, p. 171, Tables 6–9.

In the area of Japanese-occupied China, the economic situation was very complicated. In fact, there was an absence of a united economic policy or a consistent development strategy. Even the Japanese occupation army itself was divided into two forces dispatched to the different areas of North and Central China. In many cases, the two forces did not cooperate with each other. The more blunt occupation policy was exerted in North China. At first, since both the Japanese government and army wished to exploit a number of resources in North China, they linked that region's currency with the Japanese yen in order to facilitate trade with yen-bloc areas.[10] But the lack of consumer goods in North China resulted in a

---

[10]   Nakamura Takafusa, *Senji Nihon no Kahoku Keizai Shihai* [*Japanese Rule against the North China Economy during War-time*] (Tokyo: Yamakawa Publishing, 1983), pp. 103, 151.

large amount of imports from yen-bloc areas. Since the enormous import surplus was very harmful for the North China economy, the Japanese government and army had no choice but to adopt a new policy to restrain and control the trade of North China.[11]

Meanwhile, the war situation was becoming worse and worse for Japan. Hence, the Japanese government and army shifted policy after 1941 and tried to develop heavy industry in the North China area in order to support munitions production in Japan. There was, however, no chance for them to succeed, for the transportation system had been seriously damaged, labour was insufficient, and the various raw materials needed for production were in short supply.[12]

The Chinese Nationalist Government, moving their capital from Nanjing to Chongqing in Sichuan, promoted the strategy of munitions industrialization in order to support their resistance war against Japan. The munitions industrialization policy led by the National Resources Commission was developed in Southwest China, including Sichuan, Yunnan, and Guizhou. Weng Wenhao and his colleagues, believing in the superiority of the planned and controlled economy, made a big effort to promote munitions industrialization.[13] Their belief was as follows:

State building in the modern world needs to rely on economic power so that we can exist by ourselves during wartime and develop rapidly during peace time. (1) Building favorable fundamentals by a planned and controlled economy. The economic systems of contemporary countries are classified into three types. (A) Full state managed, planned economies like U.S.S.R. (B) Full governmentally controlled economies like Germany, Italy, Japan etc. (C) Mainly free competition and partly governmentally controlled economies like Britain, America, etc. ... China should adopt a mixed way. Considering the national defense as the most important problem, on the one hand the Government should take responsibility to promote state businesses, while on the other hand it should control private businesses so that they develop in accordance with state businesses in order to increase the nation's power rapidly.[14]

---

[11]   Ibid., pp. 250, 267.

[12]   Ibid., Ch. 4.

[13]   William C. Kirby, 'The Chinese War Economy' in James C. Hsiung and Steven I. Levine (eds) *China's Bitter Victory: The War with Japan, 1937–1945* (M.E. Sharpe,1992).

[14]   Weng Wenhao, 'Jingjian Fangxiang yu Gongtong Zeren [The Direction of Economic Reconstruction and our Common Responsibility]', in 'Zhongguo Guomindang Geming Weiyuanhui [The Revolutionary Committee of the Chinese Nationalist Party]' (eds) *Weng Wenhao Lun Jingji Jianshe [Weng Wenhao's Opinion on Economic Reconstruction]* (Beijing: Tuanjie Publishing, 1989, originally published in a journal of 1942).

By 1945, the National Resources Commission had become a huge economic administration with 119 business units with 63,700 engineers and workers covering the machine industry, coal mining, the electric-power industry and so on.[15]

The Shanghai area experienced an economic boom from the spring of 1938 to the end of 1941 when the Asia-Pacific War broke out. Meanwhile, the Japanese invasion was spreading throughout Chinese territory. As a consequence, the boom in Shanghai was termed 'the prosperity of a solitary island'. It was a result of many complicated factors. At first, it must be pointed out that Shanghai maintained many trade routes which facilitated the gaining of resources from foreign countries and the sale of commodities abroad, even after 1938. Shanghai could also continue to trade with inland areas under the Chongqing Nationalist Government (so-called 'Free China'). In spite of the economic blockade by the Japanese Army against Free China, Chinese merchants successively developed new routes entering Free China, and the Chongqing Nationalist Government also supported their activities in order to get necessities or raw materials. The second reason was the Shanghai market itself, which expanded rapidly. As the International Settlement and the French Concession in Shanghai became the safest spaces in China, about one million refugees arrived from other areas in China. At the same time, it was very important for the Shanghai economy that the commodities produced in the Shanghai area were exported to foreign countries, especially to Southeast Asia.[16] Under these conditions, some of the Shanghai industrialists sought to maintain exports to the Southeast Asian countries, in order to preserve markets during the difficult wartime conditions. To do so, they became supporters of the collaborator Wang Jingwei and his puppet government. In fact, those who participated in Wang's puppet regime, including He Pingxian, who took charge of its economic policy, usually insisted that their purpose was to save the Chinese who lived in the occupied areas.[17]

With regard to China's foreign trade during wartime, Table 9.4 shows the increased influence of Japanese aggression. If we break down trade statistics, we can clearly identify several patterns of trade in wartime China. Such trade patterns reflected the economic necessities of each area.

As the Japanese Government and army sought to exploit the resources in North China for their own munitions industry, they controlled the foreign trade in this area. Although they changed their policies several times, the basic trends reflected in Table 9.5 are as follows: a large quantity of resources produced in this area

---

[15]   Zheng Youkui, Cheng Linsun et al. (eds), *Jiu Zhongguo de Ziyuan Weiyuanhui: Shishi yu Pingjia* [*The National Resources Commission in Modern China: Historical Facts and their Estimation*] (Shanghai: Shanghai Academy of Social Science Press, 1991).

[16]   Kubo Toru, 'Senji Shanghai no Busshi Ryutsu to Chugokujin Shou [Materials Circulation and Chinese Merchants in Shanghai during War time]', in Nakamura Masanori et al. (eds), *Senji Kachu no Busshi Douin to Gunpyo* [*Materials Mobilization and the Army's Currency in Central China during War time*] (Tokyo: Taga Press, 1994).

[17]   He Tao, 'Wo de Fuqin [My Father]', *Ming Bao* (Hong Kong), 9 Feb. 1999.

Table 9.4   China's Foreign Trade by Countries, 1938–1945 (Value in 1,000 US $)

Imports	Year	Total (val.)	USA (%)	Gt. Br. (%)	Jpn (%)	Ger. (%)	USSR (%)	HK (%)	SEA (%)
	1938	263,938	16.98	7.93	23.28	12.70	0.62	2.75	13.29
	1939	406,984	15.90	5.76	23.32	6.55	0.00	2.60	9.43
	1940	511,469	21.30	3.99	22.81	2.69	0.01	7.19	16.12
	1941	605,487	18.44	2.19	18.91	1.99	0.03	14.47	20.69
	1942	165,758	4.28	1.98	61.79	7.43	...	4.18	7.60
	1943	159,686	5.50	1.88	63.66	11.42	...	5.90	7.81
	1944	77,815	4.56	2.33	61.89	16.86	...	6.08	3.26
	1945	21,027	7.19	1.07	56.72	9.55	...	4.78	0.37

Exports	Year	Total (val.)	USA (%)	Gt. Br. (%)	Jpn (%)	Ger. (%)	USSR (%)	HK (%)	SEA (%)
	1938	160,468	11.37	7.43	15.26	7.39	0.07	31.87	6.64
	1939	116,194	21.92	8.82	6.47	4.38	0.00	21.56	13.56
	1940	119,414	28.63	9.96	6.40	0.21	0.00	18.60	11.18
	1941	154,317	20.61	3.36	8.66	0.71	0.00	25.54	16.15
	1942	76,491	14.05	0.00	51.09	0.41	7.22	0.87	3.25
	1943	43,080	31.38	0.00	37.33	0.04	24.29	0.84	1.24
	1944	34,889	17.64	0.00	42.64	0.09	27.78	1.90	0.43
	1945	16,031	12.50	0.00	44.10	0.00	38.54	0.32	0.00

Balances	Year	Total (val.)	USA (val.)	Gt. Br. (val.)	Jpn (val.)	Ger. (val.)	USSR (val.)	HK (val.)	SEA (val.)
	1938	-103,471	-26,568	-9,009	-36,945	-21,672	-1,531	43,874	-24,429
	1939	-290,791	-39,222	-13,187	-87,413	-21,581	-11	14,454	-22,614
	1940	-392,055	-74,769	-8,525	-109,020	-13,521	-67	-14,562	-69,122
	1941	-451,170	-79,866	-8,090	-101,147	-10,957	-158	-48,185	-100,326
	1942	-89,267	3,654	-3,278	-63,352	-12,007	...	-6,260	-10,110
	1943	-116,606	4,739	-2,996	-85,575	-18,220	...	-9,057	-11,939
	1944	-42,926	2,605	-1,811	-33,285	-13,085	...	-4,071	-2,386
	1945	-4,996	493	-225	-4,858	-2,009	...	-954	-77

Source: Computed from Appendices.

Table 9.5   Foreign Trade in Occupied China, (a) North China, 1938–1941
(Value in 1,000 US $)

Imports	Year	Total (val.)	USA (%)	Gt. Br. (%)	Jpn (%)	Ger. (%)	HK (%)	SEA (%)
	1938	94,088	8.0	3.5	64.5	5.2	1.4	5.9
	1939	173,410	9.3	3.3	61.7	4.2	1.0	5.9
	1940	246,442	14.5	2.1	50.9	2.5	2.5	14.6
	1941	257,882	16.9	0.5	45.4	1.0	1.1	15.8
Exports	Year	Total (val.)	USA (%)	Gt. Br. (%)	Jpn (%)	Ger. (%)	HK (%)	SEA (%)
	1938	53,479	13.6	6.8	54.8	9.7	5.1	0.3
	1939	22,650	20.6	10.7	41.5	11.2	3.8	0.3
	1940	19,790	30.5	12.5	43.5	1.2	4.7	0.2
	1941	20,565	23.3	1.6	59.4	2.2	5.6	0.2

Source: Cheng Yu-kwei, *Foreign Trade and Industrial Development of China* (Washington, DC: The University Press of Washington, 1956), pp. 134–5, Table 44.

were exported to the Japanese Empire including Taiwan, Korea, and Northeast China (Manchuria), while most of the imports came from the Japanese Empire. We can identify this as a particular pattern of trade within the Japanese Empire's yen-block.

On the other hand, under the controlled economy directed by the Chinese Nationalist Government in Chongqing, the foreign trade in Southwest China demonstrated a different and distinctive pattern (Table 9.6). At that time, it was necessary for China's munitions industrialization to import machines or equipment to develop domestic heavy industry and the munitions industry. During the war period, Nationalist China imported such machines or equipment mainly from Germany, the USSR, and the USA. In exchange, it exported several strategic goods such as tungsten, antimony, tin and tong oil.

Finally, we need to pay special attention to the foreign trade of Central China (see Table 9.7). Shanghai continued to export many industrial products to Southeast Asian countries and to import several important resources. The total value of the exports to Hong Kong (most of which were transshipped to Southeast Asia) and the exports to Southeast Asia reached about 30 per cent of Central China's exports between 1938 and 1941.

In short, China had two patterns of Asian trade during the wartime period. One of them was represented by the foreign trade of North China, monopolized by the Japanese Empire, while the other was the trade of Shanghai with Southeast Asian countries from 1938–41. The former seriously damaged China's economy, while the latter provided at least some stimulation to industrialization in the Shanghai area.

Table 9.6   Foreign Trade in Free China, 1938–1941 (Value in 1,000 US $)

Imports	Year	Total (val.)	USA (%)	Gt. Br. (%)	Jpn (%)	Ger. (%)	HK (%)	SEA (%)
	1938	86,388	21.9	9.7	0.2	20.9	4.7	20.7
	1939	39,077	27.0	6.3	0.2	10.7	13.8	25.8
	1940	67,133	19.1	6.4	*	4.1	40.2	16.3
	1941	135,952	18.3	3.6	*	2.4	58.3	7.0
Exports	Year	Total (val.)	USA (%)	Gt. Br. (%)	Jpn (%)	Ger. (%)	HK (%)	SEA (%)
	1938	59,454	6.2	4.5	2.1	3.1	67.3	10.4
	1939	21,283	0.9	1.6	*	*	51.7	31.4
	1940	14,947	4.7	*	*	*	55.8	17.7
	1941	19,973	6.8	0.5	0.8	3.2	78.9	2.9

Source: Cheng Yu-kwei, Foreign Trade and Industrial Development, pp. 134–5, Table 44.
Note: * negligible.

Table 9.7   Foreign Trade in Occupied China, (b) Central and South China, 1938–1941 (Value in 1,000 US $)

Imports	Year	Total (val.)	USA (%)	Gt. Br. (%)	Jpn (%)	Ger. (%)	HK (%)	SEA (%)
	1938	83,462	22.0	11.1	16.7	12.7	2.3	15.4
	1939	194,497	19.6	7.8	16.9	7.9	1.8	10.1
	1940	197,894	30.4	5.5	10.8	2.5	1.8	18.7
	1941	211,653	20.4	3.3	11.3	3.0	2.6	36.6
Exports	Year	Total (val.)	USA (%)	Gt. Br. (%)	Jpn (%)	Ger. (%)	HK (%)	SEA (%)
	1938	47,535	15.4	11.8	8.7	10.3	17.6	12.0
	1939	72,261	28.5	10.3	6.9	3.5	18.2	14.9
	1940	84,677	32.4	11.1	10.1	*	15.3	14.9
	1941	113,779	22.5	4.3	16.9	*	19.8	25.0

Source: Cheng Yu-kwei, Foreign Trade and Industrial Development, pp. 134–5, Table 44.
Note: * negligible.

The Post-War Period: I, 1946–1949

After the end of the Second World War, the system of the controlled economy to support the resistance war against Japan was no longer required. The trends of the world economy were reoriented toward free trade, as suggested by the foundation of the IMF and GATT. Hence, on the one hand, led by the Prime Minister of the Administrative Yuan, Song Ziwen, the Nationalist Government selected a free trade policy in 1946. Song clearly announced his basic concept at the first meeting of the Supreme Economic Council. 'The Government should help the people's economic activities develop further, but should not control them. The Government should help people's economic activities proceed favourably, but should not intervene in them … With regard to foreign trade and foreign exchange, China must endeavor to concert with other friendly countries as much as she possibly can'.[18] According to Song's interpretation, Chinese foreign trade and foreign exchange were basically free after 25 February 1946 in order to increase imports and supply enough goods for China's national industry and the people's daily lives. The new company law promulgated in April 1946 made it clear that even companies fully-owned by foreigners would be allowed to develop. But the liberal policies of Song Ziwen did not succeed, because the sudden increase of imports resulted in serious damage to most of China's national industry, as well as a large outflow of China's foreign exchange.

On the other hand, some of the bureaucrats believed that the policies of the controlled economy during the war period had achieved positive results and suggested that the continuation of such policies would be the best course for China's economic development. The bureaucrats who believed in the superiority of the controlled economy concentrated around the Head of the National Resources Commission, Weng Wenhao. When the liberal economic policies of Song Ziwen ran into serious difficulties, the bureaucrats around Weng seriously criticized Song, forcing him to resign as Prime Minister in March 1947. The economic policy of the Nationalist Government turned to the direction of the controlled economy.

Nevertheless, the new policy of the controlled economy also failed to save China's economy. At that time, the Nationalist Government issued a large amount of money in order to raise revenue for military expenditures. As the large amounts of money in circulation brought down the value of the currency, the government could not acquire sufficient revenues to support its projects. After the spring of 1947, the vicious circle of financial deficits and currency issues resulted in hyperinflation.[19]

During Song Ziwen's free trade policy, China's imports suddenly increased, while her exports recovered much more slowly due to the insufficiency of production (see Table 9.8).

---

[18]   Song Ziwen, 'Zai Zuigao Jingji Weiyuanhui Shouci Huiyi Shang de Yanshuo [Address in the first meeting of the Supreme Economic Council]', *Dagong Bao*, 27 Nov. 1945.

[19]   Kubo Toru, 'Kingendai Chugoku ni okeru Kokka to Keizai [State and Economy in Modern China]', in Yamada Tatsuo (ed.), *Rekishi no naka no Gendai Chugoku [Contemporary China in Historical Perspective]* (Tokyo: Keisou Publishing, 1996).

Table 9.8   China's Foreign Trade by Countries, 1946–1948 (Value in 1,000 US $)

Imports	Year	Total (val.)	USA (%)	Gt. Br. (%)	Jpn (%)	Ger. (%)	USSR (%)	HK (%)	SEA (%)
	1946	560,555	57.25	4.59	0.40	0.38	0.65	4.60	3.63
	1947	451,031	50.20	6.86	1.69	0.02	0.31	1.84	6.41
	1948	211,028	48.45	8.05	0.94	0.03	0.98	1.48	7.14
Exports	Year	Total (val.)	USA (%)	Gt. Br. (%)	Jpn (%)	Ger. (%)	USSR (%)	HK (%)	SEA (%)
	1946	148,986	38.71	4.38	3.11	0.00	4.99	28.27	3.46
	1947	215,763	23.31	6.56	1.92	0.05	1.49	34.18	7.11
	1948	170,419	20.06	3.90	5.52	0.22	3.24	31.44	16.51
Balances	Year	Total (val.)	USA (val.)	Gt. Br. (val.)	Jpn (val.)	Ger. (val.)	USSR (val.)	HK (val.)	SEA (val.)
	1946	-411,569	-263,248	-19,203	2,371	-2,134	3,796	16,321	-15,166
	1947	-235,268	-176,120	-16,807	-3,465	32	1,830	65,438	-13,579
	1948	-40,610	-68,046	-10,352	7,434	315	3,460	50,464	13,078

Source: Computed from Appendices.

If we also take account of the activities of the UNRRA (The United Nations Relief and Rehabilitation Administration) the real value of imports was far more than the official trade statistics (see Table 9.9). Subsequently, a large import surplus inevitably appeared. After the controlled trade commenced, the glut of imports declined somewhat. This did not mean, however, that China's foreign trade had recovered to the pre-war level.

Table 9.9   Direction of China's Imports, 1946–1948, revised (Value in 1,000 US $)

Year	Total (val.)	USA (%)	Gt. Br. (%)	Jpn (%)	HK (%)	SEA (%)
1946	716,139	61.4	6.5	0.3	3.5	3.2
1947	608,552	57.0	8.5	1.2	1.4	5.0
1948	331,044	66.5	5.5	0.6	0.9	5.1

Source: Cheng Yu-kwei, *Foreign Trade and Industrial Development*, p. 180, Table 71. Total of commercial imports and UNRRA aid to China.

When we turn to consider the direction of trade, several interesting trends can be discerned. (1) Given the limited capacity for most industrialized countries, except the United States, to export to other foreign countries just after World War II, the United States share in China's imports rose sharply. (2) In China's Asian trade, Japan lost its past position because of its defeat in the Pacific war. (3) China's exports to Southeast Asian countries were favourably recovering in

1946–48. The total share of Hong Kong and Southeast Asian countries in China's exports exceeded 40 per cent (see Table 9.8).

The Post War Period: II, the 1950s

It is well known that the government of the People's Republic of China (PRC) initiated its planned economy after the Korean War. As the leaders of the communist government sought to accomplish radical industrialization to build their own munitions industry and a strong war economy, they adopted two sets of financial-economic policies. One called for the establishment of the planned and controlled economy to concentrate investments in heavy industry, especially in the munitions industry. The other called for diminishing the private sector, establishing collective farms or factories and strengthening the state sector. Policy-makers believed that such policies were the best way to accelerate industrialization and dubbed them socialism. In fact, however, the main trends toward the development of state-managed heavy industry were very similar to the policies of the Guomindang government during the Sino-Japanese War period (though the strong hostility to the private sector was somewhat different).

At the same time, since the development of munitions industrialization required the import of large quantities of machinery or equipment for heavy industry, the PRC government had to mobilize existing light industry and agriculture to export Chinese products in order to gain foreign exchange.[20] Notwithstanding that light industry and agriculture were also very important to the supply of consumer goods for domestic consumption, first place in the PRC's economic policy was given to exports designed to earn foreign exchange, rather than to produce goods which might boost the livelihood of the population.

According to Table 9.10, China's most important trading partner in the 1950s became the USSR, while the United States, Britain and Japan lost the positions they had held before World War II. Of course, this was an inevitable result under the conditions of the Cold War. However, we should also pay attention to the continuity of some trade patterns. On the one hand, China's trade balance with the USSR showed import surpluses because the PRC government had to import large quantities of machinery or equipment for munitions industrialization. Although China exported vast amounts of food and resources to the USSR, it could not match the vast sum spent on imports. On the other hand, China's trade balance with Southeast Asian countries (including Hong Kong) revealed export surpluses except in 1951, when the Korean War had a negative influence on trade.

[20]   Matsumoto Shigekazu, *Chugoku no Tai Ajia Keizai Seisaku, 1949–72* [*China's Economic Policy toward Asian countries, 1949–72*] (Tokyo: Institute of Developing Economy, 1975), pp. 145–9.

Table 9.10 China's Foreign Trade by Countries, 1950–1960 (Value in 1,000,000 US $)

Imports	Year	Total (val.)	USA (%)	Gt. Br. (%)	Jpn (%)	Ger. (%)	USSR (%)	HK (%)	SEA (%)
	1950	583	24.46	7.02	4.48	1.83	31.77	1.46	12.47
	1951	1,198	0.66	1.63	1.00	1.61	41.51	35.88	3.40
	1952	1,118	0.00	1.22	0.10	6.31	58.33	12.08	0.14
	1953	1,346	0.00	4.99	0.23	5.55	57.77	9.03	0.38
	1954	1,287	0.00	3.58	1.13	9.16	54.75	6.87	1.06
	1955	1,733	0.00	3.73	1.45	6.07	64.61	2.00	2.16
	1956	1,563	0.00	4.05	4.07	8.03	48.76	1.80	4.00
	1957	1,506	0.00	3.87	3.66	9.76	41.02	1.67	5.21
	1958	1,890	0.00	6.78	2.55	15.77	33.85	1.34	5.66
	1959	2,120	0.00	4.99	0.00	11.17	46.18	0.96	5.82
	1960	1,953	0.00	5.35	0.01	9.68	43.27	0.85	4.83
Exports	Year	Total (val.)	USA (%)	Gt. Br. (%)	Jpn (%)	Ger. (%)	USSR (%)	HK (%)	SEA (%)
	1950	552	17.30	5.91	3.81	2.06	27.76	28.11	0.64
	1951	757	0.01	2.05	0.13	7.58	41.12	25.69	0.88
	1952	823	0.00	1.48	0.40	5.33	50.07	20.50	0.65
	1953	1,022	0.00	2.92	0.67	6.64	47.03	16.45	0.89
	1954	1,146	0.00	2.15	1.79	7.28	51.19	11.31	2.24
	1955	1,412	0.00	2.84	4.12	7.18	47.47	10.96	5.64
	1956	1,645	0.00	2.99	3.94	6.20	46.30	10.48	7.26
	1957	1,597	0.00	2.75	3.74	6.39	46.77	10.97	8.32
	1958	1,981	0.00	3.82	1.64	7.07	45.37	10.80	8.04
	1959	2,261	0.00	4.03	0.00	6.67	49.44	8.45	7.27
	1960	1,856	0.00	4.42	0.00	6.10	44.12	10.69	8.46
Balances	Year	Total (val.)	USA (val.)	Gt. Br. (val.)	Jpn (val.)	Ger. (val.)	USSR (val.)	HK (val.)	SEA (val.)
	1950	-31.00	47.14	-8.31	-5.09	0.66	-31.94	146.62	-69.17
	1951	-441.00	-7.83	-4.03	-11.00	38.13	-186.02	-235.34	-34.02
	1952	-295.00	-0.05	-1.51	2.24	-26.70	-240.13	33.64	3.82
	1953	-324.00	0.00	-37.34	3.68	-6.92	-297.01	46.47	3.99
	1954	-141.00	0.00	-21.50	5.97	-34.53	-117.98	41.12	12.02
	1955	-321.00	0.00	-24.49	33.03	-3.75	-449.43	120.13	42.09
	1956	82.00	0.00	-14.18	1.08	-23.60	-0.41	144.25	56.87
	1957	91.00	0.00	-14.42	4.59	-44.92	129.24	150.03	54.50
	1958	91.00	0.00	-52.49	-15.61	-157.93	259.17	188.59	52.29
	1959	141.00	0.00	-14.76	0.00	-86.03	138.88	170.60	40.96
	1960	-97.00	0.00	-22.55	-0.19	-75.90	-26.38	181.71	62.63

Source: Computed from Appendices.

Table 9.11   Chinese (PRC) Trade with Hong Kong (US $ Millions)

	Imports	Exports	Total	Balances
1950	8.52	142.68	151.20	134.16
1951	429.79	182.36	612.15	-247.43
1952	135.10	162.83	297.93	27.73
1953	121.61	163.08	284.69	41.47
1954	88.48	125.68	214.16	37.20
1955	34.62	154.75	189.37	120.13
1956	28.08	172.33	200.41	144.25
1957	25.18	175.21	200.39	150.03
1958	25.39	206.81	232.20	181.42
1959	20.45	185.03	205.48	164.58
1960	16.61	191.67	208.28	175.06
1961	11.83	181.47	193.30	169.64

Source: Appendices. 1955–1957 Ex. Including Macao

Table 9.11 shows China's trade with Hong Kong and Table 9.12 presents Hong Kong's trade with China. Both sets of data reveal a large Chinese export surplus. At that time, there were many factors impeding China's trade with Hong Kong. The United Nations decided to place a trade embargo on China in December 1950 because of the Korean War. Facing such international conditions, the PRC government tended to develop its economic relationship with the USSR and the other Eastern European countries. The political situation in the PRC often prevented normal trade activities.

Table 9.12   Hong Kong's Trade with China (PRC) (US$ Millions)

	Imports	Exports	Re-Exports	Total	Balances
1950	136.99	220.52		357.51	83.53
1951	151.04	280.66		431.71	129.62
1952	145.30	91.01		236.30	-54.29
1953	150.00	94.56		244.56	-55.44
1954	121.07	68.39		189.46	-52.69
1955	157.09	31.77		188.86	-125.32
1956	181.70	23.79		205.50	-157.91
1957	197.94	21.59		219.53	-176.36
1958	244.46	23.76		268.22	-220.70
1959	180.98	1.55	18.46	200.99	-160.97
1960	207.53	2.27	18.77	228.58	-186.49
1961	179.96	1.38	15.97	197.31	-162.61

Source: *Hong Kong Statistics 1947–1967* (Hong Kong Census and Statistics Department, 1969).

Notes: 1950–58: Exports including re-exports. Original data was quoted in HK$. 1 HK$ = 0.175 US$

Even so, Chinese trade with Hong Kong did not stop and maintained a certain level of export surplus, as the PRC government intentionally promoted its exports to the British colony. The annual reports of *Jingji Daobao* [*Economic Herald*], which was one of the notoriously pro-CCP (Chinese Communist Party) economic journals published in Hong Kong, repeatedly drew attention to the export promotion policies of the PRC government. In fact, the Communist Chinese authorities dealing with foreign trade often pointed out that they themselves wanted to increase the exports of Chinese products for the Hong Kong and Southeast Asia markets, as verified by the following quotations:

> In this half a year, as we used the conditions of Hong Kong very well, our state managed trade and private trade produced lots of import and export activities and gained good results under the enemy's blockade.[21]

> Many native products in Guangdong must be sold to foreign customers ... If we want to open the foreign markets for native products at a reasonable price level, we should organize producers and private merchants and cooperate with them to struggle against imperialists and speculative merchants ... At first we should recognize that if we depend on the state managed economy alone, it will be very difficult to solve this big problem.[22]

> Regarding foreign trade with the capitalist countries, we should make one more effort to overcome the difficulties. In Hong Kong, Macao and Southeast Asia particularly, there is demand for our native products which do not have markets in other districts. If we give up this market, therefore, it will be unfavorable for us.[23]

But it was not an easy task for government agencies to promote exports through Hong Kong. The official records reveal many obstacles. At first, Communist China faced a lack of commodities for export, because the PRC government tended to

---

[21] The Department of Trade, The Central and Southern Districts Office of the CCP, 'Summary of trade activities in the first half of 1950', 1 Nov. 1950, in Zhongguo shehuikexueyuan and Zhongyang Dang-an guan (eds), *Zhonghua renmin gongheguo jingji dang-an ziliao xuanbian zonghe juan* [*Selected Series of Economic Documents of the PRC, volume on general problems*] (Beijing: Jingji guanli chubanshe, 1990), p. 276.

[22] The Department of Commerce, The Peoples' Government of Guangdong, 'Opening the foreign market for native products', 31 May 1951, in Zhongguo shehuikexueyuan and Zhongyang Dang-an guan (eds), *Zhonghua renmin gongheguo jingji dang-an ziliao xuanbian Duiwai maoyi juan* [*Selected Series of Economic Documents of the PRC, volume on foreign trade*](Beijing: Jingji guanli chubanshe, 1994), pp. 706–11.

[23] The Central Finance Committee, PRC, 'Responses to the report on the main changes in the domestic and foreign markets from January to April 1952', 14 May 1952, in *Economic Documents, Foreign Trade*, p. 555.

export large quantities of Chinese products to the USSR and Eastern Europe, while it also had to meet the consuming needs of its own people.

> At present the situation is as follows: while the domestic consumption and the foreign trade with the USSR and the Eastern European countries are increasing, the products for export become scarce. There is a contradiction between domestic and foreign consumption and another contradiction between sales for the USSR and the Eastern European countries and sales for the capitalist countries. How shall we solve the problems?[24]

Moreover, disputes occurred within the government. Some administrators insisted on exporting industrial products only and did not agree on the need to export agrarian products, while the Southern district leaders often had different viewpoints from the central government in Beijing. However, Cai Ze, manager of the China Native Products Company, was certainly more flexible in attempting to export all of the available goods, including agrarian products:

> It is a little difficult to trade with the capitalist countries at present. But each of our export organizations should not give up favourable chances and possible conditions, and should overcome difficulties to promote exports.[25]

In addition to officials like Cai Ze on the Chinese side, the British and Hong Kong governments also sought to develop trade with China to resurrect the UK's international economic status, in competition with the burgeoning influence of the United States. There were strong impulses, therefore, to increase British direct trade with China, as well as indirect trade via Hong Kong. Although the results were often limited, Hong Kong did remain an important source of foreign exchange for China.[26] And, as a matter of course, most of the exports from China to Hong Kong were re-exported from the British colony to the South East Asian countries.[27] Geo-political obstacles notwithstanding, we can still be confident in concluding that trade with Southeast Asia played an important role in Communist China's munitions industrialization policy during the 1950s.

---

[24]   The Ministry of Trade, PRC, 'This year's foreign trade situation and our policy in the future', Dec. 1951, in *Economic Documents, Foreign Trade*, pp. 688–9.

[25]   'Summarized Report of the 3rd meeting of managers', 4 Mar. 1951, in *Economic Documents, Foreign Trade*, p. 688.

[26]   Catherine R. Schenk, *Hong Kong as an International Financial Centre: Emergence and Development 1945–65* (London and New York: Routledge, 2001), p. 42.

[27]   Wang, Gengwu , *Xianggangshi Xinbian, shang ce* [*A New History of Hong Kong, vol. 1*](Hong Kong: Joint Publishing (H.K.) Co. Ltd, 1997), p. 314.

Conclusion

China followed very different development strategies at different period from the 1930s to the 1950s. If we pay attention to the main purpose and method of such strategies, we can classify them into three types. In short, they were: (1) the strategy of import-substitution industrialization; (2) the strategy of export-oriented industrialization, and (3) the strategy of munitions industrialization.

Due to the differences in these strategies and the influence of the Second World War, the direction of imports, which were mainly machinery or equipment for industrialization, changed drastically. In the pre-war period, China imported such goods from the United States, Britain, Germany, and Japan. During the war period, China imported them from the USA, Germany (before 1939), Japan (for the occupied areas), and from the Soviet Union. During the post-war period, at first the USA monopolized China's import trade and then the USSR took over the leading position from the Americans in the 1950s.

In spite of this shift in the countries that were the main sources for imports, we can find a consistent trend in exports during the period from the 1930s to the 1950s. China exported large volumes of light industrial goods and primary products to Southeast Asian countries almost every year (except for the unusual decrease in 1942–46 caused by war). China's export surplus was thanks to the trade with Southeast Asian countries. Of course, those who promoted the strategy of export-orientated industrialization attached great importance to this fact. But for other governmental leaders, who believed in different development strategies, the export surplus was also quite valuable as a means of earning foreign exchange in order to pay for imported machinery and equipment. Through this brief exploration we can see the importance of the links between Chinese economic development and the Asian regional economy, and we can also begin to gain a greater understanding of why we need to view Chinese development within the context of Asia as a whole.

Appendix 1

China's Foreign Trade by Countries, 1930–1948
(US$ Thousands)

	Imports							
	Total	USA	Gt. Britain	Japan	Germany	USSR	Hong Kong	Southeast Asia
1930	602,488	106,907	49,799	150,496	31,788	8,749	100,450	41,204
1931	487,386	109,256	40,795	98,664	28,395	8,500	75,506	27,225
1932	356,744	91,520	40,525	50,467	24,451	5,894	20,561	68,545
1933	354,517	78,374	40,585	34,870	28,459	5,786	12,722	70,887
1934	347,893	91,810	42,114	42,871	31,553	2,886	10,014	54,207
1935	333,150	63,400	35,602	50,593	37,470	2,791	7,379	56,477
1936	279,752	55,119	32,831	45,631	44,639	370	5,287	36,293
1937	279,935	55,291	32,698	43,992	42,861	113	5,590	42,499
1938	263,938	44,817	20,937	61,433	33,530	1,648	7,266	35,083
1939	406,984	64,694	23,434	94,926	26,667	13	10,592	38,370
1940	511,469	108,952	20,417	116,658	13,768	69	36,770	82,471
1941	605,487	111,667	13,273	114,509	12,056	158	87,600	125,247
1942	165,758	7,095	3,278	102,428	12,318	…	6,926	12,597
1943	159,686	8,780	2,996	101,658	18,238	…	9,418	12,471
1944	77,815	3,550	1,811	48,164	13,118	…	4,734	2,535
1945	21,027	1,511	225	11,927	2,009	…	1,005	77
1946	560,555	320,927	25,733	2,265	2,134	3,643	25,793	20,321
1947	451,031	226,421	30,961	7,613	76	1,389	8,300	28,924
1948	211,028	102,235	16,992	1,980	54	2,059	3,120	15,064

	Exports						
	Total	USA	Gt. Britain	Japan	Germany	USSR	Hong Kong	Southeast Asia
1930	411,628	60,665	28,828	99,615	10,746	25,490	72,688	18,547
1931	309,222	40,870	21,939	84,755	7,867	18,583	50,426	12,352
1932	167,616	20,398	12,779	36,545	10,143	8,296	25,726	7,689
1933	161,321	29,811	12,848	25,242	5,479	1,557	31,868	9,273
1934	181,008	31,907	16,828	27,446	6,473	1,906	34,125	12,032
1935	208,868	49,439	17,927	29,741	10,484	1,536	34,392	9,840
1936	210,002	55,360	19,278	30,415	11,639	1,251	31,657	10,205
1937	245,802	67,826	23,555	24,706	21,239	1,418	47,739	13,739
1938	160,468	18,249	11,928	24,488	11,859	117	51,140	10,654
1939	116,194	25,472	10,247	7,513	5,086	2	25,046	15,757
1940	119,414	34,183	11,893	7,639	248	2	22,208	13,349
1941	154,317	31,801	5,184	13,362	1,099	0	39,414	24,921
1942	76,491	10,749	0	39,076	311	5,519	666	2,487
1943	43,080	13,519	0	16,082	17	10,463	361	533
1944	34,889	6,156	0	14,878	33	9,692	663	149
1945	16,031	2,004	0	7,069	0	6,178	51	0
1946	148,986	57,678	6,530	4,636	0	7,440	42,114	5,154
1947	215,763	50,301	14,154	4,148	108	3,218	73,737	15,346
1948	170,419	34,189	6,640	9,414	369	5,519	53,584	28,142

Sources: 1930–41, 1946–48: China Maritime Customs, *The Trade of China* (various years); 1942–45: Cheng Yu-kwei, *Foreign Trade and Industrial Development*.

Notes: Exchange Rates: 1930–41: Maritime Customs; 1946–48: Cheng Yu-kwei, *Foreign Trade and Industrial Development*.

Imports: 1930–32 converted from Haikwan taels; 1933–36, 1946–47 from Chinese dollars; 1937–41 from gold units; 1948 from gold yuan.

Exports: 1930–32 converted from Haikwan taels; 1933–41, 1946–47 from Chinese dollars; 1948 from gold yuan.

Appendix 2

China's Foreign Trade by Countries, 1950–1960
(US$ Millions)

	Imports							
	Total	USA	Gt. Britain	Japan	Germany	USSR	Hong Kong	Southeast Asia
1950	583	142.63	40.91	26.14	10.69	185.19	8.52	72.7
1951	1198	7.91	19.55	11.95	19.23	497.31	429.79	40.69
1952	1118	0.05	13.66	1.08	70.55	652.17	135.1	1.54
1953	1346	0	67.19	3.12	74.74	777.62	121.61	5.12
1954	1287	0	46.09	14.6	117.93	704.61	88.48	13.7
1955	1733	0	64.56	25.14	105.15	1119.64	34.62	37.5
1956	1563	0	63.34	63.66	125.56	762.09	28.08	62.5
1957	1506	0	58.35	55.07	147.03	617.73	25.18	78.43
1958	1890	0	128.22	48.13	298.07	639.7	25.39	106.93
1959	2120	0	105.88	0	236.73	979.06	20.45	123.36
1960	1953	0	104.51	0.19	189.07	845.16	16.61	94.32

	Exports							
	Total	USA	Gt. Britain	Japan	Germany	USSR	Hong Kong	Southeast Asia
1950	552	95.49	32.6	21.05	11.35	153.25	155.14	3.531
1951	757	0.08	15.52	0.95	57.36	311.29	194.45	6.67
1952	823	0.003	12.15	3.32	43.85	412.04	168.74	5.361
1953	1022	0.002	29.85	6.8	67.82	480.61	168.08	9.11
1954	1146	0	24.59	20.57	83.4	586.63	129.6	25.72
1955	1412	0	40.07	58.17	101.4	670.21	154.75	79.59
1956	1645	0	49.16	64.74	101.96	761.68	172.33	119.37
1957	1597	0	43.93	59.66	102.11	746.97	175.21	132.93
1958	1981	0	75.73	32.52	140.14	898.87	213.98	159.22
1959	2261	0	91.12	0	150.7	1117.94	191.05	164.32
1960	1856	0	81.96	0	113.17	818.78	198.32	156.95

Source: China's Foreign Economic Relations and Trade Yearbook 1984.

Chapter 10

Continuity and Discontinuity from the 1930s to the 1950s in Northeast China: The 'Miraculous' Rehabilitation of the Anshan Iron and Steel Company immediately after the Chinese Civil War

Toshiro Matsumoto

Introduction

This chapter attempts to clarify the relationship between continuity and discontinuity from the 1930s to the 1950s in Northeast China by tracing the history of the Anshan Iron and Steel Company (AISC). The iron and steel industry was the most important component of the munitions industry. For this reason, its development process strongly reflected the military picture, and was a mirror also of the international order in Asia. The AISC was the iron and steel industry's second biggest production facility in the Far East, and the biggest complex in China from the 1930s to the 1950s. The company was part of the Yen Bloc from the 1930s to the first half of the 1940s, and thereafter was encompassed by Republican and then Communist China. The AISC was originally established as a production arm of the South Manchuria Railway Company in 1918, and only in 1933 did it become a separate Japanese colonial company. The AISC drastically enhanced its production levels for the military designs of Japanese imperialism. The company's main equipment was conceived and constructed in the second half of the 1930s under the Manchukuo regime, and this followed the war programme instigated by Japan to fight against the US and the UK. This programme took concrete shape in 1936, and war commenced in 1941. The AISC rapidly increased its production after the outbreak of the Sino-Japanese war in 1937, and it became a gigantic enterprise in the 1940s and 1950s. Production was planned to support the iron and steel industry in Japan, and inhumane working conditions, including a forced labour system, victimized a huge number of Chinese. It is also worth noting that the AISC suffered serious war damage several times during both World War Two and the Chinese Civil War (CCW), and production was completely suspended in 1945. Notwithstanding this destruction, the AISC resumed its pre-war maximum production levels by the early 1950s.

Anshan is located in the Southern part of Northeast China. The Northeast became the most important district in the Chinese Civil War immediately after the surrender of Japan and the collapse of the Manchukuo regime. The Nationalists and the Communists made desperate attempts to gain control of Northeast China, and the balance of power in the Northeast seesawed between the two sides between August 1945 and December 1948.[1] International political pressures from the USSR and the US further complicated the entangled process of the civil war.[2] The military, political and economic influence of these two superpowers replaced those

---

[1]   The Northeast district became an important battlefield between the Nationalists and the Communists because of the weapons left behind by the Japanese army, the heavy industries developed under the Manchukuo regime, and the region's ample natural resources. When the Red Army attacked Manchukuo on 9 August 1945, the Japanese army numbered 700,000 soldiers, as well as 150,000 Chinese soldiers organized by the Japanese army for the Manchukuo regime and other puppet territories. All soldiers carried rifles, machine guns, or grenades. The Japanese army was equipped with 1,000 cannons, 200 tanks, and 200 aeroplanes. Some of those weapons were lost during the final conflict between the Japanese and Soviet armies. It was, however, still an important task for both the Nationalists and the Communists to retrieve those weapons in order to deny them to their respective enemies. On the other hand, the pig iron output capacities in the Northeast, 2,524,000 tons per annum, accounted for 75.2 per cent of the 3,361,000 tons per annum output of the whole of China in 1945. Meanwhile, steel ingot output capacities of 1,623,000 tons per annum accounted for 89.2 per cent of the 1,819,000 tons per annum total output in the same year. See Nakayama Takashi, *Sorengun Sinko to Nihongun: Manchu 1945.8.9.* [*The Advance of the Soviet Troops and the Japanese Army: Manchuria, 9 August 1945*] (Tokyo: Kokusho-Kankokai, 1990); Makoto Hagiwara, 'Chugoku no Keizai-kensetsu [The Economic Reconstruction of China]' in Shinchi Nagaoka and Hiroshi Nishikawa (eds), *Nihon-keizai to Higashi Ajia* [*The Japanese Economy and East Asia*], (Kyoto: Mineruva-shobo, 1995), Ch. 5.

[2]   The course of the CCW was complicated by the foreign policies of the USSR and the US. Both superpowers repeatedly forced their ideological partners to compromise with their rivals. The USSR concluded the Sino-Russian Peace League Treaty with the Nationalist Government in August 1945, believing in the victory of the Guomindang, and drew up joint development plans for northeast China with Chiang Kai-shek's regime. This treaty forbade the USSR from assisting the Communists. The USSR also feared the deep commitment of the US to the northeast. Because of these restrictions, the USSR sometimes ordered the Communists to retreat from important cities within areas that the Red Army had already occupied. On the other hand, Yan'an's strong resistance to Chongqing had led the US to arbitrate between the Nationalists and the Communists. The US feared that the Nationalist government would become bankrupt and that this would be followed by the collapse of Chinese society: the Americans hoped to prevent the Chinese from accepting the CCP cadres as their new leaders. See Matsumoto Toshiro, *Manshukoku kara Shin Chugoku e: Anzan Tekko-gyo karamita Chugoku Tohoku no Saihenkatei, 1940–1952* [*From Manchukuo to Communist China: the Industrial Reconstruction of Northeast China Observed from the Anshan Iron & Steel Company, 1940–1952*], (Nagoya, Nagoya University Press: 10 July 2000), Ch. 1; Steven I. Levine, *Anvil of Victory: the Communist Revolution in Manchuria 1945–1948* (New York: Columbia University Press, 1987).

of the UK and Japan. This meant that the military environment and international order in the Northeast China region changed entirely during World War II and the CCW. As for the volume of production by the AISC, in 1943 the output of pig iron was 1,308,000 tons, that of steel ingots was 843,000 tons, and that of rolled steel was 265,000 tons. In the Japanese Yen Bloc, which consisted of Japan, Taiwan, Korea, South Sakhalin, Manchukuo and others, these outputs represented 21.5 per cent, 11.6 per cent, and 5.4 per cent respectively of total production of pig iron, steel ingots and rolled steel. The outputs of the Yahata Iron & Steel Company, the largest enterprise in Japan, were 1,690,000 tons of pig iron (27.8 per cent), 2,244,000 tons of steel ingots (30.9 per cent), and 1,744,000 tons of rolled steel (35.7 per cent).[3] The statistical bureau of Liaoning province reported in 1989 that the production of the AISC accounted for one quarter of the total iron and steel production of Communist China. The report also stated that the amount of tax the company had paid from 1949 to 1989 was equal to one-third of that paid by all the iron and steel firms in China in the same period.[4]

The AISC was therefore a focus of the military operations of each power in the 1940s, that is, in the final stage of World War II and subsequently during the CCW. The course of warfare around Anshan was also extremely complex.[5] Even after the final occupation by the Communists in November 1948, the political situation in Anshan remained ambiguous. During those difficult years, the AISC suffered war damage on six occasions.[6] The damage to the AISC was very serious, and production at the company was at a standstill in the autumn of 1945. The production

---

[3]   Shigencho-chokan Kanbo Tokei-ka ed., *Seitesugyo Sanko Shiryo: Showa 18–23 nen* [*A Statistical Reference for the Iron and Steel Industry: 1943–1948*], (Tokyo: Tekko Renmei, 1950).

[4]   Liaoningsheng Tongji-ju [Statistical Bureau of Liaoning] (ed.), *Liaoning Fenjin Sishi Nian, 1949–1989 Nian* [*The 40 Year Development of Liaoning, 1949–1989*], (Shengyang: Zhongguo Statistical Publishers, 1989), p. 131.

[5]   The ruling regimes in Anshan changed bewilderingly: (i) 8 August 1945, the Japanese army, (ii) 21 August 1945, the Soviet army, (iii) February 1946, the Eighth Route Army (ERA) or 'Red Army' of the CCP, (iv) 2 April 1946 , the Nationalists, (v) 25 May 1946, ERA, (vi) 1 June 1946, the Nationalists, (vii) 19 February 1948, ERA, (viii) 6 October 1948, the Nationalists, (ix) 31 October 1948, ERA. See Matsumoto, *Manshukoku kara Shin Chugoku e*, Chs 2–3.

[6]   The AISC experienced war damage six times: (i) air raids made by the US air force (July and September 1945), (ii) the confiscation by the Red Army (autumn and winter 1945), (iii) the despoliation when the Red Army retreated from Anshan (March 1946), (iv) the exploding of the blast furnaces by the Communists at the end of their brief occupation (June 1946), (v) the destruction by the Nationalists and pillage by Chinese residents when the Nationalists withdrew from Anshan (February 1948), (vi) upheavals during the final reoccupation and evacuation by the Nationalists, and sabotage organized by the underground agents of the Nationalists (October 1948 to the beginning of 1949). Of those instances, (ii)–(vi) occurred after the surrender of Japan, while the damage caused by the Red Army at (ii) was the most severe for the AISC. See Matsumoto, *Manshukoku kara Shin Chugoku e*, Ch. 7.

levels of the main sectors in the AISC, however, resumed their maximum pre-war levels between 1950 and 1954 (Table 10.1). This level was achieved just before, or slightly overlapped with, the period when some new equipment provided by the USSR came into production.

Table 10.1   Output of the Anshan Iron and Steel Company, 1943–1955
Unit: 10,000 tons (figures in brackets are percentage of 1943 production)

	Pig Iron	Steel Ingots	Rolled Steel
1943	130.80	84.30	26.50
	(100.0)	(100.0)	(100.0)
–	–	–	–
1949	10.16	9.32	8.03
	(7.8)	(11.1)	(30.3)
1950	51.60	38.22	32.17
	(39.4)	(45.3)	(121.4)
1951	67.63	60.32	47.61
	(51.7)	(71.6)	(179.7)
1952	82.56	79.44	63.15
	(63.1)	(94.2)	(238.3)
1953	105.55	89.03	74.90
	(80.7)	(105.6)	(282.6)
1954	150.51	99.91	84.78
	(115.1)	(118.5)	(319.9)
1955	213.55	115.23	97.62
	(163.3)	(136.7)	(368.4)

Sources: The data for 1943 is based upon Shigencho-chokan Kanbo Tokei-ka (ed.), *Seitesugyo Sanko Shiryo Showa 18–23 nen* [*A Statistical Reference on the Iron and Steel Industry 1943–1948*], (Tokyo, Tekko Renmei, 1950). The rest of the data is extracted from Angang Shizhi Bianzuan Weiyuan-hui (ed.), *Angang-zhi 1916–1985* [*A History of Anshan Iron & Steel Co.*], (Beijing, Renmin-chubangshe, 1991), pp. 311, 325, 374–5. See also Matsumoto, *Manshukoku kara Shin Chugoku e*, p. 5.

The reconstruction of the AISC in the 'Three Year Reconstruction Period' (1949–52) can be described as 'miraculous'. In 1953, the First Five Year Plan (FFYP) supported by the USSR commenced. However, at Anshan, some parts of the FFYP were launched in 1952 – that is, (i) No.7 blast furnace, (ii) the seamless tubing mill, and (iii) the heavy rolling mill, the so-called 'Three Major Projects'. Moreover, the planned output of those pieces of equipment was realized as early as November and December 1953. This meant that reconstruction in the early-1950s relied primarily on the original pre-war equipment. This phenomenon demonstrates that continuous and discontinuous factors could exist side by side in the rejuvenation of the iron and steel industry at Anshan.

How was it possible to restore this output in spite of the heavy damage sustained during World War II and the CCW in such a short period? How can we explain both continuity and discontinuity within the company as a whole? Despite the important role of the AISC outlined above, few studies addressing these questions have been published.[7]

The factors that permitted the rapid reconstruction of the AISC under CCP administration can be summarized as follows: (i) the arrival of young Chinese engineers and workers at Anshan from all over China; (ii) the know-how and the skill of engineers and workers, which was developed and nurtured by an established training system and by an exceptional enthusiasm for reconstruction; (iii) the latest technical and managerial know-how was utilised, including the flexible man-power policy of the Communists, who contained their hostility towards their ex-enemies to create a new steel production technology, and also encouraged competitiveness between the Japanese and the ex-Nationalist Chinese engineers; (iv) the experience and skills of the remaining Chinese workers; (v) the availability and cooperation of the Japanese and the ex-Nationalist Chinese engineers; (vi) captured documents on the operations of the Manchurian Iron and Steel Company (MISC) (as the AISC was known between 1944 and 1945); and, (vii) the use made of the remaining original equipment. When all these seven factors were combined, the AISC dramatically recovered its facilities, and resumed its pre-war production level within a few years. Figure 10.1 illustrates the relationship between these factors. In the first stage of reconstruction, that is, during the Three Year Reconstruction Period, 1949–52, factors (iii), (iv), (v), and (vii) were vitally important. Therefore, the rest of this chapter focuses on these factors.

---

[7]   Historical analyses of the AISC during the 1940s and 1950s have been few for the following two reasons: (i) a lack of archival material and (ii) ideological obstacles in the way of acknowledging rapid economic development under the Manchukuo regime, and its effects upon Communist China. Many historical resources were lost in the chaos during and immediately after World War II. Nonetheless, a not inconsiderable amount of material exists not only in Anshan, but also in Nanjing, Taipei, Tokyo, Washington, and London. Iron and steel is a key strategic industry. For this reason, the Communists and the Guomindang strictly prohibited researchers from using their collections until the 1980s. On the other hand, many historians in post-war Japan viewed the rise of communism in China somewhat stereotypically as either just or liberating. These views undoubtedly contain some important truths. However, general acceptance of this viewpoint has tended to overlook the positive aspects of industrial development by the colonial authorities in Manchuria.

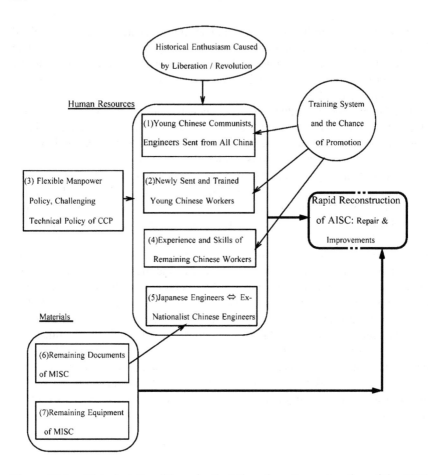

Figure 10.1   Historical Conditions for the Miraculous Reconstruction of the AISC

From War Damage to Reconstruction of the Iron-Smelting Department

We focus our enquiries on the main departments of the AISC in the following sections, that is, the iron-smelting sector in this section, and the steel-smelting sector in the next section.

(1) Serious Damage and Suspended Production

We can see from Table 10.2 that the principal equipment of the iron-smelting sector was heavily damaged by the Red Army's confiscation policies during 1945 and 1946. In the sponge iron plant, all four of the rotary kilns were cut into pieces and carried away. The Red Army took the most important parts of the three blast furnaces – namely, the mud guns, hoisting equipment, turbo-blowers, hot stove burners, pig iron casting machines, and pig ladles. In addition to the above, a loading bridge of a loading bin was completely removed and the other one was partially dislodged.[8] The weights of the machines removed from the factories were measured one by one by using track scales to accomplish the daily task given to each factory by the Red Army.[9] All blast furnaces ceased their production after the confiscation.

Table 10.2   Damage to the Iron-Smelting Department in Autumn 1945 Capacity (1,000 ton) or Number of Machines

	Original Annual Capacity (OAC)	Lost Annual Capacity (LAC)	LAC/OAC (%)
Sponge Iron Plant	80 tons	80 tons	100
Iron Blower	13	8	62
Plant Gas Washer	15	7	47
Kiln	4	4	100
Blast Furnace	1950 tons	1950 tons	100
	9	9	100

Sources: Umene Jozaburo, *Tohokuchiiki no Seitetsukai no Zenbo* [*The Iron & Steel Industry of the Northeast District of China*], Anshan: the National Resource Commission, 1946, p. 37; *Ziyuan Weiyuan-hui [the National Resource Commission]*, *Anshan Gangtie Youxian Gongsi Gaikuang* [*A Guide to the Anshan Iron and Steel Co. Ltd.*], Ziyuan-Weiyuan-hui, 1947, p. 24 (Place of publication unknown); see also Matsumoto, *Manshukoku kara Shin Chugoku e*, p. 185.

The level of damage to individual blast furnaces varied, as did the completion rates of the repairs (Table 10.3). The remaining three furnaces that were 'liberated' from destruction by the Red Army in February 1946 suffered only slight damage.[10] However, the Communist army inflicted new damage upon these furnaces at the beginning of June. Of the three remaining furnaces, the army exploded two (No.1 and No.4) and attempted to destroy the No.2 furnace also.[11]

---

[8]   Edwin W. Pauley, *Report on Japanese Assets in Manchuria to the President of the United States* (Washington: United States Government Printing Office, 1946), p. 110.

[9]   Matsumoto, *Manshukoku kara Shin Chugoku e*, Ch. 4.

[10]   Naikaku-Kanbo-Chosashitsu [the Cabinet Research Office] (ed.), *Chukyo Tekkogyo Chosa Hokokusho [A Survey Report on the Steel Industry of Communist China]*, Enterprise Edition (Tokyo: Chukyo Tekkogyo Chosa Hokokusho Kanko-kai, 1956), p. 39.

[11]   Pauley, *Report on Japanese Assets in Manchuria*, p. 112, Naikaku-Kanbo-Chosashitsu, *Chukyo Tekkogyo Chosa Hokokusho*, p. 40, Matsumoto, *Manshukoku kara Shin Chugoku e*, Ch. 4.

Table 10.3   Type of Damage to the Blast Furnaces and Perpetrator in 1945–1946

Name of Blast Furnace / Capacity per Day	Type of Damage	Damaged By	Time/Order of Recovery
No.1 / 400 tons	Explosion	CCP	September,1949 / 2
No.2 / 400 tons	Explosion	CCP	June, 1949 / 1
No.3 / 550 tons	Removal	Red Army	December, 1957 / 8
No.4 / 600 tons	Explosion	CCP	January, 1950 / 3
No.5 / 700 tons	Removal	Red Army	July, 1955 / 7
No.6 / 700 tons	Removal	Red Army	September, 1954 / 6
No.7 / 700 tons	Removal	Red Army	December, 1953 / 5
No.8 / 700 tons	Removal	Red Army	November, 1953 / 4
No.9 / 700 tons	Removal	Red Army	July, 1956 / 9

Sources: Angang Shizhi Bianzuan Weiyuan-hui (ed.), *Angang-zhi 1916–1985* [*A History of Anshan Iron & Steel Co.*], (Beijing, Renmin-chubangshe, 1991), pp. 56–69, 316; Naikaku-Kanbo-Chosashitsu (ed.) [the Cabinet Research Office], *Chukyo Tekkogyo Chosa Hokokusho* [*Survey Report on the Steel Industry of Communist China*], Enterprise Edition (Tokyo, Chukyo Tekkogyo Chosa Hokokusho Kanko-kai, 1956), pp. 39–43; Edwin W. Pauley, *Report on Japanese Assets in Manchuria to the President of the United States*, 1946, p. 112.

(2) The Remaining Structures: Reports and Memories of the Witnesses

Three reports, one written by a Japanese and two by Americans who observed the iron-smelting sector of the AISC in 1946, provide us with a description of the level of damage inflicted upon the company. Three quotations from these reports are specially extracted below. All of these historical documents demonstrate that many of the structures and sets of facilities and machinery remained untouched. All the removed equipment was transported by freight cars. The furnace bodies (four pillars of the turret, the iron skin, the iron belt, and the inclined tower for insertion), however, were left where they stood without being repaired.[12] Considerable sections of the factories and the offices of the AISC remained intact, and more than a few machines and manufacturing instruments were left undamaged in the 1950s. The damage to the blast furnaces was mostly to their key components, but the furnace bodies themselves were left in a state capable of repair and re-utilisation.

---

[12]   Naikaku-Kanbo-Chosashitsu, *Chukyo Tekkogyo Chosa Hokokusho*, p. 39.

(a) Theodore L. Johnston, a member of Edwin Pauley's mission engaged in the investigation into mining, concentration, and iron manufacture:

> In most cases the equipment removed is only a fraction of the whole installation but that fraction constituted a vital missing link that prevents the whole unit from operation.[13]

Johnston hereby placed emphasis on the following two points: (i) the various facilities that were taken away by the Soviet army were a small proportion of the whole site. However, (ii) those items removed were the parts indispensable for the operation of the facilities, and their absence caused serious problems for the operation of the mining shops, the concentration shops, and the iron manufacturing shops. Accepting Johnston's report, Pauley was of the view that it was possible to resume the operation of two 700-ton-per-day furnaces within six months by temporarily using the remaining parts of the other blast furnaces. He also believed that the resumed operation of one blast furnace would be possible in three months. In addition, Pauley also recognised that the repair of the furnace had been progressed to a considerable degree by the Soviet army.[14]

(b) Kiichi Saeki, chief of the clerical-work section (Gyomu Kacho) of the MISC:

> As far as I remember, Anshan and Benxihu were never 100 per cent damaged. *None of the facilities were removed to the extent of eradication.* As you may be aware, large-sized facilities including blast furnaces can never be removed by dismantling them, although they actually broke the equipment. In the case of an iron mill, indispensable facilities and machines are furnaces, compressors and blowers amongst others. The integrated operation in the factory could be disrupted in any of the manufacturing stages, even by removing a single motor. This nullified the capability of the furnace.[15]

(c) Edmund O. Clubb, the US Consul General Stationed in Shenyang (Mukden):

> 'Showa' plant is completely idle. Chinese claim equipment removed by Soviet(s) from 6 of 9 local blast furnaces. *Time factor prevented my verification extent dismantling but apparently furnaces structurally intact.* ... ReConstel, inspection revealed no substantial damage caused to plant by American bombing and that *estimate 70 to 80 recent removal equipment by Soviets was substantial exaggeration*

---

[13]   Theodore L. Johnston, 'Plant Inspection Report 2-A-1, Appendix 5' in Pauley, *Report on Japanese Assets in Manchuria*, p. 4. Emphasis added.

[14]   Pauley, *Report on Japanese Assets in Manchuria*, p. 110.

[15]   Yomiuri Shimbunsha (ed.), *Manshu Keiei no Kessan: Showa-shi no Ten-no* [*A Settlement of Accounts regarding the Management of Manchuria: The Emperor in the History of Showa*], vol. 6 (Tokyo, Yomiuri Shimbun-sha, 1969), pp. 261–2. Emphasis added.

if plant be taken as whole. This believed [apparent garble] even if true as stated by Chinese official without substantiating evidence, that Soviets removed over 900 trainloads, or more than 70,000 tons, loot from Anshan. Loot from that point included, be it noted, livestock, grain, household furnishings, *et cetera*.[16]

(3) Reconstruction by the Communists

The Communist army finally occupied Anshan at the end of October 1948, and set to work re-constructing No.1, No.2 and No.4 blast furnaces, the damage to which was slight. The first kindling was undertaken with No.2 blast furnace in June 1949, with No.1 blast furnace in September 1949, and with No.4 blast furnace in January 1950. After that, the repair work to the blast furnaces was interrupted for about two years. Thus, the growth in capability for manufacturing pig iron, which had been improved in contrast with the capability of steel-ingot and rolled-steel production, was curbed (see discussion below).

Until the second half of 1953, the aid from the Soviet Union had not been substantial. Initially, Communist China had to mobilise materials and capital by itself. The main pieces of equipment for No.1, No.2, No.4 and No.8 blast furnaces were designed and produced in China.[17] During this repair process, Chinese engineers and workers accumulated technological knowledge and developed some new construction methods. In addition, some methods were introduced from the USSR. For example, a special heating plant to keep cement warm in winter was built at each construction job site.[18] Therefore we believe that: (i) independent China had already acquired the ability to rebuild and operate a modern iron and steel industry, and that (ii) the Chinese were able to utilize the legacy of the puppet Manchukuo regime.

(4) Rectification of the Imbalance between Pig Iron and Steel Production

The output of pig iron in the AISC recovered to the level of 825,600 tons in 1952. Although the output was still at a low level compared with the amount of 1,308,000 tons produced in 1943, the highest in the pre-1945 years, the volume was high in comparison with the highest output of steel ingots (Table 10.1). After World War II, the AISC did not need to export pig iron as raw material for steel manufacturing. The necessity for China to create pig iron to make up for the iron and steel imbalance in Japan had completely disappeared in the post-war years.

---

[16]   Clubb to the Secretary of State, 15 May 1946, 3 pm (Received 18 May, 7.30 am, 893.60 Manchuria/5–1546: Telegram), *Foreign Relations of the United States 1946*, vol. X, The Far East: China, the National Archives II (Washington DC: College Park, 1946), pp. 1126–7. Emphases added.

[17]   Naikaku-Kanbo-Chosashitsu, *Chukyo Tekkogyo Chosa Hokokusho*, pp. 168–9.

[18]   Gu Lei, *Angang Jiben Jianshe de Shigong Gongzuo [A Basic Construction of Anshan Iron & Steel Co.]*, (Beijing: Gongren-chubanshe, 1954), pp. 29–32.

The progress of recovery in the blast furnaces corresponded to the recovery speed of the production facilities of steel ingots and rolled steel. Pauley had estimated that two or three years would be required for the production capacity of the pig iron manufacturing facilities to return fully to the level of 1943.[19] But, such a complete recovery of the blast furnaces, was actually not necessary in the early stages of reconstruction.

War Damage to and Reconstruction of the Steel-Smelting Department

The AISC had two steel-smelting mills, No.1 steelworks (with a capacity of 580,000 tons per annum) and No.2 steelworks (with a capacity of 750,000 tons per annum). All of the equipment at No.2 steelworks, with the exception of the buildings, was removed (Table 10.4). The production capacity fell from 1,330,000 tons to 580,000 per annum between September and November 1945. The AISC lost over 60 per cent of its steel-smelting capacity when the Red Army confiscated the company's equipment. Even in this sector, however, the AISC recovered its maximum pre-war production levels by 1952–53. The output of steel ingots was 843,000 tons in 1943, 770,000 in 1952, and 976,000 in 1953 (Table 10.1).

(1) The Steel-Smelting System of the AISC before 1949 and War Damage after World War II

Under the Manchukuo regime, the AISC smelted steel in two stages, the preliminary smelting stage and the refinery smelting stage. Three 300-ton preliminary smelting furnaces (300-ton tilting active mixers) in No.1 steelworks and four 300-ton preliminary smelting furnaces in No.2 steelworks were used in the first stage.[20] This smelting process was developed to protect the bottom of open-furnaces by causing chemical reactions with alkaline oxides, reducing the silicate content of pig iron.[21] This method had also the merit of saving steel scraps. The system was called the Iron Ore Combination Method, and was one of the indirect steel-smelting methods. It was reasonable and inevitable for the AISC to choose this method during World War II, because it could not import scrap steel from the US at that time, and the output of steel scraps by the AISC itself was not sufficient due to the imbalance between pig iron and rolled-steel production. No.1 steelworks was constructed in 1935 and No.2 steelworks in 1942. The Red Army destroyed the newer mill in 1945. Table 10.4 shows us the damage inflicted at that time. For example, 5,400 tons of equipment was removed only from No.2 steelworks. No.1 steelworks was left untouched.

---

[19]   Pauley, *Report on Japanese Assets in Manchuria*, p. 110.

[20]   Matsumoto, *Manshukoku kara Shin Chugoku e*, Ch. 6.

[21]   Chen Tsu-yuan, *The Anshan Steel Factory in Communist China*, Problems in Communist China Research Series EC9 (Hong Kong, the Union Research Institute, 1955), p. 42.

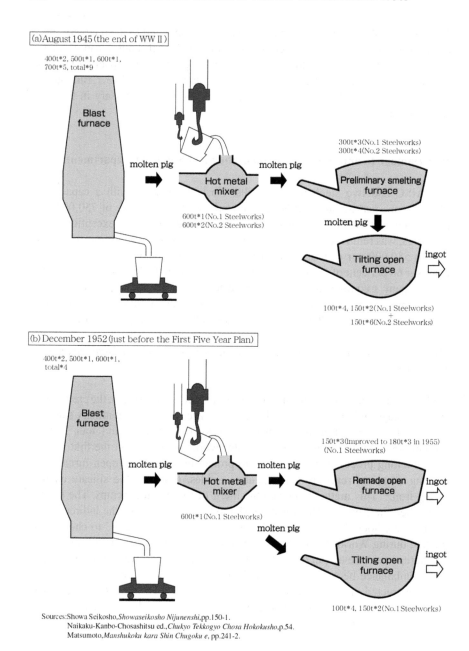

Figure 10.2   Conversion of Preliminary Furnaces at the AISC

Table 10.4   Damage to the Furnaces at the Steelworks: Number of Furnaces and Removed Furnaces (in brackets) in Autumn 1945

Furnace	No.1 Steelworks	No.2 Steelworks
600 ton Hot Metal Mixer	1(0)	2(2)
300 ton Preliminary Smelting Furnace	3(0)	4(0)
100 ton Tilting Basic Open-Hearth Furnace	4(0)	0(0)
150 ton Tilting Basic Open-Hearth Furnace	2(0)	6(6)
10 ton Electric Furnace	1(0)	0(0)

Sources: Earl L. Shaner, 'Plant Inspection Report 1' in Pauley, *Report on Japanese Assets in Manchuria*, p. 2; Suno Kunro, *Showa Seikosho Shiryo* [*A Document of the AISC*], Anshan, manuscript, 1945, pp. 4–5, 60, 63; See also Matsumoto, *Manshukoku kara Shin Chugoku e*, p. 236.

The Nationalists began repairs on No.1 steelworks in April 1946. No.1's 100-ton open-hearth was restored in the same month and started its smelting work in August.[22] The operation of the steelworks was, however, suspended again in October 1947. The spring attack by the Communist army in May 1947 forced the AISC to curtail operations and the autumn attacks in September finally stopped operations altogether.[23] Reconstruction commenced in full force after the final occupation by the Communists. No.4 open-hearth furnace (the ex-No.2) and No.3 open-hearth furnace (the ex-No.1) started their operations in April 1949. On 1 May, the Chinese Communist Party sent He Long, the vice president of the Southeast Military and Political Committee, to Anshan, and held an opening ceremony for No.1 steelworks. This was followed by the repair and opening of No.5 (the ex-No.3) in July 1949, No.6 (the ex-No.4) in December 1949, No.8 (the ex-No.5) in February 1950, and No.9 (the ex-No.6) in April 1950. All six open-hearth furnaces had thus started fully-fledged operation by April 1950.[24]

[22]   Xie Xuesi and Zhan Kelian (eds), *Angang Shi* [*The History of the Anshan Iron and Steel Industry*], (Beijing: Yejing-gongye-chubanshe, 1984), pp. 401, 460–61.

[23]   Matsumoto, *Manshukoku kara Shin Chugoku e*, pp. 137–8.

[24]   Wu Heng (ed.), 'Dongbei-qu Kexue-jishu Fazhan-shi Ziliao: Jiefang Zhanzheng Shiqi he Jianguo Chuji Gangtie-gongye-quan [Material Concerning the Development of Science and Technology in the Northeast District: From the Liberation War to the Early Period of the State's Foundation, volume on the Iron and Steel Industry]', (Beijing: Zhongguo Xueshu-chubanshe, 1986), pp. 482–5; Angang Shizhi Bianzuan Weiyuan-hui (ed.), *Angang-zhi 1916–1985* [*A History of the Anshan Iron & Steel Company*], (Beijing: Renmin-chubangshe, 1991), pp. 192–3; Naikaku-Kanbo-Chosashitsu, *Chukyo Tekkogyo Chosa Hokokusho*, p. 54.

(2) Conversion of the Preliminary Smelting Furnaces to the Open-Hearth Furnaces

The production capacity of No.1 steelworks was improved by conversion of three 300-ton preliminary smelting furnaces. Initially those preliminary smelting furnaces were repaired in May 1950 and, at first, the AISC used them in the same fashion as under the Manchukuo regime. Subsequently, however, the AISC tried to make low-silicate pig iron with the smelting furnaces. This change of production was proposed and designed by the ex-Nationalist engineers and was successful notwithstanding the opposition of the Japanese engineers. However, the production of low-silicate pig iron by the preliminary smelting furnaces was again terminated in July 1950, because it became possible to produce pig iron using No.2 blast furnace. The preliminary smelting furnaces became idle for a while. At that time, the AISC made a decision to convert the furnaces to normal tilting basic open-hearth furnaces. The experiments to introduce new production technology were carried out in December 1951.[25] After this, the AISC changed its steel-smelting method from the Iron Ore Combination Method, using preliminary smelting furnaces, to the Iron Ore Method, a direct steel-smelting method.[26] Figure 10.2 illustrates the differences between these steel-smelting systems.

The three 300-ton preliminary smelting furnaces (Nos.1–3) were reformed into No.1, No.2 and No.7 150-ton open-hearth furnaces in April 1952, July 1949, and May 1953 respectively. Originally, No.1 steelworks had four 100-ton open-hearth furnaces and two 150-ton ones. After this renewal, it had four 100-ton open-hearth furnaces and five 150-ton ones. Later, in 1955, the three reformed preliminary smelting furnaces were enlarged to 180-ton capacities.[27] Thanks to these renovations, the capacity of No.1 steelworks was much improved.[28] The rebuilding of No.2 steelworks, which had been dismantled in 1945, commenced in November 1954.

---

[25]   Wu Heng, *Dongbei-qu Kexue-jishu Fazhan-shi Ziliao*, pp. 101–4.

[26]   Naikaku-Kanbo-Chosashitsu, *Chukyo Tekkogyo Chosa Hokokusho*, p. 63; Matsumoto, *Manshukoku kara Shin Chugoku e*, pp. 239–42.

[27]   Angang Shizhi Bianzuan Weiyuan-hui, *Angang-zhi*, pp. 212–13; Wu Heng, *Dongbei-qu Kexue-jishu Fazhan-shi Ziliao*, p. 104; Naikaku-Kanbo-Chosashitsu, *Chukyo Tekkogyo Chosa Hokokusho*, p. 5.

[28]   Chen Tsu-yuan claims that 'technical improvement literally increased the bottom of the open-hearth furnaces by 56 per cent, and the cost of steel smelting was reduced by 10 per cent. As a result, though the steel-smelting installations of the AISC are smaller by 50 per cent than those in 1943, production is 19 per cent more than during Japanese days'. The percentages mentioned here might be incorrect. The increased rate of production seems higher than 19 per cent. Chen's figure, however, does demonstrate the tremendous results of technical improvements at the steel-smelting mills. See Chen Tsu-yuan, *Anshan Steel Factory*, p. 43.

Engineers, Workers, and the Manpower Policy of the Communists

(1) The Extraordinary Endeavours of the Chinese Engineers and Workers

The results of resumed operations in the early stage of reconstruction were excellent. This achievement was in the period immediately after the victories against Japanese militarism and the Nationalists, and ended over one hundred years of colonialism. A tremendous sense of historic destiny spread among the Chinese. As for Northeast China, the popularity of the Communist movement was much enhanced by the corruption of the Nationalist government following the collapse of Manchukuo.[29] Talented young engineers and students were summoned from all over China and sent to Anshan. Young workers got the chance to be leaders of each shop, and subsequently of the factories. This opportunity for promotion to positions of leadership had been closed to the Chinese under the Manchukuo regime.[30] Until the first half of the 1950s, at least, the enthusiasm among the Chinese had a great influence on their motivation to work.

The morale of the Chinese engineers and workers grew extremely high. They started their work and training at five in the morning and continued to work until late at night every day. In their records and memoirs, the detained Japanese engineers, the ex-Nationalist Chinese engineers, and observers who visited the AISC in the post-1949 period, recorded 'abnormal' devotion to the company on the part of the new Chinese engineers and workers.[31] The young Chinese developed a considerable number of technical innovations in machinery, heat control, and operative processes during the late-1940s and the early-1950s.[32] Competitions among workers were efficiently organised to maintain enthusiasm. During November and December 1952, for example, a 50-day *Hongqi Jingsai* (Red Flag Competition) was held. A new record was achieved for the shortest operation time of an open-hearth furnace – six hours and nine minutes. In the Manchukuo years, the shortest operation time had been around nine and a half hours.[33] The average time in the pre-war period had been between eight and twelve hours.[34] To report their new record, the Chinese workers despatched a letter to Mao Zedong, and

---

[29]   *United States Relations with China: with special reference to the period 1944–1949*, Washington, Department of State Publication 3573, August 1949, p. 300; Matsumoto, *Manshukoku kara Shin Chugoku e*, Ch. 2.

[30]   Matsumoto, *Manshukoku kara Shin Chugoku e*, Ch. 7.

[31]   Matsumoto Toshiro, 'The Japanese Engineers of the Iron and Steel Industry Detained in Northeast China', *Manchester Metropolitan University Discussion Papers in Economics and Economic History*, Series No.97–13 (Manchester: August 1997), p. 18. Matsumoto, *Manshukoku kara Shin Chugoku e*, pp. 290–91.

[32]   Matsumoto, *Manshukoku kara Shin Chugoku e*, pp. 239–41, 249–50, 253.

[33]   Wu Heng, *Dongbei-qu Kexue-jishu Fazhan-shi Ziliao*, p. 105.

[34]   Suno Kunro (the ex-chief of No.1 and No.2 steelworks in the Manchukuo period), *Showa Seikosho Shiryo* [*A Document of the AISC*], Anshan, manuscript, 1945, p. 47.

the reply from the leader of the Communist Party further spurred them on in their sense of mission.[35]

(2) The Manpower Policy of the Communists

Generally speaking, accumulated know-how and experience, for example connected with the design of equipment, the timing of casting materials, and the distribution of operation time, were significant in the planning and starting-up of factories. The detained Japanese engineers were a useful source of knowledge for bringing about the best performance of the furnaces and other equipment, according to the remaining design drawing and operation manuals. The Communists themselves recognized the importance of steel skills and know-how and, hence, criticisms levelled against their former enemies, the engineers from the Manchukuo and Nationalist periods, were considerably reduced. The Communists provided the Japanese and Guomindang engineers with special living conditions, in the form of food and housing, while attention was also paid to their pride as technical specialists, and they were asked to cooperate with Communist China. The AISC's captured records were re-deployed efficiently by the detained Japanese engineers who had originally drawn them up. In addition, trained Chinese workers who had remained in Anshan were gathered together to work in the factories.

The Communists sometimes instigated competition between Japanese and Nationalist engineers. For instance, Chinese engineers, mainly ex-Nationalists, sometimes ignored the Japanese engineers' suggestions, and implemented innovative new production techniques of their own. As mentioned above, the production of low-silicate pig iron using the preliminary smelting furnaces, and their later conversion to normal tilting basic open-hearth furnaces, were typical successful examples. Owing to the determined and independent spirit of the Nationalist Chinese engineers, the equipment achieved higher levels of productivity than in the pre-war years.

The manpower policy of the Communists towards the detained Japanese engineers was quite different from Soviet and Nationalist techniques. The first work undertaken by the Japanese engineers after World War II was the confiscation of factories. Obeying the orders of the Red Army, the AISC organized a bureau of confiscation, and a confiscation party for each factory. Shortly after the occupation of Anshan by the Nationalists in April 1946, the Japanese engineers switched the concentration of their efforts to reconstruction. The Guomindang's National Resources Commission forced the Japanese engineers to remain at Anshan to help rebuild the equipment. The Japanese staff of the AISC organized a group of experts, the so-called *Anshan-gumi* or Anshan Group. The Anshan Group consisted of 1,600 engineers and their families (about 6,500 individuals altogether). The treatment of the Japanese engineers by the Nationalists was harsh and discontent rose amongst them. The Nationalists intended to continue the

---

[35]   Matsumoto, *Manshukoku kara Shin Chugoku e*, p. 238.

detainment of the Japanese engineers and their families. However, under strong pressure from the US, the Guomindang regime permitted the gradual return of the Anshan Group to Japan.

When the Communists re-occupied Anshan in February 1948, most of the Anshan Group had been repatriated and its size had been reduced to some 100 engineers and their families (about 280 individuals in total). These remaining Japanese engineers, however, were the most experienced of the special technical staff. The Communists recognized that their skills and abilities were essential factors in the rebuilding of the iron and steel industry. The Japanese engineers were thus evacuated to Andong to avoid recapture by the Nationalists. The confinement at Andong lasted eight months, but the living conditions, particularly the food provided for them, were excellent as they would also be in Anshan later. The Anshan Group was brought back to Anshan by the Communists in November 1948 after their final victory in the CCW in the Northeast theatre. Thereafter, the Japanese engineers provided technical advice and tuition for the Chinese engineers and workers. Japanese and Chinese workers who had been working for the AISC since the Manchukuo years were put in charge of engineering and production.[36]

(3) The Return of the Anshan Group to Japan

By 1950, normal operations utilizing the remaining original equipment were basically attained at Anshan. In 1952, machinery from the USSR was introduced and the FFYP began in the same year (a year earlier than in the other districts of China). Steel engineers (after 1951) and technical and financial support for the FFYP (after the second half of 1952) from the Soviet Union accelerated this progress. By 1953, young Chinese engineers and workers had become familiar with operating the reconstructed factories. The Communists gained the self-confidence to operate the factories themselves, and changed their attitudes towards the detained Japanese engineers in the course of 1952 and 1953. Communist special education was now forced upon the Japanese engineers, breaking a previous promise that such lectures would not be delivered to the *Anshan-gumi*. The Japanese engineers were gradually excluded from productive activities. Even amongst the Chinese, senior engineers and older workers were replaced with younger ones. Replacement was accomplished by the early 1950s. The Japanese engineers, the ex-Nationalist engineers, and probably many senior Chinese labourers, were finally excluded from important roles in the factories. Their continued presence, however, had been necessary for immediate reconstruction during the first few years after the CCW at the very least. The last group of Japanese engineers was repatriated at the end of March 1953, six years and ten months after the formation of the Anshan Group, and seven years and seven months after the end of World War II in Asia. By this time, the AISC had almost finished the transfer of technical know-how from the

---

[36]   Ibid., Ch. 7.

Japanese staff, and a shift of management strategy from a Japanese- to a Soviet-style had begun.[37]

Conclusions

As this chapter has demonstrated, the international order in the Far East changed dramatically between the 1930s and the 1950s. The influence of the UK in Northeast China had been ineffectual since the 1930s, while Japanese power was terminated at the conclusion of World War II. The USSR and the US emerged as the new superpowers in the region. And, by the end of the 1940s, military hegemony within China shifted from the Nationalists to the Communists. The international environment and order within Northeast China in the 1950s was undoubtedly different from that of the 1930s and the 1940s. But this does not mean that there was absolutely no political and economic continuity between the 1930s and the 1950s in the Northeast region of China.

This chapter has additionally outlined the process of reconstruction in the iron- and steel-smelting departments of the AISC (MISC). The AISC suffered heavy war damage and both of the departments stopped their operations in the autumn of 1945. However, their reconstruction was achieved in only two to four years. The reconstruction of the AISC in the 'Three Year Reconstruction Period' (1949–52) was distinguished. It was a result which relied on a combination of many factors (Figure 1). The types of war damage experienced by the two departments at the AISC were different. In the iron-smelting department, many machines were confiscated or destroyed, but the main bodies of blast furnaces and other giant structures were left intact. In the steel-smelting department, the more recent No.2 steelworks completely disappeared, but the older No.1 steelworks remained intact. Both sectors resumed their maximum pre-war production levels in a few years, by rebuilding, re-using remaining equipment, and by implementing new production methods. The remaining equipment and records, and the operative skills provided by Japanese and ex-Nationalist engineers, as well as experienced Chinese labourers, were indispensable factors in that achievement. Concurrently, the endeavours of Chinese engineers and workers in the early 1950s were outstanding. An upsurge of patriotic sentiment amongst the Chinese immediately after victory in World War II sustained their great devotion to the rebuilding of the AISC. The patriotic sentiment and heart-felt devotion were mirrors of the new domestic and international political situations in Northeast China. Even so, it was the flexible and rational manpower policy of the Communists which proved the key factor, permitting other factors in the process of reconstruction to combine successfully. The CCP suppressed its hostility towards its ex-enemies, that is, the detained Japanese engineers, the ex-Nationalist engineers and the pre-war Chinese workers.

---

[37]   Ibid.

In sum, a considerable part of the material resources (the remaining equipment and records) ensured some continuity at the AISC. A quantitatively small but qualitatively important proportion of the human resources (the detained Japanese engineers and the ex-Guomindang engineers, and the trained Chinese workers) remained even after the end of the CCW. However, in terms of quantity, most of the human resources (the young Chinese communists and the newly arrived Chinese engineers, as well as newly recruited young Chinese workers) represented an element of discontinuity in the reconstruction of the AISC. Therefore, both continuous and discontinuous factors were effectively combined by CCP manpower policy. All the processes regarding the AISC presented in this chapter exhibit both continuity and discontinuity, and their complicated interlocking, in the political and economic transition from the Manchukuo regime to the People's Republic of China.

Chapter 11

The Survival of Economic Elites during Regime Transition: Government-Merchant Cooperation in Taiwan's Trade with Japan, 1950–1961

Man-houng Lin

Introduction

This chapter examines the level of cooperation between Taiwanese merchants and the government of the Republic of China (ROC) in the trade between Taiwan and Japan in the period, 1950–1961. It does this by drawing upon publications from a Japanese private company (Sumitomo) and Japan's Ministry of Foreign Affairs and Ministry of International Trade and Industry (MITI), as well as the governmental archives of the ROC deposited in Taiwan.[1]

During the period 1950–61, both Japan and Taiwan were short of foreign exchange. Japan did not have enough money to buy Taiwan's rice, sugar, bananas, lumber, and other primary products. Although the ROC took over a large number of Japanese factories in Taiwan, the ROC did not have sufficient hard currency to purchase Japan's machine parts to run these factories. Taiwan also needed fertilizer, chemical products, Western medicine, camera appliances and other products from Japan. Therefore, both governments negotiated year by year for precisely what to exchange, as well as the exact quantities of each product to be exchanged, so as to reach a balanced barter trade.

On the Japanese side, it was actually the SCAP (Supreme Commander for the Allied Powers) administration that took the principal decisions before 1952. MITI was the office in charge of foreign trade from 1945, and the leading decision

---

[1] As part of the book project, William C. Kirby, Man-houng Lin, James Shih, and David A. Pietz, *State and Economy in Republican China: A Handbook for Scholars* (Cambridge, Mass.: Harvard University Asia Center, 2001), the author has supervised several degree theses in Taiwan which have unearthed related archives and which have been written on related topics. The author concentrated on gathering materials from Japan, from Taiwan's archives for the Ministry of Foreign Affairs, the Taiwan Area Productive Enterprises Management Committee, and from merchants' biographies. This chapter summarises the findings of this teacher-student joint work, which spans the past decade.

maker from 1952 onwards.[2] On the Taiwanese side, the Central Trust Bureau was directly in charge of foreign exchange. This bureau was supervised by the TAPEMC (Taiwan Area Productive Enterprises Management Committee) in the period between December 1950 and July 1953, by the Foreign Exchange and Foreign Trade Section of Taiwan Province between July 1953 and March 1955, and by the Foreign Exchange and Foreign Trade Council of the Executive Yuan for the period between March 1955 and September 1963.[3]

Such a system of control over Taiwan–Japan trade would appear to substantiate the stereotypical view that the early post-war ROC government in Taiwan was largely a dictatorship. The command economy apparently controlled everything. This situation raises an important question: how far were the Taiwanese–Japanese business ties built up in the Japanese colonial period suppressed in the post-war period?

The existing literature would have us believe that the ROC government during the early post-war period did indeed suppress the Taiwanese elite from the Japanese colonial period. It has even been claimed that, 'the local elite stratum had turned into a vacuum'.[4] However, careful study of the evidence for this assertion indicates that it was mainly the political elite which was 'purged'. What, then, happened to the economic elite? The evidence to date suggests that there was a strong continuity between the pre-war and the post-war periods for the economic elite, in respect to trade between Taiwan and Japan, and in Taiwan–Japan trade with Southeast Asia. This chapter will present this evidence and identify the mechanisms for such continuities. Part one and part two of this chapter will deal with Taiwanese merchants in Japan and in Taiwan respectively, and part three will trace the international politico-economic background that underpinned the Taiwanese role in the Taiwan–Japan trade.

Taiwanese Merchants in Japan for the Taiwan–Japan Trade

Table 11.1 details the ROC government offices in Japan in 1951. This included the Commerce Section of the Representatives of the Ministry of Foreign Affairs stationed in Japan (Tokyo and Osaka), the Tokyo branch office of the Central Bureau, the Tokyo branch office of the China Bank, and the office for overseas Chinese.

---

[2]   Liao Hongqi, 'Maoyi yu zhengzhi: tairi jian de maoyi waijiao (1950–61) [Trade and Politics: Trade Diplomacy between Taiwan and Japan]' (Taipei: Daoxiang Press, 2005), pp. 1–2, 63.

[3]   Gaimushō keizai kyoku ajiaka, (ed.), *Chūka minkoku teki boeki kanri (fu bōeki tetsuzuki)* [*Trade management of the Republic of China, enclosed with the minutes for trade*] (Tokyo: Gaimushō, 1966), p. 5.

[4]   Peng Huaien, *Taiwan fazhan de zhengzhi jingji fenxi* [*A political-economic analysis of Taiwan's development*] (Taipei: fengyun luntan press, 1995), p. 104; Chen Lifu, *Jinji, yuanzui, beiju: xinshengdai kan ererba shijian* [*Taboo, original crime, and tragedy: the 228 incident of the new generation*] (Taipei: Daoxiang Press, 1990), p. 78; Chen Yongxing, 'Taiwan yijie yu ererba [The Taiwan medical circle and the 228 incident]' in *Taiwan yiliao fazhanshi* (*A medical history of Taiwan*) (Taipei: Yuedan Press, 1997), pp. 103–11.

Table 11.1   ROC Government Offices in Japan, 1951

The Commerce Section of the Representatives of the Ministry of Foreign Affairs Stationed in Japan (Tokyo)

Official Title	Official's name	Responsibilities
Section Leader	Shao Yizhou	General affairs
Deputy Section Leader	Wang Deli	Assistance with general affairs, contact with the Japanese government
Expert	Jiang Liang	Contact with SCAP
Technical expert	Li Yinchen	Buyers' entry and exit of Japan
Expert	Wu Dingmin	Applications for export permits
Senior expert	Zhang Youyi	Relations between Taiwan and Japan
Expert	Cheng Naichang	Treasurer
Section staff	Zheng Luda	Affairs relating to the closure of various institutions
Assistant	Ruan Shouwei	Census and statistics relating to trade with Japan, and negotiations with the Japanese government
Assistant	Zhou Zhanghou	Secretarial
Assistant	Zhou Zhuochang	Secretarial

Branch Section in Osaka

Central Trust Bureau, Tokyo Office

Manager	Wang Shenmin
Deputy Manager	He Xiaochao
Deputy Manager	Chen Xi

Bank of China, Tokyo branch

Manager	Zhang Wu
Deputy Manager	Cao Lichi

Section for overseas Chinese

Tokyo Office
Osaka Office

Source: Tsusanshō tsushōkyoku shijōkakuka, *Bōeki jitsumu shirizu, Taiwanbōeki no tebiki* [*Series on practical affairs of trade: an introduction to Taiwan's trade*] (Bōekikankōkai, 1951), pp. 125–7.

The Central Bureau was set up in mainland China in 1935. Whence in Taiwan following the Communist victory in the Chinese Civil War, the bureau stipulated trade policies and signed trade treaties with other countries.[5] From September 1946 onwards, there was a division of labour between this bureau and the Ministry of Foreign Affairs. In Taiwan, it was the Central Bureau which took full responsibility for Taiwan–Japan trade issues; yet, in Japan, the Tokyo branch office of the Central

---

[5]   Zhongyang xintuoju, *Zhongyang xintuoju wushinian* [*Fifty years of the Central Bureau*] (Taipei: Zhongyang xintuoju, 1985), preface, p. 58.

Bureau was subordinated to the Commerce Section of the Representatives of the Ministry of Foreign Affairs stationed in Tokyo and Osaka. The latter was responsible for dealing with SCAP and the Japanese government for the barter trade between Taiwan and Japan since some trade was tied up with military defence.[6]

The Tokyo branch of the Bank of China was designated by SCAP as the agent of the Bank of Taiwan to keep accounts and to provide clearance facilities for the barter trade between Taiwan and Japan. The account was denominated in US dollars and kept in both the Bank of Japan and the Bank of China. The assets and liabilities charged no interest. If the account was outstanding more than ten million dollars (at the beginning, it was four million dollars), then cash had to be used to balance the account.[7]

To carry out trade between Taiwan and Japan, Taiwanese merchants had opened 113 stores in Japan by 1951 (89 in Tokyo, 9 in Kobe, 9 in Osaka, 3 in Yokohama, and 1 respectively in Nagoya, Nagasaki and Kyoto). These individuals and the companies they worked for are listed in Table 11.2.

We can trace back the Taiwan–Japan, or even East Asian and Southeast Asian, trade network to the pre-war period for several of these post-war Taiwanese merchants. Some started to constitute this network by themselves, some followed their elder brother or father or uncle, and some had first served Japanese companies and then opened their own businesses. In addition to general trading, some were exporting rice and bananas from Taiwan, some were selling hat-making materials to Japan (and then processing these materials in Japan for re-sale all over East Asia), and some were importing western medicine, bicycles, fertilizer, flour, and other goods from Japan into Taiwan. These narratives demonstrate that some stayed in their pre-war business spheres, while others used pre-war Taiwan–Japan ties to diversify into other business operations. The following are some examples:

Huang Muyi: a native of Tainan, southern Taiwan who opened an ice company in Swatow in 1927. In 1941, he set up the Baixing Company with a main store in Shanghai, and branch stores in Xiamen, Swatow, Canton, Hong Kong, and Nanjing, conducting trade between Japan and China.[8] The store he operated in Tokyo in 1951 for the Taiwan–Japan trade continued to be known as Baixing (see Table 11.2).

Zhang Qinggang: after graduating from Taipei's Normal School,[9] he worked at the Taipei branch of the Mitsui Company. In 1925, he set up the Jierong Merchant Store as the agent for Mitsui to sell its foodstuffs, groceries, and matches with the value of sales exceeding capital invested by some ten times. Zhang turned into one of the leading merchants in Taipei's downtown in the Japanese colonial period. In 1940, as the representative of the Jierong Merchant Store and a council member of the Taipei Chamber of Commerce and Industry, Zhang attended the Bangkok Commodity Fair with seven leading Japanese merchants in Taiwan, as well as two

---

[6]   Liao Hongqi, 'Trade and Politics', p. 63.

[7]   Ibid., pp. 16–17.

[8]   Konan Shinbunsha comp, *Taiwan jinshika* [*Almanac of Taiwan's Notables*] (Taipei: Konan Shinbunsha, 1943), p. 156.

[9]   In Taiwan, 'normal schools' prepare students for primary-school teaching.

other leading Taiwanese merchants.[10] In the post-war period, as shown in Table 11.2, his store in Japan was still named Jierong.

Table 11.2   Taiwanese Merchants Trading in Japan (26 April, 1951)

Name	Company	Name	Company
Pan Zhenyu	Yaguang Business Company	Li Yizhao	Gaosha Merchange Store
Li Shikang	Xing Zhonghua Merchant Store	Lin Qingmu	Datong Trading Company
		Wu Yuchen	Zhonghua Miscellaneous Business Company
Li Huaxiang	Huada Business Company	Xu Peiyan	Xinshang Merchant Store for Foreign Goods
Zhou Chongqi	Zhonglian Merchandize Trading Company	Xie Chunan	Maoyi Merchant Store
Xu Hongyu	Shanxi Trading Company	ZhaoKangbo	Hongxin Business Company
Zhang Ziliang	Changfeng Company		
Zhang Jifei	Jianzhong Company	Chen Bailin	Hongsen Merchant Store
Huang Muyi	Baixing Merchant Store	Xu Xiantang	Gongyi Import and Export Trading Company
Wu Jingyuan	Yonglihuahang Company		
Shao Yuanpei	Minji Business Company	Han Shangyong	Xinxing Trading Company
Yang Yunzhu	Huaxin Silk Business Company	Huang Tangen	Santai Merchant Store
		Chen Fan	Huili Merchant Store
Zhang Qinggang	Jierong Merchant Store	He Yi	Yongfeng Company
Ye Songtao	Taiwan Provincial Fishery Production Cooperatives	Chu Mianqin	Jiangan Business Company
		Cai Moutian	Jinghua Business Company
Liu Azhen	Jianlong Trading Company; Dajian Trading Company	Qiu Xianjin	Taiwan Import and Export Merchant Store
		Jiang Shitou	Yongyuxiang Merchant Store
Ma Ximing	Nanyang Business Company	Li Tuanju	Xindelong Tea Merchant Store
Lin Youxiang	Zhongguang Business Company	Jian Wuchao	Wushun Trading Company
Chen Zizong	Zhengchuan Merchant Store	Chen Ajin	Kunqing Merchant Store
		Wang Chusheng	Jinlun Merchant Store
Liu Tianlu	Yongchang Trading Company	Lin Shuqi	Linweixing Merchant Store
Zhu Hanyao	Rongchun Merchant Store	Li Lianchun	Liyiao Merchant Store
Huang Dun	Penglai Sugar Company	Guo Zhenhua	Dongya Fishing Company
Ji Zhanchun	Taiwan Weaving Product Company	Lin Rende	Xinyi Trading Company
		Lin Jinlai	Sanjin Company Ltd.
Lin Keyi	Sitong Business Company	Xie Shuilong	Longji Merchant Store for Foreign Products
Huang Jishi	Guanglong Merchant Store	Lai Jinwen	Wenguang Merchant Store
Xie Chengyuan	Yiyu Trading Merchant Store	Fu Jinguan	Jinxing Western Medicine Merchant Store
Ke Shiyin	Jushui Merchant Store	Huang Tianyin	Sanguang Appliance Merchant Store
Huang Shushui	Chongde Merchant Store		

10   'Hanaka Hakkō, Bankoku oyobi Manira ni okeru Taiwan bussan mihon'ichi hōkoku [A city report of the samples of Taiwan's products exhibited in Bangkok and Manila]', 'Chōsashiryo [historical material investigated]' (Taiwanshōkōkaigisho, 1940), p. 12.

Table 11.2   Continued

Name	Company	Name	Company
Mou Younan	Chongde Import and Export Trading Co.	Huang Yuanzhu	Zhongyang Gear Company
Wen Chaozhu	Dehehua International Trading Company	Xie Jingzhi	Gongxue Company
		Lin Mugui	Sanxin Merchant Store
		Fan Jinfa	Zhongrong Big Drugstore
Xue Bengui	Huaqiao Commercial Company	Lin Yongsheng	Chengde Merchant Store
		Chen Xiushi	Taishi Merchant Store
Zou Renzhi	Wuhe Business Company	Lin Yujia	Linjianjia Ji Merchant Store
Shen Wenbuo	Dasheng International Business Supply Company	Fang Junming	Daming Trading Company
Huang Songchang	Xielian Trading Company	Lai Atong	Meiji Merchant Store
Zhu Wenyuan	Dafong Commercial Company	Zhang Ruixiang	Yufong Merchant Store
		Wu Xindeng	Wanmao Miscellaneous Merchant Store
Xia Qangpan	Daxinzhen Dying and Weaving Factory Company	Zhang Liyang	Huatai Merchant Store
Yang Shuyan	Tongji Company Ltd.	Lin Canrong	Tongrong Business Company
Zheng Jiyin	Huian Business Company		
Luo Wenshi	Dadong Company	Gu Weifu	Longchang Business Company
Zai Kegong	Tianyuan Business Company		
		Chen Xida	Chen Hefa Company
Zhaung Sichuan	Zhongxing Business Company	Yang Lianshu	Tongyi Merchant Store
		Chen Xingcun	Fugong Trading Company
Zhao Shuxun	Yatong International Business Company	Li Amu	Yongrui Merchant Store
		Chen Tiancheng	Jianyuan Merchant Store
Lin Yiwen	Huitong Business Company	Guo Yannian	Qiazhong Shanghang
Lin Binsong	Songyong Merchant Store for Imported Goods	Li Jianxing	Taiwan Coal Adjustment Committee
Zhou Xiang	Yongshun Trading Company	Du Wanji	Taiwan Coal Adjustment Committee
Guo Xuyong	Taicheng Company	You Zunde	Taiwan Coal Adjustment Committee
Cheng Yulin	Youxin Merchant Store		
Wang Zhongyi	Zhongan Trading Company	Yang Jiannong	Nanhua Trading Company
Shi Wanshui	Yongxing Trading Company	Chen Qingqin	Dayue Merchant Store
		Wang Qingzong	Taian Merchant Store
Sun Fengshan	Yuwu Trading Company	Lin Huorong	Lintong Merchant Store
Guo Qingquan	Overseas Chinese Weaving Products Co.		
Yu qiufen	Osaka Kawaguchi Trading Company		
Zhou Musong	Xingguang Company		
Wang Debei	Hualian Trading Company		
Li Zhixiang	Kawaguchi Trading Company		
Qu Minzhai	Asia Trading Company		
Wang Zhaode	Overseas Chinese Trading Company		
Huang Wanju	Daxin Business Company		

Source: As Table 11.1, pp. 127–4.

Li Yizhao: born in 1907 in Wuqi, central Taiwan, he moved to Kobe after graduating from normal school to help his elder brother develop the hat export trade to Europe, America, and Southeast Asia.[11] In the post-war period, he opened a hotel and helped establish a school for the overseas Chinese community in Kobe. Li was also vice-president of a company involved in the Japan–China trade before he died in 1981.[12]

Chen Fan: born in Nantou, central Taiwan in 1895, he formed a fruit and vegetable company in 1925 and extended its market to China. In 1929, he shifted business into bus transport in Taizhong, central Taiwan.[13] In the early post-war period, Chen was an important merchant in the export trade from Taiwan to Japan as shown in Table 11.2.

Table 11.3   Taiwanese Banana Merchants in Taiwan and Japan and their Inter-Relationships

Company on the Taiwanese side	Representative (A) (Ethnic Background)	Company on the Japanese side	Representative (B) (Ethnic Background)	Relationship between A and B
Dati Merchant Store	Chen Xingcun (Taiwanese)	Fugong Maoyi Co. Ltd.	Xie Zheyi (Taiwanese)	Mother and Son
		Wanda Shangshi Co. Ltd.	Chen Xingcun (Taiwanese)	The same individual
		Sanxing Shangshi Co. Ltd.	Xie Zhexin (Taiwanese)	Mother and Son
Dayongchanghang	Zhou Chengzhi (Taiwanese)	Yongchang Trading Co. Ltd.	Liu Tianlu	
Yongchang Shiye Co. Ltd.	Li Tingyou (Taiwanese)			
Dadonghang	Zhang Dinglan (Taiwanese)	Wanguo Trading Co. Ltd.	Li Banchi	
Gongxueshe Co. Ltd.	Xie Jingzhong (Taiwanese) Xie Jingzhi (Taiwanese)	Gongxueshe Wuchan Trading Co. Ltd.	Xie Jingzhi (Taiwanese)	Brother
Dayang hang	Cai Zhizhe (Taiwanese)	Day Yang Trading Co. Ltd.	Cai Zhiyuan (Taiwanese?)	Kinship Ties
Wuda Trading Merchant store	Lin Shengxi (Taiwanese)	Wuxing Trading Co. Ltd.	Li Lianchun (Taiwanese)	The same individual
Liyixing Trading Co. Ltd.	Li Lianchun (Taiwanese)			

---

[11]   Taiwan Shinminpō sha comp, *Taiwan jinmei jiten* [*Dictionary of Taiwan's Notables*] (Taihoku: Taiwan Shinminpo sha, 1937; Nihon Tosho, 1989 reprint), p. 37; Sumida Yoshihiro, 'Kōbe no kakyō kigyō [The business of Kobe's overseas Chinese]' in *Kōbe to kakyō* [*Kobe and the overseas Chinese*] (Kōnan daigaku sōgō kenkyūsho, 1994), p. 123.

[12]   Sumida Yoshihiro, 'Kobe's overseas Chinese', p. 123.

[13]   Taiwan Shinminpō sha comp, *Taiwan jinmei jiten*, p. 37.

Table 11.3   Continued

Company on the Taiwanese side	Representative (A) (Ethnic Background)	Company on the Japanese side	Representative (B) (Ethnic Background)	Relationship between A and B
Baixing Hang	Huang Muyi (Taiwanese)	Baixing Trading Co. Ltd.	Huang Muyi (Taiwanese)	The same individual
Yongfeng Hang	He Rongting (Taiwanese)	Yongfeng Wuchan Co. Ltd..	He Rongting (Taiwanese)	The same individual
Linweixing Shanghang	Lin Shuqi (Taiwanese)	Shui Shangshi Co. Ltd.	Ke Shiyin (Taiwanese) Ke Desheng (Taiwanese)	The same individual Father and Son
Shuixuan Trading Merchant Store	Ke Shiyin (Taiwanese)			
Inching Trading Co. Ltd.	Lin Xigui (Taiwanese)			
Xinde Trading Merchant Store	Wang Zhuhui (Taiwanese) Lin Ajiu (Taiwanese)	Xinyi Trading Co. Ltd.	Li Qilin Wang Zhuhui (Taiwanese)	The same individual
Xinyi Trading Co. Ltd.	Wang Zhuhui (Taiwanese)			
Lianqiao Business Co. Ltd..	Chen Shaohui (Taiwanese)			
Jianlong Trading Merchant store	Chen Chamou (Taiwanese)	Jianlong Trading Co. Ltd.	Chen Jianzhong (Taiwanese)	Father and Son
Jianyuan Hang	Chen Tiancheng (Taiwanese)	Jianyuan Hang, Kobe Branch	Chen Tiancheng (Taiwanese)	The same individual
Huaxin Hang	Guo Yuxin (Taiwanese)	Xinfeng Miscellaneous Goods	Guo Yuxin (Taiwanese)	The same individual
Guoji Trading Co. Ltd..	Lin Xichi (Taiwanese)	Guoji Tongchan Co. Ltd.	Lin Xilian (Taiwanese?)	Kinship Ties
Shunxing Trading Co. Ltd.	Xue Guoliang (Taiwanese) Xue Guozhi (Taiwanese)	Fuguo Miscellaneous Goods Co. Ltd.	Xue Guoliang (Taiwanese)	The same individual Kinship Ties
Wangong Hang	Wang Liyi (Taiwanese)	Wangong Industries Co. Ltd.	Shen Shuimu	
Yufeng Hang	Li Tu (Taiwanese)	Yufeng Trading Co. Ltd.	Zhang Ruixiang	
Longhua Trading Merchant Store	Xie Longcai (Taiwanese)			
Ruihe Trading Co. Ltd.	Lan Songhui (Taiwanese)	Ruixing Trading Co. Ltd.	Du Qing	
Ruixing Trading Co. Ltd.	Xie Wanhe (Taiwanese)			
Yiyu Trading Merchant Store	Xie Chengyuan (Taiwanese)	Yiyu Trading Co. Ltd.	Xie Chengyuan (Taiwanese) Xie Chengye (Taiwanese?)	The same individual Kinship Ties

Table 11.3   Continued

Company on the Taiwanese side	Representative (A) (Ethnic Background)	Company on the Japanese side	Representative (B) (Ethnic Background)	Relationship between A and B
Tongxin Maoyi		Tongxin Trading Co. Ltd.	Xie Chengye (Taiwanese?)	
Dayuan Trading Co. Ltd.	Xie Yuansen (Taiwanese)	Dayuan Trading Co. Ltd.	Xie Chengye (Taiwanese?)	
		Zhonglian Trading Co. Ltd.	Zhou Chongqi (Zhejiang)	
Xinxing Trading	Zeng Shaoji (Taiwanese)	Xinxing Trading Co. Ltd.	Han Shangyong (Shandong)	
Taiwan Xincheng Hang	Chen Qingcheng (Taiwanese) Huang Wanyi	Xincheng Trading Co. Ltd.	Huang Wanyi	The same individual
Dechengfa Trading Merchant Store	Chen Decheng (Taiwanese)	Tonghe Trading Co. Ltd.	Chen Weiqian (Taiwanese)	Father and Son
Qianshun Co. Ltd.	Du Wanquan (Taiwanese)	Qianshun Trading Co. Ltd.	Du Wanquan (Taiwanese)	The same individual

Source: Liu Shujing, *Banana Trade Network*, pp. 93–95.

Xie Jingzhi: born in 1918, he graduated from Hiroshima Commercial School. In his early years, Xie carried on stationery, book, paper, and printing businesses. After 1945, he obtained the agency rights for many brand-name products in physical education, and established a company selling products for both physical and musical education. As his place of birth was also an important banana-growing area, Xie additionally sold bananas and other fruits to Japan through introductions provided by the Japanese merchants who knew Xie through the education equipment business.[14]

Chen Xingcun: born in Taipei in 1910, she graduated from Taipei Professional Girls School. In 1932, she moved to Tokyo, graduating from the Tokyo Fashion School in 1935. In the same year, Chen returned to Taiwan to open a modified western-style clothes shop, employing 15 staff. Chen became a pioneer of Taiwanese fashion.[15] In the immediate post-war period, she was one of the leading merchants in the banana export trade from Taiwan to Japan (See Table 11.3).

Chen Xida: born in Taoyuan in northern Taiwan in 1896, after primary education he entered his uncle's store, known as Chen Hefa. When this store was reorganized as a joint company in 1927, Chen Xida became its manager. In 1931, he was elected congressman for Taoyuan. A year later, he visited several big merchant firms in Japan. Chen subsequently became a Taiwanese agent for the Kokura Petroleum Oil Company and the Showa Sugar Company. He also engaged

---

[14]   Zhonghua zhengxinsuo, *Dui Taiwan jingji zuiyou gongxian de gongshang renminlu [The who's who of individuals who have contributed most to Taiwan's economy]* (Taipei: Zhonghua zhengxinsuo, 1973), p. 504.

[15]   Taiwan Shinminpō sha comp, *Taiwan jinmei jiten*, p. 249.

in a large amount of business with the Japan Flour Company, the Japan-Qing Flour Company, and the Osaka Flour Company. In 1933, he achieved high office as the vice- president of the Taoyuan Chamber of Commerce and as president of the Taoyuan Rice Association.[16]

He Yi: born in Tainan City, southern Taiwan in 1903, he entered the transportation business for several years after graduating from primary school. He went on to work for the Anbei Merchant Company for four years before working for a sugar company in Houli, central Taiwan. In 1924, He Yi and his elder brother, He Chuan, created the Yongfeng Merchant Store for the retail and wholesale of fertilizer, sugar, and flour. In 1934, He Yi opened branch stores in various locations throughout Taiwan such as Gaoxiong, Dajia, Yuanlin, and Pindong.[17] The He brothers not only appear in Table 11.2 of this chapter on the early post-war Taiwan–Japan trade, but today their business still counts as one of the largest conglomerates in Taiwan.

Xie Chengyuan: achieved prosperity though the trading company which he established in 1926 to participate in the canned goods, vegetable, tea, and grocery trades between Taiwan and Japan. In the post-war period, Xie remained active in the trade between Taiwan and Japan. Each year, he divided his time equally between Japan and Taiwan, and he was head of the overseas Chinese organization in Japan. It was not until 1955, when he commenced serving as the director of the Taiwan Pineapple Company, that Xie spent most of his time in Taiwan.[18]

Huang Jishi: born in 1902 in Shulin, Taipei County, he visited the Dutch East Indies for two months in 1938 to investigate economic conditions under the sponsorship of the Japan–Netherlands Investigation Commission. In 1927, he had graduated from the University of Commerce in Tokyo and worked in the accounting section of the Mitsubishi Company. In 1939, Huang was sent to Tianjin to serve as director of Mitsubishi's local branch, as well as head of its accounting section.[19] In 1951, he opened the Guanglong Merchant Store in Tokyo (see Table 11.2).

Wang Zhaode: born in Dajia, central Taiwan in 1899, he moved to Kobe in 1916 and served in the Taiwan Hats and Mats Merchants Association. In 1921, he was appointed director of the Dajia office of the Maeda Store for Taiwanese hats. In 1922, he branched out on his own, establishing the Lichun Merchant Association to sell Taiwanese hats. In 1924, Wang set up a factory for processing hat-making raw materials in Zhanghua, central Taiwan. In 1925, he established the Deming Merchant Association, with its main store in Dajia and with a branch store in Kobe,

[16] Lin Shinhatsu, *Taiwan kanshin niankan* [*Annual almanac of Taiwan's officials and gentry*] (Taipei, Minshuu Press, 1933), pp. 102–103.

[17] Ibid., p. 135.

[18] Kōnan Shinbunsha comp, *Taiwan jinshikan*, p. 38; Shijie wenhua fuwushe bianzuan weiyuanhui comp., *Zhonghuaminguo mingren zhuanzhi si* [*Biographies of ROC notables*] (Taipei: Shijie wenhua fuwushe, 1957), p. 240; Bu Youfu, *Taiwan fengyun renwu* [*Taiwan notables*] (Hong Kong: Xinwentiandi she, 1962), pp. 205–10.

[19] Kōnan Shinbunsha comp, *Taiwan jinshikan*, p. 150.

to engage in the manufacture and export of Taiwan's hats. In 1920, he established the Xinzhu Hat Company Ltd. and served as the head of its standing board of directors. Wang also established the Defeng Merchant Association. In 1930, he was the standing executive of the Kobe Hat Association. Four years later, Wang was appointed chairman of the Kobe Taiwan Hat Association. He often travelled to southern China and Southeast Asia to investigate commercial conditions.[20] In 1951, Wang was still running a trading outfit in Kobe (see Table 11.2).

Wang Chusheng: born in 1899 at Neihu, Taipei, he spent the first 13 years of his working life in agriculture. He subsequently moved to downtown Taipei to look for work – in this search for employment, he first gained experience of, and a great interest in, bicycles. Through some 18 years' perseverance, Wang and his partner became the sole Taiwanese merchants to import American and Japanese bicycles, and received a prize from the Governor-General.[21] In Table 11.2, Wang's store in Tokyo in 1951 retained its pre-war name – *jinlunhang*, which literally translates as 'the merchant store which imports bicycles'.

Huang Shushui: born in Shimen, Damsui in northern Taiwan in 1899, he entered the Taiwan Marine Products Company in 1912 and worked for its general affairs department to 1915. For the next five years, he worked for a gold mining company, but then returned home to inherit the family business, serving as an agent for Japan's army and navy, as well as Japanese marine products and groceries, and earning several tens of thousands of Japanese yen per annum. For his public service, Huang was elected congressman for Jilong City in 1930 and was involved in the management of the city's affairs. In 1934, Huang served as vice-president of the Jilong Chamber of Commerce, director of the Jilong Storage Cooperatives, and director of the Marukose Fountain Water and Ice Joint Stock Company.[22] In 1951, he opened a merchant store in Tokyo for general trade (see Table 11.2).

Gu Weifu (the son of Gu Xianrong): Gu Xianrong (1866–1937) was born in Lugang, Zhanghua in 1866. In 1899, Gu Xianrong headed the Taiwanese monopoly for salt sales. In 1919, he set up the Daiwa Sugar Company and served as its director. One year later, he established the Daiwa Merchant Store in the Japanese Bridge area of Tokyo (the current diplomatic zone of the city). Gu Xianrong served on the supervising committee for Taiwan's Governor-General, as director of the Bank of Zhanghua, as president of the Taipei Chamber of Commerce, as director of *Taiwan Daily* [*Taiwan Nijiniji Shimpo*], as director of the Daiwa ice-making industry, and as director of the Longjiang Trust Bank and the Meiji Sugar Company.[23] Gu Weifu, whose name we find in Table 11.2, was only young in the Japanese colonial period. By 1948, however, he was the representative of the

[20] Taiwan Shinminpō sha comp, *Taiwan jinmei jiten*, p. 37.

[21] Lin Shinhatsu, *Taiwan kanshin niankan*, p. 66.

[22] Ibid., p. 111.

[23] Taiwan Shinminpō sha comp, *Taiwan jinmei jiten*, p. 45.

Yongyu Tea Company.[24] And, the Gu family business remains one of the leading ten conglomerates in contemporary Taiwan.

The presence of some 113 Taiwanese merchant stores in Japan at a time when the ROC regime controlled the Taiwan–Japan trade illustrates the coexistence of both the ROC government and the Taiwanese merchants engaged in such trade. The prevailing and ongoing Japanese networks have been revealed through, for example, Xie Jingzhi's extension of pre-war commercial networks in books and stationery to post-war banana exports; in Chen Xingcun's and Xie Jingzhi's extension of their educational backgrounds in pre-war Japan to post-war Taiwan–Japan trade; through He Yi, Zhang Qinggang, Huang Jishi, and Wang Zhaode making use of their experiences of working with Japanese companies; and, in Xie Chengyuan, Liu Azhen, Wang Chusheng and Gu Weifu extending their family's pre-war Taiwan–Japan related enterprises to the post-war period. Moreover, many of these Taiwanese merchants had received a Japanese education, such as Zhang Qinggang and Li Yizhao with normal school education, Liu Azhen with industrial school education, He Yi and Chen Xida with primary school education. This background also provided a basis for post-war links between Taiwan and Japan. And, all of the above-listed Taiwanese merchants had achieved entries in the *Who's Who* of Japanese colonial Taiwan. In addition to economic prosperity, these merchants held prestigious social positions such as Gu Xianrong as a member of the supervising committee of the Taiwan Governor-General, head of Taiwan's leading newspaper, and president of Taipei's Chamber of Commerce; Liu Azhen was Jilong City's congressman; Chen Xida was Taoyuan Town's Congressman; Zhang Qinggang was the director of Taipei downtown's trust cooperatives; and, Wang Zhaode was the Chairman of Kobe's hat merchants' association. These individuals certainly constituted the Taiwanese economic elite of the colonial period. Moreover, they remained active in the post-war Taiwan–Japan trade, two of them are still included in the list of Taiwan's top-ten conglomerates. All of this points to the continuities between pre-war and post-war business elites in Taiwan.

For Taiwanese merchants engaged in trade between Taiwan and Japan, it was very common to maintain liaison houses in both countries for the purpose of doing import and export business. Mother-son, father-son, elder brother-younger brother, friend-friend were all possible partnership combinations in establishing these cross-country liaison houses. Entrepreneurs on both sides, even from the same family, might have carried different nationalities, that is, the exporter on the Taiwan side was a national of the Republic of China, while the importer on the Japan side might have held Japanese nationality (see Table 11.3). Indeed, some of the Taiwanese traders on the Japanese side were executive members of Japan's Banana Import Association.[25]

---

[24]   Zhang Wojun, (ed.), *Taiwan chaye jikan* [*Taiwan tea quarterly*] (Taipei: Taiwan provincial tea commerce association, 1948), first issue, p. 47.

[25]   Liu Shujing, 'TaiRi jiaomao wangluo yu Taiwan de jingji jingying (1945–1971) [The banana trade network between Taiwan and Japan and Taiwan's economic elite]'

Among the Taiwanese merchants active in the Taiwan–Japan trade, many had acquired a strong Japanese identity during the Japanese colonial period. Some even had taken Japanese names, for example, Xie Chengyuan had been known as Uehara Shogi, while Zhang Qinggang had been known as Fukushima Shinko.[26] When Japan and China descended into war in 1937, in Kobe the Taiwanese Zheng Wang and Li Yizhao supported Japan, while mainlanders such as Wu Jingtang and Wang Mingyu were pro-Chinese.[27] Huang Shushui had been agent for supplies to the Japanese army and navy. Zhuang Sichuan, a Taiwanese studying Chinese in Japanese-occupied Shanghai, headed propaganda newspapers in the Japanese occupied-area in central China, following his graduation from school. Zhuang was subsequently described as a 'Han cultural traitor'.[28] Nevertheless, he worked as the representative of the ROC in Taiwan during trade negotiations with Japan.

(Taipei: Daoxiang Press, 2001), p. 33.

[26]   'Kōnan Shinbunsha comp, Taiwan jinshikan', p. 38; Yang Jiancheng, 'Taiwan shishen huangminhua gean yanjiu [A case study of the Japanization of Taiwan's gentry]' (Taipei: Longwen Press, 1995), Appendix 1, pp. 1–9.

[27]   Sumida Yoshihiro, 'Kobe's overseas Chinese', p. 123.

[28]   When the Wang Jingwei regime was set up in Nanjing, Zhuang established two nation-wide cultural agencies. One of these was established in Wuchang and Hankow in Hubei province, and Zhuang became its chief executive. The Japanese army entered Wuchang and Hankow on 25 October 1938, and the Wang Jingwei regime ruled Wuchang and Hankow for seven years. Qing Tezheng, 'Wuhan lunxian shiqi hanjian zhengqvan de yanbian [The transformation of the Han traitor's regime when Wuchang and Hankow were occupied by the Japanese army]', in *Wuhan wenshi ziliao wenku, vol. 2, political and military section* (Wuhan: Wuhan chubanshe, 1999), pp. 24, 36. The Japanese government behind the Wang Jingwei regime paid considerable attention to propaganda and issued some 30 newspapers in Wuchang and Hankow alone. The *Dachubao [Great Wuhan Daily]* was controlled by the intelligence section of the Japanese Army and was the city newspaper for Wuchang and Hankow until the Japanese surrender. Zhuang was the director of this newspaper. At the same time, he was the director of an even larger newspaper called *Wuhan bao [The Newspaper of Wuchang and Hankow]*, which was controlled by the newspaper section of the Japanese Army. Tian Ziyu, Huang Huawen, *Hubei tongshi [A general history of Hubei]*, Republican volume (Wuchang and Hankow: Huazhong Shifan University Press, 1999), p. 589. I am particularly grateful to Prof. Luo Jiurong for providing this information. And, according to 'Diliu zhanqu canmouchu [The military advisory section of the sixth warring zone]', Zhuang was listed as a 'cultural traitor'. *Diliu Zhanqu shouxiang jishi [A narrative record of the surrender of the sixth warring zone]*, 1946, pp.1–24 (cited in Tang Xiyong's National Science Council project report of 1990, p. 46). Zhuang defended himself against charges of treachery at the end of the war. He argued that alleged Taiwanese traitors were innocent since China had ceded Taiwan to Japan in 1895, and that he personally had nurtured Chinese culture and had taken advantage of his position as a Japanese subject to help the Chinese population. Zhuang's trial concluded that he was not guilty of treason. Xu Xueji (interviewer) and Huang Meizi (recorder), *Bainian yiwang: Zhuang Sichuan xiansheng fangtan jilu [Recalling the last one hundred years: a record of interviews with Zhuang Sichuan]* (Taipei: Caituan faren jieyan shiqi budang panluan cucang jijinghui, 2003), pp. 32–3.

Zhuang also urged the ROC government to further the trade with Japan since most of Taiwan's machinery at that time was of Japanese design.[29] He even participated twice in the standing committee meetings of TAPEMC, the main policy-making organ for economic affairs of the ROC in the period, 1949–53.[30] The interaction between Zhuang and Yin Zhongrong, the vice-chairman of TAPEMC, vividly reveals the cooperation between ROC high officials and Taiwanese merchants. When Yin was setting off for Japan to sign the first trade agreement between Japan and the ROC, he sent a telegram to Zhuang asking this Taiwanese merchant to greet him at Haneda airport. When Yin arrived, he discussed the proposals of the Ministry of the Economic Affairs with Zhuang. As Yin explained to Zhuang: 'I am representing the government to sign a trade agreement with Japan. I am not familiar with the current economic situation in Japan. You have stayed in Tokyo for a long while and are more familiar with the situation. Please share your opinions with me.'[31] In addition to Zhung Sichuan, three other Taiwanese banana merchants, Xie Chengyuan, Huang Muyi and Ke Shiyin, were appointed as representatives of the ROC's Ministry of Foreign Affairs to negotiate trade deals with Japan.[32]

Taiwanese Merchants on the Taiwan Side of the Taiwan–Japan Trade

On the Taiwan side, meanwhile, we find several Taiwanese merchants who were part-merchant and part-official in the early post-war period. Li Lianchun, the individual in charge of bartering for Taiwanese rice and Japanese fertilizer, the most important of Taiwan–Japan trades in this period, bore the same name as an individual appearing on the 1951 MITI list reproduced in Table 11.2. We cannot be sure whether they are the same individual. We are certain, however, that the official Li had strong commercial ties with the Japanese, since he was a manager of one of the biggest Japanese rice export companies in Japanese colonial Taiwan in addition to having been section head of the rice bureau of the office of colonial Taiwan's Governor-General. And, for 11 years in the post-war period, Li maintained crucial positions as head of the Bureau of Food given his expertise in Taiwan's land, soil, weather, seeds, and agricultural technologies gained in the Japanese colonial period.[33]

[29]   Zhonghua zhengxinsuo comp., *Dui Taiwan jingji zuiyou gongxian de gongshang renminlu*, p. 302.

[30]   Meng Xianghan, 'Taiwan qu shengchan shiye guanli weiyuanhui yu zhengfu qiantai chuqi jingji de fazhan (1949–1953) [The Taiwan Area Productive Enterprises Management Committee and the economic development of Taiwan after the ROC government moved to Taiwan]' (Taipei: Ph. D. thesis, Department of History, National Taiwan Normal University, 1999), p. 293.

[31]   Xu Xueji, Huang Meizi, *Bainian yiwang*, p. 47.

[32]   Liu Shujing, *Banana Export Trade*, p. 46.

[33]   Chen Jinman, 'Taiwan feiliao de zhengfu guanli yu peixiao (1945–1953) – Guojia yu shehui guanxi zhi yi tantao [The governmental management and distribution of fertilizer

Meanwhile, one of the Taiwanese banana merchants, Guo Yuxin, was also a provincial congressman.[34] Indeed, of all Taiwan's exports to Japan, the banana trade witnessed Taiwanese merchants playing the most active of roles. Before the Peace Treaty between the ROC and Japan was signed in 1952, some Taiwanese merchants were promoting the barter trade between the two countries, and they had also begun to export bananas to Japan.[35] Between 1953 and 1969 (with the exception of 1963), bananas ranked within the ten most important Taiwanese exports. Moreover, more than 90 per cent of Taiwan's bananas were exported to Japan.[36] Additionally, between 1949 and 1959, 97.75 per cent of all bananas imported by Japan were from Taiwan.[37] Many of the Taiwanese merchants active in the Taiwan–Japan trade were involved with the banana trade, for example: Chen Xincun, a woman involved in fashion design; Xie Jingzhi, a merchant in sports equipment and music instruments; Guo Yuxin, a provincial congressman; and, Li Lianchun, who, as we have already seen, shared his name with an individual at the head of the rice-fertilizer barter trade. Since bananas decay easily, they were excluded from government-controlled trade because the harvesting and storage process would prove too lengthy if handled by state agencies.[38] Even though the Central Trust Bureau managed the lion's share of Taiwan's trade with Japan for this period, banana exports were beyond its control. Hence, from 1952 to 1955, the Taiwanese Merchants' Export Company Association exported 92 to 98 per cent of Taiwan's bananas to Japan. Even when the government tried to allocate some export quotas to the banana farmers, the Japanese side co-operated more with merchants, with long-standing relations, than with the farmers.[39] The Taiwanese merchants even owned steamships to transport bananas abroad. The carrying capacity of steamships owned by the government and by the Japanese companies could not compete with the steamships owned by Taiwanese merchants. As calculated from Table 11.4, the government's share of tonnage in the 1960s was 22.71 per cent, while Taiwanese private companies represented 48.29 per cent, Japanese companies accounted for 5.97 per cent, and companies whose ownership is unclear commanded tonnages of 23.03 per cent. Some of the Taiwanese steamships, it should be noted, were built in the pre-war Japanese colonial period.

in Taiwan (1945–1953): An investigation into state-society relations]' (Taipei: MA thesis, Department of History, National Taiwan Normal University, 1995), p. 192; Shangye xinwenshe comp, *Taiwan minren zhuan* [*Biographies of Taiwan notables*] (Shangye xinwenshe, 1956), pp. 17–18.

[34] Cf. Guo Yuxin, *Yitan ershinian* (*Twenty years in Taiwan's provincial congress*), 1969.
[35] Zhonghua zhengxinsuo, *Dui Taiwan jingji zuiyou gongxian de gongshang renminlu*, p. 9.
[36] Liu Shujing, *Banana Export Trade*, pp. 3–4.
[37] Ibid., p. 11.
[38] Ibid., p. 56.
[39] Ibid., pp. 203–15.

Table 11.4   Chartered Steamships with Refrigeration Facilities Sailing between Taiwan and Japan in the 1960s

Steamship company	Name of ship	Total tonnage	Velocity (maritime miles)	Year Built	Note on Ownership
China's Steamship and Merchant Company	Hairen	3200.14	14.5	1948	Government-Managed
China's Steamship and Merchant Company	Haili	3800.00	15.9	1968	Government-Managed
China's Steamship and Merchant Company	Haiyi	2840.00	16.0	1955	Government-Managed
Taiwan Navigation Company	Taiqing	3140.66	15.0	1949	Government-Managed
Taiwan Navigation Company	Taijiao	4373.67	17.0	1965	Government-Managed
Taiwan Navigation Company	Taiyun	2840.00	16.0	1955	Government-Managed
Xintai Maritime Transportation Company	Taian	4424.65	17.0	1965	
Dacheng Maritime Transportation Company	Furen	4279.00	16.5	1945	
Dacheng Maritime Transportation Company	Fujiao	3368.00	18.0	1960	
Yongda Maritime Transportation Company	Dongqing	4610.10	17.0	1965	
Qiaoguo Navigation Company	Qiaoguo	3353.46	15.0	1936	Owned by Chen Chamo family; Wang Zhuhui also participated as an investor
Da Yang Navigation Company	Jianfu	3082.20	14.5	1941	Owned by Chen Chamo family
Da Yang Navigation Company	Jianguo	3203.29	15.0	1949	Owned by Chen Chamo family
Da Yang Navigation Company	Jiantai	2919.88	15.5	1940	Owned by Chen Chamo family
Da Yang Navigation Company	Jianxing	2902.00	17.0	1951	Owned by Chen Chamo family
Da Yang Navigation Company	Jianchang	2996.32	15.0	1939	Owned by Chen Chamo family
Da Yang Navigation Company	Jianfu	3076.00	15.0	1941	Owned by Chen Chamo family
Da Yang Navigation Company	Zhongtai	3352.00	14.0	1939	Owned by Chen Chamo family
Xinyi Navigation Company	Xinde	4121.44	16.0	1951	Owned by Wang Zhuhui

Table 11.4   Continued

Steamship company	Name of ship	Total tonnage	Velocity (maritime miles)	Year Built	Note on Ownership
Xinyi Navigation Company	Xinyi	4281.54	16.0	1940	Owned by Wang Zhuhui
Guoji Maritime Transportation Company	Guofeng	4661.00	17.0	1966	Investment held by Chen Decheng (father) and Chen Weiqian (son)
Guoji Maritime Transportation Company	Guofu	5000.00	16.5	1967	Investment held by Chen Decheng (father) and Chen Weiqian (son)
Fuxing Navigation Company	Fuqing	3800.00	15.6	1960	
Nihon Yusen Steamship Company	Yushan	2697.00	12.9	1960	Japanese capital
Osaka Commercial Steamship Company	Gaosha	2615.00	12.9	1959	Japanese capital

Source: Liu Shujing, *Banana Export Trade*, p. 105.

In terms of export value, however, sugar and rice held the prime positions in Taiwan's exports to Japan (see Table 11.5), and, in contrast to bananas, these exports were more closely controlled by the government. Sugar was a product of government enterprises, and its export was directly under the control of the state.[40] As in the case of bananas, rice was an agricultural commodity produced on privately-owned farms. However, rice was used by the government as the chief commodity to exchange for Japan's fertilizers, since the latter was desperately required by Taiwan to boost its agricultural productivity. At the same time, rice in Taiwan was much less expensive than it was in Japan, and early post-war Japan was desperately short of rice. In addition, given competition from Cuban sugar, Taiwan increasingly shifted from sugar to rice production – the latter requiring greater quantities of fertilizer. Moreover, since fertilizer was a bulky commodity, it was more convenient to buy from Japan than from Europe.[41]

The rice-fertilizer barter trade was initiated in 1952. The fertilizer industry had turned into an important chemical industry for Japan from the 1930s, with

[40]   Chen Zhaowei, 'Guomin zhengfu yu Taiwan tanye (1945–1953) [The ROC government and Taiwan's sugar industry]' (Taizhong: MA thesis, Department of History, Donghai University, 1993), pp. 42, 55, 217.

[41]   Liao Hongqi, 'Trade and Politics', pp. 51, 55–6, 60.

Sumitomo as one of the crucial manufacturers.[42] In August and September 1952, Taniguchi Yoshio, the head of the Chemical Section of the Sumitomo Company joined a Japanese merchant delegation, sponsored by the Osaka Commercial and Industrial Association and the China–Japan Economic Exchange Association, for a four-week tour of Taiwan. Taniguchi's *Taiwan Journey*, published immediately after this visit in an elegant publication by the Sumitomo Company, records the beginnings of the Taiwan rice-Japan fertilizer barter trade.

Table 11.5   Value of Particular Commodities Exported from Taiwan to Japan as a percentage of Taiwan's Total Export Values of those Commodities, 1966 (Unit: 1,000 US dollar)

	Total export value (A)	Export value to Japan (B)	B / A (%)
Sugar	67,955	25,495	37
Rice	42,954	42,954	100
Tea	9,719	561	6
Salt	2,723	2,187	81
Bananas	55,269	54,927	99
Coal	1,174	7	0
Camphor	907	131	14
Bamboo	3,503	2,252	64
Marine products	1,997	752	77
Total exports	487,959	151,628	31

Source: Gaimushō keizai kyoku ajiaka (ed.), *Chūka minkoku teki boeki kanri* 1966, p. 3.

The delegation met Generalissimo Chiang Kai-shek, Generals Bai Chongxi and Ho Yingqin (responsible for the cultural and economic aspects of ROC-Japan relations), Wu Sanlian (the Mayor of Taipei), Zhang Zikai (the Minister for Economic Affairs), Yin Zhongrong (director of the Central Bureau), and Li Lianchun (director of the Food Bureau). Taniguchi was very much impressed by the ROC economic bureaucrats whom he mixed with most. In proposing a lower price for Japanese fertilizer, Yin Zhongrong, for example, demonstrated that he understood the world-wide fertilizer market far better than Taniguchi. Li Lianchun, on the other hand, conversed with Taniguchi – up to midnight sometimes – on the desirability of further cooperation.

Taniguchi's particular aim in negotiations was to engineer the barter of Taiwan's rice for a type of fertilizer less suited to Japanese soils than the Taiwanese equivalents. The Sumitomo representative also hoped for the maximum use of US aid in the purchase of Japan's fertilizer. He achieved wide newspaper coverage

---

[42]   Hori Kazuo, 'Shokuminchiteikoku Nippon no keizaikōzō – senkyūhyakusanjūnendai wo chūshin ni [The economic structure of the Japanese empire, with particular reference to the 1930s]' *Nihonshikenkyū* [Japanese studies], No. 462 (Feb. 2001), pp. 26–54.

while the delegation was at Gaoxiong, and Taniguchi tried to use his powers of persuasion during visits to Taizhong's Chamber of Commerce, at a cocktail party offered by the Minister of Economic Affairs and the Director of the Central Bureau, at a meeting with General He and the individual in charge of the US aid programme, and, of course, during meetings with Yin and Li. He kept in close contact with the Sumitomo Company by telegram. Even on the day of departure, Taniguchi continued to forward messages to Yin.

Although the Japanese delegates were delighted to be fêted by ROC high officials, they felt uneasy about communicating in English with the bureaucrats from the Chinese mainland. By contrast, they felt more at ease when entertained by the various chambers of commerce in Taiwan. When the Japanese and the Taiwanese merchants sang Japanese songs (such as *Aisen Katsura*) together or recollected their Japanese university alumni ties, Taiwan–Japan relations were further cemented.[43]

The development of Taiwanese chambers of commerce had started during the Japanese colonial era. Some of the pre-war membership survived into the post-war period. For example, the organizers of the Taiwan Provincial Chamber of Commerce in the early post-war period, Lin Xiongzheng, Jiang Weichuan, and Huang Zaishou, had respectively been the vice-president of the Taipei Chamber of Commerce, permanent director of the Taipei General Chamber of Commerce, and president of the Yilan Industrial Association. Gu Weifu's brother and Gu Xianrong's son, Gu Zhenfu, had been a permanent council member of the Taipei Chamber of Commerce since 1937 and he headed the Industrial and Commercial Association for some 30 years of the post-war period.[44] The president of the Taipei Trade Association, Huang Jishi, who met Taniguchi's delegation, had earlier opened the Guanlong Merchant Store in Tokyo (see Table 11.2).

It was the Central Bureau which principally took charge of the rice-fertilizer barter trade. The government-owned steamships carried 70 per cent of this cargo, while the civilian owned steamships transported only 30 per cent.[45] However, in the export of rice, although the government nominally controlled this trade, according to some archival information provided by TAPEMC the entire business was actually farmed out to a private enterprise, the Longshun Company. TAPEMC tried to set limits on the Longshun Company regarding the quantity of rice to

---

[43]   Taniguchi Yoshio, *Taiwan kiko* [*Taiwan Journey*] (Osaka: Sumitomo Chemicals Company, 1952), pp. 5, 8, 10, 13, 14, 15, 18, 20, 21, 23, 25, 30, 31, 32, 47, 49, 50.

[44]   For the development of chambers of commerce in the Japanese colonial period see Zhao Youzhi, *Riju shiqi Taiwan shanggon hui de fazhan* [The development of Taiwan's chambers of commerce in the Japanese colonial period] (Taipei: Daoxiang Press, 1998), particularly p. 493 for Gu's role.

[45]   Chen Siyu, 'Shengguanhui yu Taiwan gongying shiye tixi zhi fazhan (1949–1953) [The Taiwan Area Productive Enterprise Management Committee and the development of Taiwan's public enterprises]' (Taipei: MA thesis, Department of History, National Zhengzhi University, 1999), pp. 165–9; Liao Hongqi, 'Trade and Politics', pp. 55–7; Meng Xianghan, 'TAPEMC', pp. 148, 155.

be sold. However, in 1951 Longshun dispatched a telegram in Japanese to the sales company in Japan. The latter subsequently forwarded the telegram to MITI requesting permission to be included in the Taiwan–Japan barter trade. This lobbying was successful and TAPEMC proved incapable of controlling the company's activities.[46] Significantly, listed in the membership of the Taiwan Rice Export Association between April 1916 and December 1922 was a store called Longshun.[47]

The International Politico-Economic Background

The ability of Japanized Taiwanese merchants to continue to play a substantial role in the Taiwan–Japan trade in the early post-war period essentially derived from the fact that Japan became Taiwan's most important export market from 1950 onwards. Here was another obvious continuity with the pre-war era since Japan had been Taiwan's main trading partner in the Japanese colonial period. Taking the average over the whole period 1902–37, the value of Taiwan's trade with countries other than Japan and China was four times that of the value of Taiwan's trade with China; by contrast, the value of the island's trade with Japan was four times that of the value of the Japanese colony's trade with countries other than China and Japan.[48] Yet, after the surrender of Japan in August 1945, Taiwan's main trading partner became mainland China. The mainland's share of Taiwanese trade in terms of value was: 1945: 26 per cent, 1946: 94 per cent, 1947: 91 per cent, and 1948: 86 per cent.[49] Although the ROC government moved to Taiwan in 1949, it was not until the Korean War, which broke out on 25 June 1950, that the Taiwan–Japan trade gradually resumed. From 1950 to 1966, Japan resumed its role as Taiwan's principal export market.[50] The Korean War, as well as British recognition of the

---

[46]   Archive of the Taiwan Area Productive Enterprises Management Committee, 1951, Guanyizi, No. 2202.

[47]   Ueno Kosa, *Taiwan beikoku nenkan* [Annual report on Taiwan's rice], (Taipei: Kastuppansha, 1923), p. 177.

[48]   Taiwansheng wenxian weiyenhui [Provincial Taiwan Historical Sources Commission], *Taiwansheng tongzhi* (*Taiwan Provincial Gazetteer*), vol. 4 (economic gazetteer chapter), pp. 170b–71b.

[49]   Yang Chingfa, 'Sengo taiwan keizai haten no kenkyu [A study of the economic development of post-war Taiwan]' (Ph.D. thesis, Department of Economics, Tokushoku University, 1993), p. 78; Taiwansheng zhujichu, *Taiwan maoyi wushisan nianbiao* [*The fifty-three annual tables of Taiwan's trade*] (1949), pp. 1–2.

[50]   Tu Zhaoyan, 'Zai guoji jingji yanbian zhong de taiwan jingmao guanxi [Taiwan's trade relations in the international vicissitude]' in Zhang Yanxian (ed.) *Zhongguo haiyang fazhanshi lunwenji* (*Chinese maritime history*), No. 6, Taipei: Sun Yat-sen Institute of Social Science and Humanities, 1997, pp. 556, 559; Liu Jingqing, *Taiwan zhanhou jingji fenxi* [*An analysis of post-war Taiwan's economy*] (Taipei: Renjian Press, 1992), p. 365.

PRC, led to the United States including Taiwan in the front line of defence against the expansion of Communism.[51] The role of Taiwan as an entrepot between Japan and overseas Chinese communities in Southeast Asia was the rationale which the US used to persuade Japan to sign a peace treaty and renounce its sovereignty over Taiwan in favour of the ROC government in Taipei. This line of argument also bolstered the development of formal trade relations between Japan and Taiwan.[52]

In addition to the island's central geographical location, Taiwan could serve as a point of social interaction between Japan and Southeast Asia. Since the overseas Chinese in Southeast Asia were often hostile towards Japan in the aftermath of the Pacific War, Taiwan could play a central role in dampening down this hostility by marketing the products of Taiwanese and Japanese joint ventures as being 'Made in Taiwan'. This would go some way to easing the direct psychological tensions between Southeast Asian Chinese and Japan.[53] Taiwan could also help Japan open up Southeast Asian markets because of the obvious cultural affinity of the Taiwanese and the *Nanyang* Chinese; both groups often sharing common ancestral roots in the Fujian and Guangdong provinces of Southern China. Moreover, overseas Chinese business communities were largely supportive of the Guomindang, given its attachment to traditional Chinese culture.[54]

In the 1950s, some Japanese merchants in Osaka and Kobe hoped to expand trade with the PRC, while others agreed with Prime Minister Yoshida Shigeru, as well as the US government, that trade should be reinforced between Japan, Taiwan, and the overseas Chinese of Southeast Asia.[55] Taniguchi Yoshio's business delegation belonged to the latter group. After a Japanese Foreign Office official – significantly from the same place of birth as Taniguchi – had facilitated the peace treaty between the ROC and Japan, Taniguchi's delegation visited Taiwan. The Peace Treaty became effective on 5 August 1952,[56] and the commercial mission arrived in Taiwan

---

[51]   Sun Zaiwei, 'Chaoxian zhanzheng yu guogong gaunxi [the Korean War and relations between the Communist party and the Guomindang party]' *Nanjing Shehui Kexue* [*Nanjing Social Science*], 2, 1994. See also Prof. Richard C. Kagan's remarks.

[52]   Zhang Shuya, 'Dulesi yu duiRi gouhe zhong de Taiwan wenti (1950–1952) [Dulles and the Taiwan issue in the Peace Treaty with Japan]' in Guoshiguan (ed.), *Kangzhanjianguo ji Taiwan guangfu: Di san jie Zhonghua minguo shi taolunhui lunwenji* [*Anti-Japanese war, nation-building, and the restitution of Taiwan: The 3rd conference proceedings on Republican history held by the National Historical Commission*] (Taipei: Guoshiguan, 1996), pp. 1071–92.

[53]   Zhongyang yanjiuyuan jindaishi yanjiusuo [The Institute of Modern History, Academia Sinica], *Koushu lishi* (Oral History), No. 5, 1994, p. 141.

[54]   Liao Hongqi, 'Trade and Politics', p. 50.

[55]   Furuta Kazuko, 'Osakazaikai no Chūgokubōekilon-gojūnendaishoki' in Nakamura Takafusa and Miyezak Masayasu (eds), *Katoki toshite no senkyūhyaku gojūnendai* [*The 1950s as a transitional period*] (Tokyo: University of Tokyo Press, 1997); Liao Hongqi, 'Trade and Politics', pp. 73–4.

[56]   For the Treaty of Peace between the Republic of China and Japan, see Waijiaobu (Ministry of Foreign Affairs) comp., *Zhongwai tiaoyue jibian* [*A compendium of treaties*]

17 days later. Moreover, Taniguchi clearly articulated the view that having Japanese products marked 'Made in Taiwan' would facilitate sales to the overseas Chinese (as well as to their future offspring which would double or triple the existing population of over 13 million in Southeast Asia within a generation).[57]

With the outbreak of the Korean War, South Korea, as well as the ROC, was added to the Philippines, the Ryukyu Islands, Japan, the Aleutians Islands, and Alaska as part of the United States's Pacific defence line. But, economic relations between Korea and Taiwan were not as close as their respective relations with Japan and the US. This was because the degree of economic development in 1950s Korea and Taiwan was very similar – in other words, a complementary division of labour was far more pronounced in Korea's and Taiwan's respective economic relations with Japan and the US.[58] In the division of labour between Taiwan and Japan, the ability of Taiwan to provide a geographical and social entrepot for Japan's industrial production into Southeast Asia was of crucial importance. Moreover, around 1952–54, Japan's trading relations with South Asia had been superseded by the relationship with Southeast Asia. Japan–India relations were close immediately after the Second World War because India was an Asian nation which had not been directly occupied by Japan during the war, while Japan also hoped to take advantage of British development policy in post-war India. Meanwhile, Japan shifted its reliance on Northeast China for iron-ore mining to India following the outbreak of the Korean War in 1950. Because of the San Francisco Peace Treaty signed in 1951, however, Japan was required to engage in reparations negotiations with several Southeast Asian countries. Many of these territories asked Japan to aid their reconstruction. At the same time, India's economic growth was retarded by its government's heavy industry policy, as well as the border conflict with China.[59] Hence, the entrepot role of Taiwan between Japan and Southeast Asia became even more pertinent.

Implications

In early post-war Taiwan, government control of trade was intense. When Taniguchi came to Taiwan in 1952, the proportion of trade controlled by the

---

between China and other countries] (Taipei: Shangwu yinshuguan, 1963 reprint), pp. 248–63.

[57]   Taniguchi, *Taiwan Journey*, preface, pp. 13–14.

[58]   Kurt Glaset (Chinese translation), 'Meiguo zai dongya de diyuan zhengzhi liyi [The geopolitical interest of the United States in East Asia]' in *Meiguo yazhou waijiao zheng*ce [*The diplomatic policy of the United States*] (Taipei: zhengzhong shuju, 1991), pp. 114–16 and Xie Jiazhen's term paper for Chinese economic history, National Taiwan Normal University, 2002 on the relationships between Taiwan and South Korea, 1950–60.

[59]   Hideo Kobayashi, *Post-war Japanese Economy and Southeast Asia* (Quezon City, The Philippines: New Day Publishers, 2002), Ch. 2, 'From South Asia to Southeast Asia'.

state was around 80 per cent.[60] Government-controlled trade still accounted for 30 per cent of Taiwan's total trade in 1965.[61] On average, the Central Bureau controlled about 50 per cent of trade in the course of the 1950s and the early 1960s.[62] In addition to extensive official controls, the relations between Taiwanese merchants and the government were not always smooth. For example, merchants from Southern Taiwan complained about the government-controlled barter trade of fertilizer and rice because they had been selling their own rice for years, and fertilizer affected their agricultural districts more than those in Northern Taiwan. But the government needed to control such barter trade, since the foreign exchange obtained was crucial for the government to secure the machinery imports to operate factories.[63] Because of political protests, some Taiwanese merchants were also arrested during the 28 February Incident.[64] But, plenty of evidence remains, on both the Taiwanese side and the Japanese side, to illustrate the active role played by Taiwanese merchants in international trade because of the Japanese ties built up in the pre-war period. The Japanese linkages of Taiwan's merchants included their Japanese language ability, their Japanese education and relations with former classmates, and their experience of working with Japanese companies or Japanese

---

[60] Taniguchi, *Taiwan Journey*, p. 61.

[61] Gaimusho keizai kyuku ajiaka, ed, *Zhuka minkoku teki boeki kanli*, pp. 8, 9.

[62] Zhongyang xintuoju, *Zhongyang xintuoju wushinian*, preface, p. 58.

[63] Chen Siyu, 'Development of Taiwan's public enterprises', pp. 165–9.

[64] Wang Tiandeng serves as one example. Wang was a leading tea merchant from the Japanese colonial period and into the post-war era to 1947. He joined the local autonomy petition league in the Japanese period, and, in the Nationalist government take-over period, he spoke vocally as a congressman in Taipei city and proposed lenient measures to deal with the Taiwanese who rebelled in the 28 February Incident. This incident broke out on 28 February 1947 when a woman in downtown Taipei sold tobacco in contravention of the government's monopoly sale regulation of the previous day. Anti-smuggling officials and the police terminated her selling activities with considerable and unjustifiable force. Since many Taiwanese were disaffected by the corrupt, statist, inflationary and ethnically biased rule of the Guomindang government, which followed the take-over of 25 October 1945, and, while high officials in the Nationalist administration despised the Japanization of the Taiwanese under colonial rule, this smuggling incident led to large-scale protest demonstrations and strikes. The tension was further inflamed when an angry mob was shot down by soldiers. The Taiwanese protesters turned from petitioning to calls for arrests of leading officials to bring about wide ranging reform. The government's response, however, was further suppression through the mobilization of more soldiers from the Chinese mainland. Arrests and killings of Taiwanese continued until 15 May 1947, and this incident remains a source of ethnic tension between Taiwanese and mainland Chinese in contemporary Taiwan (cf. Xu Xueji ed. *Taiwan lishi cidian* [*Dictionary of Taiwanese History*] (Taipei: Cultural Reconstruction Committee of the Executive Yuan, 2004), p. 48). Wang Tiandeng was arrested and burnt to death in this incident. See Lee Xiaofeng, *Ererba xiaoshi de Taiwan jingying* (*The Taiwanese elite who disappeared in the 228 incident*), (Taipei: Zili Wanbao, 1990), pp. 52–75.

institutions in general. This serves as a contrast with the discontinuity in Taiwan's political elite.

The contrast between the discontinuity of the political elite and the continuity of the commercial elite for Taiwan–Japan trade from pre-war to early post-war Taiwan can be further illustrated by the gap between the intellectual establishment and the politico-economic alliance. In the Cold War period, when Taiwan was allied with Japan and Southeast Asia for its politico-economic development, historical studies in Taiwan dropped the pre-war emphasis on East Asia and Southeast Asia and, instead, focused on the history of mainland China and Euro-American history.[65] Moreover, Take-Over Day replaced Establishment Day as the anniversary of the National Taiwan University (despite this institution actually having been established during the Japanese colonial period). Books held by this university, which contained an abundance of information on East Asia and Southeast Asia, were largely neglected in the early post-war period. Such study was regarded as having been instrumental in 'The Great East Asian War', which had seriously afflicted the people of the Chinese mainland.[66] This intellectual gap might be a cause of the lack of awareness in contemporary Taiwan of the ROC government's use of Taiwanese merchants and their Japanese links in the early post-war period. With resources obtained from mainland China and Japan, with American aid obtained from 1951 onwards with an unquestionably anti-communist mission, and with substantial international recognition, the ROC government was able to exercise authoritarian rule.[67] The successful economic performance of the ROC government in the early post-war period might be taken as an exemplar of favourable economic developments under authoritarian rule; that is, the argument that governments should have a strong hand in the economies of developing countries.[68] However, as we have observed in this chapter, the ROC government still required assistance from local business elites.

At the time when Taiwan was short of foreign exchange, the level of US aid was more than Taiwan earned in foreign currency through trade with all foreign countries. American aid amounted to one-third of Taiwan's capital assets from

---

[65]   Han Fuzhi, 'Fu Sinian xiansheng nianpu [Geneology of Fu Sinian]', *Taida lishi xuebao* [*Bulletin of the History Department of National Taiwan University*], No. 20 (Taipei: History Department of National Taiwan University, 1996), pp. 258–9, 292.

[66]   Li Donghua, 'Yijiusijiu nian yihou zhonghua minguo lishixue yanjiu de fazhan [The development of historical studies in the Republic of China since 1949]', *Zhongguo luntan* (China Forum), 21:1, 1985, p. 39.

[67]   Zhu Yunhan, trans. by Qi Lingling, 'Taiwan zhengquan zhuanxing qi zhengshang guanxi de zai jiemeng [The reliance of politicians on merchants in a period of political transformation]' *Zhongsan shehui kexue jikan* [*Zhongsan University Social Science Quarterly*], 7:4, Dec. 1992, p. 63.

[68]   Ishida Hiroshi, *Kyōdōgensō to shiteno Chūka* [*The Chinese world as a common illusion*] (Tokyo: Tabata shoten, 1993), p. 111.

1951 to 1963.[69] In Taniguchi's account, the ROC government in 1952 used surpluses in Taiwan–Japan trade to purchase Japan's fertilizer, but about 80 per cent of the money allocated for fertilizer purchases still had to be drawn from American aid.[70] However, while the deployment of US aid could not be entirely determined by the ROC government, the use of earnings from foreign trade could. Therefore, earning foreign exchange through trade, especially from Taiwan's most important export markets in Japan, was crucial for building the ROC's national economy. Commodities which Taiwan bartered with Japan in the early post-war period were mainly agricultural products in exchange for textiles, metal products, machinery, cars and ships, electrical appliances or materials, chemicals, cameras, and movie-making appliances and materials (see Table 11.6). Despite Japan's destruction by the US Air Force at the end of the Second World War, with American aid for recovery, and the economic boom brought on by the Korean War, Japan's economic growth rates in the 1955–60 period reached 10.5 per cent.[71] Clearly, the close Taiwan–Japan relationship helped boost the industrialization of Taiwan.

Table 11.6   Value of Particular Commodities Imported from Japan to Taiwan as a percentage of Taiwan's Total Import Values of those Commodities, 1966 (Unit: US dollar)

Commodities	Total Import Value (A)	Value of Import from Japan (B)	B / A (%)
Cotton	39,417	0	0
Lambs wool and its products	10,750	4,663	43
Artificial fibres and silk	19,861	18,047	90
Metal products	90,595	50,038	55
Machinery tools	84,420	44,045	52
Electrical appliances	26,741	16,896	63
Chemical fertilizer	16,169	10,196	62
Total imports	555,360	206,054	37

Source: Gaimushō keizai kyoku ajiaka, (ed.) *Chūka minkoku teki boeki kanri*, p. 8.

In addition, through the ties built with Japan, Taiwan became further linked with other international markets through the connections of Japanese merchants. In the post-war era, Taiwan's economy was highly dependent on foreign trade. Its trade dependency ratio was over 100 per cent in the 1960s and 1970s, and

---

[69]   Zhao Jichang, *Meiyuan de yunyong* [*The application of American aid*] (Taipei: Lianjing press, 1985), pp. 13–14.

[70]   Taniguchi, *Taiwan Journey*, p. 21.

[71]   Kobayashi, *Post-war Japanese Economy and Southeast Asia*, p. 37.

remained as high as 87.7 per cent in 1990.[72] On top of those overseas Chinese who extended Taiwan's external ties, the Japanese conglomerates opened Taiwan's external markets by importing Japanese products into Taiwan. It was not until the late 1960s that multinational enterprises opened direct international trade networks with Taiwan to share the role of Japanese conglomerates in their indirect links between Taiwan and the international economy.[73] Nevertheless, until the 1970s, the trade managed by the four conglomerates of Mitsubishi, Mitsui, Marubeni, and C. Itoh continued to constitute one-third of Taiwan's trade with Japan, and 15 per cent of Taiwan's trade with other countries.[74] In 1971, the largest 40 Japanese companies undertook about 50 per cent of Taiwan's total trade – 60 per cent of Taiwan's total imports and 40 per cent of Taiwan's total exports.[75] The Japan–Taiwan trade created in the early post-war period was therefore a stepping stone for Taiwan's global trade.

From 1953 to 1971, Japanese and American companies respectively owned 64.02 per cent and 27.41 per cent of foreign-controlled companies in Taiwan, and their investment capital represented 19.45 per cent and 54.84 per cent of total foreign investment capital, which, in turn, triggered the import of materials and the export of manufactured products. The percentage of Japanese capital in total foreign investment was particularly high in the electronic and electric appliance industries (14.2 per cent), the chemical product industry (20.57 per cent), the textile industry (85.6 per cent), the basic metal and metal product industry (91 per cent), the rubber and plastic product industries (52.7 per cent) and the machine appliance industry (46 per cent). Moreover, the American companies tended to cooperate with Taiwanese entrepreneurs who had emigrated from the Chinese mainland, while the Japanese companies generally collaborated with the indigenous Taiwanese.[76] In early 1972, before the cessation of diplomatic relations between the ROC and Japan, the Japanese embassy in Taiwan was still rented from Lin Boshou of the Banqiao Lin family which had cooperated strongly with the

---

[72]   The trade dependency ratio is the total value of imports and exports as a percentage of national income. Taiwan's trade dependency ratio for 1990 was calculated from the Directorate-General of Budget, *Accounting & Statistics* (Executive Yuan, Monthly Bulletin of Statistics, Nov. 1992), Table 33.

[73]   Taniura Takao, *Taiwan de gongyehua: guoji jiagong jidi de xingcheng* (Taipei: Renjian chubanshe, 1992), p. 86.

[74]   Yu Qingzhen, 'Taiwan zhi maoyishang (Taiwan's traders)' in *Zhangyin ziliao (Archives of the Bank of Zhanghua)* (Taichung: the Bank of Zhanghua), vol. 22, No. 6, January, 1971, p. 22.

[75]   Foreign Affairs Archives of the Republic of China, yadongtaipingyangsi 012.1–89001, p. 303019.

[76]   Foreign Affairs Archives of the Republic of China, yadongtaipingyangsi 032.4 89001 rishangzaiTai danwei. pp. 19, 20, 26.

Japanese colonial government in Taiwan.[77] After diplomatic relations between the ROC and Japan ended in September 1972 (as a consequence of Japan's decision to now recognise the PRC regime in Beijing), a semi-official association was created to maintain and progress the *de facto* relationship between Taiwan and Japan. Two of the three members of the association's board of overseers were Gu Zhenfu and Chen Qichuan.[78] These individuals hailed from powerful Taiwanese families that had prospered in the Japanese colonial period. Gu Zhenfu, elder brother of Gu Weifu, and a son of Gu Xianrong (who had welcomed the Japanese army to Taipei in 1895), even represented the ROC in semi-official talks with the PRC on cross-Straits relations in both 1993 and 1998.[79]

Unlike the assertion of previous scholars that the early post-war ROC government did not need to rely upon Taiwanese merchants,[80] it is this chapter's view that the latter's cooperation was essential for boosting the entire national economy, and indeed bolstering the new nation-state. The development pattern of post-war Taiwan should not therefore be held up as a prime example of the positive role of dictatorships in developing economies. Through the post-war Republican government's reliance on Taiwanese merchants, nurtured from the late-Japanese colonial period, in developing the Taiwan–Japan trade to uphold the national economy and polity, we can also observe the continuity of the Asian international order from the 1930s to the 1950s.

---

[77]   Foreign Affairs Archives of the Republic of China, yadongtaipingyangsi 010.18–89002 ZhongRi duanjiaohou wozaiRi guanchan (1), p. 1.

[78]   Foreign Affairs Archives of the Republic of China, yadongtaipingyangsi, 012 89013 ZhongRi guanxi xinjiagou, 500629.

[79]   http://news.sina.com.cn/c/2005–01–06/10474736190s.shtml.

[80]   Zhu Yunhan, 'Reliance of politicians on merchants', p. 63.

Index

Modern Economic and Social History Series

General Editor
Derek H. Aldcroft, University Fellow, Department of Economic and Social
History,
University of Leicester, UK

Derek H. Aldcroft
Studies in the Interwar European Economy
1 85928 360 8 (1997)

Michael J. Oliver
Whatever Happened to Monetarism?
Economic Policy Making and Social Learning in the United Kingdom Since 1979
1 85928 433 7 (1997)

R. Guerriero Wilson
Disillusionment or New Opportunities?
The Changing Nature of Work in Offices,Glasgow 1880–1914
1 84014 276 6 (1998)

Roger Lloyd-Jones and M.J. Lewis with the assistance of M. Eason
Raleigh and the British Bicycle Industry
An Economic and Business History, 1870–1960
1 85928 457 4 (2000)

Barry Stapleton and James H. Thomas
Gales
A Study in Brewing, Business and Family History
0 7546 0146 3 (2000)

Derek H. Aldcroft and Michael J. Oliver
Trade Unions and the Economy
1870–2000
1 85928 370 5 (2000)

Ted Wilson
Battles for the Standard
Bimetallism and the Spread of the Gold Standard in the Nineteenth Century
1 85928 436 1 (2000)

Patrick Duffy
The Skilled Compositor, 1850–1914
An Aristocrat Among Working Men
0 7546 0255 9 (2000)

Robert Conlon and John Perkins
Wheels and Deals
The Automotive Industry in Twentieth-Century Australia
0 7546 0405 5 (2001)

Geoffrey Channon
Railways in Britain and the United States, 1830–1940
Studies in Economic and Business History
1 84014 253 7 (2001)

Sam Mustafa
Merchants and Migrations
Germans and Americans in Connection, 1776–1835
0 7546 0590 6 (2001)

Bernard Cronin
Technology, Industrial Conflict and the Development of Technical Education in
19th-Century England
0 7546 0313 X (2001)

Andrew Popp
Business Structure, Business Culture and the Industrial District
The Potteries, c. 1850–1914
0 7546 0176 5 (2001)

Scott Kelly
The Myth of Mr Butskell
The Politics of British Economic Policy, 1950–55
0 7546 0604 X (2002)

Michael Ferguson
The Rise of Management Consulting in Britain
0 7546 0561 2 (2002)

Alan Fowler
Lancashire Cotton Operatives and Work, 1900–1950
A Social History of Lancashire Cotton Operatives in the Twentieth Century
0 7546 0116 1 (2003)

John F. Wilson and Andrew Popp (eds)
Industrial Clusters and Regional Business Networks in England, 1750–1970
0 7546 0761 5 (2003)

John Hassan
The Seaside, Health and the Environment in England and Wales since 1800
1 84014 265 0 (2003)
Marshall J. Bastable

Arms and the State
Sir William Armstrong and the Remaking of British Naval Power, 1854–1914
0 7546 3404 3 (2004)

Robin Pearson
Insuring the Industrial Revolution
Fire Insurance in Great Britain, 1700–1850
0 7546 3363 2 (2004)

Andrew Dawson
Lives of the Philadelphia Engineers
Capital, Class and Revolution, 1830–1890
0 7546 3396 9 (2004)

Lawrence Black and Hugh Pemberton (eds)
An Affluent Society?
Britain's Post-War 'Golden Age' Revisited
0 7546 3528 7 (2004)

Joseph Harrison and David Corkill
Spain
A Modern European Economy
0 7546 0145 5 (2004)

Ross E. Catterall and Derek H. Aldcroft (eds)
Exchange Rates and Economic Policy in the 20th Century
1 84014 264 2 (2004)

Armin Grünbacher
Reconstruction and Cold War in Germany
The Kreditanstalt für Wiederaufbau (1948–1961)
0 7546 3806 5 (2004)

Till Geiger
Britain and the Economic Problem of the Cold War
The Political Economy and the Economic Impact
of the British Defence Effort, 1945–1955
0 7546 0287 7 (2004)

Anne Clendinning
Demons of Domesticity
Women and the English Gas Industry, 1889–1939
0 7546 0692 9 (2004)

Timothy Cuff
The Hidden Cost of Economic Development
The Biological Standard of Living in Antebellum Pennsylvania
0 7546 4119 8 (2005)

Julian Greaves
Industrial Reorganization and Government Policy in Interwar Britain
0 7546 0355 5 (2005)

Derek H. Aldcroft
Europe's Third World
The European Periphery in the Interwar Years
0 7546 0599 X (2006)

James P. Huzel
The Popularization of Malthus in Early Nineteenth-Century England
Martineau, Cobbett and the Pauper Press
0 7546 5427 3 (2006)

Richard Perren
Taste, Trade and Technology
The Development of the International Meat Industry since 1840
978 0 7546 3648 9 (2006)

Roger Lloyd-Jones and M.J. Lewis
Alfred Herbert Ltd and the British Machine Tool Industry, 1887–1983
978 0 7546 0523 2 (2006)

Anthony Howe and Simon Morgan (eds)
Rethinking Nineteenth-Century Liberalism
Richard Cobden Bicentenary Essays
978 0 7546 5572 5 (2006)

Espen Moe
Governance, Growth and Global Leadership
The Role of the State in Technological Progress, 1750–2000
978 0 7546 5743 9 (2007)

Peter Scott
Triumph of the South
A Regional Economic History of Early Twentieth Century Britain
978 1 84014 613 4 (2007)

David Turnock
Aspects of Independent Romania's Economic History with Particular Reference
to Transition for EU Accession
978 0 7546 5892 4 (2007)

David Oldroyd
Estates, Enterprise and Investment at the Dawn of the Industrial Revolution
Estate Management and Accounting in the North-East of England, c.1700–1780
978 0 7546 3455 3 (2007)

Ralf Roth and Günter Dinhobl (eds)
Across the Borders
Financing the World's Railways in the Nineteenth and Twentieth Centuries
978 0 7546 6029 3 (2008)

Vincent Barnett and Joachim Zweynert (eds)
Economics in Russia
Studies in Intellectual History
978 0 7546 6149 8 (2008)

Raymond E. Dumett (ed.)
Mining Tycoons in the Age of Empire, 1870–1945
Entrepreneurship, High Finance, Politics and Territorial Expansion
978 0 7546 6303 4 (2009)

Peter Dorey
British Conservatism and Trade Unionism, 1945–1964
978-0-7546-6659-2 (2009)